Love amid the Turmoil

Love amid the Turmoil

The
Civil War Letters
of William and
Mary Vermilion

Edited by

Donald C. Elder III

UNIVERSITY OF IOWA PRESS ψ *Iowa City*

University of Iowa Press, Iowa City 52242
Printed in the United States of America
http://www.uiowa.edu/uiowapress

The publication of this book was generously supported
by the University of Iowa Foundation.

Printed on acid-free paper

Library of Congress Cataloging-in-Publication Data
Vermilion, William, 1830–1894.
    Love amid the turmoil: the Civil War letters of
William and Mary Vermilion / edited by Donald C.
Elder III.
    p.   cm.
    Includes bibliographical references and index.
    ISBN 0-87745-849-9 (cloth)
    1. Vermilion, William, 1830–1894 — Correspondence.
2. United States. Army. Iowa Infantry Regiment, 36th
(1862–1865).   3. Vermilion, Mary, 1831–1883 —
Correspondence.   4. Married people — Iowa —
Correspondence.   5. Soldiers — Iowa — Correspondence.
6. Iowa — History — Civil War, 1861–1865 — Personal
narratives.   7. United States — History — Civil War,
1861–1865 — Personal narratives.   8. Iowa — History —
Civil War, 1861–1865 — Social aspects.   9. Indiana —
History — Civil War, 1861–1865 — Social aspects.
10. United States — History — Civil War, 1861–1865 —
Social aspects.   I. Vermilion, Mary, 1831–1883.
II. Elder, Donald C., 1952–   . III. Title.
E507.5 36th. V47 2003
973.7′477′0922 — dc21
[B]   2002040839

03 04 05 06 07 C 5 4 3 2 1

To my great-grandfather,

Jesse Bowen, Company E,

3rd Iowa Infantry

Contents

Preface

In the summer of 1997 I was finishing up a book on William Henry Harrison Clayton, a Civil War soldier from Iowa. As historians are wont to do, I wanted to make absolutely sure that I had consulted every possible source available. Much to my surprise, on the Internet I found a reference to a set of letters from an Iowa soldier that I had never seen before. As it turned out, I saw that the individual who wrote the letters belonged to a regiment far removed from the focus of my work, but one bit of information from the website caught my eye: the letters were housed at the University of California, San Diego, (UCSD) where I had received my doctorate in history. I therefore decided to look more closely at what the collection contained.

Upon examination, I learned that Eloise Duff, and her brothers Edward and Charles William Simmons, had just donated to UCSD a treasure trove of materials generated by their great grandfather, William F. Vermilion. Much of the collection pertained to his business affairs, but it also contained letters that he wrote to his wife during his years of service as a captain in the 36th Iowa Infantry. It looked like interesting material, but nothing out of the ordinary.

After a brief perusal, I was ready to exit the website. At that moment, however, I noticed that the collection also included letters that his wife Mary had written to him during the Civil War. This put the collection into an entirely new perspective. As students of the period are aware, it is extremely rare to find any letters that soldiers received during the Civil War. Veteran soldiers traveled as lightly as possible, which meant that few would undertake the burden of carrying around an accumulation of letters. Here, however, were letters in abundance.

These letters, I knew, represented the potential to explore hypotheses about nineteenth-century women suggested by Catharine Clinton, Nina Silber, Anne Rose, and Glenda Riley. As an advisee of Professor Riley's at the University of Northern Iowa, I remember discussing themes with her along these lines that she would later develop in her writings. I now had the chance, if Mary Vermilion's writings had any sort of merit, to use primary sources to examine these hypotheses. Recognizing the rare opportunity I had, I decided that, after finishing my book on Clayton, I would journey to my alma mater to examine the collection.

Once there, it took me only a matter of minutes to determine that I had found an unbelievably rich source of information about the Civil War, for both Mary and William were extraordinarily gifted writers. Both wrote in a highly literate fashion, hinting that these were two well-educated individuals. In fact, William was a graduate of a medical college, a rarity in that age. While his spelling often left something to be desired, he provided keen commentary on the war, politics, and business conditions. Moreover, Mary was, if anything, a more eloquent writer than her husband. Although I have no definite proof regarding the educational level that she reached, I do know from her correspondence prior to the Civil War that she had attended school at some time in her life. Moreover, I can surmise that her education must have been fairly extensive for a female at that time, because she refers in her correspondence to her experience as a schoolteacher in both Indiana and Iowa. Finally, her letters from the Civil War period suggest that the author was a person whose outlook had been shaped by an exposure to higher learning. Indeed, frequently using literary references, she paints vivid pictures of the events transpiring around her. When combined, these letters yield fascinating insights into the world of two intelligent Americans caught up in our nation's greatest crisis.

These letters are of particular interest on another level as well. At a time when many northerners were ambivalent at best about the fate of African Americans, William and Mary were abolitionists of the first order. While not above occasionally using the pejorative "N" word, both felt that blacks should gain not only their freedom, but win political and civil rights as well. In moving passages they talk about the inherent worth of people of color, especially compared with the whites who were attempting to destroy the national polity.

Readers will also learn a great deal from these letters about attitudes in two states during the Civil War. When William concluded that his regiment would soon venture into harm's way, he took Mary to Indiana to live with his parents. She remained there for six months, and her letters during that period reflect the troubles which plagued that state at a crucial juncture in the war. Even after she moved back to Iowa in April 1863, her letters continued to include references to affairs back in the Hoosier State. These letters, then, allow readers to compare and contrast attitudes in two of the loyal states during the Civil War.

The main interest that readers will have in these letters, however, stems from William and Mary's relationship. They obviously loved each other a great deal, calling each other pet names of endearment: he was Peaches in their letters, and she was Dollie. They yearned for each other, and spoke often about how much they wanted to be reunited. In and of itself, the tone of their letters will not surprise those readers steeped in the literature of the nineteenth century; this was, of course, the era of Victorian sentimentalism, and the affection expressed by William and Mary seems well in keeping with this theme. But what sets these letters apart is the fact that they were written by two people caught up in the most critical test the nation had ever faced. Because they also believed deeply in the Union cause, they tempered their desire to be rejoined with their fervent wish to see the nation reunited. This dynamic tension permeates their letters, reminding us of the human costs involved in the crucible of war.

Here, then, are the Civil War letters of William and Mary Vermilion. Or, should I say, a sample of their hundreds of lengthy letters. A complete transcription of their correspondence would have produced a work comparable in size to Gibbons' *The Decline and Fall of the Roman Empire*, so I excerpted many of the letters. A good number of William's letters do not appear at all, while all of Mary's letters lack at least one passage. Because Mary's letters are truly unique, I wanted to include something from every one of her existing letters. (Many of her letters, referred to in William's, are missing from the archives.) By doing so, I hoped to capture the essence of the dialog between the Vermilions. The letters are transcribed as they were written, with three exceptions. First, Mary misspelled "their" every time that she used it, and I have silently corrected these mistakes. Second, I have occasionally added a word or a letter in brackets to make a passage more comprehensible. Third, the editors at the University of Iowa Press have standardized the format of such terms as A.M. and P.M., and have italicized book titles and ships' names consistently. Everything else contained here is exactly as William and Mary wrote it.

In putting this work together, I have relied on the help of a great many people, beginning with Eloise Duff. Not only did she, along with her brothers, donate the letters, but she and her husband, Russell, also offered me their beautiful home in La Jolla to stay in when I visited UCSD to transcribe the letters. Throughout the period in which I was writing they continued to answer my questions with amazing patience and good humor. Finally, Eloise and her brothers supplied photographs which appear in this book. I will always be in their debt.

Transcribing letters requires identifying the names and events discussed in them. As always, librarians proved extremely useful in the process. Lynda Claassen and her staff at the Mandeville Special Collections Library at UCSD were tremendously helpful during my trips there. The staff of the Golden Library at Eastern New Mexico University, especially Brackston Taylor-Young, Gene Bundy, Lilah Gainey, and Michele Wood, handled my numerous requests with impressive efficiency. The DePauw University Archives and the Iowa State University Library proved equally helpful, as did the Iowa public libraries located in Centerville, Albia, Corydon, Marshalltown, and Carroll. In addition, the staffs at various institutions also aided my cause, especially the Lincoln Shrine in Redlands, California, the Military Records Department at the National Archives, the State Historical Society of Iowa, the Kansas State Historical Society, and the Indiana State Historical Society.

Many individuals also helped me. I would like to thank Ethel Lira, who spent hours preparing answers to questions that I posed for her regarding Appanoose County. Gary Craver, another resident of Appanoose County, went above and beyond the call of duty to answer questions about his home area. Dr. Brad McConville, who lives in the house that the Vermilions built after the Civil War, also provided me with a large amount of valuable information about Appanoose County during the Civil War. Such gracious individuals do justice to the tradition of hospitality in the Hawkeye State, a land I was proud to call home for parts of four decades.

Becky Hepinstall also deserves special mention. A brilliant former student of mine, she transcribed dozens of letters for me. When she completed the letters, I checked her work against the originals to verify the accuracy of her transcriptions, and found that I needed to make only a few corrections. She also provided excellent advice and commentary, even as she was preparing to get married. All professors should be as fortunate as I am to have had a student of her caliber.

Four historians who have specialized in various aspects of Iowa history proved helpful. My good friend, Rick Sturdevant, shared his research on recruitment in Iowa. Greg Urwin offered keen insights into the experiences of Iowa soldiers in Arkansas. Robert Dykstra provided astute analysis of the question of African American civil rights in Iowa at the end of the Civil War. Finally, Steve Beszedits gave me his perception of an altercation involving the 10th Iowa at the conclusion of the war. I appreciate the help that these excellent historians offered.

Not enough can be said about the wonderful people at the University of Iowa Press. Holly Carver helped immeasurably in the process of completing this work. The anonymous referee she selected provided a perceptive analysis of my work, suggesting ways to improve upon the finished product. I would daresay that there could not be a better university press to work with.

As my students would say, I have to give a shout out to a number of individuals here at Eastern New Mexico University. My colleagues Linda and Jerry Gies, and Suzanne Balch-Lindsay, gave me excellent advice. My secretaries, Lori Collins and Amy Jordan Pool, helped with typing, as did Kelly Stapp, Susan Baysinger, Mike Garcia, Jessica Rodriguez, Diego Gutierrez, Justin Schroerer, Sandra Saiz, and Karen Ingram, our department work study students.

Many individuals supplied key bits of information. I would like to thank Bobby Roberts, Jeannie Whayne, Dan Sutherland, Ellen Sulser, Linda Pine, Mary McNamara, E. H. Dewes, Jill Costill, John

Brashar, Debbie Wafford, Stuart Campbell, Sharon Bryant, Brenda Busing, Rhonda Frevert, Linda Jacobs Green, Doug Atterburg, Carol Thomas, Shirley Grimes, Ruth Black, Susan Carter, Michael Pollack, and Rita Harlan. Any mistakes that remain in this work after the efforts of all those who have helped me are completely my own responsibility.

Finally, my greatest debt is owed to my family. My in-laws, Ward and Doris Salisbury, provided food, lodging, and encouragement on my numerous research trips to Iowa. My sons, Cam and Brian, provided diversion during my years of work. I also involved them in creating this book. Cam did extensive work preparing the maps that appear in the book, and checked sources for me. Brian also helped me with the maps and took an excellent picture that is included herein. My wife, Janine, wins my highest praise. She provided me with the support, encouragement, and love to see this project through to the end. After many years of marriage, she remains my Dollie, and I hope that I am still her Peaches.

Love
amid
the
Turmoil

1

"Still I Am Proud of My Gallant Soldier Husband"

In a memorable scene from the movie *Dr. Zhivago*, General Yevgraf Zhivago (the character played by Alec Guinness) reminisces about Russia's mobilization at the start of World War I. Commenting about how few married men chose to enlist in the Russian Army at that time, he asserts that "happy men don't volunteer." In Iowa at the start of the Civil War, it seems that many married men saw the option of military service much as Boris Pasternak's fictional character did. Based on a sampling of the individuals who enlisted in the first six regiments recruited in that state and finding their marital status in the 1860 federal census, it appears that young, single men comprised the majority of Iowa's first volunteers. But when in the summer of 1862 President Abraham Lincoln issued his call for additional recruits, numerous married Iowans chose to respond by leaving their families to fight for the concept of an indivisible Union.

One such individual was William F. Vermilion. Married for over four years, he decided to forsake his comfortable existence in southern Iowa to fight for a cause he fervently believed in.

It had been an interesting path that led William to that choice. Born in Mercer County, Kentucky, on October 18, 1830, he lived there only a few months before his family moved to Putnam County, Indiana. The Vermilions were not alone in this migration; it is estimated that 75 percent of the early settlers in Putnam

Site of the Joel Vermilion farm, Jefferson Township,
Putnam County, Indiana, 1998. Photograph by the author.

County came from Kentucky. His father, Joel Vermilion (a native
of Virginia), purchased land in Franklin Township, and began to
farm. A few years later, the elder Vermilion moved his growing
family to a farm of 160 acres in nearby Jefferson Township. Joel,
an old-line Baptist, also preached at a number of churches in the
county, thus acquainting himself and his family with many individuals. William evidently acquired more than just a growing
circle of friends through attending church — it is probable that he
also met Mary Alice Cecilia Kemper, the woman who would one
day become his wife.

Like William, Mary was not a native of Indiana. Born in Virginia on December 4, 1831, Mary had moved with her family to
Jefferson Township in Putnam County shortly after her birth. Her
father, Valentine Kemper, put in a crop in the spring of 1832, and
within a decade had become a prosperous farmer. The Kemper
family (which would eventually include three sons) attended the
Baptist church in their neighborhood, and in all probability it was
in this manner that William Vermilion and Mary Kemper met
each other.

Details about William's early life are sketchy. It can be surmised
that he attended one of the public schools in Putnam County, because in 1852 he appears on the roll of students at Indiana Asbury

Mary Alice Cecilia Vermilion, ca. 1870.
Photograph courtesy of Eloise Duff.

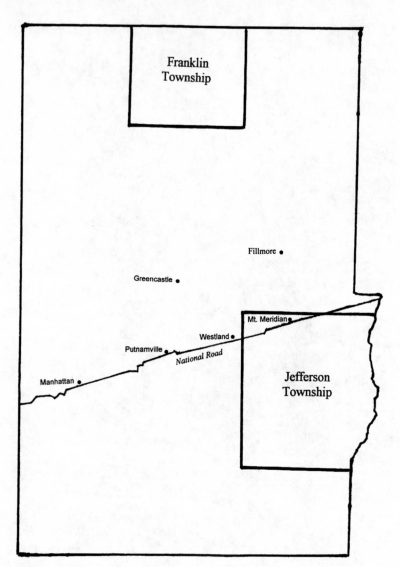

Putnam County, Indiana.

University, located in the Putnam County community of Green-castle. In 1837 the Methodist Church in Indiana had received a charter from the state legislature to create a college, and in 1838 Indiana Asbury University (known today as DePauw University) opened its doors. William chose to enroll in Indiana Asbury's school of science.

Mary's formative years are also a mystery. There are no actual school records extant, but a female seminary existed in Putnam County at the time Mary was growing up. It seems logical that Mary must have attended school, because in the early 1850s she became a schoolteacher in Putnam County. She did not remain in this position for long, however, as her father decided to relocate his family. Valentine Kemper had run the family farm successfully for years, accumulating property worth $3,000 by 1850. He chose to invest some of his money, purchasing land in Lucas and Monroe Counties in Iowa. In 1855, Kemper decided to journey to Iowa to inspect his property, and took Mary with him.

Kemper liked what he saw in this land that had become a state only nine years before. He was so impressed that he decided that same year to move his family (with the exception of a son by a previous marriage) to the southwest corner of Monroe County. Mary would soon find employment as a schoolteacher in the Monroe County community of Osprey.

After finishing his studies at Asbury, Vermilion chose to seek opportunities farther west. In 1852, he moved to eastern Illinois, settling in the community of Martinsville. While there, he decided to pursue a career in medicine. Rather than simply apprenticing himself to a local doctor, Vermilion attended medical school. After reading medical literature to prepare himself, he selected one of the most prestigious institutions of the time, Rush Medical College.

Founded in 1843 by Dr. Daniel Brainard, Rush was one of fewer than forty such institutions in existence in the United States by the time Vermilion matriculated. Vermilion entered school at a time when students engaged in a course of study that involved sixteen-week sessions until graduation. Such was the reputation of the school that the conferral of a degree by Rush gave its graduates automatic licensure to practice medicine. Vermilion gained that status in 1857.

Before embarking on his career as a physician, however, Vermilion needed to take care of some family business. His older brother, Joel Davis Vermilion, had fallen into ill health, and William thought that a different climate might help him. Upon graduation, therefore, he took Davis to the state of Texas. After seeing his brother established in this new location, William journeyed northward, but he did not return to either Illinois or Indiana. On

The site of the William Vermilion farm, "Woodside," in Chariton Township, Appanoose County, 1998. The waters of Lake Rathbun, seen in the foreground, now cover all but a small portion of the forty-acre plot of land. Photograph by Brian Elder.

April 13, 1857, he purchased forty acres of land in Section 11 of Chariton Township in Appanoose County, Iowa. He would live and farm on this acreage, which he named Woodside, for the next five years. He also purchased a building in the nearby community of Iconium, where he started his medical practice in the fall of 1857.

He was obviously good at his craft, having amassed a personal fortune of $2,200 by 1860. This was a figure comparable with other, more established, physicians in Appanoose County. But more than the promise of a thriving practice drew him to south-central Iowa. Before he began medical school William had asked Mary to marry him, and she had accepted. As the historian Anne Rose has perceptively noted, many Victorian couples postponed marriage for lengthy periods of time until financial security could be guaranteed. William and Mary followed this pattern, deciding to delay their wedding until he graduated. After that time arrived and William's career began to blossom in Iowa, the two waited no longer: they were married on February 23, 1858.

They quickly became established members of the community of Iconium. Just as the majority of the first settlers in Putnam County had come from one specific area, many of the early residents of this part of south-central Iowa had also come from the same region — in this case Putnam County. Indeed, William and Mary were able to reestablish an acquaintance with thirty-year-old Julia McCarty May (Mary's cousin) and her husband Humphrey, age thirty, who lived just across the Wayne County line in Confidence. John Wright, also formerly of Putnam County, lived there as well. These transplants had all become successful in Iowa as the 1860s started.

Unfortunately, the start of the 1860s brought more than prosperity for the men of south-central Iowa. The coming of the Civil War forced them to make a choice about military service. Initially William, Humphrey, and John opted to stay at home. But as previously noted, William did answer Lincoln's call for troops in the summer of 1862. To the surprise of many, he sought a combat assignment with the Union army instead of offering his services as a physician. Although a relatively new resident of Iconium (itself something of a newcomer, having been established in 1856), William had no trouble in raising a company of volunteers, drawn primarily from Appanoose, Monroe, Wayne, and Lucas Counties. He drew a physically imposing group of individuals to the cause: 75 percent of the men in the company were taller than the five-foot eight-inch average Union soldier during the Civil War. Because of his recruiting efforts, he was chosen by the lanky volunteers for the captaincy of the company. Upon his recommendation Humphrey May became the first lieutenant, and John Wright received the position of second lieutenant. The three Hoosiers-turned-Hawkeyes then awaited orders to report for duty.

The call finally arrived on September 21, 1862. The company gathered in the Monroe County community of Albia, and marched to Eddyville in Wapello County, where they boarded a train that took them to their training camp in Keokuk. Once there on October 4, 1862, they were officially mustered into federal service.

After a few days, William realized that he did not have to live in camp with the enlisted men. Consequently, he asked Mary to leave Woodside and come stay with him in Keokuk. She did, and remained for a month. When William thought that his regiment would soon embark on a campaign, he decided that Mary should move in with his parents in Indiana rather than return to Woodside. Accordingly, he escorted her to Putnam County. Upon his re-

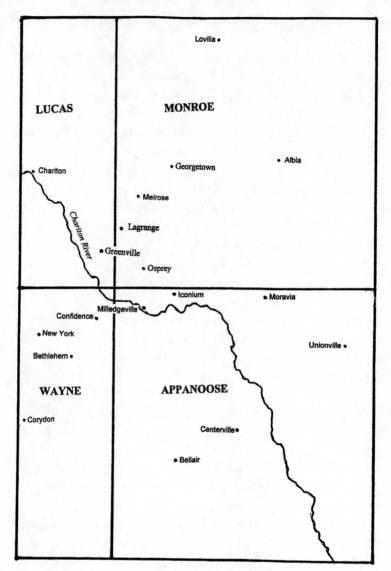

Wayne, Lucas, Monroe, and Appanoose Counties, Iowa.

turn, his regiment — now designated the 36th Iowa Infantry —
finished its training and moved to St. Louis for assignment.

The letters in the first chapter cover this period of transition for
the Vermilions. William describes the process by which his men
coalesce into a trained military unit, while Mary discusses her
growing dissatisfaction with the attitude of her in-laws towards

the war. But what comes through most clearly in the letters is the strength of their relationship.

Camp Lincoln,[1] Keokuk, Sept. 10, 1862
My Dear Mary,

We are here this morning and all right, but orderly May.[2] He is unwell. Has worked himself sick, but not bad. Will's[3] eyes are a little sore. They will soon be well.

We had a very good time coming. Got to Eddyville before sundown and got plenty of good places to stay at. Mr. Dunlap[4] took the thing in hand and made everything all right for my company, although there was another company in town the same night. All of the Appanoose boys met at the Depot and escorted us up to the camp in fine style, where they soon cooked us a very good meal. I am eating and sleeping with the boys.

Come Mary, next Monday. . . . I will meet you at the Depot. Come on the morning train.

Give my respects to all and be sure I remember you, my Dear. In all probability you can remain here 3 or 4 weeks. There is too much for me to write this morning Dolly.
Will

Camp Lincoln, Oct. 26, 1862
My Dear Mary,

Tired and weary I sit myself down to write you a few lines that you may know I am at Keokuk and all right. Well, but I have done a hard days work today.

I got on the [railroad] Cars at Greencastle. . . . Went to Terre Haute against sundown. Ate oysters for supper, gave half a dollar for a bed to sleep in till half past 10 o'clock, when I took the cars for St. Louis. Gave half dollar for a berth in the sleeping car for the rest of the night.

Got to St. Louis at 8 o'clock in the morning. Went aboard of the *Die Vernon*[5] and took passage for Keokuk. Felt too blue and indifferent to travel over the city any. . . . Had a very pleasant trip up to Keokuk at which place we landed last night at 8 o'clock. Came up to camp and shook the hands of the boys for 10 or 15 minutes and went to bed.

I found 16 or 17 of the boys sick. 9 or 10 in the Hospital. None bad sick but James Bartlett.[6]

Going away put me behind the boys in the Drill but I think I will soon catch up again.

Be in good hearts Mary. We will soon meet again. If we go to St. Louis you can meet me there.

Will Vermilion

Mrs. Rowe's,[7] Keokuk, Iowa, Oct. 30, 1862
My Dear Mary,

Last week I sent you two letters. . . . There was not much in them, but if you knew how much the boys had to ask of me, and then how much I had to do, you would not blame me for not writing more. It is utterly impossible for me to be Capt. of the Chariton Rangers[8] and do much of anything else. . . . I think I will detail some prompt man to answer questions for me. . . .

The boys are having a sad time of it just now. James Bartlett died on the 27th the inst.[9] of Typhoid Fever. John McCullough died yesterday with I think an inflammation of the bowels. Joseph Bartlett will *undoubtedly die* tomorrow or next day. Thomas Duckworth is very sick with measles and flux but we think he will get well. James C. Evans is better. He starts home in the morning. Roland was better when I got home. Jenkins[10] was better. He is about now. We have had a good many others sick but none bad. None of our near neighbors.

We are sending all who die home to their friends. We make the money up by voluntary subscription. You never saw boys more liberal. They raised in a few minutes $17.50 to send James Bartlett home. Don't imagine, because these boys have died, that we are all going to die, for there are but few sick men who take care of themselves.

The two Bartletts and John McCullough drank to excess. . . . I never knew it till a few days ago. I have been using every exertion for the last few days to put a stop to it. I have issued an order punishing severely any man who brings liquor inside the guard

lines. . . . If any man brings whisky in the quarters and I find it out
I will put him in the guard house for 24 hours.

We drew last Sunday, coats, pants and socks for the boys. Yesterday we drew arms — Enfield rifals.[11] They are good, some of them
shoot 1200 yards. . . .
Will Vermilion

Mrs. Rowe's, Keokuk, Saturday night, 9 o'clock, Nov. 1, 1862
My Dear Darling,

You see it is already late enough for me to go to bed, but I
thought I would talk awhile to my good Dolly; especially since I
received the letter your brother James has sent you. I have opened
it and read it. . . . He must be camped on a lonesome spot. But I
would not be afraid of any of the spirits of those brave fellows who
fell on that eventful day.[12]

I am sorry I missed seeing Woodford and Henry,[13] but I can't
help it now. . . .

Whisky drinking in my quarters is played out, the boys are
afraid to bring it there. I will put the first man in the guardhouse
who brings any inside of the lines. There is none drunk now. All I
have to regret is that I did not issue the order sooner.

Will is quite well and is making a good officer. So is J. Grimes.[14]
Will says he will write. . . . We have good guns. . . . The Austrian
rifals.[15] Major Woodward has gone to the governor about the rest
of our clothing. It will be here in a few days. Then we will go to
St. Louis immediately. . . . That is the opinion now of our Colonel.[16]
While I think of it the Colonel asked me to assist him in making
his brother in law sutler.[17] I did not do it. . . .
Will Vermilion

Mrs. Rowe's, Keokuk, Nov. 5, 1862
My Dear Dollie,

I received your good letter, evening before last, and was glad to
get it. You know how glad you are sometimes to get a letter from
your Peaches. It does me just as much good as it does you. . . . They
are my comfort here, Dollie, and they can come from no person

William F. Vermilion, ca. 1862. Photograph courtesy of the Mandeville Special Collections Library, University of California, San Diego.

*The staff of the 36th Iowa Infantry, ca. 1862. Photograph
courtesy of the State Historical Society of Iowa — Des Moines.*

but you. Everything from you is nothing but that pure love that
gives such comfort to the soldier in camp. Every person has (or
ought to have) one or more such persons to write to them. You are
the only one for me. Then remember me, Dollie.

I fear my dear from the tone of your letter you are not satisfied — not comfortable. I used the wrong word. I don't expect you
to be satisfied; but what I mean is I fear you are not as well satisfied
at fathers, as we both thought you would be. . . . I know how it is at
fathers. They live a different way to what I want you to live if I can
help. I am sorry almost every time I think of it.

If you can be any better satisfied by coming to Iowa — by going
to your fathers and taking money enough with you to make things
more comfortable there, go, *you shall have the money.* I will draw
money in a few days, then we will have plenty, my Dollie. I will
[do] anything — everything in my power to render you as comfortable as you can be while we are so far apart. This war will be

over after awhile. Then we will go home and stay there. It seems to me that would be the most desireable thing on earth. Wouldn't it, my darling. . . .

Mr. Sevey[18] was down last Sunday. . . . He went home well satisfied that we were caring for ourselves, which is a fact Mary. . . . Tell Henry[19] I love him and respect him. He loves his country.
Will Vermilion

Mrs. Rowe's, Nov. 7, 1862
My Good Dollie,

. . . My cold is a little better this morning. I feel a good deal better, but cough some yet, not much. If Dollie were here to pet me I would be all right. I will have interest for all the petting I lose, when I see you. Be sure of that. You will pay it, won't you Dollie. . . .

The news yesterday evening gave us all the blues. Intervention threatened, from abroad, men elected to Congress here who will vote to cut off supplys, and do all they can to depreciate the currency of the country. Do you suppose Seymour of N.Y.[20] will ever send any more men from that state to support the Government. If he does he will deceive us here. May Hell reap its full reward, amen. We live in Iowa, thank God. A state that has more than its quota of men in the field, and not one 3 or 9 month or drafted man among them.[21] No traitor in Congress to disgrace our fair fame, by voting to cut off our supplies. Whether the Government stands or falls, we will love Iowa. But I keep in good cheer, the first of Jan. will be here after awhile, when I hope that there will not be another Bondsman on American soil. Let men throw up their hands in awe; let them go to the Bible to prove that slavery is Divine, if they wish to, I am in favor of President Lincoln's [Emancipation] Proclamation. If he will add, give every negro who is willing to fight a good gun and let him slay his thousands if he can. Let him assist in making every brook in the South run red with treasonable blood. It is not as precious as loyal blood is to loyal men. The Day of redemption will come. Reformations will never go backwards.

What is Greeley[22] saying these days. You must tell me. I don't read any. . . .
Will Vermilion

Friday Evening, Nov. 12th, 1862

My Dear Love,

I wrote to you last evening, but you won't think I write too often will you? I can't write much though this time. It is nearly dark, and I must help Mother and Jane[23] a little. Henry is better today. I sat up late last night and read my papers. . . . I am in favor of *immediate*, not *gradual* emancipation. I don't see the justice of paying even loyal men for their slaves. No one thinks of paying northern men for the property they may lose by the war. Nor do I see the need of talking about colonization just now.[24] This country will need all its laborers for the next few years.

I don't really think my beloved that this war will last many months longer. Oh, may God hasten the end. . . . If our Generals only do their duty, as the men will do theirs, I don't see how we can fail now. I have read Halleck's[25] report. Is it not enough to make one's blood boil in their veins? What other government on earth ever suffered so much at the hands of its friends?

I shall not sleep any tonight, dear. Just a rumor of good news can keep me awake. If I could only see you for one hour tonight what would I not give? I *don't* get used to the separation or reconciled to it at all. It hurts me worse every day. I think of you every minute when I am awake and dream of you when I sleep. I long to see you more than I can tell. But you know all this without my telling you, don't you dear love? Still I can no more help telling you than the brook can help babbling in summer. . . . Even this poor companionship with you is so much better than none that I feel the parting most keenly whenever I say goodby to you. But I must say it, dear one. *Goodby*. Don't forget to write your Dollie and don't forget to *love* her. . . .

Dollie

Mrs. Rowe's, Nov. 13, 1862

. . . Don't let the war news trouble you, it will all come right after awhile. Burnside will fight you know. McClellan won't, you know. Rosencrans will fight, Buell would not. Grant[26] was timid on the Contraband[27] question, but he is no more. . . .

The Colonel has taken a notion to drill the Regiment. It is a fine thing, the boys will have better health if they are drilled 6 or 8 hours every day than if they lay round in camp & do nothing. Action is what they need. We will be very apt to get plenty of it from this on.

If I had known we would have been kept here till this time, you shouldn't have left me so soon. . . . Christies[28] left while I was gone and some medical students got the room they had and I had to keep the room you and I had. Had we known it, we could have had it just as well as not.

Will

Mrs. Rowe's, Nov. 15, 1862

. . . We must have by this time men enough in the field to make an active campaign of it this Winter. We will have it under Halleck & Burnside. Then for gougers we have Rosencrans & Curtis.[29] Two good men. Fighters. . . .

Sunday evening, 9 o'clock, Our regiment has to . . . act as Provo Guard for the city. Yesterday morning there was quite a fire broke out in the central part of town.[30] The firemen were there with their engines. The citizens of course were there. The convalescent soldiers from the Hospital were there. In all there was quite a crowd. . . . All — every body worked putting out the fire, till most of them were exhausted, especially the soldiers. . . . While the fire was raging, some one distributed whiskey quite freely among the firemen. They got drunk against the fire being put out. After the fire was all out 4 or 5 of them jumped on & whipped badly one of Capt. Gedney's[31] boys who was acting as guard at the commissary. . . . About the same time they threw some rocks into the Estes House Hotel.[32] The convalescent soldiers became enraged and lunged out into the street. It being a work day a great many of the 36th were in town. They became enraged also & the riot commenced. . . . The Soldiers got the upper hand of the firemen & citizens & no person could control them. Our Col. had a weak effect & retired. Lieut. Ball[33] came out & made the effort by smacking one of [the] disturbants. The soldiers threw brick bats & stones at him . . . one of which hit him in the back. *He gave it up as a bad job.* After the Citizens & firemen caved in the boys dispersed.

After the boys of the 36th . . . consulted the matter over, they concluded it was not well done. The Col.— apprehending trouble issued an order, not allowing any soldier outside of the lines during the night. Just before night, the boys (except my company; I had but 3 men out during the night and they were not in the mob) got together & concluded they would [g]o down in town & clean Lieut. Ball out. When they came to the Guard lines the Major Adjutant and the most of the line officers[34] tried to keep them back. The boys did not hurt any of them, but took them & lifted them to one side & told them to stand there & about 300 of them proceeded out, went down to Lieut. Ball's office & called for him, but were told he was under arrest. They then took a look for firemen but found none. Then they went to the Theatre. The manager threw open the door, the Citizens stood aside & the boys all went in. All in all there is a bitter feeling on the part of the soldiers towards the citizens here. . . . Keokuk has to behave from this on. Rest assured of that. . . .

W. F. Vermilion

Mrs. Rowe's, Nov. 22, 1862

My Dear Dollie,

. . . *You must not stay at father's* if it can *possibly be helped.* . . . Go to Mrs. McCarty's[35] & tell her that I want her to board you what time you stay in that country & you will pay her any fee she may see fit to charge. . . . Make yourself as comfortable there as you can. . . . I cannot stand it for you to stay at father's & know you don't want to go contrary to my wishes. . . . If you stay at Mrs. McCarty's — you can if you wish to — go & see them occasionally. I am going to write to the Old Lady about it myself. . . . This is all on that point, & as Col. Kittredge says "I hope you will attend to it immediately." Move to Mrs. McCarty's. She will be a mother to you. Julia & Emily[36] will be sisters to you. And I will even try to be more than every person to you Dollie.

W. F. Vermilion

*Colonel Charles W. Kittredge, ca. 1862. Photograph
courtesy of the State Historical Society of Iowa — Des Moines.*

Lorenze,[37] Mississippi R., Nov. 26, 1862

We are on our way to St. Louis. We will get there tonight some-time. We left Keokuk yesterday about 1 o'clock with 58 men. Lieut. Wright will be down tomorrow with the rest of our Company who are able to travel. . . .

Will came back yesterday just as we were starting. He is on board today. He is well. Your father & mother are well, & were get-ting along finely. No bad news from the neighborhood.

The Regiment is not all along this time. 6 Companies only. The other 4 will follow us. . . .

W. F. Vermilion

Benton Barracks,[38] MO., Nov. 28, 1862

Here we are at last. We are getting ready to go to Helena as fast as possible. . . . All right we are willing to go, if it will do any good.

This thing called Benton Barracks is a fine thing. It covers about one hundred & fifty or sixty acres of ground. I can't describe it. It would take too long. . . . Some few soldiers say Fremont was too ex-travagant, others say God bless him, he thought something of his men. My opinion is, if every commander in the Army had under-stood the nature & comprehended the magnatude of this rebellion as well as Fremont did, the war would have been over long ago. Don't you wish they had. The most of us do here. . . .

James Kemper's Capt.[39] was here last night. He has resigned in consequence of bad health. He had Pneumonia, & came very near dying. He is better off now however. He says Jim is well & first rate as a soldier. No better in his company. Humphrey was sick when we got off of the boat, & had to go to doctor, when he met Benthusen.

When Lieut. May saw Benthusen on his way home he took a no-tion to resign. . . . He said his constitution was gone, & he would never be fit for the service. If he went to Dixie he would die there. "Won't you get me off as quick as soon as you can Cap" says he. "If I stay here I will be sure to die," & all such talk as that. . . . I have had this disease bad ever since I was 20 years old. . . . Finally this morning I went to see Col. Kittredge & told him. . . . He objected, but said he would sign papers if nothing else would do. But says he I will go & see him myself about it & try & put him out of the notion. So he came over & talked to him & put him out of the notion sure enough. Tonight he is quite comfortable & chipper. . . . But I will tell you my Dollie what I think about it. He can't stay away from Julia and the children. . . . I don't blame him for wanting to be with his family but he ought to have known his own fortitude. Now it is perfectly right my Darling for a man even in these days of war to think as much of his family as it is possible for a man to, but he ought to have the moral courage to do what is right. I love you Dollie, I know, as much as he can love his wife, but it will make it worse for me & you here to act as he does. Don't think I don't love you Dollie, for I love you as much as it is possible for one person to love another. . . .

Will Vermilion

Benton Barracks, Dec. 1, 1862

. . . I can't & will not stand it for you to stay among the people who hate the cause I am sacrificing and risking for. To say who they are, if they think anything of me, they can't like much of [Confederate President] Jeff Davis's government. If they think anything of his confederacy I don't want them to think anything of me. And I don't want any person that does think anything of me to stay where rebel sympathizers are. . . . If you think you would get along any better at your father's, go there Dollie. . . . We could fix for you to be better off there than any other place. . . . If you leave Indiana, it will be a very long time before I see that part of God's Earth again. I would not be likely to eat mother's turkey very soon. . . .

W. F. Vermilion

Benton Barracks, Dec. 4, 1862

Good evening my good Dollie,

. . . Let me talk to you Dollie about our Field officers.[40] I don't like them. . . . The Col. I don't like at all. Lieut. Col. Drake[41] I hate. . . . He is ignorant and egotistical, two bad traits for a man. . . .

If we ever live to get home I will remember him. I can be his equal then, & he can't help it. If there would be ever so many vacancies in our regiment there never would be any chance for me, Dollie. Wapello County would get it all. Appanoose County is not known in the arrangement. . . .

Lieut. May and myself have expressed our trunks to Putnamville for you & Julia to get. . . . Tell Henry to keep in good spirits. I hope you are not staying at father's yet. . . . I don't care what they say or think about it. Just so they become convinced that I hate Traitors both North & South.

Will Vermilion

Benton Barracks, MO, Dec. 7, 1862

My Dear Dollie,

. . . Will's health is good. . . . He . . . is always ready for duty, but as backward as ever. The other day, I told Will to take the company out & drill it, (the orderly and commissioned officers were all busy) but he didn't do as I told him. He concluded Hancock[42] ought to do it as he was 2nd Sergeant. But I had put Hancock under arrest a few days ago . . . for getting drunk & breaking guard, and of course I would not let him drill the men after such conduct as that. The consequence was I put Hancock in the ranks & made Will drill the boys for a while, simply to give them exercise. Hancock hated it the worst I ever saw a man hate anything of the kind in my life. I am determined to punish him. . . . But I will not remove him as long as I can help it, for when he is sober he does the best he can, & his family needs all the money he can get for them. . . .

. . . Jake Grimes . . . is as good a fellow as I ever saw. He says the boys are well pleased with everything. . . . Will, they like first rate. He is a good fellow. Better, I never saw.

When you get this write all you think about father's folks. Tell me how you live, what you get to eat, how much did you have to eat, although I hope by the time you get his letter you will not be eating much there, for I can't bear the thought of you staying there this winter. . . . The error was my taking you there, but there I thought you would get along better than I used to. I thought they were doing better. But such people seldom improve Dollie. By this

Francis M. Drake. This photograph dates from 1865,
when he was promoted to brigadier general. Photograph
courtesy of the State Historical Society of Iowa — Des Moines.

time I guess you know why I am no better than I am. Why I never made much more than a very ordinary fellow of myself. . . .

I have just learned from the Albia boys that judge Townsen[43] is arrested for treason. . . . We hope they will hang him. We have no love for traitors here, North or South. Lieut. May says he is an Abolitionist. Says he "I wish the negroes would rise all over the South & do their part of the fighting." He wants the whole South overrun with insurrection. Such is the influence of the war on good men who are not out [for] popularity or money.

I am abolitionist full blooded. We want every negro set at liberty & if any person tried to enslave them give them a gun & let them flood the South with blood.

If the people of Indiana don't like such talking *they can make the most out of it.* . . . I like the negro better than I like traitors. I would rather live by a loyal negro than by half of the people who are living in Putnamville. It would not be comfortable for me to live there, the consequences might be bad. Men fighting for their liberties become desperate towards their enemies. If we could we would wipe them off the Earth at one blow.

Be of good cheer Dollie, time will roll on & we will go back to our Prairie home again. Up in Iowa the traitors don't rule.

If we were at home Dollie now we would be ashamed of ourselves. The quiet of home would not do us. . . .

W. F. Vermilion

Benton Barracks, MO. Dec. 8, 1862
My Dear Dollie,

The boys in the next Barracks are singing Home Sweet Home, & it makes me think of our home, our lovely home in loyal Iowa & of my good Dollie, for no place would be home without my Dollie. . . . I have just been in the Barracks & talked to them or nearly all of them. Bad Marchbanks[44] was out of tobacco & out of money. This evening when I was up to the store I thought of him & got him enough to do him a little while. He was the best pleased fellow you ever saw. He is one of the best men I have. Stop. I would not use the word "best" in comparing members of my company. *They are all good.* I can't *pick out one* private to dislike. I don't suffer myself to notice the little eccentricities of men. In fact if it is necessary to punish one of them — which is very seldom — they soon forget it. They always expect punishment however, when they violate a rule. The boys who talk to me about it say they don't hate me for it, but soon forget it. . . .

W. F. Vermilion

Tuesday Morning, Dec. 9th, 1862

My Darling,

. . . You are troubled too much about me I'm afraid dear. I don't want you to be uneasy on my account. You tell me I must not stay here love, but I am here yet. I got your letter telling me what you wanted me to do more than a week ago but I have been sick darling. . . . I am about well now but yesterday was the first time I have been out. Father was at Deer Creek[45] Sunday and heard that your trunk had come to Putnamville. When he came home and told me I could hardly wait. I asked if I might have a horse with buggy to go . . . see it — I thought there would be a letter in it. He said I might have the buggy. So yesterday morning cold as it was I wrapped up and went. When I got there Julia had just got back from Putnamville with the trunks. We both cried over them. There was a long letter in hers, *but none in mine*. There was only your shirt and blouse. . . .

I asked Aunt Anna about my staying here and she said "come along child; you are welcome." She said I might help to hire the wood chopped and that was all the pay she wanted. She must have more than that dearest. . . . She says I must not break off and move at once and hurt their feelings here. And she is right, my dear one. . . . I tell them I am going there to stay with Julia a few weeks and they seem willing to that. I am going just as soon as I can get there. Some of them would come after me but they have no buggy. . . . I couldn't stay yesterday because I went alone and had to bring the buggy home. They asked me to stop at Tom's as I passed and get Reason[46] a school book. I drove up to the door and Tom came out and was very clever. He asked if I had got my letters from the office since Saturday! And then had I heard from you and what the news was from you. In all he talked to me more in two minutes there than he had altogether before since I came. The change in his manner was so marked that I know mother has told him that I said I didn't believe they cared anything for you because you had gone to the war. It may be, love, that it really *is* their way and that they have not been so bad all the time as they seemed. I am willing to believe so darling and let it all go. Our ways and views of life are so different from theirs that it is hardly possible that they should have any sentiments or feelings in common with me. . . . I wish sometimes that I had not told you a word about them. That would have been the best way but you know dear I always told you everything. And when you asked me I told you and couldn't help it. If I have erred darling, I am sorry. Will you forgive me? And love me?

Henry is not so well. He grew worse yesterday. . . . They sent for Brinton.[47] And he says he has typhoid fever now and will not get well for a long time. John[48] says he thought yesterday that Henry wouldn't live a week. . . . Tom came out and staid all night. I can't see this morning that he is worse than he has been for several days but of course he is weaker. The doctor is coming back today. Our cousin Brothers[49] was here last night. He is out hunting land to buy "just to get rid of this 'greenback' money"[50] he said. I hope he can succeed in getting rid of all he has of it.

I see in my Gate City that William Burns has died since you left Keokuk.[51] How sad such news is! I wonder what will become of the helpless families that are left without guides or protectors. It is very dreadful. You never told me he was sick. . . . Greeley . . . is just beginning to recover his equanimity since the election. His faith which was obscured for a time is growing as bright as ever. God bless him; and all earnest workers in the cause of Right and Humanity!
Mary

Benton Barracks Mo., Dec. 14, 1862
My Dear Dollie,
  . . . You scared me Dollie when you told me how sick you had been, with diptheria. . . . But how glad I am that you are better again. . . . Don't be uneasy about my taking care of myself. I do that

better than I ever did in my life. Our diet is as good as we need to have, I think. Good bread, good coffee and tea, fresh beef, ham, potatoes, & all pretty well cooked. . . .

You are too afraid of hurting father's folks feelings, Dollie. They have but little regard for our feelings. . . . I can't stand it & I *won't stand it.* . . . I am too proud to have you stay there. . . .

Capt. Gedney, Col. Kittredge & myself had a settlement day before yesterday. I have always been thinking how mean he treated us at Keokuk, & the other day I happened to be in at Gedney's & got to talking about it. . . . He proposed that we go over and settle up. We went over and talked to him as plain as one man ever talked to another. We told him how he had treated us personally, and told him how he had favored Wapello Cty. & Ottumwa, & how he had slighted Appanoose Co. He said at first that he had done what was right. That assertion gave us a good opportunity to relate every grievance I had to relate, & you know I am generally pretty good at such things, especially when I feel right for it, which I did that afternoon. We did not stand on military eticet (that is not right is it?) But talked to him as plainly as I could in my life. In fact I tried [to see] how plainly I could talk. At last he saw & acknowledged that he had wronged us. He told us he ought to have given us something more than he had. He told us if it ever happened to our lot to be Col. of a regiment we would know then how he was situated. Says he, Gentlemen it hurts my feelings for you to talk to me the way you do. Well, says I, Col. if it hurts your feelings for us to tell you of what you have done, how do you suppose we feel, who have it to bear? We talked about an hour, when the drum beat for dress parade & we got up to leave. I went out. Capt. Gedney hung behind to change a few words with the major. He said the Col. looked as though he was going to *cry.* . . . You & Humphrey did wrong Dollie in crying peace at Keokuk. If I had contended for my rights there the regiment *never could have been organized,* unless they had made me the ranking Capt. Then I would have had the best position in the regiment. We are going to get a hearing with the commander of the post & learn by him what we can do. But rest assured they are not going to run over us, because we are from up the country. . . .

I have not heard from Wood-side or your father's for a long time. . . . I think very little about our property back [there], not as much as I ought. . . . There is a good deal of property back there to be left so loosely, but the cause requires it. If we do lose a good deal of it, it will have to go, we can't help it. But what do you suppose father's folks would say if they knew how much we had sacrificed to get into the service of the Country? They would think that I am a fool. . . .

To think that my father is against the cause I am risking everything for. . . . Let them be traitors Dollie if they want to be. They are no relatives of mine. No person who wishes people well who are trying to take my heart's blood from me shall call me brother by my consent. I feel too indignant Dollie to write any more about it. But *I love you with all my heart.* If you have the money to spare get Jane a dress worth $2 or $3 and give it [to] her. . . .

W. F. Vermilion

Tuesday Morning, Dec. 16th, 1862
My Own Love,

I have the blues a little this morning. . . . Jim McCammack[52] was here last night and I sat in the corner with my knitting and listened to him and John and John Runyan[53] talk about the war. My blood soon boiled but I said never a word. McCammack said word came yesterday that they were still fighting at Fredericksburgh and that Burnside was falling back. He was not beaten yet, but had lost ground.[54] It made me sick all over to hear this though I know it is not reliable. . . . If Burnside is whipped what will become of us? John Runyan is sure we can't conquer the South. They have too many good men. McCammack said they were fighting for their homes, their property, their lives, while the northern men are fighting for *money or fun!* They all assented to this. I made up my mind while they talked that I would go to Mrs. McCarty's as soon as I could. . . . Aunt Anna is so good to me, and has so many women there now that it won't do for me to stay there without paying her well. And I hate to spend your money, darling. I will make just a little do me as I can. I have not bought me anything for winter yet. I couldn't get to town to get them. If I can't go I will do with what I have. I can manage to get along comfortably enough. . . .

It was 8 weeks yesterday since you left me. . . .

Dollie

Wednesday Morning, Dec. 17th, 1862

Henry is better. He is eating his breakfast — a cup of coffee and a biscuit and butter.... John can't take me today. Father is shelling corn to take to the mill....

I think of you every minute. I would give everything I have in the world to have you home with me now, I would darling. Still I am proud of my gallant soldier husband. *But I love you too much.* I can't bear the separation like a brave woman might. My head is all right enough dearest, but my heart is weak and afraid. You don't know dear how contemptible these men at home all look to me now. I have no patience with them at all. I have not seen a woman whose husband is in the war since I came to this state — except Julia you know.

Goodby, my own sweet love. You know how Dollie loves you, don't you? If you come home dear I am afraid I shall *pet* you and *spoil* you till I won't know what to do with you. I will be good to you darling and try to make your home happy.
Dollie

P.S. Father manages badly I think. They are pretty hard run for money. I don't think he makes any money scarcely. He talks of renting the farm next year to John Runyan.... They say they don't get along near so well as they used to when the children were all at home. I guess it is about the same. People often think any time [is] better than the present. John stays here in spite of jeers and jibes and reproaches and scoldings such as *you* would not endure one month for all they are worth, and gets his living and every dime he can off the homestead. He doesn't care what they say or think of him. He cares for money and he means to have it. He is a queer genius that John.

I am very sorry that you don't have good officers. I know you don't like them darling and they don't treat you well. Be as patient as you can, and remember that you are serving your country — not Col. Kittredge.... Look beyond him darling to the cause you both serve. I am much afraid he will make your duty unpleasant and hard and dangerous for you. Oh dear one, be cautious.... If he hates you, love, there is no telling what he may do. Be watchful....

Thursday Night, Dec. 18th, 1862

My Dear Love,

... I got plenty of news today, but it is all bad. Burnside has fallen back across the river. He has failed so far. But worse than this is the report that the president is about to modify or withdraw his Proclamation.[55] Better a Waterloo defeat from Burnside than that he should retract one word of that Proclamation. At least we will not be kept in suspense much longer. We shall soon know. Two more weeks will bring the 1st of January. It will be a day dark with disaster and clouds of coming evils or a glorious day of Jubilee, just as our president shall stand firm or falter. His responsibility is terrible. I am beginning to fear for him. Oh, if he will only strike for the right now while he can. But we can only wait, with what patience we may. ...

... You say I must not stay here any more. I want to do just as you tell me my darling, but I am in a delicate position. They have been kind to me in their way all the time, *and now they are very kind* to me. They understand me and my wants better than they did at first. Henry is getting well now I think, and when he gets up there will be somebody to go to the post office for me all the time. He is going to take a daily paper and that would reconcile me to almost anything. At Aunt Anna's there are no men, and it will hardly be possible for us to go to the office ourselves in all weather. I am staying in this country because I can hear from you oftener than at home, and I would rather stay here on that account when Henry gets well — part of the time at least. They are not loyal but then not half the people here are. They are like their neighbors. Mother is getting right as fast as she can. I can make a conquest of her prejudices I think before long. ... They didn't think or know any better than to treat me as they did at first. I have forgiven it all. Won't you forgive them too, darling? It would all have been different if Henry had been well. I *don't* want to hurt their feelings dear. It would be wrong, and would look very badly on me. But still I want above everything else to please you. You can tell me what you want me to do and I will do it. ... I have tried to do right. If things had continued as they seemed at first I should have been gone before now. But they did better as soon as they knew how, and I ought not to blame them. I like to stay better — a great deal [more] than I did at first. Now dearest, I have told you the truth as nearly as I can, and I will come back to stay or not just as you wish. Remember that they are old and getting childish. As to the 3 boys — I ask nothing of them. God bless you darling. . . .

My darling, I want to see you more than I can tell you. . . . If I could see you a few days now I think I could bear it better. I surely could. If we never meet again my love I will wait for you *and live for you as long as I live in this world.* And you won't forget your Dollie, will you dear?
Mary

Benton Barracks, MO, Dec. 19, 1862
. . . We have not been paid any by the Government yet. . . . Fully half of the line officers are strapped, have not $2 to save their lives. Humphrey is out. John Wright is, & by the way I am nearly out, got about $25. But I will get along, don't be uneasy about that. . . .

You said in your last letter that you would stay at father's, a part of this time. . . . You have no business to stay with traitors Dollie. I don't regard their feelings. They don't regard ours. I'll assure you I want them to know (with every person in the Co.) that I act independent of the feeling of all the traitors whether they live *South or North.* If you can be comfortable at Miss McCarty's *make that your home.* I have no objections to your going to father's on a *visit,* but that is all. Let the people talk if they want to. . . . Let what I have said this time Dollie be the law. I am used to giving commands here Dollie, you know. You won't object to my giving them to you.
Will Vermilion

2

"You Are in Danger Now, Every Day, I Know"

Fate did not treat the 36th Iowa kindly during its initial period of military service. Made up primarily of men from small towns and farms who had had only limited exposure to communicable illnesses, the regiment suffered severely from various maladies both in Keokuk and St. Louis. Indeed, of all the regiments recruited from Iowa during the Civil War, the 36th Iowa had the eighth-highest fatality rate from disease. As a consequence, the War Department did not consider the regiment fit for duty until months after its muster into federal service. Finally, in December 1862, it received orders to embark for duty in the field.

What started as a simple redeployment soon turned into an adventure for the 36th Iowa. Twice along the way the regiment had to land in response to suspected enemy activity. Neither threat materialized, and eventually the regiment made its way to its destination: Helena, Arkansas.

Union forces had occupied Helena on July 12, 1862. The War Department envisioned it as a strategic point from which to initiate campaigns into the interior of Arkansas or down the Mississippi River. But the Union high command recognized that the town could also be a target for a Confederate attack, making it necessary to garrison troops there for defense. That task would occupy William Vermilion and his regiment for months to come.

While William dealt with his changing circumstances, Mary dealt with hers on the homefront. The Civil War proved divisive to

Theater of operations, 36th Iowa, 1863–1865.

many families, and Mary found that the Vermilions held widely different views on the prosecution of the war. Her husband, William, and brother-in-law, Henry, had volunteered to fight for the Union, but others in the family actively opposed the cause. Joel Vermilion, in particular, was an interesting case study involving antiwar sentiment. Originally a Whig, he had joined the nativist Know Nothing Party during the 1850s. As the historian Tyler Anbinder has demonstrated, most individuals who followed such a path became Republicans after the collapse of the Know Nothing Party. Joel Vermilion did not, however. He joined the Democratic Party in 1857 and became a bitter opponent of the Republican agenda. Three of his sons also shared his views. The disloyalty convinced Mary to move out. Fortunately, another familial relocation gave her such an opportunity. Julia May moved back to her mother's in Putnam County when the 36th Iowa moved south in December. Mary moved in with her and Aunt Anna soon thereafter.

The letters in the second chapter deal with William's impending battles in the field and Mary's continuing familial conflicts at home. William assesses the combat effectiveness of his unit as it is placed into a situation of potential danger. He also gives his wife vivid descriptions of the communities in which his regiment serves. Mary informs her husband about her adjustment to life in a household of women, and talks of the troubled state of affairs in Indiana. Both of them reveal to each other their frustration with the lack of progress achieved by Union military forces. They do find consolation, however, in their mutual approval of Lincoln's Emancipation Proclamation, and in their love for each other.

Jeannie Dean,[1] Mississippi River, Dec. 21, 1862

We will be at Cairo in an hour or two. . . . Humphrey & Will are not with us. They did not get back against we started. . . .

I am officer of the day today & have more than I can do. . . . We will not get to Helena for 2 or 3 days. . . . Dr. Phillips[2] tried to resign and could not. Don't say anything about it, the Dr. told me. . . . W. F. Vermilion

Mrs. McCarty's, Dec. 21st, 1862
My Own Darling,

I came down here last Friday. John brought me down like a gentleman — dressed himself up, and took good care of me. We came horseback. There are 5 women of us here now, and the only man among us is Billy May. Lina[3] is here now — what a good bright lively girl she is. . . .

I am sorry that you feel so bitter towards father's folks, dearest. I have often been sorry that I told you anything about it for it has caused you trouble, but I couldn't help it. When my feelings would be hurt I ran instantly to tell you — my best, my *only friend.* I don't think they treated me at first just as we would have treated them if they had come to Iowa. But I am sure now that it was because they didn't think or know any better. They didn't mean to do wrong or hurt my feelings. I have told you already what a change has come over them lately. Let us both forgive them dear love. I have fully. . . . We came here of our own accord you know and it would be wrong for us to come here and have any difficulty with them. It would nearly kill them now. *You must not write to them on the subject.* Please my love do not do this. First because *I would hate it so much* to be the cause of estrangement between you and them. And second because it would do harm. Father was crazy you know for nearly two years. He is not quite right yet, I don't think he ever will be, and a little trouble and excitement might throw him off balance and make him as wild as ever. He can't bear excitement. You would shudder to hear mother tell what they all suffered during those two years. She never told me till the other day. Let us be mindful darling of his grey hairs, and his shattered mind and do nothing that we can ever regret. Mother is as kind to me now as she can be. There is much good about her, much that I can love and reverence. And then she is *your mother*, and that makes her sacred in my eyes. I must not hurt her feelings, darling. Then Jane is a good girl sincerely attached to you and me. . . . She is intending to come to Iowa and stay with us awhile when we get home. . . . If you ever meet face to face, say what you please to them. As to their disloyalty I feel as badly about that as you do, but they are just like a large majority of the people now in this country. Not a whit worse. . . . Yesterday afternoon Lina and I went up to Mrs. Mc-Gaughey's.[4] We staid till dark. While the girls got supper we sat by the fire and talked about the war. . . . She is not at all discouraged by our reverse at Fredericksburg. She says Lincoln won't modify the Proclamation now. Her conversation cheered me up a little. We had on the whole a pleasant little visit. When we got home Sally Peck[5] was here to stay all night. She is another wholesouled Unionist. She brought Julia a letter from Humphrey. He said you were all well. These are a few simple words dear but you can't imagine how much good they do us. . . .

I am glad to hear that you are about to get your right in the regiment. . . . I hated all the time to have you submit to injustice, but I feared you would make the matter much worse. I don't want Col. Kittredge to be your enemy. He might cause you harm sometime. . . .

I fear we shall have a hard time of it in the South West, this winter. There will be a battle at Vicksburgh[6] I think before long. In all probability you will be there. . . .

Dollie

P.S. I will get a new dress for Jane when I have the chance. . . . Don't be uneasy about me darling, I shall get on now as well as I possibly can without you. That is the only cause I have for trouble. But let us be patient and hopeful. . . . This cruel separation will not last I trust very many months. . . .

Mrs. McCarty's, Tuesday Evening, Dec. 23rd, 1862
My Dearest Love,
    . . . I am staying here very comfortably. There are 5 women of us, and Julia's 3 children in family. They do the feeding themselves, and have the wood chopped. We make our own fires. And we have very good ones when it is cold. Today it is almost warm enough to do without. I sleep downstairs in the west room with Emily. This morning we waked up long before day, but were lazy, and lay and talked till Julia and Lina had breakfast ready. Generally we are smarter. . . . I wish I were with you my darling wherever you are, helping you, doing something for the cause that is so dear to us both. I ought to be dear, I feel that. You are too careful and tender of me dearest. I feel like I could endure hardships and privations as well as you. I could do and endure anything now to be with you love. To be near you now so that I could get to you at once if you were sick or hurt. But you have promised to send for me if you get sick. You must not forget that, will you my darling? You speak sometimes about me leaving this country before you come back. What do you want me to do about that? You have never told me. I can't think hardly of going back just now, just as you are going into danger. If you have fighting to do at all it will probably be before spring. I think if it suits you, that I will stay two or three months longer. We *may by that time see how the war is going*. Surely we can tell more about it then than we can now. Then if you are well, and I *can't go to you*, I will go home. Will this way be right? I don't like this country half as well as I always thought I would. I would rather live in Iowa. *I am proud of Iowa.* I am glad that *our home is there.* No other state has acquitted herself so nobly as Iowa. Besides, I think I ought to go home and look after things. I don't know that I could do any good. I might see after the stock and things at Woodside. If I can go to you at any time I want to do it above everything else. But if this is out of my power I think I ought to be at home caring for the things there. *That* would be doing something for you, and I would be better satisfied than to stay

here and do nothing. Father writes like they want me to come home. I am sorry for them. I didn't know how much they had sacrificed until I came here where no one has done anything. They will not have their reward. But I will do as you tell me what you want me to do about everything.

I am troubled and frightened, my beloved, when I think how far you are gone. . . . You know how uneasy I used to be about Matt[7] and Jimmy. I hardly ever think of them now or Will either. They are good boys too and I like them as much as any sister could her brothers, but I know a love so much deeper and stronger and more absorbing, that I scarcely think of them.

If you never come back to me dear love, I shall have no interest in life — nothing to live for. . . . There are times when the very blackness of despair gathers over my soul and I feel that I could lie down willingly by your side and die but to live without you I cannot. God pity us all!

Should you come home, my love, home with your life, I think I shall have more to be thankful for than any woman on earth. . . . It seems to me now that nothing could ever trouble me again. Life's petty cares and vexations could never touch me. I will make you a better wife darling, I will do more for your happiness than I ever did before. I used so often to do wrong dearest, so often forgot what rich blessings I had! The remembrance makes my heart ache often. Do you forgive me, dear one, for all the wrongs I did? And do you love me all the time? *All the time!*

Julia takes the separation from Humphrey very hard. She says if he were home again he should never go. Then she gets disgusted at the men here and says she would rather have a good man in the war than a "creature" like them at home. I see no wholesouled war men here hardly. . . . The warmest friends . . . in the county I have seen are women — widows too. I wish I could talk to you a long time about the war and our prospects now. It seems to us gloomy enough. But I am not in despair — I never have been about its final result. Our cause is just, and must succeed sooner or later. But I do fear they will make our victory cost us too dear.

Wednesday Morning, Tomorrow is Christmas, but we hardly know it here. Old Mr. Pentecost[8] is going to kill a turkey and has invited father and mother and me over to eat it. . . . I think all the time of last Christmas when I was at *home* getting a Christmas dinner for you. Don't you remember how you came home from Chicago in the night, and brought me 4 new books, and how glad and happy we were? Oh, were those not pleasant days, dear love? Don't you think when we get home again we will know better how to appreciate our blessings? We will love each other more and be happier than we ever have been in our lives. . . .

We read a good deal here. Of nights we take turns reading aloud. Last night we read "Among the Pines." [9] I think by the time we finish it Julia and Emily will be as thorough abolitionists as I am. A few more chapters will complete their conversion. Now dear one I must say goodby again. But I want to beg you to promise me one thing. If you get sick or unwell and I can't go to you get a furlough and come here to your Dollie. . . . I know you will hate to leave your men so much that you will not do it if you can help it. But remember your Dollie and don't stay there and die. . . .
Dollie

Memphis, Dec. 27, 1862

If it were not that I know you will be uneasy about me, I should not write you this evening. . . . For 3 days I have been sick — not bad — but unwell.

Three days ago we stopped here, were ordered ashore immediately. We went up into the Center of the City & lay on our arms all night. The authorities were expecting an attack but none came. . . . About noon we were ordered out here inside of the fortifications & here we are yet. Military men here say they are expecting an attack in a few days. I doubt it very much. . . .

The more I see of the Army, Dollie, the more I become convinced you can't be with me. Here the Women will all be excluded from the lines in a few days. Then there would be no place for you but the Rebel city of Memphis & all of our Guns are being set upon the City, so if the Rebels take it we will burn it in two hours. The attack in all probability will not be made. . . . If it does we will fight inside of fortifications. Don't be uneasy Dollie. . . .

Matt Kemper left here with his regiment some four weeks ago.

One of Dr. Hay's boys is here in the Hospital.[10] Matt was quite well when he left. Si Reed is here.[11]

W. F. Vermilion

Fort at Memphis,[12] Dec. 27, 1862

. . . This is the first I have been out all day since we came here, consequently I know but little more of things than at home. Gen. Asboth is in command of the fortifications. Gen. Hurlbert commands the place. Hurlbert I have not seen. Asboth is a blustering Dutchman,[13] goes out to do a good deal of business himself. . . .

After breakfast I walked out and looked at the guns . . . that are planted to destroy the City in case of an attack. . . . The authorities are going to take down some 90 or 100 houses. They are in the way of the range of the guns. Yesterday they put some Negroes at work tearing them [down] with a Capt. or Lieut. over them to superintend the business. After they got under headway the Officer went to dinner. While he was gone the Negroes set fire to the house and burned the house down, thinking that the quickest way to do the work of destruction. That was Negro-like. . . .

Will

Fort at Memphis, Dec. 29, 1862

My Dear Dollie,

. . . The boys are all without money. . . . I have about $30. . . . If we draw money the first of the year we will be all right. If we don't I don't know what we will do — without, I suppose. . . .

We had no excitement on our trip down till we got to Columbus Ky. There everything was in perfect ferment. . . . About 10 o'clock at night we were pulled out in line of battle on the river bank. Our Co. all went out finely except G. Owen and John Clowser, who were sleeping on the lower deck. . . . Someone told me about it and I got them out quick — you had better believe. They say they never woke up. They were awake when I went to see them. I will watch them from this on, especially Owen. Don't say anything about it however, they may turn up all right.[14] We distributed 40 rounds of cartridges to the men and then went back on board the boat. . . . The first day we got here . . . we came ashore and slept on our arms in the City Park all night. . . . The regiment stayed there a little while when they were ordered down here in the fort which is in the southern part of the City, and put by our Col. in a horse shed — that is the man. . . .

Since writing the above . . . the report came into our tent that Grants[15] army was coming into the city. . . . Soon found that it was a detachment and coming in for supplies. . . . I have not been able to learn whether the Iowa Sixth is along or not.

After Supper, I have just now talked to a Lieut. who belongs to the train that has just come from Grants army. He is very much discouraged. He says they have had a very hard time for the last two months. Thinks some other man will have to do the fighting beside Grant. . . .

Now Dollie . . . first of all things I would like to see you. . . . I would kiss Dollie and Dollie would pet me. I would love her and she would love me. I would hold Dollie's head on my bosom and she would pet me just as we used to do at Woodside. . . . While I think of it Dollie, let me tell you I want your likeness. If you are at Mrs. McCarty's can you go and get it taken for me. Send it to this place and it will follow me. I would give everything in the world for it tonight. I often lay at night Dollie and wonder if I know how you looked. So send it to me Darling. . . .

W. F. Vermilion

Helena, Dec. 30, 1862
My Dear Dollie,

. . . Yesterday I got a few lines from Mullinix.[16] He had sold my hogs, & wanted to trade calves with me. My stock was doing well. . . .

Last week the expedition left here for Vicksburg, about 50 thousands strong, with 4 or 5 Gun boats. This evening the news came here that they were fighting on both sides of Vicksburg. Every person here is uneasy here — not about the result of the fight, but it is the general impression that our loss will be great. . . . 6 or 7 regiments from Iowa are there. We will get more news tomorrow — I think — I hope it will be good. If good news ever comes, I want it now.

Capt. Hale[17] of Eddyville & myself went ashore this evening &

looked around a little. Helena is rather a hard looking place. The Town is not so large as Ottumwa. It is not so well built either. . . . It will cost us something to live here. Eggs are only 33 ct. per doz, butter 33 ct. per lb. Potatoes $1.80, & everything else in proportion. Don't you see I can't save any money?

Let me tell you how we live. We eat — sometimes hard bread & sometimes soft. Generally we have been able, so far to get very good soft bread. We have Coffee & tea whenever we want, generally 3 times a day. We have sugar cured hams, sometimes beefstake, dried fruit, butter, molasses & more, plenty for war times. We can live on it very well.

You don't know how glad I was to hear that you were at Mrs. McCarty's. You will be more comfortable there Dollie. They will be more to you than father's folks were.

You don't want me to write to father's folks. Well Dollie do you want me to risk my life in the field for the course of our Country, & respect traitors anywhere. . . . They can't talk about our Country, without saying things that will hurt the feelings of my best friend on God's Earth. How else can I help feeling bitter when they treat everything, & every person that is dear to me as they do. There is as much difference between them & me as there is between me & the traitors here. They want me to fail. They want my cause to fail. What else are they but rebels. . . . Can I love my enemies. *But Dollie stay where you are till I order different.*

No more news from Vicksburg. I have just been talking to Col. Drake. He says the news from below is unsatisfactory. We have effected a landing, but our loss is heavy. I hope the news will be better tomorrow. If it is not we will all have the blues. . . .

W. F. Vermilion

Helena, Arkansas, Jan. 2, 1863

We have been here now for two days. . . . The Fort I have not got to see yet. The boys who have seen it, say it is quite a place. . . . Gen. Gorman's [18] dwelling is situated not far away from our camp, in the edge of the town, at the foot of the blough (I don't know whether that was spelled right or not). It is a very nice little fraim house. . . .

The weather here is quite warm. . . . There was frost yesterday morning but no ice. . . . This is the climate for me, Dollie, but not the country. This is a rebel country, and you know my Dollie I don't like it. They are my enemies and I don't want to live where they are any longer than is necessary to whip them, which will take some time. The Garrillas make runs on our chain guards every few days and capture 10 and 15 at a time. This evening there is a rebel boat lying at the wharf. It has come in from White River with 40 or 50 prisoners to be exchanged.[19] The Government is playing with the rebels in the South West. We will never succeed until the Government adopts a different policy. . . .

Yesterday news came up from below that Gen. Sherman[20] had taken Vicksburg. We were all jubilant for awhile. But it did not last us long, for another boat came up with Gen. Wyman's body,[21] and the news that our forces had taken but a small portion of the rebel works and that our losses were very heavy. . . .

If we are whipped what will we do Dollie. In fact sometimes I think this government is going by the board anyhow. . . . If we had no traitors in the north to discourage us we could do better. But Dollie how can we keep up all of the time when those who ought to be our friends have proven themselves to be our enemies. Suppose the Government goes down, where is there a spot we would like in the continent. I mean the people. I can think of none. . . .

. . . The boys get mad occasionally at Col. Kittredge, at the Quarter Master[22] and etc. Then the Col. gets mad, then we the line officers get mad, the Col. threatens to Court Marshall us for counseling insubordination. Don't be uneasy about me, my good Dollie, I'll try to stay inside the ropes. . . . The Col. I think was very anxious to have us stay in Tennessee for no other purpose but to keep us if possible out of Gen. Curtis' Department. . . . The old Gen. would correct things for us and make everything all right.

The Col. still treats us mean, or if he does not do so it is done by some one in power. For instance the Quarter Master failed to yesterday to [*sic*] issue to our boys the regular rations. They had not had any coffee for several days. This morning unbeknowing to me they raised a fuss with Mr. Quarter Master and I was called in to settle the fuss. This afternoon I called on him and told him that the coffee had to come, and *it did come in a hurry too.* The Quarter Masters in the army as a general thing are very mean and I think, I fear, ours is as bad as any of them. . . .

The 43rd regt. Ind. Vol. is camped along by our side. There are two Co. in the regiment from Putnam [County]. Captain Layne[23] from Greencastle has command of one of them. . . .

W. F. Vermilion

Mrs. McCarty's, Thursday Morning, Jan. 8th, 1863

My Dearest Love,

. . . Are you forgetting me, my pet? You say, *if* I am like I used to be; and that you wonder if you know how I looked. Yes, dearest, you do know how I looked, and all about your Dollie. She is just like she was at Woodside, only she *loves you more than she did*, and, I hope, she is better. . . . Don't you remember, darling, the old happy days, and how I loved you and petted you? I didn't think it was possible for any human heart to love more than mine did then. . . . You are dearer to me now. Your very danger and suffering makes you dearer. I shall spoil you, when you come home, I know. I shall, sweet love. How I will wait on you, and do everything in the world to please you, and stay with you always. You shall never go, even to feed Rocker, without me. . . .

I got two letters last night from father and Jimmy. They were all well. . . . Father wrote the 27th. He was at Iconium the day before and saw Mullinix. He said they were well and doing well at Woodside. Jake Fees was married Christmas Day to John Scott's daughter.[24] Poor insignificant! Thom. Dykes married Bartlett's daughter.[25] This was about all the news. . . . Jim said Blue[26] was elected Captain in their company. Matt has no doubt been in the Vicksburg battle. He may be killed. But I don't feel uneasy about him. I can't feel uneasy, or interested about anybody but you, my own love. I am afraid this is selfish and wicked, but I can't help it, dearest. Julia has had no letters yet from Humphrey. She is troubled about him. Sally Denny has not heard from her husband for more than a month. He was at Oxford, Miss. then. She is nearly crazy. Poor thing, I pity her from the bottom of my heart. I don't know how soon I may suffer just such suspense. . . .

Friday Morning, My Precious Darling, I am in despair this morning almost. The news is now that instead of taking Vicksburgh and so many prisoners, Sherman was repulsed with a loss of from 3 to

5 thousand men. This news came yesterday. Oh, dear love, I am so troubled about you. I am afraid you are now at Vicksburgh or will have to go there. And I am afraid they will kill you, my love. I have not seen any papers this week and all I know is hearsay. I can't wait, it seems to me, for news. Yesterday I was in good spirits about the war, now I am appalled at our fearful loss of brave men, 10,000 of Rosecrans'[27] and 3,000 of Sherman's.

Dollie

Mrs. McCarty's, Sunday, Jan. 11th, 1863

My Own Darling,

... We have just been to dinner. We had fresh bones and potatoes stewed, and frumenty[28] and applebutter and cornbread and milk. You would have liked it. I never sit down to eat without thinking of you and wishing for you. ... I am afraid you are living hard. ... Have you nothing but your blanket to sleep on? I know I never shall get tired petting you when you come home, and cooking you something nice and trying to make amends for all the hardships you have suffered.

I saw a disabled soldier the other day. He was here. He used to live at John McCarty's, and is there now. He was wounded in both legs at Antietam. He can walk about now with a cane. Says he is going into the service again, when he gets well.[29] He seems like a very worthy sort of man, but he looks pitiable. I am sorry for a sick soldier, be he who he may. ...

Dollie

Helena, Arkansas, Jan. 11, 1863

My Dear Dollie,

... Yesterday there were some 15,000 troops here, now 4 or 5 thousand would be a large estimate. Where the 10,000 are gone I do not know.[30] You will have learned before you get this letter that Gen. Sherman failed at Vicksburg (failures are common these days). ...

Will

Helena, Arkansas, Jan. 12, 1863

My Own Dollie,

... About your coming here. I think you had better stay where you are and write me letters. ... Lieut. May will be there in a few months and he my darling will tell you the utter impossibility of you coming down here. ... I have no friends here except the U.S. soldiers and Negroes. ...

Will

Wednesday Morning, Jan. 14th, 1863

My Dearest Love,

... Indiana, they say, is on the verge of revolution. Day before yesterday they had wild times at Indianapolis. The secesh tried to get possession of the arsenal, but were prevented by the Governor,[31] who called out the militia. The Legislature broke up in a row. ... The democrats are determined that the state shall "secede" and they think now is the time to strike. They don't propose *yet* to join Jeff Davis' Confederacy, but to form a Southwestern confederacy of their own. The opposition in Ohio and Illinois are ripe for it too. They say Lincoln has violated the Constitution — in issuing his late Proclamation — and that now is their time, if ever. The Governor of Kentucky,[32] too, counsels armed resistance to the Proclamation. ... For every friend the government has in this state now, it has two bitter and malignant and ignorant foes. They were working on the roads about Westland yesterday, and in a company of 8 or 10 Abe McCarthy was the only professed Unionist. Tom Bridges[33] — you knew him, didn't you? — told that 90,000 soldiers had thrown down their arms, and gone home, in consequence of the Proclamation! And that 4 carloads of "niggers" had just been landed in Terre Haute! Another said that white men couldn't walk the streets of Lafayette without being insulted by great black "niggers," even now. My dearest, I blush to write such things about Indiana. I could not have believed such ignorance and baseness possible in a country that was so long my home, and yours. ...

Dollie

Sunday Afternoon, Jan. 18th, 1863

My Own Darling,

. . . I went to Tom's store and bought calico to make me a sun bonnet. He was very obliging. Isaiah [34] went to the office and got my letters and sent them to me, as soon as the mail came. . . . They say Henry is well, excepting his feet. . . . I had a very pleasant visit at Bournes'. [35] They are first rate people. I slept in the room where I first promised to be yours. Do you remember that rainy Sunday, years and years ago? I do, my dear one. The first time I staid there, and slept in that room, I cried nearly all night. I couldn't help it, darling. And the first time you ever kissed me, I was sitting in that room, by the fire, just as I sat last night. I thought of everything, and couldn't sleep much. But I am glad of one thing, my own love. A long time ago, I promised, right there, to give myself to you, and I have kept the promise. Are not you glad too, love? If there ever was a promise sacredly kept on earth, that one has been, and shall be, to the end. . . .

I feel badly about Humphrey coming home; not that I want him to stay if he is not able, but it will be so hard to see him come while you are left. And then you may miss him a great deal. . . . But I will try not to be selfish, not to grudge Julia her happiness. . . .

If I can't go to you, my loved one, I would rather be at home. It looks badly, dearest, for me to go anywhere else to stay after your leaving me at father's. People don't understand it, and if they knew the facts they would *all*, except 2 or 3 widow women, blame *us*, and not them. You have no idea, darling, how little genuine loyalty there is in this community. Treason is fashionable here. People say boldly that they wish or hope this state may secede, and the party now in power here are doing their best to take her out of the Union. . . .

Dollie

Friday Evening, Jan. 23rd, 1863

My Good Darling,

. . . You are in danger now, every day, I know. And then I don't get used to the separation. I miss you more every day. I want to see you worse every hour. . . . And the one thing that I always want to tell you is that your Dollie loves you, as no man was ever loved before, and that she can hardly live without you at all. I am astonished that I ever consented to your going. I don't know what possessed me, dearest. I could not bear it now as I did then. But I don't blame you, sweet love; you did right. It is I who am wrong. I wish I were braver. But I was not made for a heroine. . . . As to myself dearest, I feel ashamed of the life I am living. It is not worthy of a patriotic American woman. I ought to be up and doing [something] for the cause! I shall always be ashamed of myself, I think. And I am afraid my husband will be ashamed of me too. . . .

Emily and I have made a large bouquet of flowers. . . . They are pretty . . . but I had no heart in the work. . . . I thought a little time of a little tent pitched on the bank of the "Great River," and my heart went out to the dear lonely occupant, and I felt that to be there with you to comfort you and care for you would be a far richer boon than to be given to dwell in the palace of kings. . . . Dollie

My Cabin, Helena, Jan. 23, 1863
My Dollie,
. . . We consider there is no danger here, except from Guerrillas. . . . 26 of the 28th Iowa got taken prisoner 4 or 5 weeks ago.[36] It was in consequence of the carelessness of the commander. We don't want the 36th to be taken that way. . . .

The authorities here are organizing a negro regiment. . . . They said they could get plenty of them. . . .

I have a steel armor that covers me quite well.[37] It will resist any rifle shot. I intend to wear it, not through cowardice but because I consider it my duty to protect myself in every manner possible. Don't speak of it to anyone, Dollie. The boys here don't know it. . . . Will Vermilion

Sunday Evening, Jan. 25th, 1863
My Own Darling,
. . . Henry is sitting up all the time, and can walk a little, but he looks badly yet. He is like a skeleton almost. . . . Isaiah is not strong.

He coughs and spits blood, and looks very bad. I am afraid, darling, that he won't live long. They say Tom is very uneasy about him. They are all anxious about you now. Mother laments a great deal about you. And they haven't said one word against the war. The truth is, I think, they are badly scared about the troubles at home. They see now how the men they elected to office are keeping the promises they made, to end the war. I had a plain talk with John as we came along yesterday. He asked me, as soon as we started, what I thought of the aspect of affairs. I told him [the] war would be moved from Kentucky to Indiana and that every man who voted for this Democratic legislature would have to assume *his* share of the responsibility. . . . John didn't know what to say, and at last he burst out with "Well, I didn't think of it! I didn't believe things would go the way they have." He says father is coming around, too. He doesn't talk at all, as he did before. . . .

Spring is nearly here, darling. It will be here by the time I get home. But if you would really rather have me stay, I will, my pet. I will do anything that pleases you. I get indignant and out of patience oftentimes with the traitors here, who are trying to work us so much harm, and I feel like I must go home anyhow. They are an "abomination" in my eyes, and I want to get out of sight and hearing of them. I . . . think when you know it all you will want me to go home — home to our brave, loyal Iowa. But you shall judge, my dear one. It shall be just as you say. . . .
Dollie

Tuesday Morning, Jan. 27th, 1863
My Dearest Love,

. . . Yesterday mother gave me a beautiful new blanket. I thought you would not want it . . . and I didn't want to take it. I told her I couldn't take it home, that my trunk would be full. Did I do right about it darling? I have taken nothing from them but yarn enough to knit you and myself each a pair of stockings. I wish I could send yours to you. I am afraid you are needing them. . . .

I have nothing reliable from Illinois. . . . There was a rumor that she had seceded. . . . Eckels[38] of Greencastle says there are 2,000 men in Putnam County just awaiting the tap of the drum to rise up against the Administration. . . . He ought to be hung, and I hope

he will be some day. But the strongest side is the right side with most of the people here. They will get their reward. . . .
Dollie

Helena, Jan. 27, 1863
My Good Dollie,
   . . . I was down at Segt. Hancock's mess. . . . Dave Stewart [39] spoke up and said "when the Regt. got paid off there were a good many men who would desert and go home, that their pay was keeping them now." Several of the boys spoke and sanctioned it. . . . Well, says I "I am very glad you spoke of it boys. I have just been around to headquarters. . . . They have heard of such talk and are going to have an investigation and ascertain just what every man who has been talking so, has said." I left them all rather serious. . . .
Will

Thursday Evening, Jan. 29th, 1863
My Dearest Love,
   . . . I got a letter yesterday from Jimmy. It was the first word I had heard of him since the Springfield fight.[40] He was in the thickest of the battle. The balls flew around him like hail, and one spent ball struck him on the cheek, but didn't hurt him. That was the only one that touched him. His Capt. Blue was mortally wounded and died soon after. 15 others of his company were wounded, but none that I knew. I feel very sorry about Blue. . . . He got his commission the day before Christmas, and Jimmy said he made a good Capt. I pity his young wife.[41] Poor thing. . . .
   Allee was very sociable and clever. . . . He is troubled about affairs here. He says we are just as sure to have civil war here, as if it were here now. He doesn't know how to stand it hardly. His neighbors say they prefer Jeff Davis' government to Lincoln's. He and Amanda [42] are all right. They seem to agree about everything, and she gets on very well with his children. He has 3 at home. They will have a larger family afterwhile! Jane told me as we went up that she and young Wilcox [43] are engaged. . . . She has told no one else. They made this arrangement while I was at Aunt Anna's. She said she needn't wait thinking she would go to stay with us, for

they would never give her money enough to take her there. I told her if she would come, *you* would send her the money. I knew you would do it for her cheerfully, and she should have everything she needed while she staid. She nearly cried, and said it would be too much for us to do for her. But I think you would like to do it, dear. She wanted me to tell her what I thought about her marrying. I told her I couldn't advise her, further than to *"be sure she was right* before she went ahead." I don't know anything about the man. I hope she will do well. She likes him, I know. . . .
Dollie

Helena, Jan. 29, 1863
My Good Dollie,
. . . Wesley May and I got to talking about the old times this evening and as usual it made me a little blue. . . . My life in Illinois came up. . . . It always makes me blue, Dollie, you know for me to think of my past life. I have done so little. . . . It is an evident fact that I have not done much during the 32 years I have lived. Whether I will live to do anything worthy of a man or not is yet to be told. If we gauge the future by the past I will not. Time will only tell, I must wait. . . .

Jan. 30, 3 o'clock P.M., Capt. Phillips is back to the regt. again. The boys say he could not get a Divorce. . . . His discharge would not be accepted. The Col. says now that it was never sent up. . . . At St. Louis he tried to get the surgeons to give him a certificate of disability but they would not do it. At Memphis he wrote out his discharge on a sheet of foolscap paper, stating the cause of his disability and that he regretted very much having to resign. Some one happened to get to see it before he handed it in, and told him that was not the way to write a resignation. He, then informed we were just about to start for this place, asked Dr. Cousins[44] if he would just write it out for him. The Dr. told him he would, and send it up with the certificate of disability. With that understanding Phillips went to St. Louis and waited a reasonable length of time for his divorce as the boys call it. He thought best to come back. . . . When he came in this morning he told every person he met he wanted to see the boys, so had decided not to stay away. . . . Poor fellow. If it had been me I would have gone home. I would have as soon be dishonorably discharged from the service as to remain in it in such a dishonorable manner. Let him go, however it will suit him and his friends when he gets back where he lives in Iowa. He can tell them that he went into the service to get out of the Draft, and as soon as he found there was going to be no Draft [that would] amount to anything, he done his best to get out. I don't envy him his reputation here.

From below we have it that the water is running through the canal at Vicksburg,[45] to the depth of 5 feet, and that one gunboat has run through and gone down to get news from Banks.[46] The report says there is 3 feet of blue clay in the bottom of the channel that the water doesn't wash out. There are 16 regt. working . . . besides all the negroes they can get. . . . The News from the east is that the army has not crossed the Rappahannock (I don't know whether that word is spelled right or not). That Burnside is superseded by Hooker. I don't know whether to believe it or not.[47]

Our brigade is all here now. I believe Gen. Fisk[48] is our brigadier. We can't tell when we will go down the river. . . . But let me tell you one thing Dolly I want you to do — or rather not to do, don't be uneasy. . . . Every one who is in the army runs the risk[s] of a soldier. . . . Be hopeful then my sweet Dollie, I will come to you after awhile. When we have decided whether we have a country to live in or not. If we have no country my Darling we will have no place to live.

We all got our Commissions a few days ago and they all date on the 4th day of Oct. So you see no one of us can claim rank over another. This the Col. says will not do. Which I think is pretty true. For instance were it necessary for a Capt. to command the Regt. which is frequently the case. Would not know who to give the command to, or what command to obey. For this reason it is necessary to know who the ranking Capt. is. The question comes up, how are we to determine it? By lot, the Col. says. We tell him to show us the law and we will act as he says. He says he will not split hairs with us. "But" says he last Sunday evening "you, gentlemen, must determine this matter, or do the other thing, which others think will not be very pleasant." Be sure you are right and then go ahead Col., says I. When you have the law on your side and you want anything done, Col., *have it done*. I will submit. But sir, says I when the law is in my favor *you must expect me to have the benefit of it* if I can get at the proper authority to have it dealt out. (Not changing the subject, but just here let me tell you that the QM wanted us the other [day] to receive 20 days rations at one time, when the Regulations provides that they should be issued while in the field for from 5 to 10 days. We would not take them. The care was too much.) There are 8 of us who are concerned in this matter of rank. 5 out of the 8 are in favor of giving it to me because they say I am respected and ought to have it. You need not be uneasy when I have such backing as that. But the Col. says . . . that we did not determine the matter immediately or do the other thing. . . . I supposed he would have all 8 of us under arrest before this time. . . . The Capts. *all* say I have acted honorably in the matter so far — more so than they could have asked. . . .

I let the Company elect an orderly sergeant, after Wesley May was promoted to 1st Lieut. . . . They elected Henry Swallow[49] almost unanimously. . . . He will make a first rate orderly. He will not be a good commander but he will be clever, and can do the business well — very well.

What else shall I write about, love. That cracker — that keep sake — I guess.[50] Keep it till I come home — that is if you have not eaten it up before you get this letter. . . .

Saturday morning, early, The boys have no news, yet today, which is a very uncommon thing. In one mess, when ever any goes out and fails to bring in any extraordinary news they make him carry a kettle of water. None of them have been out yet. . . .
Will Vermilion

Friday Morning, Jan. 30th, 1863
My Darling,
. . . I would not like to live in this neighborhood. . . . There are too many ignorant people living around. I don't wonder that after you once got away, you never cared to come back much. . . . I feel sorry that I ever came back to this country, it cost us so much, then again I conclude that I have had the worth of my money. I should always have wanted to come. Now I am cured. . . .
Dollie

Sunday Morning, Feb. 1st, 1863
My Dearest Love,

. . . You know you told me sometime ago to buy Jane a new dress. Well yesterday afternoon she went to town, and I gave her $5, and told her to get me the nicest dress she could at Tom's. She brought back a beautiful dark calico at 25 cents a yard, and I gave it to her. If I had given her a deed to a farm she couldn't have been more surprised. And she was pleased as well as you ever saw a child in your life. Mother was pleased about it too. Isaiah was here yesterday. He is a good deal better than he was a while ago. . . .
Dollie

Helena, Feb. 1, 1863
Good Evening Dollie,

. . . There was preaching in the Regt. this afternoon. Brig. Gen. Fisk talked awhile. . . . It is said we will belong to his Brigade, though he will soon have command of a division. Either Col. Rice[51] or Col. Kittredge will command our Brigade. Col. Rice is of the 33rd Iowa. I hope he will get command of it, for if Kittredge gets it Drake will command our Regt. That will be bad. I dislike Kittredge but he is a better commander than Drake. . . .
Will

Wednesday Morning, Feb. 4th, 1863
My Dearest Love,

. . . Had I not better write to father, and tell him not to send me any money except $10 till I hear whether you want me to go or stay? If you would rather I should stay, I will write again, and tell him to send it. I told him in my last letter that May had resigned, and I thought he would go home with his family, and that I should go with them. . . .

I got a letter from Will last night. . . . He didn't say a word about you, except that you were quite well. I wouldn't give him much for a letter if there is nothing about my "Peaches" in it. . . .

You said, if you ever get home again you thought you would stay with your Dollie. I thank you for saying that. You won't leave me anymore, will you pet? There is no peace and happiness for Dollie, apart from you. As well had any part of my body to try and live without the rest, as for me to live without you, love. I feel like only half a being. But I will try to have patience and faith. You will come home sometime, darling, and then we will be happy enough to make amends for all. God bless you.
Dollie

Helena, Feb. 4, 1863
My Darling,
    . . . Our boys came in this morning. . . . They went down the river about 20 miles to what is called the Yazoo Cutoff and blew up and threw out the levee, which prevented the water from running from the Mississippi to the Yazoo River. . . . It will overflow a large farming district and give a good navigable stream for Gunboats to run from the Mississippi to the Yazoo. . . . The object may be to send troops across and then march them down in the rear of Vicksburg. The boys while out had a fine time of it. They came in this morning loaded with nice fresh meat. . . . I hope Gen. Gorman will send them out on fatigue duty soon again. Though this afternoon I have been told several times that he is out with an order punishing any person who commits such depredations with death. . . . If he undertakes to enforce his order it will be an unpleasant time for him. He is very unpopular with everybody here — but rebels. . . . I think he is an Indianian. He used to live about Gosport. Albert Hancock says he used to know him quite well. He is an old Democrat[52]. . . .
William

Friday Morning, Feb. 6th, 1863
My Own Darling,
    I . . . am in the east room with mother and Amanda and Jane and Esther[53]. . . . All the men are in the other room talking loudly about something — I don't know what — yes, politics it is, for I caught the words "Breckenridge," "Sherrill,"[54] "Lincoln" just this min-

ute, as Etty opened the door. This reminds me, dearest, that they have had a battle this week over in the "State of Morgan [County]." They have opened the ball at last. We have been hearing of it for 2 or 3 days, but Allee's account of it seems to be the straightest one. He says a couple of officers came to Martinville[55] to arrest 2 deserters (There are lots of deserters in this country, nearly all from the Army of the Potomac) who were there. The Copperheads gathered together and resisted the officers, mobbed them and drove them away. They went to Indianapolis and the Governor sent them back with a company of Cavalry. They had quite a skirmish with the mob, but finally got the deserters, and a good many of the Copperheads, and took them off. . . . So it seems that in the first battle the "pure democracy" have been worsted. I think before they are done with him, they will find Gov. Morton is a "whole team." He is the only hope of this state now. . . .

Feb. 8, Humphrey brings a good account of you. He says every man in your Co. likes you, and that yours is the best in the regiment. He says you are a *good man every way*. Just as if I didn't know that you are the best man in the world! He doesn't know, half so well as I do, how good you are. . . . He saw Capt. Wright's wife at Memphis going to join *her* husband.[56] She told him she had been offered $30 a month to work in the hospital at Memphis. I wish I could get a post like that somewhere on the river. Then I could be nearer to you, darling, and I would be just as safe as I am here. Can you do anything for me dear, in the way of getting me such a place — in case you should be willing for me to go? I should like it, darling.

They are all talking here about father. Last Sunday at Deer Creek, he prayed for the soldiers — all of them, and for you in particular, and for the wives and children who are left all over the country. Julia said he left nothing unsaid. He never did the like before. . . . They say it is a hopeful sign. I think it is too. . . . Humphrey says you told him to tell me a great many things, but he can't remember what they were. I wish he could. Write often now, love, for I can never hear one word about you, except what you write to Dollie. I used to hear through Julia's letters, sometimes. . . .
Dollie

Captain John Wright. Photograph courtesy of Roger Davis.

Mrs. McCarty's, Sunday, Feb. 8th, 1863
My Own Darling,

Here I am again at Aunt Anna's. Friday night I heard that Humphrey had come, and yesterday morning I came down to see him.... Humphrey has told me a great deal about you, but not half

enough, not half that I wanted to hear. He gave me the letters and the inkstand and the cracker. Thank you, my love. I wanted some little thing from you, and these are just as good as anything else. I will keep the cracker till you come home and then I will eat it. . . .
Dollie

Helena, Ark., Feb. 8, 1863
My Dear Dollie,
 . . . We have got no pay yet. Just as I was writing the last sentence my candle burned out. I had another one lying by my side. I picked it up and lit it. It burned for a minute nicely, then it grew dim, then it grew dimmer, then it went out and left me in the dark. I thought — is it possible that this great Government is no more than that candle. The candle was bright for awhile and then went out. The Government — this good star of Liberty — has been shining brightly for 80 odd years. Must it fade as the candle has. Must the light of liberty by which the American people have been guided fade and go out. Woe be unto man — to the American people — if such is to be their fate. . . .
Will Vermilion

Monday Evening, Feb. 9th, 1863
My Good Darling,
 . . . I think of you every minute, day and night. . . . I don't think Julia is half so happy as I would be if you were at home. It seems to me that I never should take my eyes off of you. I would go with you everywhere, and listen to every word you said. Oh darling, do you think you will come back to your poor Dollie? I am glad you told me about having the armor, love. I won't speak of it, and I am so glad you have it, if it will be any protection. It is right to use it. . . .
Dollie

Thursday Evening, Feb. 12th, 1863
My Own Darling,
 . . . I have been writing to Matt today, and trying to cheer him up — heavy as my own heart is. I had not written to him before

since about new year's. He says he has not heard of you and Will since you left St. Louis — nor from Jimmy since last Fall. Tell Will to write him. He sent me Gen. Sherman's address to the 6th when he left them. It is patriotic. He speaks in the highest terms of the 6th. Said "*that* was the regiment he was always proud of." "That he was willing to fight the rebels, if need be, till the day of judgment, and he knew they were the boys that would help him do it." Matt says he has faith in Sherman. I don't think he has much in Grant. Still, they say Sherman, or somebody, blundered fatally at Vicksburgh. I only hope Grant may prove himself equal to the contest before him now. I can see no prospect of Banks getting up the river to cooperate at Vicksburgh. He will not pass Port Hudson. It will be, I fear, the hardest battle of the war, and if we fail, I fear our cause will be almost lost. May God strike for the *Right.* . . .
Dollie

Helena, Feb. 14, 1863
My Own Dollie,
. . . I was on duty all day yesterday and last night. While I was going the rounds I met and rode some distance with an old rebel. He was born in Kentucky, was raised there with Gen. Gorman. He thinks a great deal of the General. . . . But says he "I hope Gen. Prentiss[57] will prove himself to be as good a man as Gen. Gorman." I told him that Gen. Prentiss was a very good man. That the loyal people of the United States thought far more of him than they did of Gorman. He had the impudence to tell me that the people of this state were loyal up to the issuing of Lincoln's *Proclamation.* I merely told him "it was a lie," and let him go on his way rejoicing.

Lieut. Pearson[58] of the Centerville Co. has 2 children, aged I should think 4 and 6 years, in his quarters this afternoon. . . . The girl is full as white as many children living North, the parents of whom are always prattling about the Abolitionists bringing Negroes North to associate with white people. Poor fools that they are, talking about Amalgamation. They believe in slavery but not amalgamation, when slavery *is* amalgamation. The former can't exist without the latter more than the viper can bite without fangs. . . .
Will

Monday Morning, Feb. 16th, 1863
My Dearest Love,

. . . I think the vicinity of Vicksburgh will be dreadfully unhealthy for our soldiers. If you get unable for duty darling, get a furlough . . . or resign. That is what I want you to do. . . . I don't counsel you to do wrong. . . . It would be wrong to stay there and lose your life, when by coming home you might save it. The army is not the only place where patriotic men are needed. I have never seen a time in my life when the services of good men were so much needed at home. . . . The greatest danger now is not from the rebels in your front, but from the traitors in your rear. . . .
Dollie

Tuesday Morning, Feb. 17th, 1863
Good Morning, Darling,

. . . It will be four months tomorrow since we came here. Four months, and I have never seen my loved one in all that time. . . . I hope dear one, that you bear the separation better than I do. I believe you do. I know you love me, darling, love me with all your heart, I fondly believe — and a brave, generous, noble heart it is — but you don't know, my good darling, I *hope* you don't know anything about the wild, absorbing, idolatrous devotion that makes separation, to me, as bitter as death. I say I hope you don't know, because it is a fearful thing to love any earthly object as I love you, my husband — as I have always loved you. It is given to but few natures ever to know such a love — and they know it but once in this world, or the next. Sometimes I wish the fearful legacy had not been mine, then again I thank God for it, I do this morning. . . . I may never see you again, but I thank God for a love that is sweeter than life, and stronger than death!
Dollie

Helena, Feb. 17, 1863
My Dollie,

... Yesterday evening on dress parade the adjutant read a set of resolutions that was gotten up by the field officers of all the Iowa Regts. here at Helena. ... They take the high ground of undivided support for the Government. Leave to the President the selection of the best course for the suppression of the rebellion. ... We denounce all opponents of the war who are in the Army as men of the [Benedict] Arnold and [Aaron] Burr School. How many men do you suppose there were in our Regt. who voted against the resolutions — for they were submitted to the Regt. for their approval or disapproval. Of all the 7 or 8 hundred there were but 7 or 8 who refused to vote for them. Thank fortune — *there was not one in my Company....*
William

Thursday Evening, Feb. 19th, 1863
My Own Dear Love,

... There is to be a grand Union demonstration at Indianapolis next Thursday. I would like to go so much if my "Peaches" were here. Gov. Yates is to be there, and Holt of Kentucky, and a good many "big guns" from different states, besides Gov. Morton and Joe Wright.[59] They will have a good time I hope, and move our torpid Unionists to a sense of their duty. I am not discouraged yet, darling. It will all come right, I think....
Dollie

Feb. 20th, 1863
My Good Darling,

I feel some better than I did yesterday. I ate a hearty breakfast, and the eruption on my face is no worse. ... I don't know what I should do without you. I couldn't get on at all, darling. ... I couldn't sleep last night for grieving about my loved one. I lay alone, in the same bed *we* slept in just 4 months ago — Jane and Etty slept in the other bed. But I don't want to make you sad, sweet love, and I will not tell you how foolish your Dollie is. . . . Father is going to town, I think, to borrow money of Amos Hibbs[60] to pay a debt that is crowding him. It is going to some of the McCammack tribe. He wants $75, I heard him say. He ought to make 10 dollars on this farm where he makes 1. You would do it, easily. . . .

If Julia goes home I should be left utterly alone. . . . It is true that "Misery loves company." Here I should have none. And above all, my good darling, I want to breathe the pure air of our prairie. I want to see people who can speak out boldly and bravely for our cause. I believe there are such people yet in Iowa, though if I say so here, I am laughed at and told that Iowa is as strong secesh as Indiana. I know it is a base slander, but the people here don't know it. I hate rebels and despise traitors more every day I live. I can't think of you, my pet, and not abhor them. . . .
Dollie

Thursday Morning, Feb. 26th, 1863
My Own Darling,
 . . . You say I am "the only true friend you ever had." I am glad darling — not that I am the *only* friend you ever had, but that you knew I have been your *truest* friend. I have always wanted to do good, my darling, and I have loved you more than all the world before has loved you. . . . And I am *proud* of you. I know you are *good and true and noble*, and I feel every day that you are the *only real friend your Dollie ever had*! All the happiness I ever knew in my life, I found in your love. I never shall know any apart from you. All I ask of Fate is that you may be given back to my arms just the brave, loving, true-hearted darling that you are. I don't want you a grave Senator or President weighed down with cares and responsibilities. Ambition, never of itself, even when gratified, brings us happiness. That comes, when it comes at all, through the exercise of the affections. Don't you remember Lord Napier — the hero of the Crimean War?[61] While he was on the highest rung of the ladder of Fame, and a whole nation were singing his praises, some were talking to him about it, and he said "I would give it all to be at home a few days with my wife and little girls." It didn't satisfy his heart, and it never can satisfy the heart of a good man. Then,

my pet, don't get the blues because you think you have not accomplished as much in life as you ought. You *have* accomplished a great deal. Think of the thousands, who with better opportunities, have done far less. And you will do much more. You are young yet, darling. *I* have faith in you, and *I* know you, dear one. . . . I don't want you to get discouraged and make yourself unhappy. You must not do that. Dollie must not let you do it. . . . You needed your Dollie there to love you, and pet you up, and comfort you; just as she needs you to love and comfort her. . . .

Dollie

3

"I Want to Know Whether Our Government Is Really Worth Dying For"

Ulysses S. Grant enjoys a well-deserved reputation today as the Union general most responsible for the North's victory in the Civil War. Without question his military masterpiece was his spring campaign of 1863 that resulted in the capture of Vicksburg, Mississippi, on July 4 of that year. Defying conventional wisdom, Grant had moved his troops across the Mississippi River from Louisiana into Mississippi, cutting himself loose from a secure supply line and placing his command in a region where the Confederates outnumbered him. But Grant pulled off the maneuver adroitly, defeating smaller Confederate forces in detail and eventually bottling up a sizeable enemy force inside Vicksburg. He then starved the defenders into submission. This feat, coupled with the capitulation of the Confederate garrison at Port Hudson, Louisiana, a few days later, gave the Union control of the entire course of the Mississippi River.

Grant's triumph had come only after months of failure, however. He had initially hoped to conduct a traditional military campaign to subdue Vicksburg by utilizing the route of the Mississippi Central Railroad as a secure supply line while he advanced southward. Confederate cavalry commanders, however, spoiled Grant's plan by destroying his supply base at Holly Springs, Mississippi, and tearing up miles of railroad track in December 1862. Forced to fall back, Grant recognized that he would have to devise a different strategy for capturing "the Gibraltar of the West."

Nothing if not resourceful, Grant formulated six different plans to achieve his goal. Among these was an attempt to utilize inland waterways to reach the high ground north of Vicksburg along the Yazoo River. Accordingly, on February 7, 1863, Union forces breached the levee along the Mississippi River south of Memphis, allowing a flotilla of federal vessels to sail through Moon Lake into the Coldwater River. From there, the fleet would eventually sail into the Yazoo. If all went well, this campaign would give Grant the opportunity to reduce the Confederate fortress through an amphibious assault.

This operation included the 36th Iowa. Although the regiment did not do battle during this foray, it fought valiantly farther upriver to aid Grant's setup of Vicksburg. The infantry's first combat experience was all for naught, however, as the Union high command called off the campaign on March 20, 1863.

In the following letters to Mary, William discusses the abortive effort to assault Vicksburg. While attempting to give Mary an accurate depiction of his activities, he is careful to reassure her that he is not taking unnecessary risks. Meanwhile, Mary devotes a large portion of her letters to telling William of her decision to move back to Iowa. The historian J. Matthew Gallman has noted how northern women relied on a network of family and friends to sustain them during their husbands' absence during the Civil War, and Mary's relocation seems well in keeping with this trend. But the move was not an unmixed blessing. Initially pleased with the more positive attitude towards the war that she finds in the Hawkeye State, Mary soon realizes that disloyalty existed even in her adopted homeland. Because of the strains they faced, both William and Mary spend a significant amount of time in these letters describing their longing to be reunited with each other, if only for a brief moment.

On board Steamer *Mariner*, Feb. 26, 1863
Dear Dollie,
. . . Yesterday we started about 2 o'clock for the Pass. It took us till nearly sundown to get through the Pass into Moon Lake. . . . [The Pass] runs from the Lake across the country into what is called Coldwater, which empties into the Yazoo a way up above Yazoo

City. There are . . . 5 Gun Boats and 10 or 12 transports. It may be that we are to go down and recconoiter the Pass. . . .
Will

Friday, 9 A.M., Feb. 27th, 1863
Good Morning, My Love!

. . . I am afraid sometimes that you will think hard of me for staying here. But indeed, darling, I could not do otherwise. If you were here you would see how things are, and you would not blame me. . . . My going to Aunt Anna's, after you left me here, made such a talk that it annoyed her to death. She was afraid it would break up the friendship of her family and theirs, and remember they have been friends for 25 years, and expect to die in the church together. She likes me almost like one of her own children, and wanted to keep me there, but she could not in peace. It was troubling her, and I couldn't stand that. She is a widow and alone . . . and almost as friendless as I am, as regards her political faith. She hasn't a friend to stand by her, but 2 or 3 other widows. Abe isn't worth a charge of powder. She is old, and getting frail, and your Dollie couldn't be willing to stay and bring trouble into her family. . . .

Mother said yesterday that she couldn't bear the thought of my going home, for she was afraid she would never hear from you at all then. *She is good to me, darling.* And if I were to go anywhere else to stay I would have to tell them what you say, and the *reason* I leave, and that would make an awful rupture, my dear, never to be healed in this world. *I dare not do it on father's account.* He is old, darling, and his mind is shattered, and I believe it would make him completely wild again. He would rave about it publickly in his preaching, as he does sometimes when he is troubled about anything. You don't know what a condition he is in, my sweet love, and I have never told you all, because I didn't want to hurt your feelings. The doctors say his brain is diseased. He was *mad* for 18 months. There were days and days where he would walk all the time, all over the woods west of the house, crying and groaning with a *drawn knife in his hand.* He would declare that wicked spirits were trying to force him to commit some horrible crime, and he didn't want to do it. At other times he would be quiet. . . . They were afraid of him, and had to watch him. He is not right yet, and the least thing throws his mind off its balance. For instance the other day John got a valentine — an ugly, silly thing. He showed it to us, and while we were looking at it, and laughing at John, father happened to come in and see it. He was like a wild man in a moment and tried to burn it. He took it as a deadly insult to himself. It took them all to quiet him. They try to keep everything from his knowledge that would disturb him. . . .

Dollie

Monday Evening, Mar. 2nd, 1863

My Dearest Love,

. . . I forgot to tell you yesterday about the good time the Unionists had at Indianapolis last Thursday. They say there were 85,000 people there. Dr. Brinton was there. . . . He heard Andy Johnson[1] speak 3 hours. . . . Holt was there, and plenty of "big guns." Two men were shot and killed who hurrahed for Jeff Davis, and the Copperheads didn't "resist," as they say they will the draft, in the Spring. . . . It is said the K. G. C.'s[2] are holding meetings all around here. Old Charly Bowen and his son-in-law Bill Hurst[3] are spoken of as prominent members. . . . There is no doubt there are plenty of them all through this state. Speaking of them stirs up mother. She hates them with all her heart. And she is right about it. We hear too that the gallant *Queen of the West* is captured. . . . I hope it is not true, but it may be. Col. Ellet is a daring fellow,[4] and I don't think he would see this boat captured. His father was killed on the *Queen*, I think, a few months ago[5]. . . .

I dreamed last night that I saw you, and you laid your head in my lap, and I kissed you and petted you, and combed your head, and pulled out all your grey hairs. Oh, I *loved* you so much in my dream. Nobody combs your hair and looks for all the grey ones now, do they, Love? I am afraid they will get a long ways the start on Dollie before you come back. Do you think much dear, about the happy days we spent together at Woodside? Do you think people were ever happier in the world?

Dollie

Coldwater, On board Steamer *Mariner*, Mar. 4, 1863
My Darling,

. . . I told Lieut. Wright to take 4 or 6 men out in the woods and kill a beef. He *grinned* in his way and said he didn't want to go for fear they would do *something with him*. . . . "Stay here with the men then, I will go" says I. 5 or 6 boys volunteered immediately (they all wanted to go) and out we went into the cane after the cattle. . . . At last we found 5 or 6, and of all the shooting you ever heard we had it. The boys were perfectly wild. They could not hit a cow 10 steps hardly. I was trying to keep them from shooting each other all the while and at the same time trying to get a shot myself with my revolver. At last I got to shoot and killed a pretty good beef. Don't say anymore I can't kill anything. . . .
Will Vermilion

Thursday Evening, Mar. 5th, 1863
My Own Good Love,

. . . I am uneasy about you now that you are gone from Helena. I fear you are in grave danger now. . . . But I won't talk to my darling about this. It is just as it is and we can't help it, and I don't want [to] make you sad, love, by telling you how weak and foolish your Dollie is. You want me to be brave, and I do try, my pet. And I believe God will take care of you. "His loving care is round about all His children." I am comforted when I can believe that. I wish we were good Christians, dear one. Don't you? We ought to be. How much better we could bear all our troubles. . . . But I can't make myself good, or humble. I am afraid I never shall be. . . .

I dreamed a sweet dream of you last night. I told you I would. I thought you had come home to stay, and we talked and talked, and never got tired of talking to each other. At last, I thought, we concluded to go to Mullinix's to see Rocker and just as we started I woke up, and it was all a dream. I was here alone, and my dear one was far off, and in danger. I always feel worse when I first wake up in the morning than any other time, for I have to remember it all in detail then. I love you too much darling. I am afraid that it is wrong, and that I shall be punished for it. Do you think I do, my love? If I could love you as other people love, it might be better for us both. But I can't help my nature. God made my heart as it is, and surely he will not judge it harshly. . . .

Reason is naturally one of the best boys I ever saw, but he has not had any mental training, and he has no manners. He is bright and quick, and will make a smart lad if he had the chance to learn something. I . . . got him in the notion to take a newspaper all by himself. He has money enough. Last Fall he sold $34 worth of stock and pocketed the money. . . .

Dollie

On Board Steamer *Mariner*, March 6, 1863

My Own Darling,

. . . You seem to think I will miss Lieut. H. G. May. Not much Dollie. He never did much service, *very little*. . . . Wesley makes the best officer. He is much the smartest and much the best business man. He is not egotistical. . . . He, Henry Swallow, and I do it all for my Company. . . .

Will

Monday Morning, Mar. 9th, 1863

My Dearest Love,

. . . I want to know whether our government is really worth dying for or not. . . . Sometimes, my good love, I feel like I am willing to have the war *end* anyway, so that you can get home once more. If I lose you, my beloved, what will the country be to me? What will I care whether it is free and happy, or not? Oh, darling, I can hardly bear to think of it. *You are worth more to me than 10,000 republics!* If I had the power, this morning, I would bring you home to my arms, and we would live our days out together, and as for the government, take our chance with the rest. Are you ashamed of your Dollie, your poor, tired Dollie, when she talks this way? She can't help it, sweet love. It is my *heart* that speaks like that. Don't blame me, dearest. Sometimes I am patriotic, and I feel that it would be a glorious thing to live, or die, by your side, in defense of a country so just and holy. But my heart is truer than my head. . . . I see you every night in my dreams, and when I awake and find you gone, I can't tell you how desolate I feel. I know you are braver than I, and nobler. I hope you bear the separation better. I don't want you to suffer as I do, my precious one. . . . Tom says he has his $300 all ready, if he is drafted.[6] He would rather pay $1000 than be shot at one round, he says. John thinks it would ruin him to go into the service for 3 years. It would *nearly* ruin him to give $300, but of the two evils, this is considerably less than that. . . . Dollie

On board Steamer *Mariner*, Tallahatchie River, Mar. 10, 1863
My Good Darling,

. . . Dollie, go to the map and look what a short distance it is from the Mississippi River across to the Yazoo, and you will know something about how fast we have traveled. 15 days clawing this far and it is 20 miles to the Yazoo yet, so you know our progress has been slow . . . simply because we could not get on in these rivers with our fleet. . . . The Lavina Logan — Col. Kittredge's boat — was fired into by the Guerrillas. One man of the regiment was hurt[7]. . . .
William F. Vermilion

Wednesday Morning, Mar. 11th, 1863
My Own Good Love,

. . . There is great excitement I think, from all I hear, about the expected draft. The Knights of the Golden Circle are busy everywhere, in every nook and corner. Henry says there are not 10 Democrats in this township who do not belong to the group. They were prowling around here trying to see John last night, but he didn't get home from his work till after dark. One fellow, named Owens,[8] came in the house and talked treason awhile to Henry — said the determination of nearly every man was to die here at home, if they *have* to die in the war, and he said they had better not attempt a draft. When he started he told Henry to tell John to "be sure to come up to his house, as soon as he got home." We didn't tell John anything about it. I don't believe he will have anything to do with them, but I don't know. . . .

I had a spat with John just now. He asked me what would be the result if all the men who should be drafted should pay the $300? I told him I guessed the first result would be plenty of money to pay the soldiers already in the field. But he need not be afraid that they will all pay the exemption. Then I said "John, why not stand bravely up by the government now? Has it ever failed to protect you? Has it ever wronged you in any particular?" "No, he guessed not." "Did you ever hear *anybody* say that the government had wronged or oppressed them?" "No, he didn't know as he had." "Then it must be a good government, why not sustain it?" "Well, he always hated a nigger; and when it comes to fighting with niggers he could not stand it." Well, as to the first, now, I don't love niggers either, and I don't want Indiana to be a slave state, as she will if she joins the slave confederacy. But have you *seen* a negro since the Proclamation? "No, he believed not." "Have you heard of one in the neighborhood?" "No, he didn't know as he had." "Well, as to their fighting, they are going to fight on one side or the other. We can't help this. The only question is, shall they fight for us or against us? Would you rather they should fight with the rebels and kill your friends? Or fight with your friends and kill the rebels?" That was another question. He couldn't look at it that way. The idea of fighting with negroes was what he looked at. "Why, it is the very question. You think it isn't respectable to fight with the negroes. Which would be more respectable for you, to be shot by a nigger, or have the nigger stand beside you, to shoot the rebel?" Well, he would rather not have either. He believed in making the niggers do the hard work — ditching, entrenching, and the like; but he didn't want them to fight. "[George] Washington and [Andrew] Jackson were good enough Democrats, were they not?" "Yes, certainly." "Well, they enlisted the niggers and encouraged them to fight bravely, gallantly, and then thanked them warmly for their services. They were willing to have them fight." "Were they?" That staggered him. . . . You won't blame me, will you love, for talking to him so. I never allude to the subject, till he brings it up himself. Then I tell him facts, and talk mildly to him. He can be well led, I find. I have already got mother and Henry and Jane and Reason on my side. . . . Father never speaks on the subject, and we never do before him. . . .

Dollie

Friday Morning, Mar. 13th, 1863
My Own Darling,

. . . I cannot help knowing the danger that you are in, I cannot put it aside one moment. . . . and I don't want to think of anything but you. . . . If anything should happen to you I want you brought to me, to our own dear home. I *want* to do all that love can do for you, and then lie down by your side and never wake any more. I don't want to live without you, dear one, but I want to sleep by your side, even in death. I can't talk about it, *my only love.* Don't blame your poor Dollie. . . .
Dollie

Monday Morning, Mar. 16th, 1863
My Own Dear Love,

. . . I got 2 dailies Saturday. . . . They say that Yazoo City has been captured, and the rebel fleet destroyed by the Yazoo Pass Expedition. . . . There may have been hard fighting, we may have lost many lives, but I can't know. I must wait and wait. Oh, darling, how do you think I live? How can I bear the thought of what may have happened to you, my own sweet love? I hardly know how I have got through the long hours since I heard it, and it may be days yet before I can hear one word from you. Oh, dear, it is so hard. Sometimes I am almost wild with fear. Then, I know you are in God's hands, and I believe he has saved you through the danger. But I pray heaven you may never know such torturing anxiety as your poor Dollie suffers now.
Dollie

Near the Rebel Ft. Pemberton on the Yazoo River,[9] Mar. 17, 1863
My Darling,

Here we are stopped at last before the Rebel Ft. Pemberton, commanded by General Loring of Virginia. He is a one arm man. He lost his arm in Mexico. Our force is commanded by Gen. Ross. I think he lives in Ill.[10] The first day we came here our Gun Boats

pitched in like they were going to take the fort immediately, but after firing for awhile they backed off. The last shot the rebels threw killed 3 men on this Gun Boat. . . . The next day our forces did no firing, but during the night planted a land battery. . . . From that time to the present there has been some artillery firing every day except Sunday. The Infantry has never been engaged yet. . . .
Will

Wednesday, Mar. 18th, 1863
My Own Dear Love,
    . . . Henry can hardly walk. . . . He doesn't seem to care. He is just the queerest genius I ever saw. The longest-faced deacon couldn't help laughing at his absurdities. He torments everybody but the cat. That is his special favorite, and he never gets tired of talking to it. He is a pretty hard case, but I think everybody likes him. I do, very well. They say when he was gone soldiering he preached "hard hell" sermons to the boys regularly. He seems to have a special gift that way. He is as honest a boy as ever lived. Anyway there is more to him than I thought. . . .
Dollie

Friday Morning, Mar. 20th, 1863
My Darling Love,
    . . . I put you[r] letter under my pillow, and I thought I could dream of you. But I didn't. I dreamed of a battle somewhere, all night. I could hear the drums beating, and cannon booming, and the shout of the distant soldiers. It troubled me. . . . It is just 5 months this morning, darling, since you left your Dollie. It seems years to me. Does it seem a long time to you, my pet?
Dollie

On board Steamer *Promise*, On the Tallahatchie River, Mar. 20, 1863
    . . . Since I wrote to you, we have made a great fuss and done nothing at all. . . . The boys were all anxious to go in but there was

no use. The Infantry could not be used so we fell back to the boats. It was the first time I ever heard a cannon ball shot. I can't tell you what kind of a noise they make. It is peculiar to war, not peace. . . .

Before I quit let me answer your inquiry about our Chaplain[11]. . . . He is always with us, especially if he thinks there is going to be any fighting done. While we were down before the fort, we were ordered out one day to make an important reconnaissance across the river from where our main army lay. We had to march through thick cane brakes for about a mile and a half. We did it all right and so did the Chaplain. . . . He attended the funeral of Orderly Swallow. I asked him to. He said "Of course, that is a part of what I am for." And let me say here that my Company conducted the affair as nicely when they buried him as I ever saw. . . .
William F. Vermilion

Monday Morning, March 23rd, 1863
My Own Dear Love,

. . . Henry . . . heard that martial law is declared all over the state. The sale of arms and ammunition is prohibited from this on, and all the arms now in possession of the citizens is to be taken in charge by the Provost Marshals. . . . They have "waked up the wrong passenger" in arousing Gov. Morton. Henry said old Charley Bowen and his clan were vowing boldly that they would shoot any man who came to take their guns. . . . They were charging around at a dreadful rate, Henry said. We shall see whether they will shoot or not. I don't hear of the Unionists opening their mouths anyway. I don't know whether they are cowed down or just *biding their time*. I heard that it leaked out slyly that Dr. Brinton has a barrel of powder in his house. I don't know whether it is true. I think matters will change for the better before long. . . .
Dollie

On board the Steamer *Promise*, Mar. 23, 1863
My Dollie,

. . . Let me tell you my plan of managing the Negro. It is this: Press every Negro man into the service and make them do work,

and if necessary give them guns and make them fight, but leave the women and children at home for their rebel masters to take care of. . . . If the Government succeeds they will all be free anyhow. . . .
Will

Tuesday Morning, Mar. 24th, 1863
My Good Darling,

It is still raining. It rained all night again. A good deal of damage has been done, they say. Fences and bridges have been washed away, and things overturned generally. I haven't *so far*, heard of anybody saying that it "was all old Abe Lincoln's fault," or that it is an "abolition" flood! This is about all the comfort I can find in thinking about it. It is gratifying to know there are *some* things for which the abolitionists are not held accountable. . . . The yard and the meadows are green and fresh. I think the flowers are coming up at Woodside. I wish we were there, my darling. Don't you? How happy we should be! How could anything ever trouble us any more. I sit sometimes, and shut my eyes and imagine I am there, and my love is sitting near me, or lying in the lounge, and the fire is burning cheerfully, and the hearth is swept clean and bright, and the Post and Tribune are lying on the round table at my side. I think I could get up and put my hand on every familiar object. Then I open my eyes, and it is all gone, *all gone*. My only love is hundreds of miles from me. . . . He is in danger, in deadly peril all the time. I know not what may have happened [to] him, or what he may be suffering, or how much he may be needing his faithful Dollie at this moment. And the thought makes my heart sick, and I go off . . . and cry. . . .
Dollie

Sunday Afternoon, Mar. 29th, 1863
My Own Dear Love,

. . . I got a letter from Tom Kemper. . . . Tom and his wife and 2 or 3 of his children have had typhoid fever. . . . Another boy, about 10 years old, died last Sunday.[12] He wants me to come and see them, but I have no way of going. And if I had, darling, I should be a little

afraid to go. I might get the fever. If I were to get sick, sweet love, I don't know what I should do. You would never have any Dollie, any more, I expect. There is a great deal of sickness in the country. There is smallpox in Greencastle. I am going to be careful, darling. . . .
Dollie

Thursday Evening, April 2nd, 1863
My Own Good Love,

 . . . In the afternoon I was going to town to take my letters, but Jane proposed that she would go. I told her if she went I would make the hominy. . . . I was so glad to be alone a little while. I had not had one half-hour to myself since you left me. I thought I was getting [to be] a stranger to myself. But now everything was quiet, my head didn't ache, I could think. I could write a good letter to my dear one. I worked with all my power, and had just got a good fire made and my hominy about half done when I heard the everlasting whistling, and saw the boys coming home. I was sorry, sweet love. I was wrong, for it is their house, not mine, but I couldn't help it. . . .
Dollie

On board steamer *Mariner*, Yazoo Expedition, April 5, 1863
My Dollie,

 . . . We did not get into much danger, but one day we got where the shells whistled close to us. We closed within a mile or such a matter of the rebel fort, held as a reserve in case we should be needed. The rebels either saw us or guessed well where we were, for they threw several shells that burst near our right. The noise was peculiar. One of the Co. K boys says it went like someone repeating the word "now" very rapidly. Several of the shells burst close to us, but no one was hurt. After that I was on picket at the most exposed part of our line, but nothing occurred there of any note. We had but very few adventures of any importance. . . . Of course some of our boys think they have seen the Elephant[13]. . . .
William

Tuesday Morning, April 7th, 1863

My Darling,

... At the election yesterday the Republicans elected their men by 17 majority — every one of them. That is pretty well for a township where the "Knights" thought they had everything their own way, isn't it? Henry says they looked "awful."

There is quite an excitement now about Dr. Brinton. He has been selling whisky ... without a license. ... They are making a political matter of it. The Copperheads are trying to get a little revenge. John has to go before the jury tomorrow to testify. For my part I have no sympathy for any man who sells whisky, be he Union man or butternut. ...

I am a very coward when I think of you. ... I saw you last night in my dreams. I see you almost every night almost. You are always well and cheerful and bright, and I am so happy for a moment while the dear vision lasts. ... I can't help longing to see you, to hear your voice, to feel your kisses on my lips, *to live with you again, all your own Dollie*, and I can't help telling you when I write to you. ... Sometimes I fear my letters do you harm rather than good, and I don't want to do you harm. I can't love a little as most people do, dearest. It is unlike my nature. ...

Dollie

Friday Morning, April 10th, 1863

My Dearest Love,

... There is not much war news ... but the little there is, is encouraging. Even from Vicksburg the reports are more cheering. They say Grant is inaugurating a new "plan" for the reduction of the rebel stronghold. What it is I don't know, but I will hope it may be successful. Sometimes I am almost out of heart about matters in his department; then I remember he has a Heart.

Our soldiers often send good news to us at home; thank God, we can now send a little good news to them. The elections have gone right. Everywhere nearly the Union has triumphed. ... From Rhode Island and Connecticut, and Cincinnati and Missouri, came the good news. Treason is rebuked, and our brave soldiers encouraged and sustained. You will only have the rebels to contend with now; Traitors in your rear will not trouble you anymore, and the soldiers have done it, my darling. Didn't I tell you, weeks ago, that they will save the country in a way they never dreamed of when they left home? All hail to the brave, loyal men who knew their rights, and dared maintain them! Where can Copperheads hide their loathsome forms when all our army of patriots comes home? Then will come *their* day of reckoning. Oh, may it come soon. . . .

Dollie

Helena, Arkansas, April 11, 1863

My Darling,

. . . The Adjutant General [14] of the United States was here and made a short speech to the soldiers. He told them that the Government was going to arm every Negro who could be induced to take up arms against the rebels. . . . General Prentiss (and by the way he is confirmed as a major general) spoke awhile. He said if any man did not like the course the Government was taking, he must keep it to himself or he would deal with them severely. He is a good man. . . . Since he came the trade Gen. Gorman had established with the rebels has been stopped. . . .

W. F. Vermilion

Sunday, April 12th, 1863

My Own Darling,

. . . I am grieved to hear of so many of your men being sick, but I could expect nothing else. You are careful of your health, and that is why you escape. Do be cautious, sweet love. . . . Oh, I wish I were with you, darling. . . . I know you will tell me that I couldn't live there, and you know best, but still I want to be with you. . . . You don't know how much I could endure, love, only to be near you. But your Dollie will do as you tell her, as near as she can. And you won't blame her for wanting to stay with you, will you, my love? I got a letter from Will. . . . He wishes it would be so that you could be at home with me, but they couldn't do without you there. He praises you darling, says he never knew how good a man you are, until since you both left home. I am glad. . . .

Dollie

Monday Evening, April 13th, 1863

My Dearest Love,

. . . Nearly every night I see you, and talk to you, and love you and pet you like I used to at home. And last night I dreamed troubled dreams, and nothing about you my darling. I am in suspense to hear from the battle at Charleston. I am afraid that our forces have failed. . . . If the news is bad I shall be almost sick. I shall hate it so bad for your sake. It would encourage you so much to hear of a victory there. . . . I am getting afraid that our Monitors[15] and ironclads are not going to do as much for us as we have promised ourselves they would. But we will know when we hear from Charleston. They will have a fair trial there. . . . I can imagine, my dear one, how much good it does you, away down there, in your comfortless tents, to hear good news. . . .

Dollie

Helena, Arkansas, April 13, 1863

My Darling,

. . . Some little excitement . . . in regard to an article in the Chicago Times, purporting to have come from the soldiers of Iowa before Greenwood.[16] The article is pretty hard. We don't know anything about it, only we know our men never sent that paper any such article. Some fool in some Iowa Regt. might have sent the article on his own responsibility. But it is a base lie on the Iowa soldiers. They are not such cowards as to send that paper such articles as that is. . . .

William

Tuesday Evening, April 14th, 1863

My Dearest Love,

. . . I am not well enough to write a long letter this evening. My head aches so I am nearly blind. I have a severe cold, and sore throat. I have the head ache more lately than I ever did in all my life. I don't know what causes it. Mother says it is because I "study" too much. I think not. . . . It is cloudy and really cold today. A good log fire would be pleasant.

Darling, whenever I am sick I want to see you so much worse. I don't know how to do without you any longer. I think one kiss would cure me now, love. . . .
Dollie

Thursday Morning, April 16th, 1863
My Beloved,

. . . Are you *sorry*, dear love, that I said I wanted to go home? Are your feelings hurt with me for it? You won't think I am forsaking you, will you? Or that I don't love you? It is because *I do love you* that I want to go. *God knows I want to do right*. But I am afraid I have done wrong. . . . I remember a letter I sent you, and I have often wished I had not sent it, for fear it might be wrong, and might do harm. I had the blues, I was hurt, darling, and I had no one to talk to but you. I felt then that I had no friend but you, and you had none but your Dollie. How could I bear it, love, to hear a man say that "the Northern soldiers have gone South just to steal the Southern men's property, and he didn't blame the rebels to kill them, and he would kill them if he were in their places," and much more like it. I heard John Runyan say that, sitting here with all the family — and father — around him and not one of them said a word of reproach to him. . . . Mother has often said that if James and Davis had lived,[17] they would both be in the war now, for "Their politics was for the North" she would say. I wish they could have. . . .
Dollie

Friday Morning, April 17th, 1863
My Dearest Love,

. . . If I get home, dear pet, I will try never to cause you any more trouble. I will do *entirely* as you want done. I could not always do as you wanted me here. . . . I part in peace with them all, but Runyan. . . . I have nothing against him, know nothing about him,

but his *treason*. Mother wanted me to promise this morning that I would come back next winter if you shouldn't get home before then. She said I could pass the time, and she wanted me to come and stay as long as I would. I told her it was too hard to come by myself. She wanted to give me a blanket or coverlet, but I could not take it. I *could* make room for it, dearest, but I am afraid you wouldn't like that. Would you, my precious? She said she intended to give us something, if you came here again. I may never see one of them again in this world, and I don't want to leave on bad terms. . . .
Dollie

Sunday Morning, April 19th, 1863
My Dearest Love,
. . . Six months ago today my love was here with me. . . . There is meeting at Providence [18] today, just like there was that day. I have never been there since then. I shall never be again. Tonight I shall sleep alone in the bed we slept in the last night you were here, and in the morning I shall start away as you did. No, not as you did, for I shall leave no loving, sorrowful heart behind me. If I could only know that you were entirely willing for me to go, I should go cheerfully. . . . I put all your letters — 57 of them — in my hand box. They are more precious than anything else I have. I may lose my trunk; I shall not lose them. I don't dread the trip at all. I think I can get along. . . . They say there is a danger of war with England. We have enough hardships on our hands now, and I hope it is not true. England is treating us very badly, but we had better bear it just now. There will come a time to punish *her*, after our own war is finished. I don't believe the government will go to war with her now. I am not much afraid of it yet. The sympathies of the English *people* are with us, but the English government hates us. . . .
Dollie

Helena, Arkansas, April 19, 1863
My Darling,
. . . There are too many men of our Regt. sick. It is frightful to think of. When we go on dress parade we take out about 200

men. . . . It is true here we generally have out about 150 or 160 pickets. Counting them we only have some 350 men for duty. . . .

The news from Grant is encouraging. It is reported by the last boats up that 5 gunboats ran the blockade a few days ago and the same night some 2 or 3 transports passed down. . . . The same report says Grant has marched across the Peninsula to where the Canal empties into the river. . . . It is thought he intends crossing . . . over and then attack[ing] Vicksburg in the rear. . . .

Our major has *resigned* in consequence of bad health. His place is now to be filled by some Capt. of the Regt. and there is going to be quite a strife over it. . . . So far as I can learn there are 4 wanting it. Capt. Varner, Hale, Joy [19] and — well you may guess the other Dollie. Capt. Varner is Co. A and from Albia. He claims it because he thinks he is the ranking Capt. Joy thinks he should have it because he assisted the Col. in getting his position. Hale says he should have it because he is the best man. I would like to have it . . . because my friends want me to have it. . . .

Will Vermilion

On board *Die Vernon*, April 21st, 1863
My Own Dear Love,

. . . I got on the cars at Greencastle last night the 20th, at 10 o'-clock P.M. and came through safely without changing cars or having any bad luck at all except that it rained all the time till 8 o'clock this morning and that our locomotive broke through the road this side of Paris, about 1 o'clock, and *turned over*, and we had to stay there till half past six this morning and had to go without anything to eat till 10 when we ate breakfast at Pano. . . . I have got along without one bit of trouble darling, so far. I want you with me worse than I can tell you, my sweet love, but I can travel along fine so far as *getting along* is concerned. A nice looking old man and his niece got on the train at Terre Haute going to Keokuk. Their seat was next to mine all the way and we got a little acquainted last night. We came on the boat together and he looked after my trunk and got me a ticket to Keokuk and a state room. He asked me to let his niece room with me, as he was afraid she would be lonesome. She is a very quiet nice looking girl and I couldn't refuse, though I would rather have been alone. I have a ticket now and a check to

Keokuk. . . . I am very tired and sleepy my precious one, but I wanted the first thing I did after washing and combing my hair to tell my darling where . . . and how I am. . . . I have had just as pleasant a trip dearest as I could have without my precious love with me. I don't mind traveling alone now. I am glad I can, for I may get to you some day. It is hard to have to go the other way now when my heart is at Helena. . . .
Dollie

Keokuk, April 23rd, 1863
My Dearest Love,

 . . . We went [from Greencastle] finely till, a few miles past Paris, the locomotive and wood car broke through the road and turned over onto the side. It went down ever so many feet. The conductor and all hands worked hard all night in the rain and the mud, but they couldn't remove it. They sent back to Terre Haute for another locomotive and more hands, and these got there just at daybreak. But still they couldn't remove it, and they built a new track around it and took the cars over one at a time, by hand. At half past 6 we started again, after sitting there over 5 hours. . . . I slept a little towards daylight, and when we started I rubbed my eyes and brushed my hair, took a long look at my likeness of my far off darling, and in my heart asked God to take care of us both and reunite us again, then I ate an apple for breakfast and felt better. . . . We stopped at Mattoon a few minutes and through the window I saw Dr. Rynerson[20] get off the train. He didn't see me. . . . He stood there a few moments and walked away with a carpet sack in his hand. He looked so bad that I hardly knew him, thin and sickly and exceedingly sad. I felt wicked towards him, I am afraid. I didn't want to speak to him. At 10 o'clock we got breakfast at Pano. It cost me half a dollar, but I was so hungry and weary I didn't grudge it. . . .
Dollie

Lagrange, Iowa, Friday, April 24th, 1863
Dear Love,

It is quite early. I have just got up and washed, and the next thing that I mean to do is tell my darling how I have got on. I left

Keokuk yesterday morning, and got to Eddyville about 2 o'clock. I bought a ticket on the stage to this place before I left the cars. I[t] cost $2. We were taken from the cars to the hotel, and didn't leave town until nearly 4. Came to Albia to supper at 7, changed coaches there and started again, and got here about 11 o'clock last night. The ride from Albia was very tiresome, and I feel sore this morning all over. . . . A girl coming up from Keokuk stopped here with me. I am at the Miller House. I think it is a hard place. They are getting breakfast. My fellow traveler is still in bed snoring. The landlord talks like he can get me some sort of conveyance out to father's. Says he will try after breakfast. I want to start pretty soon. I am glad I am so near home, my darling. You are glad too, are you not, sweet love? I will write you long letters when I get there, and I hope I shall get long ones from you, dear one. I have had no bad luck at all since I started, and no trouble. But it has cost more than I expected. I paid $8 from Greencastle to St. Louis, 5 on the boat to Keokuk, 3.50 to Eddyville, and 2 here. . . .
Dollie

Home, Tuesday, April 28th, 1863
My Own Darling,

. . . I am at father's. I am well, and so are father and mother. But I must go back and tell you all that I have done and heard and seen since I came. I have not been idle a minute hardly. I got here about 10 o'clock Friday. Father was working in the field with a small boy to help him, and mother was getting dinner. They were not looking for me, but they were very glad. Father I think was more rejoiced than I ever saw him. That afternoon people came in to see me, and the next day, and the next. Everybody came, love. I didn't realize that we had so many friends, darling. I know it was for your sake many of them came, with words of hope and encouragement. . . .

Yesterday Allie[21] and I went to Woodside. We stopped a few minutes at Mr. Maiken's to talk to Mary and Mrs. Maiken. . . . They say their boys and Jacob Grimes think there is hardly another such man in the world as you. Bartley states that the men in all the other companies acknowledge that there is not in the regiment another Captain as good as *his* Captain. You know, dear love, that Dollie is glad to hear such things about you, don't you? But she knew it all before now. . . .

. . . The people here don't know much about treason. It seems to me that the people are all loyal, all friends. I am better satisfied here my love, if I could only hear you say that you don't think hard of me for coming. I loved you too much to stay where there were so many traitors. . . .

Dollie

Helena, Arkansas, April 28, 1863
Dear Dollie,

. . . Yesterday I was detailed on a General Court Martial at Gen. Ross' Head Quarters. . . . This afternoon E. W. Parkhurst, the Baptist, the man Humphrey May wanted *for chaplain* of this Regt. had a fist and skull fight with Levi Zintz. A. J. Day[22] who is 4th Corpl. stood by and urged them on. At the time he was Acting Sergeant of the Camp Guard. As Corpl. he should have stopped them, and arrested them if necessary. As Sergeant of the Guard it was his indispensable duty to arrest them both and report them to the Officer of the Day. . . . I will reduce him to the ranks. . . . As to Parkhurst and Zintz I had them at work for it all the afternoon. . . .

Will

Wednesday Night, April 29th, 1863
My Dearest Love,

. . . Mr. Grissom[23] has just been here, and says he is going to start for Helena tomorrow. He will take letters to your company if they are ready soon. I wish I had known it yesterday and I would have written you a great deal more. . . . I wish I had time to send you some little presents, but I can think of nothing he can take but a pair of socks. I expect you have plenty of socks, darling. But Dollie knit those *for you.* You will like to wear them better on that account, won't you love? I will send you some postage stamps too. Mr. Eads[24] says it is hard to get them at Helena. . . . I send you *love.* You know that, and that I would do everything for you if I could. *God bless my husband!* If you are not coming home very soon, and can get it, won't you send me your likeness by Mr. Grissom? I want one dear love, I want a large one. I don't know how to do without seeing you any longer. And put a lock of your hair with it. It has grown long enough by this time to give a little lock to Dollie, hasn't it? I will go to see Mr. Grissom as soon as he gets home. Father says he is almost a Copperhead, but he will take our letters safely and quicker than they could go by mail. Send me a sprig of cypress. I want to see what it is like. Send me any little thing you can dear one that your hands have touched. . . . Father is very uneasy about the mare — I have named her Capitala and I will call her by that name in my letters. He stops his plow today to go and see her. He thinks a great deal of her. He says he will do the very best he can for you. I know he will. . . . We are going to watch Jake as well as we can. . . . I think he may do a good deal better now I have come home. . . . I hope he will. You have lots of friends watching him. Marchbank's little boy[25] was the friend who sent word to Mullinnix about his cutting the grove. The children couldn't stand that. . . . Father has some money for you here, somewhere near $100. I have been so busy since I came home that I have not had time to look around hardly. . . . But I am not going to neglect my "Peaches" to do anything else in the world. . . . Don't forget to send your letters to Iconium. It is the best place. . . . More people have sent for me since I came home than I can possibly visit this summer. It is so different from Indiana, my love. There it was hardly respectable to be a soldier's wife, here it is a passport to the hearts and homes of all good people. I am going to visit as many of our friends as I can. They like you and I like them all for that. I hope your Dollie is a better woman than she used to be. She tries to be better, my dear one. She wants to be worthy of you. I know I can never do enough for you. . . .

You know father wrote once that I had to pay for my board in Indiana and I thought Julia had told something about it. I was mistaken. It was Mr. Eads said you were going to pay my board there. Mullinnix told father. John was very indignant over it and thought I had Union friends enough to board me till you came home. He laughs and says he will keep me one month for you. It hasn't been told to anyone else I guess. Of course I care nothing about it darling, and I only speak of it because I thought Julia had told of it. We don't owe anything for my board, my darling. I am glad of it. I have no hard or unkind feelings toward any one of them, except

John Runyan. I am afraid I can't forgive him for what he said. But we won't talk about such things now. I am home, and *we have friends*, good friends. Humphrey was here yesterday to see me. . . .

Everybody talks about my looking so bad but I *feel well* since I came home. I can stay here very comfortably. But don't tell Teater[26] darling, but that I am going to [do some] house keeping sometime during the summer. Father and mother both send their love to you. Father says tell you he will do all he can for you. Mother believes God will bring home *all her children.* . . .

Dollie

Home, Friday Night, May 1st, 1863

My Dearest Love,

I sent you these letters yesterday by Mr. Grissom, who is gone to Helena for his son. . . . I have had no letter from you since I came home. . . . You said you would send me a letter to Osprey but none has ever come. I am going to send to Lagrange and Iconium to-morrow to see if any have come there. If you sent some to Indiana, I think there has been time for them to get to LaGrange. Martha Hickcox[27] is going there for me. . . . I see that the people are friends. I have not seen a Copperhead, nor heard a disloyal sentiment uttered since I started home. You don't know, my love, how much stronger I feel. I'm afraid I was getting, as you say in the army, demoralized. . . .

Father and mother have done a good deal for the cause. They have given 3 brave, young hearts, and 6 strong arms to help save the country. It was all they could do. Now I can do much for them. And when I can do nothing else, I am willing to work to raise corn, to pay taxes, to help sustain the government, and carry on the war. A sacred cause makes even the humblest labor dignified and holy. But I know another way — I know one, as noble a soldier as ever drew a sword, whose lonely hours, perchance, I can beguile, and whose heart I can sustain and encourage by loving, cheering words, sent in the "letter from home." Do you know such a one, my pet? Do you know how much your Dollie loves you? Do you know how intensely, how *entirely* she loves you? God bless you, my precious one. . . . Have you read General Thomas's speech at Lake Providence?[28] It is in the Tribune I sent you yesterday. We cannot say anymore that the government has no *policy*. It has a policy, clearly announced at last, thank God. This announcement is a long step toward a great victory, it seems to me. It is *right* and *just*. . . . Nearly all the neighbors have been by to see me. They say they are glad I am back. And I could be glad, darling, if I knew you were *pleased*. I am afraid you think bad of me, love. I can't bear that. . . .

Saturday morning, We look for Capt. Wilson and his wife [29] here today, so I will write early. I am well except my throat. . . . I hope to get a letter from you this evening, and if [I] do it will cure me. . . . Mr. Sheeks takes a daily paper, and he says he will bring mine, when he goes for his. By the way, how does John Sheeks get along? His wife,[30] they say, is a rank traitor. The worst, if not the only one, in the neighborhood. John has been writing some disparaging letters home, about the "nigger" war, and she shows them to the neighbors. Poor fellow. I am sorry for him. It is hard for him to be there risking his life, and not one friend at home to say a kind word about him. It is no wonder he falters, is it, darling? His father and mother [31] are all right, but that is not enough. John Teater's wife [32] is the same way, I have heard. . . . Father is "laying off" corn ground. . . . As I came through Iowa I couldn't help noticing the many old, white-haired men, and little boys — some hardly as tall as their plow handles — that were working in the fields. I knew . . . where all the young men were. But the farming is going on better than you would think. They have to work harder, but I have heard no one complain yet. Some say their girls must go into the fields. . . .

I have $109 put away for you. 75 I brought home with me makes 184. Besides, I have a little change in my pocket book. This is all, darling. Tell me what you want me to do with it. I shall use only enough of it to buy a summer dress (I would not do that, if I knew I should not see my Peaches this summer), and paper and postage. I want you to have all the money when you come home, my pet. Father is going to look after Bartlett and Dooley [33] in a few days. He thinks he can get what they are owing. . . . I have spent so much money, love, during the last 8 months that it makes me feel bad to think of it. . . . I am going to be saving now, sweet love, till you come home. Then my fine clothes will do me some good. The new silk dress I bought in Keokuk I have never had on, since the day we went to Providence. I wore it when I had my likeness taken for you. But when you come home I shall need it. I will dress better than I used to, dear one. I used to do wrong about it and I hurt your feelings sometimes I'm afraid. I didn't mean to do wrong, but I see now that I did. Won't you forgive me, my dearest? Forgive me all the wrong I have done, my husband, and I will try never to displease you again. I will try to be worthy of your love. . . .

Dollie

Later, Capt. Wilson has just been here. . . . He is all right. He saw Matt 2 or 3 days before he came home. He says he looked fine, and there was never a better soldier. He told me a good deal of his experience. It is a wild, rough life, but he liked it pretty well, till he lost his health. . . . I had to tell him all about Indiana. He knows nearly everybody there that I do. He liked Henry very much, and tried hard to get him in his company. He thought father prevented his going; he saw him and talked with him on the subject. He had never heard of Henry's going. . . . Mrs. Wilson's people are all traitors, and she had a stormy time, all alone with them, while he was gone. . . .

P.S. Mother sends her love to you, and says tell you she feels anxious about you. She wants to see you and her boys come home together. She hates rebels and traitors with all her might. She reads a great deal, but only war news. She says she wants you and Will to watch over and help each other, and to both be good and true patriots.

4

"Since I Came Home
I Am Entirely Satisfied
with Iowa"

It has been said that "He also serves, who sits and waits." This was the case for the 36th Iowa from April through June in 1863. While campaigns of crucial significance took place east of the Mississippi River, the 36th Iowa remained at Helena, guarding an outpost that had become a backwater of the Civil War. Occasionally federal troops would venture into the countryside around Helena to gather information on Confederate activities, but the Iowans in William's unit participated in only a few of these scouting expeditions. All William could do was watch the steady stream of regiments sailing down the Mississippi to reinforce Grant and hope that others could strike a mighty blow for the Union cause.

The letters in this chapter focus on William and Mary's reaction to the events taking place in the war's eastern and western theaters. William reveals his growing frustration with the leadership provided by Colonel Kittredge, and tries to acquaint Mary with the workings of the military justice system. Mary, gradually becoming acclimated to life in Iowa, tries to inform William about the state of his business affairs back in Iowa. She discusses the possibility of moving to Helena to be near William, and is disappointed by her husband's response. Both reflect on how their long separation has heightened their affection for each other.

Helena, May 2, 1863
My Own Darling,

. . . For the last week Gen. Gorman had been sending every day about 150 mounted men out on the Lagrange Road on reconnaissance. Yesterday morning they ran into an ambuscade of three or four hundred rebels some 10 or 12 miles out, and got pretty badly cut up. Out of 140 men — all of the Third Iowa Cav.— they lost [42] killed, wounded and missing, . . . so I learned this evening. Of that number 3 were killed, 9 wounded, and the rest were missing. . . . This is about all I know of the fight.[1] They claim that the rebels outnumbered them 4 or 5 to 1, that they on first sight of the enemy made a charge forward, when the enemy closed up in the road behind, and surrounded them entirely. . . . There were none hurt from our neighborhood. Oliver Breeze went through all right. One of the Delay boys from near Centerville was wounded in the hand, not seriously. 2nd Lieut. Stanton[2] from Appanoose Cty. had one arm badly injured. . . . About 1 o'clock there were some 2 regts. of cavalry sent out, and I think 2 of infantry. They came in this morning and reported . . . no enemy to be found. Of course such a report is just what we expected to hear.

The news from Vicksburg this evening is good, if true. They say our force has reached the rear of the rebels and have torn up the railroad for 10 [or] 12 miles, that they are advancing on the rebel fortifications, and have captured 3 of their largest batteries. When the boats left they say firing was going on all around the rear of Vicksburg clear up to the Yazoo River. If all of this be true we may expect stirring news from that direction soon.[3]
W. F. Vermilion

Helena, Arkansas, May 5, 1863
My Darling,

Sergeant Brashar[4] is out calling the roll. Lieut. May is up superintending it. The Regulations require that one commissioned officer shall be present at every roll call. . . . The other evening I was up attending to it myself and giving the boys a little lecture. After

I was through I looked around and there stood the Col. That night the boys had done first rate, but the Col. was somewhat drunk and of course he had to complain some. . . . Almost once a month he takes such a spill. He drinks very hard, but still I have but little trouble with him any more.[5]

Will Kemper is improving finely. . . . I was down to see him . . . and found him sitting up eating his supper. He had good light bread, tea, potato soup, roasted potatoes, and some nice well cooked cherries. . . . The hospital he is in is nothing but a regimental concern in tents, but it is *well managed.* I think I know something of how such a concern should be conducted, and I have been there enough to [be] the judge of that. John Westfall[6] is there from my company as nurse, and he makes a good one too. . . . We have now, in the hospital, Will Kemper, Will Davenport, John Smith, Will Grissom, Samuel Wright, John Clowser, and Elijah Manley.[7] Wm. Worthington[8] was returned to the company today to make room for someone who is worse off than he is. On the day after tomorrow we will start Mr. Worthington and Will Grissom up the river. . . .

When you get rested you will go to Woodside . . . won't you Dollie? You would not be at home till you got there to see Noah and all of the other stock. You will want to see them as bad as I would, and that is pretty bad. I want you to write me everything. All about how Teater is getting along. If you think he is doing right tell me so Dollie, and if he is doing wrong tell me. . . . Notice if Teater is cutting any of the grove for wood. I don't want that done if it can be helped.

We all feel more sanguine than we ever have before. Grant is moving in the right direction this time. The rear is the place to make the attack. I have some hopes that if Vicksburg should fall with our army in the rear then Grant will capture most of [their] army. . . . The paper today says Hooker is on the move. If that be correct, there is going to be stirring news from that direction. . . . W. F. Vermilion

Wednesday Morning, May 6th, 1863
My Dearest Love,

. . . I write this to tell you love, that the money you sent me, reached Iconium yesterday. There is $430 for me, and some for father, our boy says. He may be mistaken about the amount. I sent him to the office last evening to take my letters and get my daily and Mr. Phillips[9] sent word to us by him about the money. It had just got there, I don't know by what means. It is at Phillips's. . . . Rocker is getting better. He is able to get into mischief whenever he finds a chance. While he was at Mullinix's he learned a trick of bursting the hen's nests and eating all the eggs he could find. The children would often have a race with him to see who should get them first. They thought too much of him to scold him if he beat them. Now my precious love, I must say goodby. . . . Don't get the blues, my love, if you don't get the major's position. . . . You have the love and confidence of your men. Are you not glad of that, my pet?

Dollie

Helena, Arkansas, May 6, 1863
My Darling,

Will Kemper is still improving. . . . All the boys are improving, but Davenport. He is having a spell of Typhoid Fever.

Our Court Martial progresses slowly. . . . There is no case, I believe, from our regiment. . . . We are unlucky, for Capt. Phillips ought to have been *arrested* and tried for treason. It is a shame that such a man should be allowed to leave the service, and draw his pay from the government. For some time before he left, he was in the habit of writing letters home for the boys, which he always filled with *treason*. He wrote one for John Wafford[10] of my company. . . . Today I got a copy of it, and took it to Wafford, and asked him if it was his letter. At first he hesitated, but then acknowledged that it was. I asked him if Phillips didn't write it. He hesitated again, but finally acknowledged that he did. I told him that treason could not exist any longer in my company if I knew it. . . . Traitors shant receive payment from the Government, on my certificate if I know it. And the most of the Copperheads in my company are just beginning to learn the facts.

Henry Maiken got a letter today from his wife[11] in which she stated that you had been there. . . . Henry's wife said you looked first rate. I was so glad to learn that. You must get *fat* like your mother against I get home.

The *St. Louis Democrat* of the 2nd says Hooker is on the move. That he has crossed the Rappahannock.[12] We hope for good news from there soon.

May 7th, A report came up late this P.M. that [at] Port Hudson,[13] 12,000 prisoners, and a large amount of guns [were captured]. . . . The report of Grand Gulf is confirmed.

I am not very well this evening Dollie. . . . I have Rheumatism in my legs. I have just taken a full dose of opium. Guess I will have a good time sleeping tonight. . . .

W. F. Vermilion

Helena, Arkansas, May 9, 1863

Mr. Grissom . . . brought in 3 letters, some papers, 1 dollar's worth of postage stamps and a pair of socks. Thank you for them all. I needed the socks. So I did the postage stamps. . . .

Iconium is a mad place for you to get your mail at love. . . . It is a bad place. Then they will devil you to death Dollie, with horrid tales of one kind and another. For instance they had it going that I had been killed, and a great many other things, that you will hate to hear. . . .

I have written you 3 or 4 times, Dollie, that I don't think hard of you in the *least*.

W. F. Vermilion

Sunday Night, May 10th, 1863
My Own Love,

. . . I am afraid yet that I did wrong to come home. But believe me, dear one, I came for your sake, more than for my own. You know when anything hurts me I feel miserably, and it was very hard, darling, to hear such things said about you. It was more than I could bear. In any other house but your father's I would not have borne any of it. But I tried always to remember that it was *your father and mother*, and brothers and sisters. And I remembered the reverence and respect that was due them from me, and that I had gone there of my own accord. I wanted to do right, love. I tried to do right. As to your writing to them about it, my love, I have nothing more to say. I thought for your father's sake, and mother's, that it would be best to say nothing. They are old, and feeble, and I would have spoiled their feelings. But in my heart, dear, I can't blame you. It was not for any regard I had for *traitors*, that I asked you to forgive, but regard to your *parents*, as such. . . . You won't own Runyan as a relative. Tom has disowned him too. I didn't know that till Jenny told me the last night I stayed there. Not because of his treason. I think Tom does not object to a genteel traitor but because at the Dan. Vorhees[14] meeting at Greencastle, he got very drunk, took off his coat in the street and made a general spectacle of himself. . . . Tom said he was never so mortified in his life and that he never should call him brother again. But father and mother knew nothing of this. The children keep all such things from them. The boys knew him well before he ever married Ellen, but they said nothing against the match. . . .

. . . The arch traitor Vallandigham is arrested at last, and is to be tried for treason.[15] If he is punished as he deserves it will be worth a great victory to us. . . . Burnside is wide awake. . . .

Sunday Evening, May 11th, I have been thinking all day, in truth ever since I read your letter yesterday, darling, of some plan by which I can be nearer to you, and can go to you if you should be in a battle. . . . I shall get my daily papers tolerably regularly. If you should go to Vicksburg, or get in a land battle anywhere else, I shall learn it from them in a little while. . . . Then as soon as I hear of the battle darling let me go to Keokuk without waiting to hear from you by letter. Then you, or someone for you, my pet, if you should be hurt, telegraph to me there. The telegram would get there before I could, but I should not be long going, and then if you wanted me I could go right on to you darling. If you were safe I could come home, and get back by the time a letter would get here. . . . I would a thousand times rather do it dear one than remain in suspense. . . .
Dollie

Helena, Arkansas, May 10, 1863

My Own Darling,

... John Smith [16] is dying. ... He has kept his faith here as he did at home, but now he has to go. His is another family left desolate by this infernal rebellion. I hate so much for so many of these boys to die, who came just because I did, but I can't help it Dollie. John has had peculiar habits of his own, habits that I could not control. For instance he would eat meat when he ought not to have done it, but there is no use in talking about his not taking the right care of himself now. ...

Will Davenport is not any better. ... Elijah Manly is not so well today as he has been. ... Will Kemper is walking about. ... Don't think Dollie because so many of our company are dying that we are worse off in this respect than anyone else. Some of the other companies have lost as [many as] 12 or 13. The Unionville [17] Company has lost 12 or 13. Each of the Albia Companies have lost heavier than we have. If Smith dies it will make 8 for us. All of the others have lost more than that, but one. That is the one from Centerville. They are too *Devilish* to die. ...

The news from Hooker has been so conflicting for several days. ... This evening the word is that he has been reinforced by 70,000 fresh troops, and that he is again in Fredericksburg. I do hope it is true. If it is and he was not too badly cut up in the fight last week he surely can go into Richmond. If he does, Dollie, and Gen. Grant takes Vicksburg, which I think he will, this war must close by fall. Grant never has done a great deal of great Generaling in this war, although his men have done some of the hardest fighting of the war. At Vicksburg I hope there will be some Generalship used in place of so much fighting.

Gen. Prentiss is still fortifying this place. He is having rifle pits dug and batteries planted on most of the hills around the town. ... Helena will soon be quite a hard place to take. ...

Capt. Fee [18] of Centerville is under arrest. I don't know the charges. Probably not much. It is getting quite fashionable here for a superior to arrest an inferior when he does something he dislikes. I don't hardly think there is any danger of Col. Kittredge arresting me. I was told this morning from a reliable source that he is afraid of me. . . . We have no contentions any more. While we were gone down the Pass, I took some of the boys out and killed a beef one day without any orders. Afterwards, I told the Col. about it. He said it was all right. Yet I had asked him if I might, and he told me no. I wanted some beef for the boys and I was going to have it.

Monday Night, May 11th, John Smith died last night at 10 o'clock. . . . I have not been to the hospital today. But I understand Will is running around. Davenport is better too. . . . Mr. Grissom is here yet. He wants to get Will Grissom to go home with him. . . . He will never be able to do military duty. I have tried to get him discharged but I can't. He is marked for up the river.

All the news from the East is bad. Hooker has been driven back again. He is at Falmouth. Stoneman did well but it will not do us any good.[19]

Grant is doing well. . . . Reports say he has already invested Jackson.[20] I hope it is so. . . .

W. F. Vermilion

Tuesday Morning, May 12th, 1863

My Dearest,

. . . I was troubled about Hooker's failure, but it seems it is not so bad as we thought at first. . . . I think we shall hear better news from that Department soon. I have not lost faith in Hooker. And I listen for good news from Grant. His "plan" now promises better I think. Oh, I hope he will succeed. We haven't heard from Matt since he started on his last expedition. The 6th is mounted now on mules. While they were out before, they "confiscated" Matt said enough horses and mules to mount themselves without any expense to Uncle Sam. Only a few of them had saddles, but they really didn't mind that. They are getting to be a terror to the rebels in that country. . . . Mr. Dunlap was here to supper last evening, and he asked if you were as zealous in the cause as ever. He says there are plenty of traitors in Iowa, but I have not seen one yet, my darling. . . . I see no one but friends at any rate. And I bear our separation better here my love where I see nearly every body else making sacrifices and suffering for Truth and Right and Human-

ity. It does make a difference my darling. Not that I *love* you pet one atom less, but it sustains me in trying to do right and to be worthy of my noble soldier love. I know you want me to keep up my spirits and be hopeful and patient and I will dear love. In Indiana I could not. I never want to go there again, unless I could go with a *Regt. of Union soldiers* darling, just such spirits as yours and Matt's, who would not be afraid to "smite in the name of the Lord." I am wicked enough sometimes my dear one to feel like I should like to go there in such company. Were there no traitors in our northern states, this bloody and cruel war could not last two days. Were it not for them you would not be hundreds of miles from me in deadly peril of your life, my brother would not be sick, perhaps dying in a dreary hospital among strangers. Thousands of our noble soldiers would not have been lying last week cold and stark on the bloody battlefield of Chancellorsville. . . .
Dollie

Helena, Arkansas, May 12, 1863
My Own Dollie,
    . . . This morning I saw some 700 or 800 prisoners going North. They have just been taken by Gen. Grant. They were a motley looking sort of fellows. All or nearly all were dressed in butternut. They wore roundabouts.[21] Some were barefooted, some had on no shirt. All were very dirty. . . . One fellow asked me for a chew of tobacco. I told him I did not use it. Some of them said we could get Vicksburg but we could not take Richmond. Some one told him that we had it all ready. He looked around and told some of his comrades that we (meaning the Federals)[22] would know d__ned well when we got that place. But the news is still . . . that Richmond is taken. . . .

May 13th, The 5th Kansas got into it out some 10 miles while on their return from the scout.[23] We were all kept ready to move at a moment's notice. . . . This evening the forces that had been out on a reconnaisance for some time returned. The cavalry had a little fight last night and another again this morning. They lost a few men killed and some wounded. . . .

Will McNully is not very well. He has diarrhea. He would eat too much and of the kind of food he ought *not* to eat. John Smith did the same way. I told him some 10 days or 2 weeks before he died if he did not diet himself he *would die sure*. "I know what my stomach calls for Capt" say he, "and I am going to eat it and I think I will get well immediately." So he did. I got him in the hospital as soon as I could, but it all did no good. There are a few others who will go the same way if they don't pay more attention to their diet. I tell some of them of it almost every day. But they tell me that when they do diet themselves they don't get well. Of course they don't. But few bad cases can be cured in that way. But all may be helped. Bad cases can be modified and recent light cases . . . cured. All or nearly all of the cases of bowel disease die, where they pay no attention to what they eat. If I get a little unwell I cure myself by bathing and dieting. Such treatment is better than medicine here. In fact the Doctors have but little medicine in the Army. . . .
W. F. Vermilion

Wednesday Night, May 13th, 1863
My Own Darling,

This has been a good day to me. A day to be marked with a white stone[24]. . . . My tulips are in bloom, and I must go to see them. Father brought me one, and I am going to send it to you. I will send it with a kiss, my love, for you. . . . I wish it could be as sweet when you get it as your rose was when it came to me. But tulips are not sweet. But it is Dollie's flower, and it came from *home, our own home, my love*. . . .

Father is going to Iconium tomorrow. He will take Rocker and get shoes put on him. Cunning old Rocker! I think there isn't much the matter with him now, only a little moral obliquity. He runs and capers over the prairie, and when he comes home to supper, like a colt. But when we try to ride him, he is *very lame*. I am ashamed to tell such a thing of Rocker, but it is a sad truth. Won't it go some ways toward knowing the doctrine of the total depravity of human nature? I believe he has a notion that he has done duty enough to have a long furlough; to eat his oats and enjoy himself in peace. And he has, my love. But he oughtn't to want a furlough till his master comes home. . . . Father saw Dr. Gibbons,[25] too, to-day. He says Humphrey is dreadfully downhearted, since he heard of Will and Sam Wright being so sick. . . . I know he was uneasy about them. . . . I talked awhile with Mrs. Sheeks yesterday morning. She is all right, I assure you. But she is troubled about the way John's wife acts, and talks. She and her mother are traitors. The old lady says John is nearly heartbroken. It is hard, dear one, for him to have no one to say a word of kindness or sympathy to him. . . . If he isn't a good soldier, no doubt this is the secret of it, and I can't wonder at it. Isaac Sheeks[26] writes that they have plenty to eat, and good enough for anybody. They say some of them have written ridiculous stories about the way they have lived, but I don't pay any attention to such things. I don't even know who wrote them. But I know you will never find 100 men in a company, every one of whom will be good and honest and truthful. . . . I am always glad, darling, when you tell me about how you are getting on with your men. I don't want you to have trouble with them. I know it vexes you, and makes you unhappy. But some of them will be sure to do wrong sometimes. I hope not very often, for your sake, love. . . . In one of your letters, dearest, you said when you come home you thought you would not live on a farm any more, and asked what I think about it. I think I *want to live with you, my darling*, live with you always, never to leave you or be separated from you. . . . It won't matter to me whether your home, *our* home, shall be on a farm, or in town. Any place that pleases my love will please me. . . .

. . . This is my birthday love, I never thought of it till this minute. . . .
Dollie

Sunday Night, May 17th, 1863
My Own Darling,
. . . I am sorry you were not well. . . . I am afraid you were worse than you said. Always tell your Dollie when you are sick, and tell her all about it, won't you, sweet love? You never told me you were sick at all — or I never got the letter while you were down on the Tallahatchie. Will spoke of it, and several of the boys wrote about it. . . . I always want you to tell me everything, good or bad. Tell Dollie everything, as she tells you. I am glad that Will is doing so

well. I hope he is almost well by this time. . . . I have not been well since yesterday. I was quite sick last night. . . . I shall be better in a day or two. I miss you so much when I am sick, love. . . . I wanted you to take me in your arms, and kiss me, and love me. I have missed you all day today. *I miss you all the time*, everywhere, my pet. We have had a house full of company today. Let me tell you who were here. David Evans and his wife, and Lucy Hancock, and Mrs. Grissom, and Mr. Thornton Davis[27] and Mr. Christie. All staunch unionists, every one of them. There was later news in my dailies, than any of them had heard, and Davis read all the late news to the rest. I wish you could have been here, my dear one. David Evans looks pitiful. He can't walk upright. He says if it hadn't been for you he would have died. . . . He told me a good deal about you being so good to the sick boys. Their lieut. he said never came to see them, if they sent for them. But you always did, even if you had been there just before. Mr. Grissom said a soldier from the 36th — I don't know what company, but not yours — staid all night at their house a few nights ago, and spoke in terms of the highest praise of you. . . . I hear it from all quarters. And I know it is true of you. And I am so glad that you are appreciated, glad for your dear sake, pet, not for mine. I would know you are good and love you just the same if every man in your company hated you. But I want them to like you because you are good, and it will please you, and make your duty so much pleasanter. . . .

Monday, 4 o'clock P.M., . . . Stonewall Jackson is dead. I think there is no mistake . . . about this. And it is said Gen. Van Dorn.[28] I wish I could hear just from Vicksburg. . . . Have you heard that the convalescent soldiers at Keokuk have arrested H. Clay Dean?[29] I don't suppose they can do much with him unless they hang him outright. He has been traveling all over this state and Illinois organizing lodges of the K. G. C. He ought to be *suspended*. . . .

It is 7 months today, dear, since we got to your fathers. I didn't think then that I could live 7 months without ever seeing you once. . . . When you come home, we will just pay ourselves, won't we darling? We will be so happy then, that we shall be more than paid for all we suffer now. . . . I am uneasy about you, all the time, dear one. But I am more anxious since you told me you were not well. I can't help it. If you should get sick I don't know what I

should do. . . . But I hope you are not sick. . . . I am afraid you don't get the letters I send you. . . . Father says Mr. Phillips takes all possible care to have the mail go quick from his office. I am going to send all my letters there. . . .
Dollie

Tuesday Night, May 19th, 1863
My Own Dear Love,
    . . . I am afraid, darling, that the only consolation afforded us, in thinking of that 6 days fighting, is that at least Hooker hurt the enemy, as much as the enemy hurt him. You know we hoped for a great deal more than this, expected a great deal more. . . . I don't feel half so troubled over it as I did over Burnside's repulse at Fredericksburg last fall. *That* hurt me as if it had been a great personal calamity — which it really was dearest. This failure is not so bad, though our loss is heavier. So is the rebel loss much heavier, from eighteen to twenty thousand the rebels admit. . . . You know Secretary Chase[30] is a careful prudent man, and he said the other day that he thought he hazarded nothing in saying that this war now approaches its "termination." Vallandigham is to be sent South for two years. . . . The sentence is a mild one, I think, but it will do. H. Clay Dean is likely to bear him company, I hope. I will send the account of his arrest by the soldiers. . . . I am glad it was the sick soldiers who dared to do it. They should be honored for being true to their cause. . . . There is a rumor that Gen. Curtis is suspended by Gen. Schofield.[31] I hope it isn't true. General Halleck talks about taking the field at the head of the Army of the Potomac in person. I fear he wouldn't be any better. . . .
    There is to be a Union meeting over near Dr. Gibbon's next Saturday. . . . I don't know yet whether mother or I will go. We can't all go off at once and leave the house alone. There are over $800 here belonging to you and the boys, and if we were all gone some "unhallowed scamp" as father Vermilion says, might walk off with it. What if he should come for it some day when I am here alone? I expect I should make a valiant fight, with a woman's legitimate weapons — the broom stick and the shovel! I wish I had a revolver, dear one, and I would learn to shoot. In times like these it is right I think for every woman to know how to defend herself and her

property. If she never has occasion to use her knowledge so much the better. Oh, I don't know what made me think of this. . . . I don't think there is any danger of such trouble up here. . . .

Wednesday Morning, 6 o'clock, My Darling, Mr. Childs and his wife[32] have parted. . . . I don't know what the trouble is, the old jealousy and their bad tempers I believe. This reminds me of Jo. Marchbanks. You know that his wife and Mrs. Mayers[33] wouldn't let him go to the war! He has been acting very badly since, and they came near parting. She told him to sell anything they had and get money to take him to the regiment, and *go*. But he didn't want to go then. They have surely repented that they didn't let him go at first. It is a lesson to Mrs. Mayers. . . . This is the 20th. 7 months ago to day you kissed me for the last time, love, and left me. It seems long ago darling. I can hardly believe it has been only seven months. In 7 more I believe you will be at home with your Dollie. Oh, darling, can I wait? I am anxious to hear, my love, how you have settled the contest about the major's place. I don't care, dearest, how it goes, if *you don't care*. . . .
Dollie

Helena, Arkansas, May 19, 1863
My Dear Dollie,
    Yesterday was a hard day's work for the Regiment. In the forenoon they had to go on Brigade drill and in the afternoon we moved from the hill where we were camped down here right on the river bank. We are now about one mile above town, with our tents running up just as close to the bank of the river as we can get them. It will be healthier here, I think, and it is much more pleasant. . . . We will be handy to water here and then the facilities for washing and bathing will be good. The men can bathe every evening if they wish. Then we have plenty of nice shade trees. . . . Will was doing finely when I saw him last. Davenport was doing very well, too. But Dollie he is not right on the war question. Yesterday when we were moving some of the boys found a letter of his that had been dropped from some of the baggage. It was from Sam Davenport in reply to one Will had written home to Sam and his father[34] in which he pitched into the Union men at home and the

abolitionists generally. Sam says his father was well pleased with the letter and so was he. Sam thinks the time may come when the Democrats and Republicans will have to try their courage over in that section of the country. I am sorry Will Davenport is the Orderly. I am sorry I suffered the company to elect him but elections have played out in Co. F. I will make the appointments if there should be any vacancies hereafter and I will put loyal men in. The Lieut. and I would each give considerable now if Levi Brashar were orderly. . . . The boys all like him, and he is moral and loyal to the core. Will Davenport can never get any higher if I can help it. . . .

Noon, Dinner is not quite ready and while Harve Ryckman [35] is getting it I will talk to Dollie. . . . We live very well yet. We have plenty of good *Irish potatoes*, and onions — and by the way, I can eat as many of the latter as you but not quite as many of the former as you used to. The onions agree with me finally now. They cost right smart but still we get them. . . . I will finish this tonight after the boys all go to bed. That is the best time I ever have to write. Everything is quiet then.

8 O'clock P.M., Mr. Grissom will start home tomorrow or next day. We have succeeded in getting the privilege of sending Will as far north as Keokuk. There I think he will be discharged. . . . Samuel Wright ought to go North too. . . . I wish they were all well, and if they can't get well I wish they were at home. Many sick soldiers could get well who die here if they could be sent North to their own climate. Of all treatments, that is the best. Of course they don't all get well, who are sent North, because in many instances they are not sent soon enough.

Later, I have been thinking lately — just today — that if I knew we would remain here during the summer and I could get a good loyal family for you to board with I would have you to come down here. . . . But you could not stay with a rebel family my Dollie and I fear & almost know there is no other kind of people living here. . . . Of course I would have to be on duty every day and I don't know that I could get the privilege of remaining outside of the lines any of the time with you, but if everything else was certain and satisfactory I would go and try Gen. Prentiss for that privilege. There is no officer in the regiment who has his wife here, in fact it would not do under such uncertainties as we are laboring under now, for we may be called upon to go to Vicksburg at any time although it seems now as though we are going to remain for some time. The Post will have to be guarded and one division makes none too many. . . . This afternoon Gen. Ross sent round some very good orders about civilians passing the lines. On all of the most important roads we have instructions not to let them pass at all. They can't visit the fortifications any more. . . .

I have been hunting for something for the last week to send you but I have not got any thing and there is nothing here to sell but sutler's goods. Nothing worth sending my one love.

W. F. Vermilion

Helena, Arkansas, May 19, 1863

My Own Dollie,

What do you suppose makes me write so often to you. I never write to anyone else, not even on business. . . . I will keep doing it because I do love you so much. I have never written to father's folks yet, and more I don't intend to. I would like very well for mother and Jane to hear from me but I can't afford to write — not even to them — as long as the rest of the family holds the principles they do. I love mother but poor old lady she can't read my letters when I write them to her, and I don't care about others, especially those who have no sympathy for me while here in the field, before the enemy and exposed to all the dangers incident to war, reading anything I say to anyone I love or respect, so all of them will have to become loyal or never hear from me. I may be killed or wounded and if they ever hear of it they will have to learn it without my order. Father is old and has not got a very strong mind, but I am in no way responsible for that. . . . But Dollie if he were all right in mind he would not be a loyal citizen. It is not in his nature to be. Neither is it in the nature of Thom or John to be. . . . All large, generous souled men are loyal. Men of small minds are all traitors. Some good Union men are small minded, that is in the power of thought, but they are generally free and honest. I would give almost any amount in dollars and cents if it would only make my brothers good men. But Dollie it is not my fault. I have done as much for them as they ever did for me. They never did anything for me. . . . Men who hold such bitter hatred towards the Government as they do can't if they are honest wish anyone who is serving the Government well. . . . If they want to hear let them be compelled to ask me to write to them. If they ever do that I will first ask them if they love their Country. If they say they do and will support it, I will write, otherwise I will not. I have no time here to write to anyone who has love and sympathy for the rebels and hatred for me. And I consider every man who hates the cause in which we are engaged as my personal enemy and I will have nothing to do with him unless he joins the rebel army, and then I will treat him as I expect to treat all other rebels. I wrote to John Runyan and told him the time might come when he and I would meet provided he had the moral courage to fight for his principles. That if the Government did not succeed in putting this rebellion down soon that such traitors as him should and would be attended to, that the cause they were pursuing would bring war to their own doors, and if it did come I wanted to go North. That I loved and respected rebels in the South compared with such men as him. I also told him that I hoped I would never see or hear from him again. . . . He is no kindred of mine. Neither is any other traitor or if they like the term any better Southern sympathizers.

Will

Camp near Helena, Arkansas, May 21, 1863
My Own Dollie,

What little the people knew when they used to say that the Government could not get white men to command Negro troops. . . . Several sergeants, and for that matter I might say several privates of our Regiment have received commissions. Many other good men of several companies have failed not because they were not well recommended but there was not room for them. Lt. Col. Wood of one of the Indiana Regiments — the 46th I believe — expected the Colonelcy of the first regiment here.[36] He said he was not afraid but they would make good soldiers. Col. Pyle[37] of the 33rd Mo. is now gone to Memphis to get the appointment of Brigadier General of an African Brigade. *He is a good man.* . . . He is a Methodist preacher, and first went out as a chaplain, but was made colonel when General Fisk was made brigadier. . . . His command as Colonel of the 33rd Mo. is a good position. Yet he will take and even seek the position of a brigadier of a Negro brigade. I hope he will get it because I hope all such positions will be filled by good men, and I think he is one. No one from our company has asked for any position yet. . . . In fact I hope they will not. We need all the good men we have in the Company for our own use. . . . Jacob Grimes is as near right as a man can be. He thinks the Government should arm every negro man in the Southern Confederacy. . . . They will be better off in the army than any place else in the United States during this great rebellion. 1st Lieut. Clifton[38] of Co. H our regiment has just asked me to assist him in getting the position of Lieut. Colonel in a regiment that is now forming here. He is an old Mexican [War] soldier and a very good officer. . . .

Mr. Grissom started home this evening. I could not get anything I wanted to send to Dollie but an Orange. I sent all 3 of you one piece. Eat them. They will soon spoil. . . .

W. F. Vermilion

Friday Evening, May 22nd, 1863

My Own Dear Love,

. . . I felt very sorry to hear of John Smith's death. Such things are so sad darling, so terrible when I stop to think of it all. You say he kept his faith. It did me good to hear this darling. This being so, no one ought to grieve for *him*. They must grieve for their own loss. I wish I could tell his mother and father that I am so sorry for you, my dear one! I know how it hurts you for one of those men to die. I thought about it often before you spoke of it, dear one. I wish I could comfort you. I know you have done all you possibl[y] could for them. . . . I know you were so sad when those letters were written, and no wonder. John Smith dying and the bad news from Hooker were enough to make you sad. But you must not be discouraged, my love. Hooker failed indeed but Grant has not yet. . . . Grant is for something besides digging ditches. We have no news of importance since the capture of Jackson. . . . There is also a report that Rosecrans is to take command of the Army of the Potomac, and Gen. McCook[39] of the Cumberland. I hardly credit this. If Rosecrans is our best general — and this seems admitted by everyone — we need him just where he is. He surely has enough to do now, and the work is just as important I should think. For the sake of the west I should be sorry to hear of that change. . . .

One Hour Later, While I was writing a while ago, who should come in but old Mr. May?[40] He had come all the way over here to see if I had heard through you of Sam Wright. The last letter they got was dated the 5th, and they were so uneasy that they couldn't wait till their mail day. I was truly glad love, that you had spoken of Sam in your last letter saying he was walking about. . . . I read to the old man what you had said about Sam and all the sick boys. It did him a good deal of good, and it will do Sam's mother still more when she hears it. . . . Humphrey and all of them over there are well. Old Mr. Evans[41] had just got a letter from Cunningham and he said he helped to arrest Clay Dean. You know he had been all this time in the hospital at Keokuk. He has got to do some good service at last. . . . As to getting my mail at Iconium you seem to hate it, darling. . . . Don't be afraid of that, will you my darling? They can't frighten me about you, for I hope I shall have as late news as any of them, and I won't listen to them. I have heard of some of their stories already dear, and I cared less for them than for the wind that blew around me. . . . Iconium is a bad place, love. There are but few Union men there they say. . . .

If it is a good day tomorrow father and I are going to Humphrey's and to the Union meeting. I want to see Julia and Billy. When he was here the other day I asked him whom he wanted to see worst, and he said "uncle doctor and uncle Wesley." I hope he will see both before long. Old Mr. May is in good spirits about the war. Everybody seems to be. I do hope it is going right at last. . . . Dollie

Saturday Night, May 23rd, 1863
My Own Love,

. . . Father and I have been to the Union meeting. . . . Very early this morning I went up to Mr. Sheeks to see if there was any mail there. . . . Then I dined and we went over to Humphrey's and stayed till after dinner, and then walked down to the speaking, which was about a quarter of a mile from there. Humphrey is not well yet by any means. . . . Julia and the children are well and look much like they did. They're good sound *abolitionists*. . . . They were looking for us and had a good dinner. Mr. Roy's[42] family and Jane Sheeks were there to dinner. . . . We talked about war, and had a very pleasant visit. But it hurts my feelings to be where Humphrey is, dear one. I can hardly bear to stay in sight of him. He was with you so long. And he wears clothes just like yours. It is so hard for me to see him at home, and you are gone, my pet. . . .

The day was beautiful and there was a large crowd at the speaking. They had martial and vocal music. There were two good speeches by Mr. Sharp and Senator Estep who was elected on the Mahoney[43] ticket. Both are strong Democrats. Their mothers soaked them in hickory sugartroughs with the bark off. Sharp made an excellent logical speech giving the *true* history of our politics for the last 30 years. Both were withering in their denunciations of traitors. I don't see how the Copperheads could stand it. Estep is Capt. of the Wayne homeguards, and they say exceedingly wide awake, keeping 5 scouts out all the time. The Copperheads are afraid of him and hate him cordially. He told them he was going to speak throughout the county and give them fair warning that they couldn't sport their butternut seals and copperhead breastpins near here. If they didn't stop giving encouragement to the rebels, the Government would make provisions for them if it never did anything else, and *they would have to go to their friends.* He was very bitter and pretty rough. He read the telegram from Indianapolis about the Copperheads firing into soldiers' houses, and told them if they did it in that county, "their boats would be chartered for hell in less than 24 hours." He said he was for his country under any and all circumstances, and if that would injure the Democratic Party, the Democratic Party might go to the devil. . . . Both sustained every measure of the administration and told the traitors that it would be a happy exchange to send them off and fill their places with loyal negroes. I wish you could have heard them, love, and seen the enthusiasm with which the people received every word. You would have felt that the soldiers were not forgotten by their friends at home. Estep was crippled by a fall from his horse and had to stand on his crutches, but he told them he was going to talk to the Union meetings that were advertised at New York and Lagrange. . . . I saw everybody that we know over there. A great many asked about you. I don't know how many came up to look at your likeness in my breastpin. They said that was the kind of pin to wear, a soldier's likeness. . . .

I have been to Woodside today. . . . When I got to the barn I saw Capitala in the pasture. She played around Rocker and tried to make acquaintance with him, much to his disgust. . . . Teater was plowing corn with Jake. . . . He is in as good order as he ever has been when he works. I can't account for the change darling, since I came home, but I think it is because they expect you home before long. . . . Rocker didn't behave very well. As I was going through the bottom I met a boy with a wagon load of poles, and he got scared and broke his martingales[44] and "cut up shines" considerably. I had to whip him and that made him very lame for a few minutes. But I gave him a good drink at the [Chariton] River, and he forgot all about it after that. . . .

Perhaps Teater is all right about the war. He says the Copperheads are very plenty in that neighborhood. They are exulting over that letter of John Wafford's a great deal. . . .
Dollie

Helena, Arkansas, May 24, 1863
My Own Dollie,

. . . I got two letters from you. . . . The one on the 14th was a good long one, and in it you have discussed your "plans" thoroughly and await my opinion. I don't know what to say about it Dollie. . . . We are not any too strong to hold this place, now that Price[45] is in Arkansas. After Vicksburg falls, there will be in all probability an expedition fitted out to clean this state of the rebels. Then we may have to leave here. In that case you are as well off where you are as anywhere else. . . . Even if you come to Keokuk it will be hard to get a telegraphic dispatch to you because there is no line from here to Memphis. And after all hard battles it is very hard to get to send any private dispatches for some time. . . . But Dollie we are not likely to get into one of those hard fights if Grant is successful at Vicksburg. . . . So don't suffer any uneasiness on that account.

If there were a good loyal boarding house in town and I could get to stay outside of the camp any portion of the time I would be sure to have you come down and stay as long as we remain here. But everyone tells me that a loyal family is a very hard thing to find in Helena. . . . It is altogether a mistake about Col. Kittredge having his wife[46] down here. She came as far as St. Louis with him last winter but when she left there she went home and she has never been with the Regiment since. General Fisk had his wife here last winter and took her down the Pass with him. But my Dollie I don't want you to be exposed as she was while on that trip. I don't mean to the enemy but to everything else that a fine woman should shun. She went & carried her revolver all of the time, not to defend herself with against the enemy but to deter the soldiers from insulting her, so she told [E. W.] Parkhurst — he says. But to finish this subject, if I find I am going to be exposed to any extent I will make sure arrangements as you have spoken of. . . .

On the day before yesterday the 5th Kansas Cavalry and the Dubuque Battery[47] had a sham fight. The cavalry charged at full speed on the Battery while they were firing blank cartridges at the rate of 2 or 3 in a minute. . . . The battery belched their fire and smoke directly at the cavalry, yet on they came at full speed urging their horses on till they were right among the cannon and took them. In making the charge the cavalry had to ride through a boggy place in the ground which caused several of the horses to fall. The horses behind were in full speed and of course could not stop. . . . Some 4 or 5 men were badly hurt. . . . In those sham fights someone is always hurt, and generally one or two killed. Yet sham fighting is the best practice men can have.

I received a letter from Henry this morning. He pitched into Dan Vorhees. He said John Runyan spat at my letter. He said he was glad I had written such a letter to him. . . . I am sorry Henry wrote to me for I did not want to write to any of them. Now I feel that I am under some obligation to him. He has written to me and *I know he is loyal* but I don't want anyone who is not to ever read anything I write to my friends. I will never write to John or Thom, no never, unless they become loyal men, which I think will never occur. . . . Poor old Mother, I am sorry for her, but Dollie I am not in the least responsible for the unhappy state of things there. They work at their own destiny. I want you to tell me all you did for them while you were there. *I don't want to owe them one cent in any way. . . .*

Henry Maiken is going to try to get commissioned in the Negro Regiment that is forming here now.[48] He wants a lieutenancy. . . .

Jacob F. Grimes was going to make application but he is afraid of his health. Jake has bronchitis badly. Don't say anything about the boys wanting such positions Dollie till they succeed. Then we will not care who knows it. . . .

Wm. F. Vermilion

Tuesday Morning, May 26th, 1863
My Dearest Love,

. . . You need not feel bad my own love, about my going to Iconium often. . . . I shall have to go sometimes myself but I won't stay 3 minutes, and they shall not worry me about you or anything. I will do as Aunt Anna used to tell me. When I would get troubled about anything in Indiana, she would say "Set your face like flint, my child." [49]

Father went to Milledgeville this morning to try to sell your corn. . . . The buyers were going to Ottumwa this morning and father didn't see them. They are giving John 16 cents. That is very little but it is as much as one can get probably. . . . The caterpillars have killed the crab-apple grove entirely. I am very sorry about it. They are worse than they were last year. . . . Teater says Smith's folks take it very hard about John. It is hard, my darling. . . .

Dollie

Tuesday Evening, May 26th, 1863
My Own Darling,

. . . I am sorry that another one of your men is dead. I am afraid that many of them will not diet themselves as you do. . . . They don't know, as you do, how it will benefit them. And they will not be as likely to regard their diet there as they will at home. If poor John Smith had been at home, and you had given him the same directions about his eating, he would have obeyed them implicitly, I think. I am glad you are careful of your health, my pet. I verily believed you could not endure the hardships of such a life 3 months, when you went away. And you have been healthier than any of them. I think it is so, because you have cared for yourself better. . . .

If only Hooker has not failed! But he will not lie idle long. He is not the man to remain quiet and inactive. . . . He *must* succeed, or he will make a worse figure before the world [than] even McClellan. But I have not yet lost faith in his generalship or patriotism. . . . The discipline of the army is very good, much better than it was before. We still have a fine army in excellent condition. If he were disposed to remain idle during this campaign, the President would not allow it. I think our worthy "Father Abraham" is in deadly earnest at last. He has learned that the only way to end the war is to whip the rebels, and be merciless to end the war. . . . If once the tide of success turns strongly in our favor nothing on earth can save the rebels from a speedy doom. I may be too sanguine . . . but let me be in as good spirits as I can. I have suffered disappointment enough to teach me not to be so hopeful, for disappointments could make me sick. . . . One perhaps ought not to be to selfish, in times like these, but I can't help it, my pet. . . . Every heart knoweth its own bitterness, as it does its own joy. I rejoice for our country, and our cause, and you gallant soldiers and their supporting families, but I think first of my own heart's treasure.

Wednesday Morning, May 27th, If you come home before winter you will not want to sell the cattle I think. . . . Cows are pretty high. Good ones older than Milcho rating at from $18 to $20. . . . I am going to Mullinix's . . . and I will have Allie drain Muley dry, and let her get fat. She will bring more money that way than any other. If the oxen get fat shall we sell them, or do you want to keep them? These are things I don't know much about, love, and you must tell me. . . . A good many think cattle are higher now than they will be this fall. . . . Father says if our young steers have to be sold this fall — that is if you and the boys are still away — he is going to buy them for Matt. . . .
Dollie

Wednesday Night, May 27th, 1863
My Own Darling
    . . . Matt was at LaGrange [Tennessee] on the 16th. They had just returned from another raid. This makes three within a month. . . . They were gone 5 days this time, went as far as Senatobia [Mississippi], had a hard time, and came near being "gobbled up" by a large body of rebels. They kept them at bay, till they finally got be-

yond their reach. They didn't want to fight. They had too much plunder along. They had over 1000 head of horses and mules, and all the negroes who wanted to go with them and some who didn't. They all got back safely, but one man from their company who was captured. He says Gen. Smith has done the rebels more harm in 1 month than Denver[50] did in 6. He takes and destroys everything. The women with streaming eyes will beg them to spare their houses or niggers or corn or bacon, or whatever they have. In reply they ask for the keys to the smokehouses, and if they refuse to give them up a few sturdy blows soon sends in the door. Matt believes in making war after this fashion, with all his might. He says he stood guard over rebel property long enough. When they move now they have no long train of provision wagons, requiring a regiment or two to guard it, but they take a little coffee and sugar and a few crackers in their haversacks, and depend on the hospitality of the southern planters for the rest. It is astonishing he says how the hams and chickens agree with them. . . . Matt is seeing a good deal of service, and learning something of the world, isn't he dear?

. . . Since I came home I am *entirely* satisfied with Iowa. I don't want to live anywhere else. If you wanted to move I would be willing to go for your sake, love, but I don't want to move on my own account. I sat in the west door this evening and watched the sun sink to rest in a bed of gold and purple clouds. I looked over the landscape and thought what a goodly prospect it was. What a beautiful country! How lovely were the dark green hill slopes, and the rich foliage of the distant woods! I sat and looked for a long time, till I almost grew sad. I wanted you to see it too, dear love. Don't you get homesick sometimes when you think of Iowa? When you remember that it is *May* up here; you know that is our favorite month. There are more wildflowers than usual. . . . I keep a pot full on the table all the time, to make sure the room looks homelike. . . .

I read a late speech of Wendell Phillips[51] today. He says this war will not be ended by an event. . . . He doesn't think it will end soon. But it *will* end, and the end will be as glorious as we dare hope. . . . I have had no letter from Jane or any of our folks in Indiana. . . . I won't write any more I think unless they answer my letters. Mother wanted me to promise to write every week to tell them about you, but I told her I couldn't promise to write her every week, but I would write as often as I could. . . . Would you write any more if you were in my place, before they write to me?

I like Jane, darling, as well as if she were my own sister. You know I went there prepared to like them all and expecting to — just as if they were my own blood, as well as yours. But Jane and Henry were the only loyal ones, and I could not love the disloyal ones. I loved you too much. And the love of my Country, and Justice, and Right, and Humanity were too strong in my soul. It was a disappointment — a sad one to me. . . . When you come here we will talk it all over, and then we will bury it, my pet, and forget it. I often think it is a great pity that I went there. If I had not gone we would never have known it. But it may be all for the best.

It is going on for 11 o'clock, my darling. Don't think I have the blues, love, for I haven't. *But I want to see you.* Perhaps I shall in my dreams tonight. Sancho Ponza said "Blessed be the man who invented sleep." [52] I say Blessed be the man who invented dreams. . . .

Friday morning, They are going to have a "big meeting" at Milledgeville this week. . . . I feel so bad, darling, to go anywhere without you that I would rather stay, unless it is a war meeting. Father has joined a company of volunteer Homeguards belonging about Melrose. They are going to draw arms. I am glad of it. Every man — loyal man — should be armed, let them be old or young. The surest way to prevent any trouble is to be fully prepared for it. Don't you think so, dearest?
Dollie

Helena, Arkansas, May 27, 1863
My Own Dollie,

Early this morning I received two letters from you. . . . I also received one from Jane. She wrote me a good letter. . . . It is short, and I am going to put it up with this and send it to you, so you may know just what she has said to me. She is a good sister and I take all I said to you about writing to father's folks back, especially so far as she is concerned. Write to her if you want to Dollie, but tell her not to let anyone else see your letters till after she reads them. In all probability, if I write to her Thom or some of the other boys will get the letter and read it before she gets to see it. . . . Yesterday or the day before I got a short letter from Henry. . . . He is a good loyal boy but I do hope he will not go into the service again.[53] He can't stand a camp life any more if he is much sick. . . .

On the day before yesterday the 5th Kansas Cavalry and the 3rd Iowa cleverly went out on the Little Rock road on a scout. Some 3 or 4 miles out they ran into an ambuscade of rebels and got pretty badly cut up again.[54] They fell back and sent a runner to town, but of course by the time the reinforcements got there the Guerrillas were all gone. . . . The 5th Kansas lost 5 men killed, some 20 wounded, and about 50 captured. The 3rd Iowa lost some 8 or 10 wounded, and 2 captured.[55] Some 2 or 3 days ago there was a boat sent down to Friars Point [Mississippi] for the purpose of getting some negroes and mules. There were 8 or 10 white soldiers and 1 or 2 negro companies sent down on the boat. Coming back the rebels fired into them some distance below here. They who were on the boat say that the negro soldiers fought like good fellows.[56]

I believe in most instances the negroes will fight equal to white men. As the 1st Arkansas was going down the river from here they were fired into by the rebels and after the Regiment had landed for the purpose of fighting it was all the officers could do to keep the negroes back. . . . They drove the rebels off and went on their way rejoicing.

Vicksburg is the only thing, or point, that one inquires after now. . . . Pemberton may concentrate his forces on some one point and cut his way through, but he can't take anything out if Grant keeps on the lookout. . . .

W. F. Vermilion

Friday Evening, May 29th, 1863
My Own Love,

. . . This morning early Mrs. Sheeks came by going to Hickcox, and brought me a letter from you, and my papers, and 3 oranges, and a little book — Letter Writer — that Mr. Grissom left at their house last night. . . . Father was at Iconium today, and they there say he brings a terrible account home. He says the boys are all sick and tired of the war, and want to come home. That they live very hard and can't eat at their tables without vomiting, and the like. Now this is Iconium talk, my dear. I don't know whether Mr. Grissom ever said one word of it. If he did he must have been intimate with Will Davenport and a few others like him, while he stopped at Helena. . . . You have a few bad men in your company, darling, who are no doubt traitors at heart, and they would be glad to get out of the service at any sacrifice of honor or manliness. . . . I expect your company is just like the others. They all have a few bad men in them. . . . The most of them give a very truthful account of how they live, my dear. The good, loyal men are very far from grumbling. . . . What a series of brilliant victories Grant has won! I am glad he has succeeded so much beyond even our fondest hopes of him, because I have doubted him. . . . I would have been glad last winter if the President had removed him from that command. But he has taken Vicksburg, he has won us such a victory as has not gladdened our hearts since Corinth,[57] nor then even, and how joyfully we forget the 5 long months of ditching and digging! Grant is everybody's hero now. . . .

Darling, you said you were thinking about letting me come down to Helena to stay awhile. My heart gave a great bound when I read that. I do want to go to you, love, if you can't come home. . . . I could do with very common lodgings, I would submit to any inconvenience to be near you. . . . I hope General Prentiss will let me come, he has a new wife of his own, and I hope he loves her and wants to see her if she isn't with him. Women are not such bad things in the army, darling, General Grant keeps his wife near him or with him all the time. She gets captured sometimes but he always gets her back, you know. Seriously, dear one, I wish I had $1000 of my own, and I would spend it all to stay near you, till you come home. . . . I am glad you have a pleasant camp on the river. . . . Won't musketos eat you up? I think Will will be careful of himself and keep clean. Matt is dirty . . . but he seems to thrive on it pretty well. Will cannot. We have heard from Jimmy through some of his comrades. His eyes are better. Otherwise he was well. . . .

Father was at Woodside. . . . He saw Mr. Dunlap going over to look at Milcho, and he went with him and sold him the cow for 19 dollars. It is a pretty good price, but I don't know if we ought to have sold her. . . . The man from Milledgeville is going to look at the corn. He offered $37 for the pen, but father wouldn't take it.

He thinks there are between 200–250 bushels of it. He says he will take $40. I hate to see our things sold off, darling. But it may be for the best. I think it is to sell the corn. Father saw the young steers. . . . He said he would give me $20 a head for them. . . .

Thank you for the oranges, my pet. Mother and I ate one. . . . The others I will keep till you come home. I am glad you can get them. They will be so good for you. . . . Get everything you can, love, that will do you good. Humphrey May starts to Kentucky next Monday. He will be gone 4 or 5 weeks. He will stop at Aunt Anna's for awhile. He will get to there from Indiana.

Dollie

Saturday Evening, May 30th, 1863
My Own Love,

. . . You are severe on poor John Runyan, love. But I am not going to apologize for him. I think he deserves it but because he married our sister I would not make an open rupture with him. . . . I am sorry for mother and Jane. . . . Poor Jane, she can't help it, and she has trouble enough without my hurting her feelings or neglecting her. . . . I hope she will some day come to Iowa and live near us. I would be very glad. Only think, love, of the moral courage it required to be loyal, and she was loyal. Surrounded with outspoken treason, no one to tell her the facts about anything or talk to her on the subject, no papers to read, or at best treasonable ones, and yet she was loyal all the time. Could you or I have [done] more? Jane is worthy of our love my pet, and we won't throw her away, will we? If she ever writes to you, answer her letters darling, and say a few gentle loving words to her. It will do her untold good. . . . The poor child never hears a loving word said to her. She told me all her trials one day, while we were out in the pasture gathering willows. It was a sad story. She said she wanted me to tell you all about it, and how she lived — after you came home, not before, because she didn't want to annoy you with her troubles, because you had troubles of your own and so much to do and think of. . . . She said she often thought that if she married and left that home she would never go back, even to see them, as long as she lived. They are not good to her, my darling. I don't know why. She is the best one in the family. And if the rest don't sympathize with you and wish you well, I know she does. She loves you more than she does any of them. We won't throw her away, my precious. . . .

As I came home with my flowers I stopped a little while at Hickcox's and saw Jane Pennebaker. I feel sorry for her. Her husband[58] is at Vicksburg, and she has not had a letter from him for two weeks. He is in Steele's[59] [division] and she knows he has been in some of the hardest battles of the last week. . . . She is quite cheerful and seems anxious to hear that our cause is triumphant, as that he is safe. I am glad for her that she can bear it so well. She has 3 babies to take care of. That doesn't leave her much time to grieve. I used to like her before either of us were married. How little we thought then of what the future had in store for us. Both of us come back to our old homes! I promised to go see her before many days, and hear how she is getting on. Mark Hickcox was at Vicksburg too. His folks are very uneasy about him. I read a letter from John Hickcox. I know he is a good soldier. . . . I sent by father today and bought some letter paper today and a pair of shoes and a dark brown dress. It is a very pretty piece. I must make it up next week, but I don't know how I am to be still long enough. I don't need it unless I go to you during the summer. Father saw Mullinix at Sam Dix's[60] trying to buy a horse. . . . He said a traveler came along and told the latest news from Vicksburg, and Dix couldn't hold his head up. I guess he and most of Iconium will put on mourning. How sorry we feel for them, don't we darling! John is rejoicing over the good news. Cy Phillips is having a jubilee all by himself. He says he has fallen 10 cents on the good [news], on his goods. . . . The war has come much closer here to the people than it had before you went away. And then they have waited on this so long, and so much depends on it. . . . An evening or two ago Mr. Ely[61] called at the gate and asked about you, and then about the news. I told him and he was so glad, and asked me again and again if I were sure it was true. I told him I was pretty sure this time, and I took my latest daily out to the fence and read the dispatches to him. He laughed gleefully over it, and said "it was mighty good, it was just good enough," but he wanted our boys to get them all, every last one of them.
Dollie

Sunday Night, May 31st, 1863
My Own Darling,
    . . . The latest dispatches say Vicksburg is not captured yet. But
Grant and everybody is still sanguine of success. . . . Grant will
fight with desperation, and so will his brave Western legions. . . .
I don't see how he can retreat, if he should be overwhelmed or
beaten. Unless Rosecrans draws the attention of the rebels to his
movements, I am afraid they will withstand his efforts.[62] Father
says I must not be scared so easily. He is not alarmed, but is confident Grant will succeed. He thinks so many western soldiers,
with fighting Generals to lead them, cannot be whipped by any
force the rebels can bring against them. But if they are it will be
so dreadful for us. . . .
Dollie

Monday Evening, June 1st, 1863
Dear Love,
    . . . Perhaps I shall go by Mr. Grissom's. I would have gone be-
fore now, but father didn't want me to. He *has* been talking treason I guess since he came home, and they are all indignant about
it. . . . Mrs. Maiken "pitched into" Grissom about the way he
talked. She told him she supposed he ate with the boys, and he
looked very well. He said traveling agreed with him. He may not
have said half that they report. . . . I shall hear all about you when
Mr. Wright comes. He is the "blackest sort of abolitionist" and I
can believe him. . . . Old Mr. Graham was here yesterday. He says
he gets very satisfactory letters from Manoah,[63] I believe that is his
name. He makes no complaints. No good or honest man does, you
need not be uneasy about that, my darling. . . .
Dollie

Tuesday Night, June 2nd, 1863
My Own Love,
    . . . I went to Mullinix's to day, and found them all right. . . .
When I went he met me out at the gate, and asked me how I was,

and . . . when had I heard from Doc, and how was he getting on all before I could get off my horse. They were very glad to see me. The children were gone to school but they came home before I started. They were nearly wild when they saw me, and Rocker. . . . John is altogether right. You need have no fear about him, love, though the copperheads have done their best to win him over. . . . He says "he has a bushel of faith." He has found a *disloyal chapter in the bible*, and he wants me to tell you that he doesn't believe in a word of it. I think he is wrong about it being there. I ate all the strawberry pie I could, for you dear one. . . . I didn't see Mr. Grissom yesterday. John says he talked very fair, to him and Mr. Eads, about you all. But he couldn't tell much news. It is said that he told some of your men while he was there that "greenbacks" were worthless up here, wouldn't pass currently and they were distressed over it, as they had nothing else to send their families. Tell them not to be afraid of the "greenbacks," darling. They are good as gold. . . . While I was traveling I often heard people refuse to take anything but "greenbacks." I would have declined anything else myself, if it had been offered me. It is a bad sign to see any one afraid of "greenbacks." That was one of the signs by which I could always tell the traitors in Indiana. . . . I think of going to New York Saturday. I would like so much to go if you were here to go with me, but I don't know whether I can go alone. I know very well that I would not go that far without you, to anything else in the world than a Union meeting. But it is a duty we owe the soldiers to go to these. . . . I shall make up my mind before Saturday. . . . John said Mr. Stewart and Dr. Richards[64] both wanted to know of him yesterday if he ever saw me, or heard of me since I came home, and why I never come to town? He told Richards that he guessed there were too many copperheads there for me to want to come often. He said oh, no, there were plenty of people there who were not copperheads, and they would be very glad to see me. . . . He claims to be loyal, but loyal men are not afraid to speak on the subject here. When I hear of one who can't express an opinion about the war, I know he is one who *would be a traitor if he dared*. He wants to be, but is too cowardly to risk the consequences. . . . You often speak of Jake Grimes, love. I am a little afraid that, as the Indians say, he has 2 tongues. . . . I read his letter to Humphrey May, and it is intensely patriotic, as near right as can be. He has written the same kind of letters to Mr. Maiken and Mr. Phillips. But John heard Mr. Cambridge read one that he got from him the other day, and it was altogether different. Had the ring of another metal entirely. He also heard one read last week from John Wafford to his brother. He said Jake was trying to get promoted and when he was with the officers he was a strong war man but *he was all right when he was with him.* I just tell you this as a hint darling. . . . I don't want him to deceive you like Davenport did. But don't let this annoy you one moment. . . .

Father is going after his new plow to day. . . . He'll feel very independent, riding and plowing 4 furrows at once. I'm thinking there won't be much work left for the young men to do, when they come home from the war. There is going to be a Union meeting at New York next Saturday. A great many are going from here. Miss Jolly[65] has trained a choir of 12 little girls to sing patriotic songs. They are to be dressed in white, with blue and red sashes. They will look very sweet, and they sing quite well. . . . The copperheads of course get very indignant, but so much the better. That proves that the lesson is working. There was one at Lagrange — a glorification rather, that was over the good news. . . . and Jane May and some more women came very near fighting. . . .

Dollie

Thursday Evening, June 4th, 1863

My Own Love,

. . . I wish you had sent me Henry's letter. I have no doubt they are very angry at me. I don't think Henry and Jane are, but I know the rest blame me altogether. . . . But that won't trouble me much, so long as *one* loves me, and has faith in me. I know Jane fully intended to write to me often, when I left there. I think they won't let her. I know they think me an "unhallowed abolitionist," and that I have turned you against them. . . . Though I acknowledge the *abolition* part! They may think that I have told you horrible stories, though I hardly believe they will accuse me of telling what is untrue. I did not tell you *more* than the truth, my dear one. But I know they will never imagine for one moment how hard I tried to keep the peace and avert your displeasure from them. When I wrote about them I tried to give the best aspect of affairs, not the worst, except about Runyan. That was precisely true, and I might have told you twice as much, and told you months before I did. But I didn't mean to tell you at all; and would not if I had not thought he was coming there to live. I couldn't stand it then, darling. Tell me all they say about me, or *you*, won't you, love? You need not be afraid to write to Henry. I don't think he will be apt to show your letter to any of them. He got a letter from you last winter when he was sick in bed. I gave it to him and that was the last I ever saw of it. I don't think any of them got to read it. Henry is a strange being. He is exceedingly rough in his behavior at home. He doesn't like them much and there is open war about all the time. He seems to think, as boys of his age sometimes do, that it is not *manly* to say or do an obliging or kind thing *at home*. And this is the fault of his training. He was never taught the beauty of gentleness. I have heard him swear at mother, till it almost made my blood run cold. They of course can't put up with his temper very well, now. They don't look below the surface, darling; *they don't know what is the matter with him*. He is naturally bitter and sarcastic, and his bringing up has fully developed these traits. Aside from . . . that I verily believe he is "more sinned against, than sinning;" he is a very noble fellow. He has a good mind, if it were educated with strong, deep feelings that he doesn't understand, and doesn't know what to do with. I am sorry for him, love, from my heart I am. But if he knew I said so, he would swear at me, and say he didn't want anybody to feel sorry for him. . . . I have heard father tell him often that he never had been anything but a trouble to him since he was a little child, and he never expected anything but trouble on his account. Of course his only answer would be an undutiful retort from Henry that would more than justify his prediction. Then taking it all together my love, it is a most unhappy household. And I think the reason — I hope it is not wrong in me to say it — lies solely with *them*, not with their surroundings. If they would only be kind and loving, one toward another, the whole trouble would vanish. . . . You want me to tell you what I gave them. I have told you dear, I got mother and Jane each a dress, and gave Jane a few trifles. I sent your likeness to town and got one taken from it for mother. I gave $1 for it. She wanted it so bad that I tried to get her one, but it was bad, it doesn't look a bit like you. *I* never would have known it. Mother gave me a dress when I started for home. I didn't want to take it, but I couldn't refuse without hurting her feelings. She gave me yarn to make two pair of stockings last fall. . . . I had nothing else but my board, and I think I worked enough to pay for that. I don't feel like we owe them anything in this way, darling. Sometimes I thought I would buy them several dollars worth of presents and send back to them, when I started home. Then I thought that we *owed* nothing, and I ought not to spend your money that way. . . . If we were at home I would like to send for Jane, pay all her expenses, and keep her a year with us. If we can still do anything for her, love, I want to do it. . . . Do you ever get any home papers in Helena — Iowa papers I mean? If you don't, shall I send you one now and then? I am proud of our Iowa papers, dear, next to our Iowa soldiers. I am proud of Iowa anyhow. She has done, and is doing, her duty so gallantly. . . .

I hope Henry Maiken has got his lieutenantcy. . . . How would you like to be Colonel of one of those regiments? Is your Court Martial ended? Tell me how you get on with your men, and how you and the Colonel are getting on. Who is Major, love? You never said. . . .

Mr. Davis came over yesterday to see my dailies and hear the latest news. . . . I never saw a man so excited and enthusiastic. . . . I didn't hear him talk any. I was sitting out under the locust tree reading your letters when he came, and I didn't come in till he was going. He is very bitter against the copperheads, and says all he thinks without any fear of consequences. The Providence[66] and Milledgeville churches are getting up a movement to purify themselves of traitors. They are going to combine all the loyal elements of both churches, into one church, and leave the copperheads and tenderfooted Unionists out in the cold. Old Mr. Christie is leading the movement. I told him yesterday that when he got that work accomplished I would go to [a] meeting. He doesn't like to go very well himself till it is done. I don't blame him.

Did you ever hear, love, that Mr. Bill Argo has been expelled from the church for treason? He has been "out in the cold" some time and Redenbaugh,[67] and several others down there, but I forget who they are now. This is right, my love. When a man proves himself a traitor to his country I don't think he ought to be allowed membership in a loyal church. . . . The weather is very dry. If it doesn't rain soon there will not be good crops. Gardens are burning up. . . .

Dollie

Helena, Arkansas, June 4, 1863

My Dollie,

Will Kemper and several of the boys start home in the morning. . . . They are not able for duty here. If they will take good care of themselves they will be well against their 30 days are out. . . . I have given him money to buy you a good Gold pen with. If he gets it use it every time you write to me, and be sure and think of me all the time. . . . If Will gets it keep it till I get home Dollie, and if I never get home keep it with you always.

I went to see Col. Drake the other day to see if he would be willing for me to go home if Gen. Prentiss will give me a furlough, but he would not give his consent. . . . There is no use in an officer trying to get a sick furlough. . . . Govt. says better discharge them. . . .

Will F. Vermilion

The camp near Helena, Arkansas, June 4, 1863

My Darling,

. . . We have no more excitement here about Price. Some say he is in our front. . . . I don't think he can take this place with 10,000 of his Arkansas rebels. . . . If he does make the attack we can hold. . . . This is a very well fortified place and then the country in the rear of town is a continuation of hills which are the most natural fortifications I have ever seen. On many of them, we have Batteries planted and rifle pits dug so it seems as though every avenue into the town is so commanded as to make it impossible for a rebel army to get in here. . . . If it does come to a fight I hope our regiment will acquit itself as the other Iowa Regiments have always done. . . .

W. F. Vermilion

Friday Night, June 5th 1863

My Own Love,

. . . We have had company today. Dr. Hays and his wife,[68] and Mr. Christie and his wife. Mrs. Hays says I won't go to see her, but she is going to follow me up, and have a good talk once in a while anyhow. . . . They take it hard about Jennings.[69] His mother says if he had been killed in battle, while he was fighting in defense of his country, they could bear it much better. And I know she could. But she is quite cheerful, for all. She says she is not going to give way to trouble, it could do no good, and she has her family to live for, yet. She is as strong in the faith as ever — more so I believe, and you know how she used to be, love. She wanted to hear all about you, and sent her respects and best wishes to you. She says you are the right sort of a man to go to this war, and the right sort of an officer to lead men to their duty. She was afraid Mullinnix was not right, and has never been to see them since they moved. The old doctor coughed and talked and wheezed just like he always did. He just got back from Missouri a few days ago. He told us all about his adventures down there. He didn't see the 18th Iowa at all. He heard of Jennings's death at Rolla, and didn't go on to there. . . . He gives a gloomy account of the state of affairs among the citizens. Of course they are in a bad enough way, but who can help it? I enjoyed their visit, and I think they all did but poor old Mrs. Christie. She doesn't enjoy anything. She says she never will again. Her mind is broken. I am so sorry for the poor old woman. She is one of the victims of this unholy rebellion. Her dead son and son-in-law were two more! Capt Wilson has been here since I commenced writing. He came to borry [borrow] something of father, about the teams, for tomorrow. He thinks there will be a very good time. He says there may be some trouble. Carr Fenton and Jim Wafford[70] say they are going to hurrah for Jeff Davis. Wilson thinks they won't but once. He says he would have no more compunction about shooting a man who does that in his hearing, than he would have about killing a wolf in his yard. I predict that those two traitors will be very quiet tomorrow, very quiet indeed!

Dollie

Helena, Arkansas, June 7, 1863

My Dollie,

. . . Sell that heifer if you can. . . . And the oxen and mules too if you think best. . . . Sell the corn. I think it will get wasted very much where it is. . . . The paymaster is here now and will pay two months' pay, that is if Col. Kittredge gets here to certify the muster on the 30th of April on which we are — or should — be paid. He mustered the Regiment for pay on that day and then went on furlough without signing the muster and pay rolls. Col. Drake has been to see the paymaster and he says he can't pay us unless the Col. gets here to sign them up properly. . . . I will send you some 200 or 250 dollars. I want you to have all the money I have, except what it takes to keep me. . . .

We have no Major yet. The discharge papers never came on till this morning for Major Woodward. Of course we could not ask Governor Kirkwood to commission anyone else till the place was vacant. In the meantime the Adjutant [71] wrote home and had his friends petition the Governor to appoint him. . . . He ranks as 1st Lieut. and has no military right to the position. The Capts. of this Regiment made their Companies, and their Companies the Regiment. If it had not been for me the Regiment never would have been filled. The Adjutant did nothing of the kind. He was simply taken from his Law Office by Col. Kittredge and Governor Kirkwood and given a good position without any effort or expense on his part. . . . Some one of us . . . is entitled to the position and we will not quarrel much among ourselves as to who shall have it. But we will quarrel and I fear the worst results if Adjutant Hamilton should get the commission. It is the opinion of nearly all the line officers that Col. Kittredge and perhaps Lieut. Col. Drake have already . . . recommended the appointment of Hamilton. Col. Drake has sold out the interests of our section of the county to Ottumwa. It was through them that he got his appointment. I was right Dollie at Keokuk and you and Humphrey May were wrong. . . . Our section of the country was wronged in the organization of the Regiment. . . . There was without a doubt a prepared plan to manage the Regiment to the advantage of Col. Kittredge and his friends.

But we stopped him in part by refusing to make his brother in law Sutler. . . . If he can get the Adjutant prompted to Major he will appoint his brother in law (who is now Sergeant Major)[72] Adjutant. If he succeeds he will have trouble. Be sure of that. . . .

W. F. Vermillion [*sic*]

Helena, Arkansas, June 8, 1863

My Dear Dollie,

. . . Since yesterday morning some 20 boats loaded with troops have passed down the river. Among the troops were the 6th Iowa. Greenwood Wright[73] was down at the wharf but could not get to see Matt. . . .

I send you a letter I received from Will Teater. . . . I send it so you may know what a mess you are getting into. Be careful Dollie. Let Teater keep the oxen till you can sell them. Let your father take care of the cattle. Tell me if Mullinix is loyal. I will not be drug into their quarrel. . . .

Will

Tuesday Night, June 9th, 1863

My Own Darling:

. . . I am glad you sent me Jane's letter. . . . She speaks too well of me. I don't deserve half she says of me, love. I have never received a word from her yet. I don't think it is her fault, surely. . . . Only think of the difference (Is it her patriotism makes the difference, or is she patriotic *because* she is different?) between her and the rest of them! They have never written one line to you since you have been in the service; *She* writes to you to write *me* lots of letters. How unselfish that was, my dearest. . . . If Jane were only away from there, I would not care half so much. Isn't she a good girl, love? I know you would like her if you only knew her. . . . I believe she really feels oftentimes that I am the only friend she has. I was not long reading her character when I went there. I understood her and was kind to her, and that was all it needed to attach her to me. Nobody had ever been much kind to her before, and . . . at first, she hardly seemed to know what to make of it. If a happier day ever dawns upon us, love, we won't forget Jane, will we?

I think the last year has tried the strength of the Confederacy to the utmost. We cannot deny but they have made a brave fight of it, but it is hardly in human endurance to stand another year of such war as our generals are waging now. The rebels don't acknowledge that their confederacy is toppling to its fall, or course. They will not, till it comes crashing about their heads, and they are hopelessly buried in the ruins. If we had pursued our old policy of fighting them at every disadvantage on the field, while we stood guard over their property at home, and returned all their fugitive negros, they might have carried on the war, quite as long as we could. But all this is changed at least, thank God! There is *war* in their land now, bitter, desolating, unrelenting war. They can't help seeing that their cause is growing more and more desperate and hopeless every day. I think the leaders see it very plainly, but they are holding out as long as possible, trusting that some strange freak of fortune may yet save them. I read a very sensible letter this morning from Jim Hickox[74] dated the 30th ult. He has been scouting through a good portion of Miss. He says the country is nearly "cleaned out" on their side of the Tallahatchie river. . . . Two or three more raids will relieve them of the balance of the corn and cattle, and then they will be utterly destitute. They have a good crop of wheat, but nobody to harvest it. The white men are all in the war, "and we have the niggers" says Jim significantly. He thinks the wheat will be lost. The Mississippians express themselves as very tired of the war. . . .
Dollie

Wednesday Night, June 10th, 1863
My Own Dear Love;

. . . I got a letter from Matt to day, dated the 29th. . . . He thinks of trying to get a furlough and going to see you and Will. . . . I don't suppose he is anything like the Matt we used to know, only in the warm, affectionate heart he carries somewhere under his dirty soldier's coat! I believe after you, my love, I want to see him worse than anybody in the world, but still I would rather he would go to see you than come home, because I think it would gratify you. He knows more about war than you ever will know, I hope and trust. . . . I went to Mullinnix's, as I told you this morning. They were well, and looking for me. John quit his plowing right straight, and came in to talk. Allie said he was dreadfully afraid I would come and he wouldn't have any good excuse to go to town. We talked about you, and the war till Allie got dinner — she had a good dinner, fried chicken, and good biscuits, and coffee, and strawberry pie — and then he took my letter and went to the office. . . . John says he is going to stay at home now and work beautifully till he gets ready to be drafted. Cy. Phillips is appointed enrolling officer for 3 townships. . . . John thinks there will be considerable jayhawking and bushwhacking here this summer. If the copperheads wish it, he is very willing to try a round at it. I don't think there will be.

How are you this morning, my pet? Did you suffer like you used to, when you had your billious attacks?[75] Did you vomit so much? I wish I knew all these things, and a thousand more, darling. But if I could know that you are well *now*, I could do without knowing anything else. We have no stirring war news. . . . Wasn't that a brilliant affair of Grierson's? How very far in the shade it throws all rebel cavalry raids! It took a western man to out Stuart[76] them, and teach them a few things they didn't know, in cavalry daring! I am glad he is already made a brigadier.

John knew all about the war in Iconium. He says it was a copperhead fight all round, and the only pity is that some more of them were not shot. There were 11 shots fired and only one took effect so far as they know. Though some think 1 or 2 men are dead in the brush somewhere. They have hunted a good deal, but could find nothing of them there. . . .

Sammonds has written home that Parkhurst has got a second Lieutenancy in a negro regiment, and Jo Funkhouser[77] same position. You can perhaps do quite as well without Parkhurst. . . . He needs the pay, and if he won't abuse his niggers he may do very well. I wonder if Henry Maiken succeeded. Tell me, my dear. I think he would make a better officer than Parkhust. . . .
Dollie

Helena, Arkansas, June 11, 1863

My Darling,

... The Government owes Lieut. May ... near $500 but he can't get it till he is mustered out as an enlisted man and then mustered in as a Lieut. and it can't be done till it is ordered by Corps Headquarters, which has never been done yet. It is owing to Col. Kittredge's imbecility that it was not done months ago. I told him he would have to send to Gen. McClernand [78] and have it ordered, but he said not. The consequences are Lieut. May and 4 or 5 other Lieuts. can't draw any money till they can hear from below. And if they can't have the muster dated back to the date of their Commissions they will lose all the Government owes them. ...

Will

5

"I Knew Somebody
Had Lost Friends, and
I Feared It Was I"

Once the Confederate high command realized the severity of the threat to Vicksburg posed by Grant, they responded with a counterplan. Lieutenant General Theophilus Holmes, commander of the Trans-Mississippi Department, suggested an assault on Helena. Believing that the city was a vital link in the logistical system supporting Grant's campaign, Holmes felt that its capture would force Grant to divert troops from the trenches surrounding Vicksburg. Requests by Grant for reinforcements already had reduced the Union garrison at Helena by the end of June 1863 to just over 3,000 healthy soldiers. Aware of this, Holmes proposed bringing an attack force of nearly 10,000 men, a fielding which would give him an overwhelming numerical superiority. His plan was approved, and Holmes quickly began to prepare his campaign.

In spite of the long odds the Union defenders would face in the ensuing battle, they did have certain strengths. First, months of control of Helena had given the federal garrison ample time to construct a series of formidable defensive positions. Four strategically placed batteries, designed to provide mutual fire support for each other, sat along a series of low hills forming a semicircle west of the city. Trenches ran between these positions. Closer to the town itself the defenders had constructed Ft. Curtis, whose guns controlled the roads leading into Helena which an attacking force would most likely utilize. Superb military engineering would allow the Federals to neutralize to a certain extent the Confederate numerical advantage.

The Union navy supplied another equalizing factor at Helena in the form of the *U.S.S. Tyler*, a gunboat which provided valuable military support throughout the war. A commercial steamboat prior to the conflict, the *Tyler* had been commandeered, armed, and used by the federal government to support offensive operations on the inland waterways of the western theater. Its finest day came on April 6, 1862, on the first day of the Battle of Shiloh. Although some historians today downplay its contribution, many observers at the time felt that fire from the *Tyler* and its sister ship, the *U.S.S. Lexington*, proved crucial in stopping the Confederate assaults on the opening day of the fight. This repulse allowed the Federals to hold on, receive reinforcements that night, and win a crucial victory the next day. Assigned to patrol the Mississippi River in the summer of 1863, the *Tyler* would fortuitously arrive at Helena just before the battle.

Finally, the Union soldiers at Helena were led by a commander whose determination and battle experience had earned him the Union military's and public's respect. Brigadier General Benjamin Mayberry Prentiss had made a name for himself, as the *Tyler* had, on the first day at Shiloh. When the Confederates began their attack that Sunday morning, many Union soldiers ran away in a panic. Prentiss, however, rallied the troops under his command and stood firm throughout the day. Surrounded by the enemy and low on ammunition by the late afternoon, Prentiss finally had no choice but to surrender himself and his command. This defense of a vital position, known thereafter as the Hornet's Nest, made him a national hero. Exchanged after the battle and promoted to major general, Prentiss received an appointment as the Commander of the District of Eastern Arkansas on February 3, 1863. Five months later, his leadership had significantly improved Helena's forces.

Unaware of such Union strengths, Holmes began his move on Helena in late June 1863. He had managed to assemble only 8,000 soldiers instead of the 10,000 he had envisioned, but Holmes boldly pushed on anyway, confident of success. His eagerness blinded him, however, and led him to rush his attack decision.

Although he planned his assault for the early morning of July 4,

Holmes imprecisely relayed these instructions. Some subordinates took his orders to mean that the attack should begin at sunrise, while others understood them to call for the commencement of activities at first light. Compounding the difficulties, Holmes had not properly reconnoitered the approaches to Helena. For that reason he learned only at the last minute that the abysmal road conditions around Helena would prevent him from deploying all but a few of his artillery pieces. Finally, for unexplained reasons one whole Confederate brigade failed to go into action against Prentiss at all.

In spite of these obstacles, the Confederate assault might still have worked had it not been for the tenacity of the Union defenders. Every federal unit fought well, and the fields of interlocking fire arranged by Prentiss allowed the defenders to quickly neutralize the one breakthrough the Confederates did achieve. The *Tyler* provided murderously accurate interdicting fire — a fact which made it obvious that had the Confederates succeeded in taking Helena, they could not have held it for long. By noon it became apparent to Holmes that he could not conquer Helena at that time, and he ordered a cessation of the assault.

The 36th Iowa saw its first test of combat on that Independence Day. Although not as heavily engaged as other regiments, the 36th held its ground and provided effective supporting fire for the other units. The Iowans remained in position, expecting a renewal of the battle, but soon recognized that Holmes would not resume hostilities anytime soon. The 36th Iowa fully savored the victory, a joy sweetened by other war news.

The letters in this chapter reflect this tumultuous period of the war. William describes the Battle of Helena and its aftermath, balancing his account of the bloodshed with assurances of his well being. Mary discusses her brother Will's return on furlough, and her response to the battle. Her observations about her brother's newfound appreciation for her husband as a leader resonate with those historian Reid Mitchell has discovered as typical of Union soldiers' perceptions of officers in his seminal Civil War study, *The Vacant Chair*. The overwhelming majority of companies that made up Union regiments were recruited from the same locale, which meant that enlisted men knew their officers prior to the conflict. Military life showed these officers in a new light to the men. Those officers who were incompetent or morally bankrupt soon lost favor with their men, while those who "led by example" (Mitchell's phrase) earned lasting respect. Will Kemper had not thought much of his brother-in-law before the war, but, as indicated in Mary's letters, that attitude soon changed. The tide was beginning to turn by mid-1863, and the couple's letters collectively document the multiple aspects of Northern satisfaction during the pivotal month of July.

Friday Night, June 12th, 1863
My Own Good Love,

. . . Father got a letter from Matt yesterday written the 3rd inst. . . . They have quite a hard time, that is constant hard service — but he believes it is right, and it is what they ought to have been at all the time. I guess there never was a set of fellows better satisfied with things in general, and themselves in particular, than they are now. . . . They have earned the right to glorify themselves a little, I think. Matt has never been reported sick, and, excepting one dose of oil, and a few pills, has never taken a particle of medicine, since he went out. . . . He says he wishes I would go to see him this summer. I would like very much indeed to see him, but there is *one* other soldier that I long to see for worse. Do you know who it is, love? We are still in suspense, like everybody else, about Vicksburg and Port Hudson. The news seems to be good. But the loss, on our side, has been frightful. It makes me sick to read the long, sad list. They say Hooker is about to move again. . . . There will be stirring times in South West Missouri, I think before long. I fear so at least. I am sorry about Curtis being removed. I never like anything I heard of Schofield, till since his appointment. He seems to be doing well, so far. We are looking for Jimmy [to come] home, a little.

Don't you wish you were here with me, pet? How much we should have to tell each other. . . . No words can tell you, my dear one, how much I want to see you. Your own heart can imagine it, partly, for I know you love me, darling. But you can bear the separation better than I. I am glad that you can. You are stronger minded than I am. You are better than I am, love. You can stay away contentedly because you know it is *right* that you should. *I* know it is right, but feeling is stronger than reason, with me, *and [I] want to see you so much.* You must not blame me, for indeed I do the very best I can. I think I could make a good soldier *with* you, darling, but I am a poor one alone. I think there is hardly anybody in the world *so alone* as I am. But I must not have the blues again tonight. . . . It is just 11 o'clock. I must quit writing soon. My eyes are a little sore. . . . They hurt me a good deal when I write of night. I fear I shall have to write only in day time. I should hate that. . . . I like to talk to you of nights, when everything is so quiet, better than any other time. We have a nice glass lamp, and burn coal oil. It may be this light that hurts my eyes. . . .

Saturday Morning, My Love, Will is here. He came last night about 1 o'clock, and surprised us all completely. . . . We all got up and sat up and talked till day was breaking. Then we went to bed again; and I took the headache and couldn't sleep one minute. But that is nothing, I heard from you sweet love. . . . Will is looking better than I expected. He says tell you that he is all right; and he wishes you could have had some of the fried chicken for breakfast this morning. He brought me a gold pen that cost $4 at St. Louis. It is a splendid one and suits my hand exactly. But my darling, what made you send me such a costly pen? But I won't scold about it. *I thank you, my dear one.* I am writing with it now. I will keep it as long as I live. . . .
Dollie

Sunday Night, June 14th, 1863
My Dearest Love,
    . . . We have had a great deal of company since Will came. . . . Mark Maiken and Johnny [1] came early this morning. Old Mrs. Ely [2] was here. I never saw her before. . . . I have done nothing since Will came but cook and talk. I hope we shall be alone some tomorrow. I never saw any one seem to enjoy himself more than Will. He . . . is gaining in strength rapidly. I can notice quite a change in him already. I think we will send him back to you all right at the end of his two weeks. I am very glad indeed that he came home. I think it is better for him, and then I can hear so much about you. . . . He thinks a great deal of you. He says the better he becomes ac-

quainted with you, the more he likes you. And that is the way with all the good men in the company. They can't help liking you. I can't tell you, love, all he says in praise of you. . . . He thinks his boat would have been wrecked before now if you had not piloted it through. Mother firmly believes you have saved his life; and she wants me to tell you how grateful she is to you, and how much she thanks you for all you have done for him. And I thank you too, my dear one. He says there are not many such men as you, and he doesn't blame me now for liking my Peaches pretty well, he does himself. How glad I am pet. But didn't I know it all before? *I* knew you long ago, darling. . . .

Dollie

Helena, Arkansas, June 14, 1863

My Darling,

. . . Why has Doctor Hays wife never been there my love if they are unconditionally loyal? But I need not talk so my Darling, for I know he is all right unless he belongs to the Knights of the Golden Circle. They are organized all over that country, and they have a lodge in Iconium. . . . You recollect don't you Dollie of hearing occasionally one and two years ago that they (the infernal rebels living in Iowa) were going to hang me. Then it made no impression on me whatever, but since I have been here in the Army I have learned beyond a doubt that they did in their secret meeting make arrangement to take my life first thing, in case there had been any trouble in the country near [there]. . . . Traitors in Iowa are as mean, if not meaner, than those in the South. As to the Copperheads in my Company, there is one beauty. They are subject to my order, and have to do as I say. . . . I am glad we have them here. I am not glad that they are rebels, but as long as they are, I am glad that I have some of them to deal with.

Some of them were talking about President [Lincoln] and using Copperhead language pretty freely. I took the Articles of War out and read 2 or 3 articles to them concerning soldiers using more respectful language toward the President and Congress and told them that I was going to enforce them strictly, and then turned and walked off. Since then I have not heard a whimper. Of course they talk and array themselves but they know better than to talk treason before me. They all make good soldiers. They do duty, all but John Wafford. He plays sick. . . .

W. F. Vermilion

Monday Afternoon, June 15th, 1863

My Dearest,

. . . Will is the best fellow in the world darling, to tell me all about you, and how you live, and what you say. He tells some funny jokes on you. I think he "enlarges" on some of them. He says you get more letters than all the rest of the company. Sometimes he goes into your tent and sees you reading your letters, and he sees how long they are, and he wants to hear the news and asks if your letters are from home. Then he repeats the question 2 or 3 times, and after [a] while you look up innocently and ask Did you say anything? Then he renews his question and you reply by an affirmative that can't be written, but which we all use sometimes, and go on quietly with your reading. And that, he would make us believe, is the way *he* hears from home. Of course I take all such reports as this "with a grain of salt." He is only "letting on." But I am glad if you get your letters dear, and I want you to read them just as much as you please. That is what I send them for.

Mary Maiken says Henry is going to get a Captaincy in the negro regiment. . . . I suppose it is all a hoax about Parkhurst and Funkhouser getting positions. I don't believe much I hear, and I guess it would be safe not to believe anything. Bartley Maiken[3] wrote home the other day that all the other companies grudged them their captain. They thought they had the best captain in the regiment "and that's just what we think too" says Bart. I tell you these things sometimes, sweet love, because they do me good, and I think they will gratify you. . . . Don't you like for me to tell you? I tell you everything, darling. . . .

Tuesday Evening, Will and I did go to Mr. Maiken's to day. . . . I think he wanted to see Jake Grimes worse than anybody else. I was glad to see Jake too, darling. He is *all right*, and defies them to produce one letter of his containing a disloyal statement, and *they don't produce it*. He battles with them all the time, and says just what he pleases. I guess he has told them some very unpalatable truths. They pitch into him constantly. After dinner to day he and Will rode up to town to stir up the copperheads and hear them hiss. Will was anxious to hear them. He doesn't see any in this neighborhood. But *two* sickly looking fellows in blue coats were too many for that nest, and they wouldn't open their lips. They can manage one by surrounding him and concentrating their fire — to change my metaphor a little — but 2 were too many. They might suffer from an attack in the rear. . . . Jake looks very bad, dearest. I was astonished to see him so thin and with such a color. I don't believe he will ever get well or live very long. . . . Will says he is looking worse than he did when he got home, but Jake thinks he is picking up, and doing finely. He seemed very glad to see me, and he told me his experience, and about how mad he used to get at you about your abolition speeches, and what a mean copperhead he used to be. I told him I had intimated to you a fear that he was not just right, and he said he wouldn't have you doubt his loyalty 1 minute for his 3 year's pay. I am very glad, my love, that our suspicions about him were unfounded. He has heard plenty of it since he came home. He seems indignant over it, and I don't blame him. . . . He showed me his bombshell. What an ugly thing it is, darling. It isn't a bit like I had imagined. I laughed to see how glad the boys were to see each other. They thought they had been apart 3 or 4 weeks. They went out and sat down by themselves in the shade and talked a long time. They both said they hadn't enjoyed themselves half as well before since they got home. They say they don't care a snap for anybody who doesn't wear brass buttons, and I don't believe they do. They were not half so glad they were soldiers before they came, as they are now. I think they will be getting "homesick" pretty soon. Jake speaks very highly of you. He says there could not be any better captain. I don't think there could either, my darling. . . .

Mary Maiken says for me to tell you never to hint to Henry that she was not just wild for him to go into the negro regiment. She wants him to do as he likes about it. I think she will be disappointed if he doesn't get the position. Mr. Maiken and the old lady are just like they used to be. He sits around in the shade and talks about the war, and she pitches into lazy people. She doesn't love them any better than she used to. C. C. Trim's family are the objects of her particular aversion just now. . . . Mr. Stock[4] has been here to day. I never saw anybody hate copperheads worse than he does. He feels like killing them where ever he finds them. . . .

I am writing with my new pen, sweet love. It is a good one. I never saw a better. The first part of this letter was written with Will's pen. He said *you* used to use it, and I wanted to try it; but I couldn't do much with it. I had to get my new one to finish my letter. . . . I would not have had such a costly one, if I had known it, love, but I shall not scold you. How could I scold you, my precious one? I wonder what you are doing just now? May be you are sitting in your tent writing to your Dollie; and may be you are busy and hurried with no time to think of her at all. . . . Jake says you say you feel badly sometimes because you don't get home sick. Why darling! Do you think you ought to do penance sometimes for not being low spirited and home sick? I don't, dear one. I always knew you would never get home sick like most men, but still you loved our home, didn't you pet? I think if we ever get home again, we will make it the happiest spot on earth. It will be such a good home, such a real *home* that you can't help loving it. . . .
Dollie

Helena, Arkansas, June 18, 1863
My Darling,
. . . I will tell you about my cook. He is one of those Reliable Contrabands that have already figured so largely since this war broke out. From his appearance I took him to be about 40 years of age though I have not heard him say one word on the subject of his age. He will weigh from appearance about 140 pounds. . . . His hair and beard are not much gray yet, which is positive evidence to me that he is a brave fellow and has never been scared, or at least badly scared. His front is not very beautiful. He is about 5 feet 8 inches height when walking, but if he were dead and straightened out his length would be near 6 feet. But then I think none the less of him as a contraband in consequence of that, for I think it impossible for him to help it. At least good men say that class of people can't help such things here in the south. If they could and would my cook would look much better. Speech is bad. Talks too fast and lisps considerably. . . . As to his cooking qualities as far as we have

tried him, they are good. He makes good light bread, fries fish well, much better than old Mrs. Rowe. The coffee he gets up just as well as anyone in this camp, contraband or no contraband. The dishes are always clean when he washes them. And the clothes now hanging on the line that he washed this morning look very well for this section of Dixie. As to his opinion of the various questions of the day I have not heard him express himself fully yet. He says his Master b[r]ought him and about 200 others to Mississippi from old Virginia some 15 or 20 years ago. . . . Only 2 were handcuffed during the trip only for a few days. That they started sometime in August and landed on the old Plantation in Mississippi, which is 15 miles above here on the river, on Christmas day. . . . Since that time he has worked constantly for the same family — that is till last August when he came here, and went to cooking for some of the 3rd Iowa Cavalry. He staid with them all the time till a few days ago when they started to Vicksburg. He said "I be too feared ob de big guns down dar." So he came over and hired to me. We . . . intend giving him 8 or $10 a month for cooking and washing. . . . If he proves to be a good worker he can make several dollars each month by working for the boys. He was worked while in Mississippi by an overseer. Says they used to shoot the "niggers" when they got mad at them and especially when the negroes refused to be whipped. He told me yesterday evening that he was shot once in the back, but he turned and whipped the man that done it. Afterwards the driver got help and whipped him. As to matrimony he says he was never married. That he took up with a woman over in Mississippi and lived with her for a long time. That they have several children and that he always cared for her just as he would have done had he been married to her. He talks some of taking up with one over here but I tell him he had better not. The officers have been after him several times to go into the army but he says they won't have him when they get him. . . . He is slightly clumsy in consequence of some deficiency in one of his legs. If they come after him while he is cooking for me I will have him rejected. Then they can't take him. He is the 4th negro we have had to cook for us. The 3rd man. Last winter while we were messing with Company A we had an old negro woman awhile. She was a good old negro and a good cook. All the others we have had have been of no account but this one. . . . He gives his name as Doctor Robinson. I tell the boys to call me Captain now altogether. It will not do for two as important men as he and I are to be called by the same name. So I will give way as he is a stranger and may have some concern or scruples about having his named changed. The officers of several other companies have contrabands [who] work quite well. We will keep Dock in preference to any other. . . .

W. F. Vermilion

Helena, Arkansas, June 20, 1863
My Own Darling,

. . . It is all false about Jo. Funkhouser seeking a position in a Negro regiment. . . . No one of my company has made application but Henry Maiken, and you may tell Mary she need not be uneasy about his getting the position. There are too many good applicants ahead of him. . . . Tell me all you know about the fight at Iconium. . . . The people around Iconium have written to the boys about it but their reports are not satisfactory. . . . You are going to have trouble in Iowa this summer. . . . There are too many mean people there to let this exciting Summer pass over without showing their hands. George Stewart, Dr. Phillips, William McDaniel[5] and all their kindred hate the soldiers and their Free Government too badly to pass on much longer without doing one injury if they can, without doing any injury to themselves, or running any risk of being hurt.

You want me at home so bad now. . . . You would surely be ashamed of me if I were lying around as I used to. . . . Do you think there is any excuse for men staying at home to make a good soldier look forward, and see his condition 10 or 15 years hence. I know it is hard for a man to lose these years of his life . . . but better that than to lose all, every thing that man should hold sacred. Look forward my Darling, if such a thing is possible, to the complete destruction of our liberties, and where are we, what are we worth? What a dark age it would be to you and me. It seems to me we would be like a lost child in a cave wandering on forever. Oh Liberty, sweet Liberty, may you and I always be friends. For 30 years I have appreciated your virtues. . . . You have never yet laid the hand of oppression on me. Now that the bloody dagger is pointed at your heart shall I step aside and see it thrust in? No, no, sweet Liberty, let me die by your side. . . .

W. F. Vermilion

Helena, Arkansas, June 23, 1863

My Darling,

. . . Col. Kittredge is keeping his wife here in camp. . . . If I were situated as he is you could stay here my Dollie, but she must see things every day that would shock your modesty. I don't know anything about her disposition but it must be very hard for a woman to remain here and retain all the fine feelings she should have. Their tents are right on the river bank and there is scarcely a day but — yes, scarcely [an] hour in the day — that some of the boys are not in the river bathing. She has to remain in her tent all the time [except] while she is gone to her meals. Do you think you could stand that my Darling? You are not much for staying in the house.

When the 6th Iowa went down the river John Collett went on the boat to see his brother,[6] and while he was on the boat pushed off and John had to go on to Vicksburg. He saw and talked with Matt. He said he looked fine. . . .

We have nothing later than the 16th from Washington. . . . Reports said the rebels were in Pennsylvania from 40 to 50 thousand strong and that Hooker was falling back on Washington and Lee following him up closely and fighting with his rear guard. . . . There appeared to be a movement to get McClellan a command again. . . . He should never command again in the Union Army. I have lost all confidence in him since his evidence in favor for Porter. He was a traitor.[7]

W. F. Vermilion

Wednesday Night, June 24th, 1863

My Dearest Love,

. . . How did you learn, dear, that the "Knights" were plotting to take your life? This is so horrible. I can hardly credit it. Such things would not surprise me now but 2 years ago there was a different state of affairs. . . . Thank God their courage was not equal to their malignity. You ask me again what I think of Mullinix. . . . I believe he is perfectly loyal. . . . John told me that Brandon[8] and himself were the only democrats who didn't belong to the K. G. C.'s, and he said Brandon would if he could see — or something like that. He says Brandon is a copperhead, one of the sneaking sort. . . . Albert Hancock was here to day. He goes about breathing vengeance against the copperheads. He says he wouldn't stay up here for anything in the world. Lucy says that he thinks there never were two better men than you and West May. His health is improving finely. He is going to tell you all about our traitors when he goes back. Father saw William Irvine[9] to day. He wants to go back to Springfield to get away from the "coppers." He says it would do him more good to kill one of his brother in laws, than to shoot Jeff Davis himself. . . .

Friday Night, June 26th, My Darling, Mary Maiken told me that Henry wrote . . . that you were going to start home in a few days and he would send him money by you. I didn't know what to think of it dear one, or whether to believe it or not, but I looked for you all night. If you started in a few days from that time, you ought to be here by this time. I don't look for you any to night. . . . Yesterday we went to Woodside — Will and I. . . . Teater was plowing with two of Cy's[10] boys to help him. . . . They had to tell me all about their difficulty with Mullinix. I answered them just like you had done — that I knew nothing about it, and could have nothing to do with it, but that I knew you would do just what was right, and I was disposed to do all that was right. They told of the letter they sent you, but I didn't hint that I had heard of it. . . . They are very mad at John, but they don't talk near so vicious as he wrote. I think he imagines that Mullinix was writing to you a great deal about him and that I was doing so too, perhaps, and trying to prejudice you against him, and he thought he wouldn't be condemned unheard, and now when he finds that you know nothing about it, and that John hasn't written to you for three months, he feels a little "cheap" over it. . . . I told him I hoped they wouldn't quarrel over our property while you are gone. . . .   .
Dollie

Helena, Arkansas, June 25, 1863

My Darling,

I have just come home from Col. Kittredge's. He asked me to come up this evening and play a game of euchre with him, Col. Drake and Mrs. Kittredge, and of course I went. . . . The days and nights here are so long sometimes we have to have some kind of amusement and euchre is as harmless as any other when conducted properly. I have never seen [a] 1 cent bet yet since I have been in the service, and if I remain my 3 years out I want to go home and be able to say the same thing. The army shant demoralize me. At home I swore, here I never do. I never gambled anywhere and I never will. . . . There is no reason . . . why a man should not be just as moral here as anywhere. Good men are when badly disposed apt to find excuses here for being immoral, but when they talk to me I tell them it is right to the reverse. That there is enough here to disgust any man in whose nature the moral character predominates. . . . All those who are naturally immoral are extremely so here. Nearly all men who used bad language at home do the same thing here. But very few are any worse here than there. . . . I don't like his wife much Dollie. She is not very smart but thinks she and the Col. know it all. When in fact the Col. is not very smart. Last winter he said Col. Rice of the 33rd Iowa was not *smart* enough to command a brigade. That he knew much more military than Col. Rice. But now Col. Rice is far ahead of him. Col. Kittredge doesn't learn anything. . . . Since we have been in brigade drill we see that the 36th is badly deficient in drill. . . . But all this deficiency is not my fault, it is Col. Kittredge's and Col. Drake's. . . .

Wm. Dooley (Jake Dooley's boy)[11] has been playing some of his games again. He is the worst boy in the regiment but I have always been able to control him until this morning, and in fact it was not properly my work this morning. Some 3 or 4 days ago while I was detailed on some business and Lieut. May was in command of the company, Dooley while out on drill slipped out of the ranks in the forenoon, and came to the quarters, in the afternoon he slipped off and did not go out at all. Lieut. May had not noticed it at all. When the regiment came in I asked him why he did not take Dooley out to drill. He replied he had. I told him he had not. Well he said he would put him on picket for it. . . . So that night the Orderly detailed him and he went quiet enough. . . . This morning his regular turn came, but he refused to go. The Orderly came and told me. I went to him and told him he *should go*. He swore he would not. I tied him up and went and told the Colonel I wanted a guard house prepared. . . . He had it done, and I put him in and confined him to bread and water. I am going to keep him there on that diet until he repents and if he never does repent I am going to have him court martialed, in which case he will *suffer severely*. . . . Reports today say the siege goes on slowly at Vicksburg. I heard of a private letter from there to some one in the regiment the other day that was rather rich. The day before it was written some portion of our forces moved up a little but were still out of sight. They could hear the rebels talking plainly. Some one in the rebel fort gave the order for a certain detachment of troops to move. What for, said those to whom the order was given? Why, the Yankees want to dig where you are and you will have to let them have room. So they moved out and the Yankees dug.

W. F. Vermilion

Friday Night, June 26th, 1863
My Darling,

Yesterday we went to Woodside — Will and I. We had a pleasant ride. He felt better than he had for several days. We went around by Linder's to look for the cattle. We found 8 that I knew. . . . Teater told me of someone who has been offered $37.00 per head for three-year-olds not as large as Tuck. . . . Teater was plowing with two of Cy's to help him. He says he has the best corn in the neighborhood. Everything seemed doing very well. . . .

Dollie

Helena, Arkansas, June 26, 1863
My Darling,

. . . Poor Jane. . . . I would give half I have got in this world in the way of property to have her with us in Iowa, and I believe we could get her there if the war were over. She has a good mind my Darling. She writes the best letters of any of them. . . . There was father [who] couldn't read my letter — that short note to John Runyan. But Jane could and she never had any opportunity to learn anything either. Her letters make me feel more like doing all I possibly can to get her away from there. If she doesn't marry before I get home she must come and live with me. . . .

Jane or Henry once sent me a bunch of papers and among them was a Republican Banner. That gave an account of the Enrolling book being taken from several of the offices in the county.[12] Milt Scott[13] was Enrolling Commissioner for Jefferson Township (at Mt. Meridian). The rebels numbering about 50 blacked themselves and went to Scott's house and demanded the books. He gave them up and they went away. . . . The same night about the same number of men went to Squire Sills'[14] house and demanded of him his books. In place of giving him the book for this year, he gave them the old books of last year. They did not know the difference. While they were there some young man who was in Sills' house started to run. They fired at him but did no damage.[15] The Editor gives an account of some instances the books have been stolen. In others the rebels would be killed. In several instances they had stopped the work lest the threat should be carried into execution. . . . Are you not glad you and I are not citizens of that County. We once lived there Dollie, but we don't partake of the nature of the people who live there now. . . .

W. F. Vermilion

Saturday, June 27th, 1863

My Own Love,

. . . This afternoon Jake and Will have gone to Greenville to a Copperhead meeting. I did not want them to go much, but they said it was the last chance to hear a Copperhead speech, and they want to be able to tell you all about our northern traitors when they go back. They wanted to hear a live Copperhead express his true sentiments. . . . I am afraid there will be trouble up there today. Both parties are getting ready for it. . . . Affairs are not half as bad here now as they were in Indiana all last winter, but Will and Mr. Hancock and Jake think it is bad enough here. . . . Will thinks we are now more unprotected than we ought to be and I don't know but we are. I do wish my love that you could send me a revolver. Darling, would there be anything wrong in my learning to protect myself? Though I am not in the least afraid for myself, I am only afraid for that if things get much worse the traitors may burn or steal our property and possibly try to rob the house. . . .

Later, I got a letter from you this evening love, dated the 16th. You are not coming home as they said you were. Oh, dear one, I am so disappointed. I thought I was not expecting you much. I told you I was not. But pet I didn't know how my heart was set on it till I read your letter. But I will try to be patient, sweet love, and not complain. I would make a poor soldier, dear, unless my duty kept me always near my captain. Then I could do pretty well. . . . Will has suggested a good plan to ascertain whether you get my letters. I am going to try it. I will number 1, and the next after that 2, and so on all the time. . . . If any of them fail, darling, you can tell me then without any trouble. The boys are going to start back Monday morning early. They thought at first they would start tomorrow, but then they concluded it would be throwing away one day of their furlough. . . . I hate to see Will go back unless he were stronger, but I don't tell him so.

Father got a letter from Matt dated in camp near Vicksburg. He said they could see the shells bursting constantly over the doomed city. They were fortifying their portion on Snyder's Bluff[16] and were working very hard. They were in good spirits. . . .

Sunday afternoon, I have been baking and stewing all day. I have cooked a boxful of dinner for Will to start with. Bread and butter and cakes and pies and roasted chickens and I am sending you a jar of butter and 2 or 3 scallions. I would send you a boxful love, if he could take it and the weather was cool. I am afraid your butter even won't be good when you get it. I am going to send you a pillow. Now you needn't laugh. I don't want your dear head laid on your rough overcoat or blanket any longer. I can't bear to think of it when I lie down in a good bed. Will is very willing to take it. He says he knows just what cap will do when he gets it. When he gives it to him he will sit down and laugh till I can almost hear him up there and saying "well, Will, I never thought you were quite that queer, but that won't break any bones."

We have had company all day. Old Mr. May and Humphrey

and Mr. Wright and Mr. Cassaday [17] are here yet. Humphrey looks badly. . . . He has not much news from Indiana. He didn't see any of your folks, nor hear anything about them except that Martha has a baby at her house and father was staying at Sills' the night his house was mobbed. They said he never got out of bed even during the attack. It was said that Sigler Duckworth[18] headed the mob that attacked Scott's house. Sill's wife says she can swear to him. They were all blacked of course. Humphrey says they will be well punished for it. I hope so, but they must catch them first, you know. Matters are worse than they were when I left there. . . . They are burning houses and stealing horses, that is the worst feature of it. He says there is a far better state of feeling in Kentucky than in Indiana. There the copperheads are not even attempting to run a candidate for governor. He was at the Perryville battlefield.[19] Our friends there were all well. Aunt Sally McGoughey, he thinks, could fight a regiment of Copperheads herself. She hates them enough. . . .

Mary

Monday Evening, June 29th, 1863

My Dearest Love,

. . . Will is gone, dear one. . . . He went off seemingly in fine spirits, but I know he is afraid he will get down sick again. He coughed badly, and he has no strength hardly. He has taken good care of himself since he came home only I think he ate too much. But he couldn't get strong.

I should be glad, for your sake only, if you could get the major's position. You could ride. I care more for that than anything else. I don't care for the additional pay, love, or the rank. So a man serves his country in a time like this, what need it matter how he serves it, or in what capacity? If you don't get it my pet, don't get the blues over it. . . .

You would laugh to hear Mr. Wright telling about you. . . . He told me yesterday that "society" is a great deal better in camp than it is here. He says people needn't be afraid of the soldiers becoming demoralized. They are better than the men at home — better than they were at home. . . .

Dollie

Tuesday Afternoon, June 30th, 1863

My Darling,

... While I think of it pet, I want to know whether your time counts from the 9th of August when your company was organized, or only from the time you were mustered into the service in Keokuk? Will says it counts from August, but others say not. ... *Where is Hooker?*[20] What do you suppose he is doing? Isn't all of it most strange and unaccountable?

I have got me a pet dear, what do you suppose it is? I ... will have to tell you — a little puppy! A cunning little brown and white fellow, named Beppo. Father has one too, so when you come riding up here some night you had better beware of the dogs or you might not get in. They are both Shepherds. I am going to try to bring Beppo up to be a sensible dog. I think that he will be fun for he is always getting into mischief already, and that is a good sign, they say, for babies, and why not for dogs? He's sure to get on, if mother doesn't kill him, which I am a little afraid!

Wednesday Morning, July 1, Father brought me a good long letter last night my love, written on the 18th ult. You want me to burn them all. I can't do it, sweet darling. You don't know how much I think of them or how much good they have done me. I promised to do anything you wanted me to, but you mustn't take advantage of me that way, will you dear? I couldn't have lived all this time without your letters. ... But if it will please you I will promise to give them all to you when you come home to stay, and let you do as you please with them, provided you are right good to talk to me all the time, provided you talk to me "late." If you don't I shall just go off and read over my old letters every day. Won't this do my pet? I can't promise any more. I know I shall cry when you burn them, even if you are going to stay with me. Why dear one, I couldn't burn them now for all the money in the world, nor even because you want me to. ... Taylor Lucas'[21] wife[22] throws his letters on the floor and stamps on them. That may be for her and for him, but your Dollie loves you, and loves your letters, and everything that is yours. ... I am glad that you have found such a good old cook. ...

You must watch "Doctor Robinson" and make him be cleanly. . . .
When the war is over darling, I want you to bring me a good negro girl to do my rough work when we go to house keeping again.
I would rather have one than white help, a great deal, if I could get
a good one. And I think it is right for everybody to keep one who
can, till some provision is made for them by the government. I have
heard plenty of people up here wishing they could get one or two.
Julia May said she wanted to get one or two as soon as they get their
farm back again. As we went to Indiana you know she "wanted to
kill" every one we saw. How people do change in this world! I have
not changed about it, for I always wanted one. What do you say
about it, my love? May I have a contraband?

There is a report that Banks has been repulsed again at Port
Hudson with terrible loss.[23] Mother saw Dr. Ivens[24] yesterday and
talked with him about Will. He said it took all they could do to
save his life, when he was sick. I am so afraid he will get down
again when he gets back. . . . He is a good fellow dear and I want
him to live to come home again. I like him better I believe because
he likes you so much. . . . He says there are not many such men and
the more he sees of you the more he thinks so. He never cared anything for you he says, until he worked at Woodside a month you
know once, and found out that you were "a real good fellow," but
still he didn't know that you were half as good a man as you are. I
told him he didn't know yet how good a man you are. He said
"Well he didn't blame me for *liking you pretty well*." I guess he
doesn't. . . .
Dollie

Helena, Arkansas, June 30, 1863
My Darling,
 . . . When we were at home I always went to bed early, but when
I get back I am going to adopt a different rule. You must sit up and
talk to me till my time for going to bed. You shant prepare the bed
and tell me I am tired and must go to bed. If you do we will have
some kind of difficulty. You may think Dollie you will do as you
please when we get to living together again. All this time you are
your own boss, but just wait. We will have military law when I get

there. Here we command and of course we will have to do the same thing when we get home. It will be impossible for me to give up all of our authority at once. . . . Won't you be afraid of me?

You have often asked what I want you to do if I should not get home. Get me home if you can, bury me on some nice loyal spot of ground, plant flowers over the grave, and then don't forget to go to that spot Dollie. That is all except live on what property I leave you. I don't want to sleep in the land of traitors. I couldn't rest well. . . . But I think I will get home. This Government will surely be saved and I will surely get back to our old home to live with my love. . . .

W. F. Vermilion

Thursday Evening, July 2nd, 1863

My Dearest Love,

. . . Mr. Henry Delay[25] was here this evening. He talked a good while about the Copperheads. He says he feels as if he could take the lives of a few of them without the least trouble. He told me about an anonymous letter that George Stewart got last winter from Helena. They all accused you of dictating it, and . . . some of them seemed almost [ready] to buy the ropes to hang the abolitionists. From what he remembers of the letter it must have been a good one. . . . He says Mr. Grissom is taking in sail, denying he ever told all the stories about the way the soldiers live, etc. Will Grissom has been writing some very strong letters from Keokuk. He says if any of his relatives sympathize with the rebels, he disowned them and will never have anything to do with them. . . . I asked him how Mullinix stood now in regard to the war, he said he was a first rate union man. "He is just as good a loyalist as any man of his party can be." I don't think you need have any doubts about him, my love. We surely can't all be deceived. . . .

Will can tell you how things look at Woodside, and about the young cattle. They are very big. Will said he wished he could see some way of getting Denko down to Co. F. He would be appreciated by the others. I told him Co. F would be entirely welcome to him. . . .

It is said that Banks has captured Port Hudson, and that Hooker has been relieved from command from the Army of the Potomac, at his own request. Nobody can remember the name of the general who superceded him. . . . I hope this is not true. Hooker would not surely ask to be relieved just at this juncture, with Lee's Army in Pennsylvania and Maryland. What competent general — if indeed there is ever to be a competent general found for that army — would be willing to assume command at this moment? If it is true Hooker will be laid on the shelf, among all the rubbish that this war has accumulated. . . . I have hoped better things of him. I am glad to see in my papers that the rebels have made a raid into Indiana.[26] That is just the best thing that could happen. . . . The Hoosier blood is up wonderfully, and they are after the rebels, bent on hanging the last one. There were about 250 of them. They were sweeping through Wayne County at last account. I don't care what damage they do. The more the better, as they treat friend and foe alike. They have no time to stop and parley with their Copperhead allies. Some of the traitors about Mt. Meridian used to say that they were not afraid of a rebel invasion. "The southern men wouldn't hurt them because they were not their enemies." Perhaps they are changing their minds!

Dollie

Helena, Arkansas, July 2, 1863

My Darling,

. . . This morning an order came around notifying us that all the forces at this place were required to fall into line of battle at daylight, and remain there under arms until half an hour by sun. This shows that there is some danger or that some General has a scare on him again. . . .

If Hooker is not the man to manage that army who is, unless it is Fremont? Meade I know nothing about. I would give the command of that army to Fremont for 6 months and if he could have the full support of the Government and all of the subordinate officers, and he should fail too to accomplish anything, I should feel very much like giving up the contest. It seems as though that Army is to gain no great victories during this great rebellion. Every time there is a chance to do anything in that department, a change of commanders becomes necessary. . . .

Later, For some time I have been thinking about selling the

horses in place of the oxen. I am afraid the horses will be stolen. See Teater and if he can gather the corn with the oxen and you have not sold them when you get this, sell the horses if you can, otherwise sell the oxen. . . . Tomorrow is the 4th. We are going to have Roast Chicken for dinner. We gave 75 cents for it. . . .

W. F. Vermilion

Saturday Evening, July 4th, 1863

My Own Dear Love,

. . . About that fight at Iconium I have already told you, love, all I know. The excitement died away, and I never inquired or heard any more about it. They all are gone from the old house. Dunover[27] took the women and children to Ottumwa. . . . You think we are going to have trouble here in Iowa. I would not be surprised, provided our armies [that] are in the field are not successful. If they are I don't apprehend any danger. The Copperheads are mean enough to kill us all if they dared. But they don't dare, and this is what will save us. If they do attempt mischief, blood will run like water, for the Unionists are terribly in earnest.

Sunday Morning, July 5th, My Darling, You know that Hooker is removed, sure enough. Let us hope once more that they have found the right man at last. I know nothing of Gen. Meade. He has taken the helm in a trying moment; if he guides the ship skillfully and safely through the storm, so much the more will he deserve our praise and gratitude. Our latest news is he was fighting a desperate battle with Hill and Longstreet[28] near Gettsyburgh, with the chances seemingly in his favor. His address to the army in assuming command is very modest, and, after Hooker's humiliating gasconades, I am glad to see that he makes no promises. From Vicksburg the news is of the favorable. The latest dispatches are about Logan's blowing up one of the rebel forts, and fighting desperately at close quarters.[29] There is no further news from Indiana, only that the Copperhead crowd, or mob, in Sullivan County is quelled, and the soldiers go back to Indianapolis. . . . Father was right sick last evening. . . . He has made him a pallet on the grass, under the locust trees, and seems to be taking solid comfort. Mother, with her cap flying, and a huge turkey wing in her hand, wanders about trying to find a cool spot to "locate." Poor mother! I wish she could find it and I would "emigrate" with her. Beppo is crying in the yard because nobody talks to him. He is getting on bravely, and is already worth 5 dozen common dogs — to play with. He is getting spoiled, as everything I love always does! What is the reason, pet? When I go out he runs to shake hands with me, and when he gets in mischief and I box his ears a little, he looks so sorry and lies down, rubbing the wounded spot with his paw. . . .

Monday Night, July 6th, My Own Love, For two nights I have dreamed troubled dreams about you being sick, and in danger, and about desolate, haunted houses, where I was lost and frightened. The remembrance of my dreams has clung to me all day. How foolish it is, love, but I can't help it. I hope I shall have a good, sweet dream of my loved one tonight. . . .

I want you [to] send me a revolver, darling. I will try my best to learn to use it well, and then if I ever have occasion to use it in earnest, I will remember that I am a soldier's wife. Now I know, my pet, that a few years ago you never dreamed that your softhearted Dollie would ever come to this, and just as little did I dream that my love would ever put on his sword and be off to the war. Times have changed fearfully and whether we wish it or not we must change with them. We might situate down and grieve ourselves to death over the spectacle that is presented to us — our country bleeding at every pore, thousands of our bravest men falling and lying in a hundred bloody fields, our nearest friends absent and suffering, our homes all broken up, our hearthstones cold and desolate, and what would it avail? The dread broom would sweep on all the same. For my own part, sweet love, I feel like grieving and more like fighting every day. Are you astonished at me? Do you blame me? I hope not, dear. The war is upon us, dire and fearful, and we must fight it through or be ruined. I feel like deserving victory by trying to achieve it. . . . You think if the war continues we shall have trouble before our Presidential election. I don't fear it then, darling. If we can escape till next June we shall be safe enough. A dozen regiments, and more, of our scarred, war-torn veterans will be home by then. If there is a prospect of trouble here, they will stay at home, and they will keep the peace in Iowa! I don't think there is any danger — at least any immediate danger — further than this: They may steal our horses, or burn our house, and they may possibly come here to rob us of our money. This last is what I am most afraid of. I don't know whether any Copperhead knows of my having money, but they may, as the first you sent was counted out in Phillips' store, and word sent to me that it was there. . . .

You can't make me say, my dearest, that I would be ashamed of you if you were at home. . . . We need you at home. I verily believe that you could do more good to the cause here, than where you are. It needs men to work for it here, as well as fight for it here. The trouble is not that we have sent too many men, but that we have sent too many good men, and left too many bad ones here. If you were at home careless and idle I might feel — no, I can't say the word, love, even then. But you could not be idle. You would not be, and you could do much good I know. . . .

Later, There was a celebration today at Melrose. . . . Dr. Lind and Dr. Hays and Mr. Mericle[30] were the speakers. They had a nice dinner set, and plenty of music. And best of all there were no traitors hardly present to mar the harmony and good fellowship. . . . Mr. Christie was telling me about it as they went home. Nearly all Iconium was there. . . . I guess they meant the loyal portion. . . .

Tuesday Morning, Have I told you that there is to be a grand Union meeting at Iconium on the 18th inst? Estep and Sharp are to be there. . . . There is to be a similar meeting at Uncle Billy Evans'[31] grove. . . . How are you going to like Col. Stone[32] for Governor, Dear? I am pleased with the nomination. He is just the sort of man Iowa needs for Governor now, I think. . . . There is likely to be an exciting time up there, until after the election. How thankful I am that Iowa soldiers weren't disenfranchised because they were patriotic! They will elect Col. Stone. . . .
Dollie

Helena, Arkansas, July 6, 1863
My Darling,
All Hail this morning. Vicksburg is ours, and everything in it.[33]
Helena is *not* taken. We did the best work here on the . . . 4th

that has been done since the war began. We fought at least 4 to 1 and placed at least half our number Hors de Combat.

My company is all right. The boys all behaved well. Corpl. Matt Walker[34] was on picket where the line was attacked. He exchanged 20 odd shots with 1 rebel but did not get him. He killed 1 other certain, and the boys say 2. . . . We fought under cover. The loss in the regiment as far as has been ascertained is 1 killed and 4 missing. . . .
W. F. Vermilion

Tuesday Night, July 7th, 1863
My Own Love,

. . . I have no war news from Pennsylvania. . . . It is said that Meade has won a complete victory after the severest fight of the war. . . . The rebels are said to be utterly routed, and trying to escape. Pleasanton[35] was expected to cut off their retreat. . . . There is no estimate yet of the loss on either side, but it is heavy — especially in officers. We have captured from 15 to 20 thousand prisoners. . . . But why can't somebody make a dash into Virginia now and capture Richmond while it is left almost at their mercy? From Vicksburg we have news up to the 29th ult. . . . The rebels thought Johns[t]on[36] would yet be there in time to save them. We have heard from some of the boys' letters that the 6th regiment is doing duty as sharpshooters at Vicksburg now, lying in their trenches all the time. . . . Bragg has at last slipped away from Rosecrans, and got to the mountains. . . .

The great Copperhead state convention is in session now, at Des Moines City, I believe. We should soon know who they want for governor of Iowa. The Unionists hereabouts are hoping they will nominate Mahoney or Clay Dean or someone of their "martyrs," but they are too cunning — knowing that our soldiers will vote — to do anything of that kind, I think. . . . Capt. Ben Jones[37] has just been home on a furlough. He passed through Melrose on his way to Bloomfield last Saturday. . . . I wonder if you didn't see him while the 3rd Cavalry were in Helena. . . .
Dollie

Helena, Arkansas, July 7, 1863
My Darling,

The smoke has now cleared away and we can see we have gained one of the finest victories that have been gained since the beginning of the war. At daylight on the morning of the Fourth Lieut. General Holmes with an army estimated at various numbers ranging from 12,000 to 22,000 men attacked this place and were handsomely repulsed with a loss of 1,500 killed and wounded, and 1,000 prisoners. Our loss will not exceed *150 all told*. The rebels were commanded by Holmes, Price, Marmaduke, Parsons[38] and some others. On the morning of the fourth we had 3,800 men *all told*. Out of that number there were many engaged as teamsters, nurses, musicians and so on, so our fighting number did not much exceed 3,000. . . . My company and 3 others of the left wing of our regiment supported the Dubuque Battery. It did good work. . . .
W. F. Vermilion

Helena, Arkansas, July 8, 1863
My Darling,

. . . Here we are on the 8th of July, but 8 days of the month have passed as yet, and what has occurred. Even here on the Mississippi River we have accomplished more than has been accomplished for the last year. Vicksburg has fallen and with it 31,000 rebels, and between 100 and 200 large guns have passed into our hands. . . .

I told you this morning how many of the Union boys were thrown into the fight here and how many of the rebels were precipitated against us. . . . General Prentiss said today that we had but 3,500 men in the fight and that we fought the rebels at least 5 to our 1. . . . Lieut. Gen. Holmes commanded the rebel forces. In the attack Gen. Price commanded the center, Gen. Parsons the rebel right, and Marmaduke the left. The attack was made simultaneously all around our whole line. They drove the Pickets in at daylight. The signal gun fired from Fort Curtis in a few minutes afterwards. The forces had all been under arms for half an hour, and when the gun fired each regiment moved off quickly to the position assigned it. Of our Brigade the 33rd Iowa moved down quickly to Fort Curtis to support in case the rebels would make a charge. The 29th Iowa being nearer Brigade Headquarters and nearer the point of attack got under way next and were thrown into the hills on our extreme right to support our Pickets. Our regiment was divided. Three companies were thrown into the rifle pits around Battery A on the hills, which is the 1st Battery on our extreme right. Four—and mine was one—were left at the levee to support the Dubuque Battery. The other 3 companies were thrown under the hill on which the 29th Iowa was fighting, to support them in case the rebels should make a charge. As soon as the 3 companies went into the rifle pits they commenced firing, and continued with more or less success until the end of the engagement. As quick as the Battery got into position and commenced work the sharp shooters commenced firing at them across the bottom. That gave us work plenty to do. We could see them running from one tree or stump to another, or to reach them. They were at least 800 or 1,000 yards off and on higher ground than we were, but they were advancing and kept advancing until we fired several volleys into them. In the mean time they got their guns in position on the hills across the bottom, and commenced throwing shell and solid shot at us at a rapid rate, at the same time throwing their rifleballs so fast as to make the air whiz with them. I am a good dodger. We remained in that position for 2 or 3 hours, when we were ordered over to the other part of the regiment, where the Quartermaster had something for us to eat. This was near 10 o'clock A.M. After eating breakfast all the companies went onto the hills and relieved the 29th Iowa. I was ordered to keep my company back as a reserve. Soon after our boys went into it the rebels fell back and the fight ceased. About this time we heard from our left and learned that we had taken about 1,000 prisoners and had killed and wounded 600 or 700 [by] the time the fight had ceased.

July 9, Today we have learned that the rebel loss will reach fully 3,000. Of that number near 1,500 are killed and wounded, the rest are prisoners. The prisoners were sent to Memphis. . . . Several Col. were killed. They were . . . buried with the common soldiers. In the center where they took one of our batteries and then commenced a charge upon Fort Curtis, the hills and hollows were covered with their dead and dying. Several men who visited the battlefield immediately after the fight told me they could have walked on them. They are all buried on the field.

The news is all good from every direction today. Bully for Meade, Bully for Grant, Bully for Rosecrans, Bully for every loyal soldier.

If I get time I will sketch you a map in the morning giving you a better idea of the way we were placed here, but you know it will not be much account. I am a poor map maker. . . .

W. F. Vermilion

Thursday Morning, July 9th, 1863
My Best Love,

. . . Old Mr. Ely was here yesterday evening, and told me th[at] John Wafford's wife[39] had just got a letter from him, later than any other from Helena, and he said she needn't expect any more letters, as the rebels had obstructed the passage of all mail boats above Helena, and that the 36th was gone to Vicksburg. I don't know, love, whether to put any faith in this or not. Mr. Ely said he didn't believe one word of it. I asked him if he thought Wafford would write such things if there was no foundation for them in fact. He said he thought he would do anything that is mean. The old man is dreadfully out of patience with the copperheads, old Mrs. Finton[40] and John Sheeks' wife in particular. If it were not that John is a soldier the conduct of these two women would hardly be tolerated these days. Everybody is sorry for him. Mrs. Finton says the quicker your men all die and are killed off the better. She says very hard and hateful things about you, but I will not repeat them love. I care nothing about them. . . . She can't get to you to kill you by putting a "big sack on your head" and as for her efforts to injure you in any other way, they will prove about as futile. Ely said that John Sheeks has got his blood up at last, and has written some very bitter letters to his wife and to Jim Wafford, denouncing their principles, and threatening to help kill all the "danged Copperheads" as soon as he gets home.

I thought I wouldn't say a word about the good news I have heard, but I can't help it, darling. It is not confirmed . . . but at any rate I can rejoice in the hope that it is true. Mr. Phillips brought the news from Moravia night before last, and yesterday a stranger brought the same word from Chariton, that Vicksburg and Port

Hudson both surrendered last Saturday! We have news also that Meade's victory over Lee was complete, and that General Dix[41] is bombarding Richmond!

Beppo is the finest little fellow in the world, though he does all manner of mischief. He pulls off my flowers, and girdles the stalks with his teeth, and scratches off my moss, and all such things, but he pays me in beguiling many a weary hour by his playfulness. Just now he is making a terrible racket about something. I must go and see what is the matter.

Dollie

Saturday Night, July 12th, 1863
My Own Darling,

I am going to try to write to you a few lines tonight my loved one, though for two long days I have not written one word. I could not write, I don't believe I can now, but it is right today. I am in some trouble, darling. Last Thursday I heard of the battle at Helena, and up to this minute I have not heard one word from you, sweet pet. Do you wonder that your Dollie is almost crazed? That she can't write or do anything? Every day we send for the mail, and get it, but there is nothing from Helena since the battle. This morning I got your letter of the 28th. Yesterday I got one written the 30th ult. That is the latest I have, my love, though Mr. Maiken and others have letters written the 3rd inst. But none of us has a word since the 4th. I hardly know how I have got on since I heard it, nor how I shall get on till I hear from you. . . . If I do hear that you are well and safe the happiest woman in the state will be your own poor Dollie, if I hear bad news what will I do sweet pet? God help me! I fear everything for you are still living, I fear you are wounded and suffering, and I can't get to you. If you had only agreed to the plan I proposed, oh, if you only had my precious one, I should have been in Keokuk many hours ago, and I might now be far on my way to you. As it is I was afraid to go, lest you would send me no word there, and I would miss my letters here. But if I hear that you are hurt I must try to find you. Oh, my love, I must find you. Sometimes I think you are safe, then again I am afraid to hope for it, almost. A soldier's life is hard, but nothing, it seems to me, can be worse than this suspense, unless it be having our worst fears realized. . . . Oh darling, I love you too much. I have loved you more than I love all on earth besides, or all in heaven. I am afraid I have sinned in my wild idolatry, and God has punished me. I can't write. My darling, I can't write. . . . Darling, my own best darling, won't you forgive me for this? If I hear good news, I shall write you such long letters, but now I cannot. I don't know what to say to you, dearest one. My heart is too full to talk. I can't cry. I wish I could. God bless you and save you, my too dear husband, is the constant prayer of your

Dollie

Helena, Arkansas, July 12, 1863
My Darling,

I have taken a few moments and scratched you a rough map of our battle field. . . . I have marked with red ink where the principal fighting was done. The square is Helena, with Fort Curtis in the West part of it. It is built on the lower point of [a] long hill which is cut through in several places by streets. The place marked "Battery C" is where the rebels . . . captured that Battery and then made a rush for Fort Curtis. As quick as the rebels got possession of Battery C the guns from the Fort threw a few shots at the guns and dismounted about all of the guns.

From our position we fired across the bottom . . . and did good execution. The distance was from 800 to 1,000 yards. Some of the rebels got much nearer however, but the position proved too hot and they ran back. About 10 o'clock A.M. we left the levee and went across the bottom . . . under Battery A. So afterwards we relieved the 29th Iowa and they came down and rested.

Gen. Prentiss and the Chicago papers are making the people believe that he, Prentiss, and some Illinois troops did all of the fighting. When in fact Gen. Salomon [42] did the managing and Illinois didn't have any troops in Helena or near here on that day.

As to the time from which we have to serve I have heard no one speak who knows. It is my opinion we will have to serve 3 years from the time we were mustered into the United States service provided the Government needs us for so long a time. But from present appearances the rebellion is going under long before the expiration of our 3 years. . . .

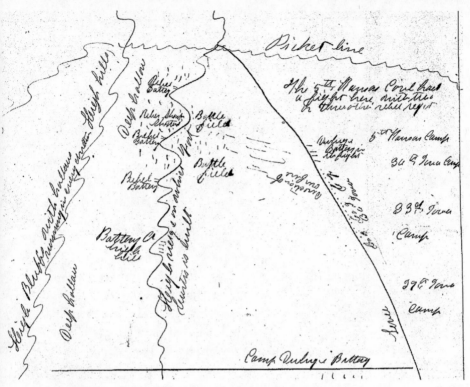

Helena Battlefield, hand drawn by William Vermilion.

If the Copperheads of Indiana want to try the strength of this Government I am perfectly willing.... Good statesmen have talked to them and told them what the consequences would be if they persisted in their course of treason, but they have heeded them not until the crisis is near at hand, and if it does [c]ome I hope the loyal people will meet it as it becomes patriots. Such times as these will bring suffering to people where there is as much treason as there is in some portions of . . . Indiana. I am not a citizen of that state, neither are you my Dollie.... We will henceforth and forever live among loyal people and where we can speak our sentiments freely. For these reasons I don't want to live in Appanoose county anymore. There are too many mean rebels there for us my Darling.... The blood of our ancestors is extinct in their veins. They can no longer claim to be the descendants of the noble Washington. They should be proud of Aaron Burr....

W. F. Vermilion

Monday Night, July 13th, 1863

My Darling,

Thank God! The news has come and it is good. Oh, Thank God! I am so thankful and so happy, my sweet precious love. I feared you were killed, or wounded. I feared everything bad. I feel like another being now. But it was providence, my pet, the good God watched over you. Let us both thank Him. It is after midnight. Mr. Hickcox came up from Moravia with the mail, just a little while ago. He brought me two letters from Will dated the 5th. Oh, my dear one, you don't know, you can hardly imagine, I think, how I have suffered since last Thursday. I was nearly wild. We heard of the battle, of the desperate fighting, and that our loss was 230. I knew somebody had lost friends, and I feared it was I. How could I help it, my dear one? I was afraid I should never have to write any more letters. But my "Peaches" is safe! Thank God, dearest! I couldn't rejoice at the same time I heard of the Battle of Helena. That put everything else out of my mind. But I shall jubilate now, love, and I know I can be glad, more than any of them. Haven't I more to be glad and thankful for than anybody else in the world, almost?

. . . In one of your letters I got last week you ask if I won't be afraid of you when you come, and say I won't get to do as I please then, because you are going to exercise your authority. You are all wrong about it, darling. I won't be much afraid, because the Bible says "perfect love casteth out all fear," and I shall do just as I please, sweet love. You'll see if I don't. For I shall please to do just whatever my "Peaches" wants me to. I haven't a quarrel till you come and we won't much then, will we? I think not. Oh, I do love you so much, my precious one! You don't know how much. God bless you!

Tuesday Morning, July 14th, I see I wrote on the wrong page last night, but you won't care, will you, pet? I was so glad and happy that I hardly knew just what I was doing. Why, my dear one, I had almost given you up for lost. If you had fallen your poor Dollie's heart would have been broken. I could not have lived over it. Oh, love, it makes me shudder yet to think of it. Have you ever thought how we have been graced and spared as a family since this war commenced? Many families have sent 4 fit young men to the war but not one so far as I know, has 4 out yet. They have all lost one, or more. It could name almost a score of such instances. And we have been spared. At Helena, at Springfield, at Shiloh, and Vicksburg, in Will's severe sickness — all the time, my darling. God has been good to us. Let us be thankful! I think now that I will trust Him for the future, and whether I can help it, if you get into another battle. . . . The people here were dreadfully uneasy about you all. Even those who [have] no immediate friends in your Company seemed as eager as any others to hear. Father was very anxious. When I read him the good news last night, I believe he cried. He says he is glad now that you have been in a battle — a battle that went all right. Mother was much uneasy about you. . . . Yesterday was the longest day I ever saw. I worked hard till 2 or 3 o'clock thinking to pass the time better, from there till night I could find nothing more to do, and I wandered around like a restless ghost. . . . Dollie

Helena, Arkansas, July 13, 1863
My Own Darling,

You have often asked me how the majorship has been decided in our regiment. . . . The commission has come at last and Adjutant Hamilton gets it. A Lieut. is appointed over me and we have to stand it. But I am not going to let it pass without telling Col. Kittredge what I think about it. . . . His object now is — no doubt — to appoint his brother-in-law who is now a sergeant major, adjutant, then all his relatives who are in the regiment will have commissions.

We have no news from below and nothing from the East except that Lee has recrossed the Potomac. . . . I wanted him to stay in Pennsylvania. He was doing us a great deal of good. Perhaps Meade will follow, and perhaps he will keep him from falling back on Richmond. And the news is that the attack has commenced again on Charleston, and with pretty good success so far.[43]
W. F. Vermilion

Tuesday Night, July 14th, 1863

My Own Dear Love,

. . . People have rejoiced over the good war news till they don't know what to do next. They had a good time, they say, at Iconium a few nights ago. At Lagrange they had a general good time — speeches, and a torchlight procession, and so on. The Copperheads were out with their drums and lamps! This is what we all expected, love. Let our brave soldiers win a few more victories, and there can't be a Copperhead found in the state. But we know them, and we shall not forget them soon. Father says [to] tell you that he heard George Stewart counting out the votes for Governor the other day. He said Col. Stone wouldn't get his own regiment, nor his own county's, and all such nonsense. He heard officers of the army say so and so. His candidate is named Fisher.[44] I don't know anything of him, only that he is a Copperhead Democrat, and that Stewart helped to nominate him. . . . But I don't want to talk about politics, love.

I want to save all the money I can for you. You will need it when you come home, my darling, and I want to have a big roll of "greenbacks" for you. Since the late victories I don't feel afraid at all of being disturbed here, or of losing our property much. . . . Were you ever so glad, pet, of anything in your life — except your own victory at Helena — as when you knew that Vicksburg had surrendered and Lee had been beaten and routed in Pennsylvania? And it was all done in two days. Verily we have had no such Fourth of July since the days of '76. Have you noticed the change in the progress of the war, love, since the Government adopted the policy of freeing the slaves, and arming them; treating them as human beings, and friends, not as chattel or enemies? Darling, if I had never believed in God or Justice before, I should do so now. I couldn't help it. You remember how for 2 years, as a nation, we denied that the "nigger" had anything to do with the war; we spurned their help offering. Thank heavens that it only took 2 years of reverses and suffering to bring the Government to its senses, and make it willing to begin to do right. Only a few weeks ago the new policy was inaugurated, and see what a change! Is it not a good thing to have God on our side? Have you seen the rebel account of the battle of Gettysburg? It was rather rich. In their dispatches of the 5th they claimed that Lee had won a plentiful victory over 150,000 federals, killing from 10,000 to 20,000, and capturing 60,000 prisoners. One of the Richmond papers said "We see now a prospect of peace, but let us have no peace except on our own terms." It is a bad rule that won't work out, you know. Is not the "prospect of peace" just the same, only on slightly different terms? We "fanatics" up here think it should be. I am very anxious to hear from Meade's army, and also from Indiana. The last dispatches I have seen from there said Morgan with 5,000 rebels had crossed the [Ohio] River with the avowed purpose of reaching Indianapolis, and were marching on New Albany. Resistance to the Government will soon be played out in Indiana if Morgan does his duty. Every blow he strikes will tell wonderfully in our favor. What do you suppose the traitors there think now of their dear persecuted brethren of the South? They have invited them there — by their treasonable conduct. . . . I imagine they have less time now to abuse "old Governor Morton" than they had last winter. . . .

I am glad, my love, that you want Jane to live with us, if she is not married when you come home. I don't believe she would marry if she knew you would come home and she could come to us. She has almost told me as much several times. She told me that she didn't want to marry. I believe she likes Wilcox, but she would wait a year or two, and so would he. If she could stay with us a year I hardly think she would have him at all. I am afraid he is not good enough for her, I know he isn't half good enough for what Jane might be. . . . In my last letter I told her if she would come to us when you come home she should have the money. . . .

We have read Gen. Prentiss' official report of the battle at Helena. It is better than we had heard at first. You know his figures, love. Oh, how thankful I am that my dear one escaped all harm! It seems like a wonder to me yet. You must tell me all about it, won't you, dear? Did you think you would be hurt? I am so glad your men all did so well. If one of them had shirked I should have hated it so much. Shake hands with Corpl. Walker for me, dear, and tell him Bravo! That was a cool thing for a young Iowa boy, wasn't it? I was scared almost to death about you, my dearest, but now that I know you are safe I am as proud of the victory as you can be. But I don't want you in another. You didn't get to eat your roast chicken for dinner on your Fourth, did you love? Did you have any dinner at all, or breakfast? Did you lie all night Saturday in the rifle pits? Were you not sick almost from the heat and exposure and loss of sleep?

Dollie

Wednesday Night, July 15th, 1863

My Best Darling,

. . . They have two nice flags fluttering to the breeze in Iconium. It did me good to see them. One is on Phillips' store, the other on the old Osborn house.[45] They are making neat preparations for having a good time Saturday. . . . One of Mr. Chapman's[46] children died of flux today. It was dangerously bad. The disease is spreading chiefly among children. . . . We have been hearing for a day or two rumors of serious trouble at Corydon. A few days ago a rebel from Mo. came there and Estep had him arrested. The Copperheads, with the sheriff at their head, then arrested Estep. While they were both in custody a squad of militia came from Mo. after the rebel. They rode into town, formed around the flagstaff, and cheered the old flag. One of the men dismounted and asked the editor of their paper there, why he didn't cheer? The editor said he wasn't ready to, and the soldier knocked him down. Another asked the sheriff to hurrah for the Union. He said he wouldn't do it, and the man knocked him down, placed his foot on his head, and in that posture made him give 3 cheers for the Union, and 3 more for Abe Lincoln! They then took their prisoner, and quickly went off.[47] The Copperheads complain of such inhuman treatment. Humphrey May was there at the time. "The way of the transgressor is hard."

I got a short letter from Jane this morning. . . . She had received a letter from you that did her more good than she could tell. . . . She said the Copperheads were active dreadfully, being determined to resist the draft. She and Henry were at a Union picnic at Fillmore on the 4th. They had a good time, and there wasn't a traitor there. The Copperheads had a picnic of their own in George Hurst's[48] pasture. I believe she and Henry will keep their faith in spite of all of them darling. The last paragraph in her letter I will quote for you:

"I hope I will get to come to Iowa yet. I am not of the notion of going to living [there] this Fall. I have had a little difficulty with M. W. I think we are not very good friends." I was glad to read this love, though it is perhaps only a "lovers quarrel" to be made up in a month. If it should be more I don't think Jane will break her heart about it. . . .

Dollie

Friday Evening, July 17th, 1863
My Darling,

. . . They had a great time at Iconium last night rejoicing over the good war news. . . . I have heard of the surrender at Port Hudson, and the attack on Charleston,[49] and the utter rout of Lee. Are you not in better spirits than you have ever been, about the war, my good darling? Only think what we have heard darling, the last two weeks. From almost every quarter the news is good, except New York! There for 3 days a lawless mob has turned the town into a Pandemonium.[50] I wish them joy of their Copperhead Governor!

You mustn't think, my dear, that your victory at Helena is not fully appreciated. It is in Iowa. Though Gen. Grant did take the wind out of your sails a little. If he had put off entry into Vicksburg a few days longer, there would have been more said about Helena. . . . The Gate yesterday put Holmes' loss at from 2,500 to 3,000. A few hundred rebels, more or less, are not much these days it seems. . . . I will quit and talk to Beppo. He is disconsolate because I wouldn't let him tear the carpet. . . . I don't want you to fight anymore, my love. I am afraid you will never escape so well again. I do want to know all about how you felt, darling, in battle, and what you did. I know you did all your duty, perhaps more. I think you would be rash, my darling. . . .

Dollie

Helena, Arkansas, July 18, 1863
My Darling,

. . . Wait till the war is over and I get home . . . and I will prove to you that I meant what I said when I told you I would stay with you when I get home. . . . This separation is too painful to allow the thought to enter my brain of ever repeating it unless I am compelled to under circumstances similar to the present. I am not to blame now love. . . . Even our happiness at home requires that I should be here and here I am. Nothing else [matters] but the cause of our beloved Country. . . .

W. F. Vermilion

Sunday Morning, July 19th, 1863
My Dearest Love,

. . . Father has gone to Mr. Sheek's to get my mail, and while he is gone I will tell you about the Union meeting at Iconium yesterday. It was the best meeting I was ever at, darling. I almost cried because you could not be there. . . . We started about 9 o'clock, and went down in the wagon. When we got to Mr. Maikens' the roads were all alive with wagons and people. The meeting was in his pasture, just below the barn. It was a nice day and there was an immense crowd out, and the *happiest* crowd I am sure ever gathered in Appanoose county. Everybody felt good, I think. The utmost harmony prevailed all day. There wasn't a copperhead to be seen. They say the traitors down there are all converted, but they can't be very zealous converts, for I don't think one of them was out yesterday, not even Davenport. But the day passed *more the less pleasantly* on that account. . . . Miss Jolly was there with her choir and sang . . . "The Battle Cry of Freedom," and other pieces. I saw Mr. Stewart and his wife, and Louisa.[51] They were very glad to see me. Mr. Stewart's health is very poor. He is nearly carried away with the good news. He said he had been up every night, but one, since the fall of Vicksburg. Glorifying. They try to have a special Jubilee over every victory, but of late the good news comes so fast that *it* crowds *them*.

There were 3 good speeches, by Sharp and Estep, and the Provost Marshal of this district. His name is Shannon.[52] He is a preacher, and a very pleasant speaker. . . . He has been in the service, and was 8 months a prisoner in the South. During that time he says he "done up" Tennessee, Mississippi, Alabama, Georgia, No. and So. Carolina and Virginia. He knows them better than he does Iowa. He is very ugly, but he said he would leave it to that audience that he was not a handsome man. In fact, he flattered himself, that he was an uncommonly dashing *institution*. Then he paused, and asked them to look at him well, and behold an *abolitionist*! Then he told how he was brought up in the South, and how, at the beginning of the war, he entered the service a proslavery Democrat anxious to save the Union if possible, but *to save slavery any how*. The first thing that tended to his conversion was lying in a filthy prison pen, with a negro soldier standing guard over him. He told how they were treated in the South; how filthy and *lousy* they were, their clothes all wore out, and they patched them with old bits of carpet, and the *patches wore out*; how the Southern women tormented them, and would bring their little children and hold them up to "look at the nasty Yankees," how his comrades died off, one after another, and were buried among their enemies. But I need not try to tell you all he said, darling. It was a good speech, and will do good. Estep followed him in one of his mirth-provoking philippics against traitors. He made a better speaker than I ever heard him before. One remarkable thing about him, dearest, is his resemblance to you, both in looks and manner. 20 persons I know have spoken to me about it. You haven't a brother who is half as much like you. The only difference is, he is not *half so good looking*, nor, I am sure, half *so good* a man. . . .

How much you will have to tell me dear, when you come home! Will we ever get done talking, do you think? You must remember every thing to tell me, pet. As for me I write you such long letters and tell you everything I know so I won't have anything left to tell when you come. Yes, I will have *one secret*, love, and I will get close to you, and whisper it in your ear, so that nobody in the world shall hear it. Wouldn't you like to know what it will be, darling? But if I tell you now, it won't be a secret, will it? But I won't keep my love in suspense. I am going to tell you if I can; *how much I love you*! You will let me love you as much as I please if you are a hero, won't you dearest? *You* don't think I shall be *afraid* of you do you? Afraid of my Peaches?

I heard bad news from Humphrey. . . . Little Anna [53] was about to die of the flux. . . . Chapman's children were no better. I wish I could hear from Anna May. I do hope she shall not die. Julia thought last winter that if Humphrey came home safely she would never see any more trouble. . . .

Monday Morning, July 20th, I am not well this morning. I have head ache badly. . . . Mr. Teater has just been here, darling. He was at the mill, and came on up here to "settle up" with you, and get in his note. He had an account against you for road tax and seed oats and feeding the cattle, and some leather he used about the harness, so we fell $1.60 in his debt. I paid it off. His charges were reasonable. . . . He charged $1 a month for feeding the cattle. I told him what you said about selling the horses, and he was quite willing to let them go. He said he was uneasy a little himself about their being stolen, and if you wanted to sell them he could make out with the oxen. . . .

Dollie

Friday Evening, July 24th, 1863

My Dearest Love,

Just as I was putting up my letter to send you this morning, Mr. Teater came in. He came to tell me that he could not get the money to pay for Capitala. His plans had failed. . . . So that trade is no trade you see, love. I don't care much for she is worth more than $100. He was going to start to Oskaloosa next Tuesday, and father told him if he could sell both the horses while he was gone for $180 to let them go; or if he could sell Capitala alone for $125 to do it. . . . Teater says that Capt. Gedney is at home, and that he says as he came up the river he sent orders going down for the 36th to repair to Alton Ills. I can't believe, though, that you are coming to *Alton*. Why that would be almost home, and I could go to you at once. But what do they want of you at Alton? If there is any truth in the report, they must be either to guard prisoners or enforce the draft in Ills. Whatever Capt. Gedney *has* told is no doubt true, but perhaps he has never heard of this in his life. I wish I could see him, dear one, long enough to ask him all about you. If it were not so far to Bellair[54] I would go and see him. But it is far, and I have no one to go with me, sweet love.

. . . Father came home from Iconium yesterday just as I finished the first page of my letter. . . . He brought me lots of news, 3 papers and 3 letters; one from Will, and 2 from you. . . . One was an old one that had been delayed somewhere, the other was dated the 16th inst. . . . But you wouldn't have waited so long, if you had known your Dollie would be sick, and how she would pine for a letter from her "Peaches," *her only love.* I am sure you wouldn't, but you didn't know it. . . . If this war ends and you come home once more, I never will let you leave me again, dear one, never, as long as I live. . . . You shall go whenever you please, and *I'll go with you.* Won't you let me, my own love? I am going to put fetters on you as soon as you come home, but they shan't be *very* harsh.

Charleston I think is almost taken. . . . The Mercury[55] of the 15th admits that nothing can save the city but their bayonets! If that is all their hope they are doomed. Lee's army has escaped for the time, but Meade is on his track. On the whole, Lee's invasion of the North has been a hard blow on the rebels, and a grand success for us, though we did lose the best part of our victory when Meade allowed him to slip across the river. But I trust he will redeem that blunder. . . . We know Lee's army must be demoralized; it can't be otherwise. Their own defeat and flight, and the news of our victories in the South and West, and the complete failure of the New York mob, could have no other effect on them, I think. Morgan is completely whipped in Ohio, and his forces . . . captured. Rebel invasion of the North has "played out" darling, and so have copperhead mobs. . . . The President has "set his foot down firmly" about the enforcement of the draft in New York. Thank God for that! It is worth more than Gettysburgh to me. I am just beginning to feel that our country is safe, love, with our "Honest Abe" at the helm. . . . We must keep up our courage a little longer, my own love! As we kept our hearts from fainting through the darkest hour of the long, dismal night that is passing, surely, now that we see the dawn already breaking, we can wait with patience for the glorious sunburst of perfect victory, and universal Freedom! *It will come,* sweet love. . . . Will we not remember this July as long as we live? It is a lucky month for us, and I count every hour as precious to me and our cause. *6* days more, and it will be gone. . . .

I wrote to Jane last evening, darling. You said you had not written to any of them since the battle, and I know, if they have heard of the battle, they are very uneasy about you. Mother and Jane and Henry are. . . . I told her about the good Union meetings we have here, and how we have all been rejoicing over our late victories, and I "pitched in" pretty strong. I can't help it, dear one. They shall know my sentiments. We risked everything for our cause, and we loved our country, and were true to her, and stood by her in the darkest hours of her peril, and that we have a right to be glad, and we will be glad, and say what we please. It will please Jenny. Dollie

Helena, Arkansas, July 24, 1863

My Darling,

. . . You have not been uneasy about me this time have you? If you have you ought to be scolded a little for our Scout didn't amount to anything. . . . We traveled about 30 miles and never saw an armed rebel. They have all disappeared. . . . I walked all the way but about a mile. The Chaplain let me ride that far. . . . We came upon a rebel Hospital some 6 or 8 miles out. There were 18 wounded rebels in it. They were Missourians and belonged to Marmaduke's Brigade. . . .

Sell all of our cattle as soon as you can. . . . I think you had better sell them all together except the oxen, if you don't otherwise you may have the cows and heiffers left on your hands. . . . Keep the horses if you think best. . . . Teater has no right to the horses after the crop is gathered. . . .

Be cheerful love but don't think the war is going to end immediately. . . . If this were a war between nations it would have ended on the 4th day of July, but it is not. It is a war of life or death with the rebels and of course they will fight just as long as they possibly can. . . .

W. F. Vermilion

Helena, Arkansas, July 25, 1863

My Own Dollie,

. . . We heard the other day that James Hickcox had been killed by one of our own men.[56] Somehow or other I hated it more than usual on hearing of the death of a soldier. He must have been a good boy and then it will hurt his parents so badly. You thought if you could have seen Capt. Jones you could have learned much about me. I think not Dollie as I have never seen him since he was at our house in Iconium. The 3rd Iowa Cavalry is divided, one half under Lieut. Col. Clay Colwell has always been in Missouri. The other half under Col. Bussey[57] was here nearly one year. . . . Capt. Jones is under Col. Colwell.

Jake is not better. . . . I was down to see him this morning. I saw his surgeon also and I think I have the arrangements made now to have him discharged as soon as this pay day is over, which will be the forefront of this next week. I want him discharged as badly as if he were my own brother. . . . When he gets back up home I think it will be better with him. . . . I believe he is a little in love with Mary Westfall.[58] He says she is loyal and her father I know is getting to be. If it were not for his wife my love he would be a pretty good man. He says he is glad the negroes are going to be freed. That he thinks now he would suffer himself burned before he would vote for any man who has given his sympathies to the rebels. He seems to be very anxious to keep in the same opinion so he can show rebels about home when he gets there, that he is true to his country.

The officers of our regiment are playing out very fast somehow. Mine is the only Company that has 3 commissioned officers for duty. . . .

W. F. Vermilion

Sunday Evening, July 26th, 1863
My Beloved,

. . . The capture of Yazoo City and Jackson is confirmed. . . . Father was over to Chapman's this forenoon. They are nearly all sick. Another one of the children he thinks will die soon. . . .

Tuesday Morning, One of Mr. Stone's children died yesterday. I have not heard from the other sick people over there, to day. . . . By the way, Jimmy is in a great way about enlisting in the regular service for 5 years. He wants to do so, and I expect he will, if he has not already. I am sorry he has taken such a notion. I want him to come home, but if he is bent upon it, it will do no good to talk to him about it. He says he would rather be a soldier than anything else in the world. He has never said a word to us about joining the regulars — he is afraid we will oppose him perhaps — but the other boys have written home about it. Two others of his company are going with him — Isley and Couchman.[59] What do you think about it, my darling? What I am afraid of is, that at the end of the 5 years, if he should live, he will be a good soldier, but good for nothing else. . . . Oh, my love, we have just heard bad news. Jim Hickcox is killed. The news came this morning in a letter from Ira Gilbert.[60] Mr. Hickcox and George[61] were at Mr. Gilbert's[62] when they brought out the letter. He was killed while on picket, somewhere near Jackson. 30 of the regiment were wounded. Ira gave no names. He was not with the regiment himself. He was left sick at Snyder's Bluff, so he could not give any particulars as yet. We fear Matt is among the wounded. Father is greatly troubled. We are all afflicted at Jim's death. He was a good boy, and such a good soldier. And he and Matt have been like twin brothers ever since they left home. . . . From my heart I pity his poor mother. I am going down there this afternoon, but I can do them no good. Only God can help them bear their great trouble. May He, indeed, be near them.

Later, Father has been down to Hickcox's and read Ira's letter, but there is nothing more in it than I told you. He says they take it very hard, and he does himself. They always send Jim's letters up here for us to read, for he always speaks of Matt in them, and we would send Matt's to them. In this way we learned a great deal about him, and he was such a whole-souled, good hearted fellow, and such a good soldier that we all thought a great deal of him. Dollie

Helena, Arkansas, July 26, 1863
My Own Darling,

. . . At sun up in the morning we have Reveille. Soon after we have breakfast. At half past 7 guard mounting, policing and so on and if there is any fatigue duty to do the men generally have to report at that time. . . . At 6 o'clock P.M. we have dress parade. Then at twilight roll call again, and half an hour later taps at which time all the lights of the men have to be put out. Company officers burn theirs as long as they wish to. . . . When there is danger of an attack we are all called up and go into line of battle a little before day. We generally stack our arms on the parade ground and return to quarters until half an hour by sun when we take our arms and return to our every day duties. For several nights now one Company of our regiment has been sent to the rifle pits to keep watch during the night. . . . Company F has never been out yet. . . . The indications be that we are going to march across Country, probably to Little Rock. At any rate there is going to be something done. Government is surely not going to keep so many troops here simply to hold this insignificant place. If it does Helena [will] cost more than half a dozen such places are worth.

Judging from the news in the papers today Uncle Abraham is going to push the Draft ahead in the city of New York. . . . Those traitors have put themselves in opposition to the Government and are just as much rebels as Jeff Davis himself is. I wish more of them had been killed. In fact I wish all of them had been killed who were daring in the least to oppose the laws. . . . Some of the papers say that Governor Seymour is going to bring the State authorities of New York in conflict with the General Government. That the Governor says the Draft must be suspended until the Constitutionality of the law is tested by the Courts. If the report is true it may cause trouble.

We expect to hear in good time from General Gilmore[63] that Fort Sumter has fallen and that it is again in our possession. . . . We have lost enough of men trying to storm the rebel strongholds. It is best to take it slower and make a surer thing of it. Look at Vicksburg will you? Every effort made there to storm their works proved a failure. So it was with Banks at Port Hudson. Yet both places fell and at last without the firing of a gun. It takes a little longer but what of that. There are men enough falling in this war to wrap the whole country in mourning anyhow. . . . Had Lee staked and fortified himself on Maryland Heights we could have ended this war in two months without losing 1,000 men. But he knew it and trusted to his ability to retreat. Let him go, we can't help it now. Meade may catch him yet and force him to fight a decisive battle. . . .

W. F. Vermilion

Tuesday Evening, July 28th, 1863

My Dearest Love:

I have just come home from Hickcox's. They are in great trouble, but they bear it very calmly. I am so sorry for the old lady.[64] She is sick too, but I think she has grieved herself sick. Jim was her favorite among all her children. Indeed he was a favorite with all the family. . . . I did get a letter my pet, just one letter from you. I feel sorry about the way the majorship has gone, because I know you hate it. Don't let it annoy you, dear one. If you should get your company detached from the regiment you would never get any more letters. I'm afraid they would all be sent to the regiment. Henry's company was always separated from the rest of the regiment on detached duty and he never got any letters hardly. . . . John Morgan is captured at last, with the last 500 of his guerrillas.[65] This is good news indeed. We have one subtle enemy the less to watch. We have reliable news from Charleston up to the 18th. Everything seemed going right although our loss had been heavy. . . . We heard nothing from Matt. . . . I expect to hear bad news from him when I do hear. Company E must be nearly all wounded. One of them was killed, and 6 wounded while crossing the Black River. Then Jim was killed and 30 more wounded near Jackson. There can't be many able for duty. A few of them were left at Snyder's Bluff sick. . . .

Wednesday Morning, My Darling, There was a man here a few minutes ago to rent Woodside. His name is Armstrong, and he has lately moved into that neighborhood. . . . Father told him he didn't know anything about what you would want to do with the place next year. I thought he looked like a copperhead who had moved to escape the draft. . . . If he had talked to me I should have asked him if he is a Union man, and always had been, before I would have talked with him about Woodside. If he is not there would have been no reason for any word on that subject.

Old Mr. Christie is . . . raising money to build a church at Uncle Billy Evans' and he comes over here and drums me for a little help, and says he knows *you* would help him, if you were here. I tell him I don't care anything about his meeting house, till the war is over,

but that I will tell you and if you want to give him anything, he shall have it. I get away from him that way. He is a good *old* man, and he is going to be quite a help to this neighborhood, I think. He stirs them up about a good many things. He is to preach at Milledgeville next Thursday on *The Union.* . . .
Dollie

Thursday Afternoon, July 29th, 1863
My Own Darling,

I have been very unwell to day, but I must write to my "Peaches" anyhow. I will write a little, if I can't say much. I have not been quite well for several days, and so I didn't get any better, I took some pills last night. They have made me right sick all day. I think I shall be well again in a day or two now. Don't be troubled about me, darling, and imagine I am going to be bad sick. I don't think I am, at all. I should be better today, if it were not for the medicine I took. Pills always make me sick, you know, darling. Last night, just at dark, I got the map you sent me, and the half dollar enclosed, but the letter you spoke of starting has not come yet. But I hope it will this evening. I want a long letter so badly, my pet. I thank you for the map. I can understand it very well. It is plain as can be. I can't understand much about it without looking at some map, for in my head *Helena is always on the east side of the river.* . . . And some day, my love, I want to go there and see where you have spent so many long months, and where you risked your life in battle. If I can't go while you are there, darling, now, sometime after the war is ended, we will go back there together. . . . No other place in the South can have as much interest for me. . . .

Little Annie May was buried today, at uncle Billy Evans' grove. She died yesterday. I am sorry for Julia, love! If I had been well enough I would have gone to the burial. I wish I could have gone and seen her while she was sick, but I was not able after I heard of her danger. . . . We have late letters from all the boys. Jimmy says they expect to go to Little Rock before long. Half of the regiment was already gone somewhere. He says they had a glorious "jollification" over the fall of Vicksburg, in Springfield. The town was all illuminated. . . .

Friday Morning, My Good Darling, Catharine Thompson[66] sent me a long letter to send, last night, that they had just got from one of Francis's brothers, in the 29th. He gives a more detailed account of the battle, than any other I have seen. He says he was near enough to hear the rebel officers giving command. Sometimes they would order the men to such or such a point, and the "rebs" would swear that they had *Iowa men to fight*. He says our boys were as cool and steady as though they were trying their skill on that many squirrels. For his own part he did better than he ever expected he would. He has a wonderful opinion of *Iowa soldiers*. And indeed, he is far from being alone in that opinion. Everybody admits that Iowa soldiers have covered themselves and their state with imperishable laurels. Today, my love, I would rather you should be a soldier from Iowa than from any other state in the Union. Other states have done well, but Iowa has excelled them all. Every loyal man and woman is proud of the record of our state for the last two years.

Dollie

P.S. You have never told me love, how you liked the butter and honey I sent you. Was it all good? Did the gooseberries keep well? What did you do with them? If you don't tell me anything about them I won't know whether to send you any more if I have the opportunity. . . .

Dollie

Thursday Evening, July 30th, 1863
My Own Darling:

Mother has been very sick since I wrote to you yesterday morning. She is much better now, and can sit up a little. She had colic. Yesterday afternoon she took worse suddenly. . . . She was quite wild, and she lost her memory entirely. She could not remember *anything*. She asked where the boys were, and where you were, and how I came to be here, and a hundred such questions. She said we never had told her about your going to the war, or that the boys were gone. . . . I did the best I could, and after awhile she got better, and grew calm. This morning she was rational. . . . There was a speaking at Milledgeville yesterday. Provost Marshall Shannon spoke. Some men were there recruiting for the 8th Cavalry. They got 6 volunteers but I don't know any but Bill McCoid[67]. . . . Tell Will that John Sullivan has enlisted in the 8th Cavalry, and his father is moving heaven and earth to get him released[68]. . . . He has written now to Gen. Baker. . . .

Friday Evening, My Dearest Love, You can resign, can you not. It does seem, my pet, that I can't get through this winter without you. I don't want to do wrong, or to counsel you to do wrong, but I don't think it would be. This is what I am afraid of, darling, or one thing I am afraid of — if the war lasts a few months longer, the new conscripts will be left to do garrison duty at Helena and everywhere else, and the trained soldiers will be sent into the Gulf states after the retreating confederacy. You will get in a strange climate, and so far from home that I shall never hear of you scarcely, and a thousand dangers would beset you, darling. I can't be a Spartan or a Roman, love. I can't be anything but your own sweethearted, loving Dollie. *I don't want you to go.* Besides, I don't think you can stand active service. Father got a letter from Will to day 5 days later than yours, and he said you could hardly walk when you came back from the scout. Poor darling! how sorry Dollie was for you. I do love our country, and our cause, but I love you *more*. . . . Mother is getting well again. She has been up all day. She has no symptoms of another attack now. Mrs. Hickcox will stay with her tomorrow, if we go to the Union meeting. . . . They are making extensive preparations for it, and I think they will have a good time. If you were only here, my dear one, I should want to go. I often feel like it is not *right* for me to go to such places while you are in danger, and may be sick, or suffering I know not what. Two weeks ago [the] Hickcox's all went to Iconium, and they enjoyed themselves very well, and that very day Jim was lying cold and stark in his bloody grave. But they didn't know it. Such things are so dreadful, dearest. I wish I could never think of them any more.

They have been getting a good many recruits for the 8th Cavalry, for instance Bill Delay, and Ben Head, and Pete Talkington, and Jake McIninch,[69] and others that I don't know. When the officers came around I didn't suppose they could get one. They will likely get several tomorrow. Capt. Wilson is trying to get up a company of homeguards. I don't know how he is succeeding. . . .
Dollie

Helena, Arkansas, July 30, 1863

My Darling,

... I have just returned from a visit with Dr. Lambert[70] of the 6th Iowa. ... He says Matt is quite hearty. He has never reported on the sick list since he has been out. He my Dollie is the kind of soldier to have. No doubt he does all his duties properly. ... Dr. Lambert had no money for me this evening. ... Just as I expected. I guess he never will have any money when I see him. What would you think of me Dollie if I were as poor a financier as he is. He will never pay his debts while the sun shines. Were he to draw $5,000 per annum he would not keep any money. I doubt very much if he funds his good natured wife sufficient to keep her and her children. ... When he was as poor as Doctors ever get (and that is quite thin you know) I gave him money. ... He took it and used it more freely than I would have done myself and now when I want it back he never has any. But let him go on rejoicing with his white shirt collars. I am fine without it. ...

Sell the cattle to the best advantage as soon as you can. Get Government money for them. That is the best currency [in] these times Dollie.

W. F. Vermilion

6

"I Will Never Forget All the Bitter Experiences of the Last Year"

The stories of Frederick Steele and Samuel Ryan Curtis, both Civil War generals from Iowa, have remarkable similarities. New Yorkers by birth, they each earned an appointment to West Point. Neither intended to make the military a career, however, for they both resigned their commissions and entered the private sector. During the 1850s, the two chose to move to Iowa, and by the end of the decade had been elected to Congress. Similarly, the War Department made Curtis a brigadier general in 1861, and gave Steele that rank in 1862. Finally, both experienced their greatest success in the state of Arkansas — Curtis at the Battle of Pea Ridge in March 1862, and Steele through his capture of Little Rock in the summer of 1863. Losing few men, Steele maneuvered the Confederates out of the capital of Arkansas, capturing enemy soldiers and material along the way.

The 36th Iowa participated in this successful campaign. As was the case with many of the regiments accompanying Steele, the 36th Iowa did not engage the enemy while en route to Little Rock. The entire campaign from Helena to Little Rock provided a test to the regiment of a different sort: the 36th, which had done little marching up to this point in the Civil War, had to exert themselves mightily during the advance to Little Rock.

The letters in this chapter center on the Little Rock campaign. William does an excellent job of telling Mary about the military side of his activities, providing interesting insights into his understanding of Union strategy. Mary tells William of the extreme happiness in Iowa over the positive war news, but also describes incidents from both Iowa and Indiana that demonstrate a growing antagonism to the Union cause. Although many historians discount the importance of the antiwar groups discussed in this chapter, it is obvious that prowar Northerners believed that these groups posed a serious threat, and the letters convey this sense of foreboding. The couple also discusses a time when Mary apparently ended her relationship with William. A Putnam County doctor had shared information with her about an incident involving William sometime during the couple's courtship or after their marriage. Because Mary corresponded with the doctor's wife from the time of her move to Iowa until the moment of William's arrival — when the discourse between the two women abruptly stopped — the incident must have occurred prior to their marriage. They quickly put the painful episode to rest in these letters, however, and pinned their hopes on the nation's reunion in the coming year.

Helena, Arkansas, Aug. 1, 1863

My Own Darling,

I wish I could sit down by your side this evening and talk to you. . . . I would tell you how at first I wanted to see you even before I left Greencastle. Then that night when I got to Terra Haute [*sic*] and had to wait for the Cars it seemed as though there was no stranger at the Hotel but me. . . . No person knew me and I knew no one so I went to bed and directed the landlord to have me wakened up at 11 o'clock. I believe it was when the cars were to start. But I needn't have given that trouble for I did not go to sleep. . . . I lay there thinking of my poor Dollie whom I had left and you don't know my good love how badly I felt. It was the first time I had ever left you to be gone any length of time. Always before when I had parted from you I knew we would meet again — if nothing happened — in a few weeks. But then I was going to the wars, and leaving my love far behind. I did not know that I would ever see her again, but it was my duty to go and when I know my duty I always try to do it. So when the cars whistled I was at the Depot ready to step into the cars and speed away to my brave boys at Keokuk. Soon after I got aboard the train I went into a Sleeping Car and took a bunk, more to get off by myself than anything else. I wanted to lie and think of Dollie. She was all I cared for. . . . We got to St. Louis about 10 o'clock A.M. There again I had not a single friend. . . . I went down to the Keokuk Packet Landing and ascertained that I would have to wait till 4 o'clock P.M. before I could get passage up the river. I engaged passage and went immediately to my room and there dreamt of Dollie all alone. Oh how I wanted my love with me during that trip up to Keokuk. . . . When I got back to old Camp Lincoln I had too much to do to get the blues much. But my love you know you were never forgotten and you know you never will be as long as I live. At Keokuk I found Humphrey not very well and with the blues. I cheered him up all I could but I had not the courage I should have had, yet I knew what our duty was and I had courage enough to do it. Even there my love you know I thought as much of you as he did of Julia. Don't you my love?

When I sat down I thought I would tell you something more about the battle here. . . . You asked me in particular how I felt. Not in the least as I had always expected. While at home and long after I came into the Service I thought if I ever got into a battle I would be scared at first. But if I do say it myself it was not the case. No doubt I was excited more or less. So was everybody else, but I don't think any of us were scared. At first when we went to the Levee and took shelter it was necessary for someone to get on the top of it and break the weeds down so the boys could see to shoot. I told some one or two of them to get up on the top and break them down. During the time the bullets were flying rapidly. All were busy firing, and no one seemed to think of the weeds. At last Cpl. Shutterly [1] said he would climb up. . . . Just then the thought struck me that I was using others to do what I could do myself. So Cpl. Shutterly and myself broke them down. While we were at it the bullets whizzed around us thick and fast, but we were not hurt. After that one of the Artillery boys got his arm shot off just above the wrist. . . . I thought I would go and see that his arm was properly bandaged. As I went to him a cannon ball passed very near by my head. I felt the air as it passed, but it did not hit me. A miss, you know, is as good as a mile, no odds how near it comes. . . . Lieut. May was sitting at a pool of water, bathing his face — he was sick — and as cannon balls passed over him one fell into the water just in front of him. He took off in another direction and walked on. Why or how we all escaped I can't say, but we [did]. . . .

Aug. 2, 1863, Lieut. Wright and 5 of our boys . . . were detailed 6 days ago to go as guards on a boat that was to carry supplies to Gen. Davidson's[2] Command up on the St. Francis River. They went up 5 days ago and should have been back last night but did not get here. . . . William Dooley died on the 31st of July . . . of Jaundice and Pneumonia. He was only in the Hospital 4 days. . . .
W. F. Vermilion

Sunday Morning, August 3rd, 1863
My Own Dear Love,
 . . . I will tell you about the Union meeting. . . . We went in the morning and took our dinner and stayed all day. There were a great many people. Mr. Shannon spoke nearly 3 hours. I can't better describe it than to say he made a tremendous speech. It wasn't fine by any means, and it was exceedingly bitter, but it was *good*. He is quite as rough, in a different way, as Estep. I wish I could tell you what he says about life in the South, and the story of his long captivity there. He says what he doesn't know about the Confederacy he's very sure he doesn't want to know. He is a Southern man and slaveholder — if the rebels haven't stolen his niggers. He says it was his curse to be born and raised, not among negroes, but among *slaves*. I wish you could hear him talk to Northern traitors. He said he was never going to run for office here, nor enter land, so he could afford to call things by their right names and tell the truth. And the truth as he tells it, is enough to give them a lively foretaste of what they may expect in the fiery home to which they are all hastening, as he says. In regard to them he has a platform with just one plank, which he read. It is the 26th verse of the 7th chapter of Ezra. You can look it up in your Bible, love. He made an exceedingly happy "hit" of it. After his speech there was an intermission, and we ate dinner, and the little boys deafened us by trying to beat the head out of the 10 or 12 drums they had on the ground. Then Mr. Barns of Albia made a speech that was rather tame, and not listened to much. Then Dr. Hays and John Bryant[3] offered some

resolutions which were adopted, and Mr. Shannon made another short speech. He said there were 150 men to be drafted from the county. The arrangements are all completed, and up. They are very anxious to get that regiment organized at once. Then he talked awhile to the ladies, advising them how to treat Copperheads, and finished by telling them to "love God and their country, pray for the soldiers, and write letters to them." Then the glee clubs sang several songs, and then the meeting was over, and everybody went home feeling the better for having been there. I wish my own darling could have been there. . . . Father has just come back and brought your letter of the 24th. No, love, I wasn't uneasy about your scout, for at the same time I got your letter telling me that you came back. I would have been uneasy if it had not been for that. . . . My heart cries for you, darling, *my* darling. I sit here and look along the road the way I used to see you coming when you came to see me in the days long ago, till my eyes get blinded and I can't see the road even. Do you remember those old days, love? You didn't come often, you know. I don't think you were half so glad to see me then, as I always was to see you. But I didn't tell you then I was glad. I thought I should have time enough for that. I loved you very much then, but not as I love you now, my dear one. In those days I never dreamed of a love like this that absorbs my whole being now. I had faith in you then, now I know you are good and noble. Darling, I don't know how I have lived all these long months without you. . . . If you could know just how I feel about it, love, I am sure you would be sorry for your Dollie. I am not afraid, dear, that you will ever leave me anymore, if you get home this time. *If you only get home.* We will live together as one. . . . I live in the past, and in the hopes of the future. I try to be as oblivious to the present as I possibly can. . . .

Dollie

Monday Night, August 3rd, 1863

My Own Darling,

. . . I just stopped at . . . Mr. Maiken's. . . . I gave him the order that was in your letter, and he paid me the money. I asked him all about the cattle trade. . . . He thinks he can sell to very good advantage, but if he can't he will take them to Chicago himself. In either case, he says he will take ours, or so many as will do at all, including Muley and the oxen, and sell them with his and do the very best he can with them for you. Would I be satisfied with this, and I told him I would. . . . He can sell them better than I could, and I am not afraid to trust him. The arrangement suits him as well as me, as he wanted to get a good lot together. . . . Mr. Maiken advised me to sell the oxen, if I had to hire a team to gather Teater's corn. He said the oxen would eat half your part of the corn before spring. He says he is going to sell all of his stock that he possibly can, and as soon as he can. He thinks the drougth is so general, and so severe, that stock will not be worth anything scarcely this fall. . . . I came home by Mullinix's. . . . John says he heard Davenport make a speech since he came home, and he talked right. He speaks very highly of you. Says you are the most *independent* man he ever saw, and that you care no more for Col. Kittredge than you do for him. John says he talked a good deal about you. He doesn't speak very highly of Lieut. Wright.

Beppo has annoyed me all the time I have been writing. The door is open and he will come in, and then he will tear my apron, or carry off my mittens, or climb up in a chair to get a snap at my fingers, or some other mischief. I have had to whip him two or three times, but he doesn't care much. I wish I could know where you are, and what you are doing right now. There is a rumor up here that your regiment is ordered to Texas. And another that it is to come North and recruit. . . .
Dollie

Helena, Arkansas, Aug. 4, 1863
My Darling,

. . . You must send me a . . . Dictionary. . . . I want one and can't buy it here. There is no such a thing in Helena. . . . I have $250 to send you. I expect I will have to express it to you. . . .

We don't know but we all think we will start in the course of 3 days to Little Rock or some other place out West. There is an expedition being fitted up here for something of that kind. It is only about 120 miles from here out there. The country between here and there is high and dry. . . .
W. F. Vermilion

I was just ready to go to bed but thought I must talk to you a little while first. . . . When I get to see you I intend to talk to you all the time. No body else shall say anything to you while I am about. . . . You can talk to them now my love as much as you want to but then you must talk to me.

Somehow or other I have been thinking about Dr. Rynerson's folks today. . . . I never feel very pleasant when I think of those old times my darling. Did you see him or his wife[4] or hear anything about them while you were in Indiana? If you did, tell me all about it, won't you Darling. Don't you suppose they would both be glad if I should fall before the end of this rebellion? It seems to me they would love. You used to disbelieve what I said of them. I wonder if you do yet. But let me talk of something else or quit and go to bed. Which had I better do? Go to bed I reckon. Then I can give my thoughts full scope without babbling my Darling. . . .

Wednesday Evening, Aug. 5th, 1863
My Own Dear Love,

. . . I am sorry to hear that Jake Grimes is so bad. I don't think he will ever get well, darling. He has written home since he got to Mound City, and says he is well cared for, and will get well there if he ever can anywhere. . . . I do not want all the good soldiers to come home. The country can't well spare her best men, to say nothing of their families and friends. . . . Have you read the President's order relating to colored soldiers, love?[5] Isn't it noble? It is nothing more than *right*, of course, but it is a cheering sign to me that the Government is determined to do all that is right by all her soldiers. Our "Father Abraham" is *all right* at last, and it is this fact which encourages me to hope for peace this fall, as much as our successes in the field. I believe I am quite as thankful for this as I am for Vicksburg. The Government has at last adopted a policy just and noble in the eyes of God and the world! And it cannot recede now if it would. Secretary [of War Edwin M.] Stanton says that when the negro blood that was shed at Milliken's Bend and Port Hudson[6] shall flow again through his veins, he will consent to return the freedmen of the seceded states to slavery, but not till then. I am uneasy about matters at Charleston. . . . I don't know much about Gen. Gilmore but I hope he is the right man in the right place.

Mrs. McCully has a sister who has just come out from Greencastle, Indiana. She says when the men of Morgan's invasion reached there, they raised 200 volunteers in 4 hours. Many of the worst Copperheads enlisted at once. She thinks Morgan did good service to our cause in that state. . . . The people there are more united now than they have ever been. I am anxious to get a letter from Jane and hear who volunteered from our old neighborhood. I think I will get one before long. . . .

Jim Evans has volunteered in the 8th Cavalry. He thinks he will try soldiering again. Henry Isley and John Hall[7] have also volunteered. . . . I wish no more men would volunteer. I want them to draft and give all men an equal chance to serve their country. For every loyal man who volunteers now, some Copperhead perhaps will get to stay at home. Our "Democratic Party" is in a good deal of trouble now. Fisher has decided to run for Governor. There is terrible fluttering among the "unterrified." I think Mahoney will *make* Fisher run. . . . Those who still claim to be loyal want General Tuttle.[8] Mahoney says he is no better than Stone. . . . Darling, have you any faith in the rumor . . . about an alliance being formed between Napoleon and Jeff Davis? I know we have had a great many alarming rumors about intervention, and everything else almost, but I attach more importance to this. Jeff Davis is desperate now, and I have no doubt but he will attempt something of the kind. He may get help from Napoleon if he can make it to his interest to help him. Considering the aspect of affairs in Mexico, . . . I am very much troubled about it. . . .
Dollie

Helena, Arkansas, Aug 6, 1863
My Darling,

We have learned nothing more about our expedition, only that Gen. Steele will command it. Gen. Prentiss goes to Memphis and takes command of that post. I wish he had remained here, not that he is a great man but *he hates rebels* and that is the kind of man we want to serve under. General Davidson's troops hate him very much. They wanted Prentiss to go so badly.

. . . Dollie, there will be no telling how long it will be before I

will get to go home. . . . You go to work and dispose of our stock. . . . Counsel your father and Mr. Maiken. I don't think it will do to depend on my getting home in time to dispose of the stock and I know you — that is among you, you can sell them as well as I could. . . . Set the price on Jake yourselves if you sell him. . . .
W. F. Vermilion

Friday Evening, Aug. 7th, 1863
My Own Darling,

 . . . I am troubled some about our stock. The price is down now, and if the drougth continues it will get worse I am afraid. . . . There was a man at the meeting yesterday buying horses for the Government. Father told him about Jake and he promised to send a man to see him next week. . . . We have no use for them now, and I am afraid this is going to be a hard winter on our farmers. The less stock we have the better, unless we raise some corn. . . . 3 or 4 men have spoken for the cattle. I will get father to look around a little, too. . . .
Dollie

Helena, Arkansas, Aug. 7, 1863
My Darling,

 . . . On dress parade last night we were notified to have our Companies in readiness to march. . . . The army is being organized for the Western expedition. . . . If nothing happens I feel pretty sure I will get to go home as soon as this campaign ends if nothing happens more.
W. F. Vermilion

Saturday Morning, Aug. 8th, 1863
My Dearest,

 . . . I have learned . . . that whenever we have stock to sell and can get a good price, this is the time to dispose of it. All the comfort I have now is in knowing that everybody else had made the same blunder I have. . . . Mr. Eads has several young ones for which he was offered $16 apiece; now he is trying to sell them for $10 and can't get it. I should have kept a sharper lookout, but I felt sure that you would get to come home in time to see to selling the cattle yourself. But then if I had looked ever so sharply I couldn't have foreseen the rebel invasion of Pennsylvania or the long droughth, and these are "what's the Matter" as you would say.

I wish you could send your money home some other way darling, than by express to Phillips. My objection is just the same as yours — everybody will know how much you send, and all about it. Mr. Phillips would do all he could to oblige you, I think, but there are a great many bad people in the world, and I would rather not have it known that I have much money. But if you have sent it love, why it is all right. Your Dollie will take good care of it for you. . . . It would make you feel sorry if you could see how some of the women spend the hard-earned savings of their soldier husbands. In some instances the money is all owing in the stores before they get it at all. They buy a great deal more finery than they need to. The real truth is darling, that a good many women up here *seem to* enjoy themselves better than ever before. They have considerable money to spend and nobody to control them. . . . It is not so with all, dearest. But it is an easy matter here now to distinguish between the true-hearted, loving wife and the Frivolous, careless one. . . .

We had a rumor in the paper yesterday that Jeff. Davis is dead. . . . It would be good news to me, and to you my pet. I don't think [Vice President Alexander] Stephens would attempt to keep the Confederacy afloat. . . . I am afraid we shall have war on our hands with France or England, or both, if our civil war is not ended soon. Neither one of them would insult or provoke us if our hands were not tied down. . . . I am sorry you met with such poor luck dunning Lambert. . . . I expect he will be as worthless as ever when the war is over. . . . The flux is presiding in Uncle Billy Evans' neighborhood. One child died yesterday. Another one of Myran Swift's boys — George[9] — has enlisted in the 8th Cavalry. Mullinix is afraid he will be drafted, and he says if he had the money to bear his expenses, he would go to your company at once. . . .
Dollie

Sunday Afternoon, Aug. 9th, 1863

My Dearest Love,

I have been thinking all day of that 9th of August one year ago, when we went to Iconium together, and went *home together*, and it has made me very sad darling. But I feel glad that any year of the time is passed. . . . I never look at the possibility hardly of your being gone two years longer. Oh my dearest, that must not be. . . . I feel sure it won't unless we have a war with France for England. I am still very uneasy about that. It would be so hard now after we have almost reached the fair haven of peace, to be thrust back upon another bloody and tempestuous sea of strife. . . . I don't think there will be much more fighting after the fall of Charleston and Mobile. . . .

. . . I don't want to buy things that I don't really need, and I don't need much until you come home. And then love, I shall not need *anything*. I shall have all I want. I shall be richer than any princess ever was. Last winter I used to ride along the National Road[10] and look at those comfortless mud-walled cabins (you remember them, darling) and feel like I would be willing to live in one of them all my life if I could only have you with me, and care for me. I don't think I shall ever care much for surroundings again, only what will make you comfortable and happy. I shall be happy with you my pet, if you conclude to live in a *tent* after you come home. . . .

Monday Evening, Aug. 10th, I went into my room a minute ago to get my paper out of my trunk, and almost stepped on quite a large snake lying on the floor. I was so scared (I was always afraid of snakes) that before I could do anything it ran under the bed. . . . I was too cowardly to follow it and hunt for it among the trunks stowed there. I am going to make a *raid* in there presently when the shower is over and it gets lighter. If I don't kill him or "take" him I shall be afraid to sleep in there anymore. I shouldn't fancy waking up in the night and finding a snake in my bed, ugh!

Well, I have just had a big hunt for my snake, love, but I couldn't find him anywhere. I guess he escaped outdoors while I was getting the shovel to kill him, and getting over my scare. If he will stay away now, it is all I ask of his snakeship. But what has become of the long letter I was going to write you this evening. It is all scared away I'm afraid. . . .

Tuesday Morning, Aug. 11th, This is a cool, clear, beautiful morning. There is no trace of the storm left. But how it *did* rain yesterday morning! For an hour it looked as if we should have another deluge. The travelers who stopped were a couple of preachers going home from quarterly meeting. They stayed till after the storm, and after supper, and then went on to Melrose. They are good Union men. One of them lives somewhere between Lagrange and Albia. He has a brother-in-law in the 36th. He said he knew you from reputation. He has seen a good many of the boys who have been home on furlough, and they all speak in very high terms of "Capt. Vermilion." I have heard that often since I came home to Iowa. It pleases me pet, and it makes me so sad too, because it reminds so forcibly of all I have lost while you are gone, sweet love. . . . While I think of it, love, I want to tell you that the Copperheads have nominated Gen. Tuttle for Gov. at last. I sincerely hope he won't accept. If he is an honorable or loyal man he can't, on that treasonable platform. . . . I want the 36th to give as good an account of themselves on the day of the election as they did on the Fourth. . . . Tuttle can't be elected, but I don't want him *near* elected. Think of Byington[11] and Mahoney going to the army for *their* candidate!
Dollie

Helena, Arkansas, Aug. 9, 1863
My Darling,

. . . I am sending my money to your father in care of H. K. Steele[12] of Albia. . . . The amounts marked you will pay out. . . . Mrs. Hancock is $50.00, Mrs. Carpenter[13] is $45 . . . Mrs. Tucker's[14] is $15.00 and Will's $50.00. The rest will be mine, which is yours my Dollie. Get your father to go over and get it of Mr. Steele. Tell your father to pay him for his troubles.

I will rent my farm next year provided I can to a good loyal man. . . . I would let it be idle forever before I would let a Copperhead have it. Tell Mr. Christie that there are too many rebels in his church for me to give anything to build a meeting house. When the war is over I will see about it. . . . See that my taxes are all paid at Centerville Dollie.[15]

W. F. Vermilion

Helena, Arkansas, Evening, Aug. 9, 1863
My Darling,

. . . We have to start on and get someone to agree to cook for us, for Dock can't go. I don't blame him much. And his family is here. And then he might get picked up and sold into slavery again. He is pretty sharp and is making money and saving it. The other day he came into my tent and told me he would change some silver for greenbacks. I told him I would change some. Lieut. May also spoke up and said he wanted some. Dock took out his purse containing some 15 to 20 dollars in silver. I looked at it and thought about it being worth 15 or 20 cents premium. I told him it was worth more than the greenbacks. "I nose dat, dat what I want to swap fo." So I did not take any. . . . He was sharp enough to know greenbacks would buy goods and that was what he wanted to change for. He intended to use the money. . . . The quicker we start out West the better. . . . The weather is warm but not so bad as you will imagine. In fact my Darling I would rather risk my chances on that trip than here in this sickly place. A few days ago I saw a cpl. from the 3rd Colorado regiment Infty. . . . Had marched from Denver City to Mo. And from there to this place (they came with Davidson's command) and had lost but 3 men, and one of them was killed by accident. As a general thing marching is healthy. . . . If I had got the position in the regiment I am entitled to I would get to ride. Col. Kittredge is commanding a Brigade, and as neither the Lieut. Colonel nor Major is here the Cap. of Company A takes command of the regiment. They will not let me ride if they can help it. But let them have their way this time. . . . A drunken low life Col. and Governor who puts my destiny in his hands, shall be remembered as long as I live. . . .

W. F. Vermilion

Helena, Arkansas, Aug. 10, 1863
My Darling,

... The boys are all in a jubilee over the prospect of a change.... Our Old Dock will not go with us.... We have got another man to go with us though.... We want him to Jayhawk for us as much as anything else. As we pass farms he must slip out and get chickens and fruit.... You must not be uneasy about me my love.... We have to work to put this rebellion down and my Darling we have never done much of it. Other regiments have been on the march almost constantly. We have nearly always been still. We may not have much of it to do, but if we do it will be nothing more than our share of the work. Look at the 2nd, 6th, and 7th Iowa regiments. What work they have done. Shall we complain even if we are called upon to work now?
Will Vermilion

Aug. 11, 1863, . . . Dollie, you work too hard.... Please don't do it love, not but what I want to have the work done. I want you to get a girl to do all the hard work. You have money enough my Darling to pay it. You won't have good health as long as you work so hard.... When we were keeping house you always worked hard and you were sick a good portion [of] the time....
W. F. Vermilion

Tuesday Night, Aug. 11th, 1863
My Dearest Love,

... Mr. Maiken has taken his cattle and ours, and gone to Chicago with them.... He only *took* 5 of our young steers and the oxen and Muley. He said the other steers were not fat enough to do at all. I fear you will not like my selling out the best ones and having the rest left on my hands. But I couldn't avoid it darling.... Mr. Maiken weighted all our cattle here. Father saw the table of weights, but couldn't remember, only that the oxen weighed over 3,200p. I am getting two cents and a half for the steers, and a cent and a half for Muley. I believe though, Mr. Maiken will pay me every cent they bring above the expense and trouble, if he should

find a better market than he expected. There is not much hope of that however. I guess I will get $225.00 for them anyway. . . .
Dollie

Thursday Evening, Aug. 13th, 1863
My Own Dear Love,

. . . I have the weights of all the cattle I sold to Mr. Maiken. . . . They weighted 3,164 lbs., and came to $79.10. That is pretty well for them. . . . The other 5 steers weighed 5,256 lbs and came to $191.40. The cow, 1,016, came to $55.24. Are you satisfied about these my pet? If you are not, if you think I have not done right, you must tell me, dear one. I will do as well as I can.

Darling, can you guess what I have been doing today? I have helped old Mr. Hickcox build an *oat stack*! Father had his oats to stack this afternoon, and when those men came he went off with them, and thought he could get George Hickcox to help his father. But George was sick, and I told the old man I would help him; so I pitched up the bundles and he built the stack. When we got about half done it fell down, and we had it to do all over. We got done at last and I was pretty near exhausted. I could not help make another one today. But . . . I believe I am a very good hand at such work. You did not know I could boast any such accomplishment, did you love?

Later, Father . . . sold Capitala for $100 and brought me the money. The man offered $75 for Jake, and he offered to take $80. They would have given it, but they were afraid he was taking "big head." But they will be here to look at him again in a few days, and perhaps they will take him. . . . I have put the $100 away for you. That makes the even $1,000 that I have, saving for you. . . . And I will keep it for you, every dollar of it, till you come home, if somebody doesn't rob me love. I am afraid of this somewhat. I asked you to send me a revolver, but it has not come. Are you not willing for me to have one dear? If I had a chance I would buy one, but I would much rather have one that *you* had sent me. I should feel safer if I had one and knew how to use it. It would break us up to lose this money, my pet. I think I ought to have some means of defense. . . .
Dollie

Friday Evening, Aug. 14th, 1863

My Own Darling,

...I am so afraid you are gone to Little Rock. You will have hard marching and hard fighting out there, and it makes me sick with fear to think of it. If you get sick or wounded, my love, way out there what will you do.... May the good God watch over my love! I cried darling, when you told me how you felt when you left Ind. My sweet dear! I thought your Dollie suffered enough then for both of us. But I will pay you darling for all that when you come home. I will spend all my life paying you. I will never forget all the bitter experiences of the last year my pet. I often think if you were here now that the longest life would be too short to prove all my love and devotion. But you shall never see one moment's trouble, my dear, if your Dollie can shield you from it. Oh, if you were only here. If you never come, *life has nothing for me....*

What made you get to thinking of Rynerson, my pet? You must not do that. It is seldom indeed that thoughts of them even cross my mind. I love my husband, and I *don't* like his enemies. I never think of them scarcely. You wanted me to tell you if I saw them while I was in Indiana, and all I heard about them. It was not much, and was nothing good. I heard no one speak well of Rynerson. Aunt Anna told me a good many very mean things about him. I saw him a moment as I came home. I told you about it dear, but I will tell you again, as perhaps you never got my letter. I started from Greencastle at 10 o'clock P.M. and when we got about Paris Ill. our locomotive ran into a ditch, or something, and upset. There was quite a smash-up, and we had to sit there in the dark and rain all night. You talked about feeling lonesome my pet, and having no friends as you came back: how do you think your poor Dollie felt that long night? I can't tell you love, and I don't want to now. The only thing that kept my courage up was the thought that I was coming to *loyal* Iowa, to *our home*. The next morning we started again and soon got to Matoon, and as soon as the cars stopped Rynerson jumped off the train and stepped along the platform just before my window. He didn't see me. We had been in the same train all night. How thankful I felt that we got into different cars.

I didn't want to see him or speak to him. The sight of him made my blood almost boil. He looked thin and haggard as a man always will look sooner or later who had done wickedly. I did used to think he was my friend, love, but I don't think so now. He tried to injure you, my darling, and I shall never forgive him for that. But then he didn't injure us pet, did he? He didn't know me, and above all *he didn't know you.* He didn't know what love could accomplish. He caused us trouble for the time, that was all he did darling, but don't thank him that it was no worse. If I ever was thankful for anything in my life, sweet love, I thank God that you came back and took me in your arms, and forgave me, and loved me. If you had been less noble than you are, you never would have come back for me. I don't know what he thinks of us now, or whether he wishes us harm, and we won't care my own darling what he thinks or wishes, will we? I don't think he will ever cross our path again. When I compare his conduct with yours love, how utterly contemptible it seems to me now. But then I didn't know it dear. But he is a poor subject to waste so many words on. . . .

We got a long letter from Matt. . . . Matt says their share of the battle at Shiloh was nothing compared to the charge at Jackson. The balls and shells fell in front, behind, around him and the shells ploughed up the ground under his feet, but he adds "2 years from the day they entered the service the regiment marched with flying colors into the blackened capital of Miss." He is grieving sorely about the loss of his friend Hickcox. . . . He had marked his grave, and has his money and what little property he had left in his possession, and is going to send them home. . . .

Friday night, Little Billy May is no better yet. They think he will die. I am so sorry. The flux is as bad as ever . . . in that vicinity. There are cases in almost every family. Julia has sent for me to go there. I am a little afraid. I am sorry for Julia from my heart, but she has her husband with her. If I were to go and should get sick I would have nobody to take care of me. For your sake my love, I want to be careful. If the disease comes to me at home, then I must do the best I can. There are no cases on this side of the river now. . . . I think perhaps I will go. . . . I shall hate it so much if Billy dies. He is a good child. Poor Julia. They have been unfortunate every

way almost since they came home. The only horse they had died a few days ago. He has no team at all now. . . .
Dollie

Home, Aug. 15th, 1863
My Dearest Love,

. . . The signs are better I think in regard to "French mediation." The news of the fall of Vicksburg and the rout of Lee seem to have had a good effect in Paris. . . . In the last 4 weeks our Iowa traitors have been doing their best — or worst — to imitate their brethren in New York. They are getting desperate but we have faith in our noble Governor. . . . You have heard of the trouble in Keokuk County I suppose.[16] I will send you the report of one of Gen. Curtis's Staff Officers. . . . Gov. Kirkwood doesn't believe in speeches nor blank cartridges to disperse Copperhead mobs in this latitude. Byington and the other apostles of "peace" are out now in a new manifesto to the faithful entreating them to go to their public meetings *armed*, and ready to defend their speakers! Let them try it. It didn't pay particularly at South English. If they "sow the wind, they will reap the whirlwind." I think it is the last card of frightened and desperate bad men. . . .

Later, The age has gone by when long wars were possible I think. Now the destruction of life and property is too great, too awful. No nation can sustain such a war as this many years. And ours has lasted two years and a half. The country could endure the loss of property but not the frightful loss of men, of her best men. I think a great deal depends on the way the elections go this fall in the Northern states. . . . Kentucky has done well. If the North generally follows her example, I think it will prove the last feather required to break the camel's back. I have no fear for Iowa or Ohio. I wish I could say as much for Indiana and Illinois. I don't know much about New York or Penn. Union victories in our elections will be an onset of sure defeat to the rebels, and they will accept it as such I think. Northern traitors know this, and hence their desperate and frantic efforts to bolster up their failing cause. They will not succeed my love. A righteous Providence will not let them succeed. I want them defeated pet. I want the defeat to be complete, and utter, and overwhelming. They are just as much our en-

emies and the enemies of our country as the bolder rebels you fought at Helena. Iowa soldiers have the privilege of fighting *all* their foes. The cowardly ones they can't reach with their muskets; they can *with their votes*. . . .
Dollie

Clarendon, Arkansas, Aug. 16, 1863
My Darling,

We marched into this place yesterday evening. . . . We were 4 days marching from Helena to this place. It was a hard march. We averaged full 15 miles a day. I stood it first rate, much better than I expected. . . . There is much excitement. Only one division — ours — is here from Helena. We look for two others in a few days. Gen. Davidson and command are here about 7,000 strong. We will remain here for a week or 10 days, then go on for Little Rock. . . .
W. F. Vermilion

Monday Evening, Aug. 17th, 1863
My Own Dear Love,

. . . I don't think you will ever want to live at Woodside anymore, and I don't either. There are so many traitors over there love, and it doesn't seem like home now. It doesn't look like it did when we left it. There is not a flower nor a blade of blue grass to be found in the yard. It looks like it did when we first went there. . . . I know you would rather live in town somewhere, and I think you ought to my pet. I shall like any place where *you* are, sweet love. I would be willing to live at Woodside always if you wanted to live there, but I know you don't, and I don't blame you dear one. We can find us a little home somewhere, can't we love? I think it will be the happiest home in the world, don't you my pet? Matters are very quiet up here now, more so than they have been before since I came home. But it is not so generally in the state. Perhaps the excitement has not reached this out-of-the-way corner yet. . . . C. C. Cole[17] speaks at Centerville next Saturday. He is a good war Democrat. Shall I tell you the joke [the] Christies have on me? They think it is a little rich that I am not "above suspicion," and it will show you how people feel here. I wanted to get old Mr. Hinton[18] to make me a keg to put up pickles in, and I got father to speak to him about it, which he has just done. The old cooper hesitated and made excuses about the keg, and at last said "Well, just tell me one thing — is she *for the Union?*" Father told him yes, I was an abolitionist, a very black one. "Oh, well tell her I'll make the keg right away." And if I hadn't been an abolitionist he wouldn't have made it for me, as if I had never seen a pickle!

Tuesday Forenoon, Aug. 18th, Father is going to write to Matt. . . . They only have 18 men in Company "E" now. They are anxious to get back to Tennessee again. In 11 months from yesterday their time will be out. I wonder how many of the 18 will live to see that day! I trust it will find them all safe at home. It surely can't be that the war will last till then. 10 months ago today my darling we got to father's in Indiana. What a long, long 10 months! Does it not seem longer to you than any two years ever did before? It seems like an age to me sweet pet. . . .

I am very anxious about matters at Charleston. I think Gilmore will succeed after awhile, but it is hard to wait so long. There is talk of another leader for the Army of the Potomac. Isn't it enough to make one heartsick darling? Don't you wish they would give that command to Rosecrans? I do wish it so much. He could lead those scarred veterans into Richmond. . . .

The 8th Cavalry boys are gone. 7 went from this township. Matt Hays has gone again and his younger brother.[19] Many boys have gone not over 17 years of age. I hope the draft will be hurried along. The 8th is to rendezvous at Dubuque. There is a rumor that they were sent there to keep an eye on the traitors up there. They say George Stewart is nominated for Representative again in Appanoose County. . . . Stewart of course will be sent up again. It is too bad, darling. . . .
Dollie

In Camp near Clarendon, Arkansas, Aug. 17, 1863
My Darling,
    Yesterday morning I mailed you a short letter. It was . . . the best I could do at that time for I was tired and there was more noise in camp then than I ever heard at one time almost in my life. I told

the boys they had to stop it or I would have to resign. . . . We have no surgeon with the regiment. Our two assistants are both left at Helena. . . . Doctor Sawyer,[20] our first surgeon, is Division Medical Director. He has too much to do to attend to the regiment as it should be. . . . Yesterday morning they talked of having me detailed. But they soon found there was some difficulty in it. The medical department is a separate thing in the army and my commission is in the army regularly detailed. The necessity of the case may cause them to waive the irregularity. . . . My objections are — there is so much work. No one man can do it and do it well and of course I don't want to do it any other way. If they would give me a good Hospital Steward and plenty of drugs and nurses and then furnish me a horse to ride I might take the place, not otherwise.

The cavalry have been crossing the river ever since yesterday morning. The 1st Iowa is crossing now. Davidson's 7,000 cavalry I suppose will go in advance and the infantry in rear. . . .

. . . I do hope I will get a good lot of letters from Dollie. I know they are on the road. She has sent them and they are good ones too.

I will put this up now love and take it to the office lest they send the mail out before I get there. . . . It would not do you know to sit here scribbling too long and not get to send it at all. Then you would think your husband didn't love you. You must not think that my good Darling, for I do love you more than all else in this world. . . . Do you ever hear from father's folks?
W. F. Vermilion

Tuesday Night, Aug. 18th, 1863
My Own Darling,
. . . Mr. Brown is here. He lives in Drakesville now. He says Col. Drake was home on a furlough expecting to stay several weeks, and that he received a dispatch from Gen. Steele on the 10th inst. recalling him at once to his regiment, as the expedition was about starting. He started back next morning after staying at home only four days. Brown says he was highly pleased at the prospect of going into Arkansas. He said the country is healthy and the water good, and he didn't think the army would march more than from 6 to 10 miles a day. And he didn't think they would have much fighting to do. He said if the war didn't end before, he expected to

winter in Little Rock.... I don't know what has brought Mr. Brown up here.... His two oldest boys are gone to the war. They are in the 8th Cavalry. One is 16, the other only 15 years old. He tried to keep them from going he says, but he couldn't do anything with them so he just gave them certificates and told them to "pitch in." He thinks they will do well and I hope they may.... We have talked about nothing but the war since he came. He got a letter from his brother at Fillmore Ind. last week, and he writes that the Copperheads are as malignant as ever, determined to resist the draft to the last.... Brown says Col. Kittredge is sick and that Col. Drake said he would never get up again. If he dies love, I fear you will have a worse officer in command of the regiment than ever. Brown says Col. Drake is a good man but he doesn't think he has the qualifications of a good Colonel....

We got a letter from Jimmy this evening. He is all right, only his eyes are very weak and sore. I got a good letter from Matt yesterday. He is in good spirits but it seems he can hardly bear to speak of their late battles. He says we up here talk lightly of a "gallant charge" little knowing what the horrible words mean. He knows what happens after, and the thoughts of it are enough to make one sick, and long and pray that they may be spared forever the sight of another "gallant charge." He won't talk about Jim Hickcox.... I am afraid our brave Gen. Blunt is about to be trapped out in the territory. He can master the situation if anybody can though[21]....
Dollie

Thursday Night, Aug. 20th, 1863
My Own Dear Love,

10 months ago today I saw you look back, one rapid glance only, as you were whisked away from me. That was the last look between us darling.... There was such a look in your dear eyes, pet. I can see it yet. We have lived apart 10 long months my love. And today I miss you so much and feel the separation more keenly a thousand times than I did the day you started. That is how I forget you my darling. But courage my pet. 10 months more I think will see us living in our own little home, all the happier for the long bitter separation....

General Tuttle has accepted the Copperhead nomination for Governor in a rather tame letter. He doesn't say a word about *their* platform but he lays down his own, which isn't a bit like the convention's. I am sorry he has accepted but if a brave man will ruin himself, why let him. I hope he will be beaten as badly as Fisher would have been, but it is not likely.

When father was in Albia he saw some soldiers just from Vicksburg. They knew all about Matt. He is doing well, says he doesn't want to come home till his time is up. He sent home his overcoat and Jim Hickcox's . . . money. Father got a letter from Will. . . . He didn't say anything about you. I wish he would always tell about you in his letters darling. Why can't he I wonder?

Saturday, Aug. 22nd, 1863, I heard yesterday that Billy May is getting well. . . . He is a good child, and he thinks a great deal of his "Uncle Doctor." Two more children from that neighborhood have been buried this week. Old Mr. Wright and his wife are out from Indiana.[22] They are at Greenwood's. . . . The old man is a good Unionist, but his wife was a Copperhead last winter. . . .
Dollie

Clarendon, Arkansas, Aug. 20, 1863
My Darling,
    . . . If you can't sell our stock for money, down the money, and we can't well keep the stock, though if we could till next June they would bring a good price. The steers I mean. I am afraid they are too young and light to take to market, though you and Mr. Maiken must be the judges. It won't break us if we don't get a big price my Darling.
    . . . No one can get a leave of absence now till this expedition is over. . . . Don't be uneasy love. There is not half as much danger of bullets as there is of sickness, and I am missing that so far. . . . Some think Price will run. It will be better for our cause if he stands and fights though we may lose a good many men. We must fight him before this country is cleared of rebels. . . .
W. F. Vermilion

In Camp 6 miles in the rear of Clarendon, Ark., Aug. 21, 1863
My Darling,

. . . A great many of our regiment are sick. I learned this morning that another one of our boys died in Helena a few days ago. His name was Robert Hardin.[23] He lived near Moravia and was as good a boy as I ever saw in my life. He did not suffer so long as some of the boys have had to. . . . Lieut. May is quite sick. He went to the Hospital this evening. . . . Will Kemper is quite well. So am I my Darling. My health is as good as it used to be in Iowa at this season for the year. . . . I don't know what I would weigh. Probably 145 or 150. That is enough, [is it] not?

We don't know when we will have to fight. . . . Our forces will have artillery. That will give us a great advantage. . . .

W. F. Vermilion

Monday Night, Aug. 24th, 1863
My Dearest Love,

. . . I went over to Julia's yesterday afternoon as I told you in my letter. . . . They are all well but little Billy. He is getting well but he can't sit up any yet. Julia is pretty cheerful. Humphrey seems very sad and doesn't talk much. He says he doesn't grieve about Annie any, that he knows it is better for her, but he is troubled about something I think. They don't think they will get their farm back before spring. They have a bad house where they are. I am afraid they have got behind a good deal. Humphrey isn't able to work any scarcely. I didn't hear much news love. Old Mr. Wright says affairs are worse in Indiana now than they have ever been before. The authorities have been trying to arrest the leaders in those mobs that destroyed the enrolling books in Putnam County, and there were 400 or 500 traitors collected and armed near Manhattan somewhere to defend them. They are after Sig Duckworth, (the leader of the Copperheads about Mt. Meridian) and he has run off and *come to Iowa*! I hope they will follow him and take him back. I should think they would from what I hear. I guess he is watched out here. He is a very mean man. His father is here too. Mr. Wright and his wife are going to stay out till fall. I hope I should get to see them. Julia is coming over here as soon as Billy gets well. She had the flux herself but was not dangerous. The sick people over there are getting well. . . . I didn't sleep much last night. It was the first time I had stayed there without you since we were moving. I thought of you every minute. . . . I don't want to go back unless you go with me. I missed you so much. But I miss you more every day, let me be where I may. Last night was the first I have stayed from home, I believe, since the first week I came home. I would rather stay at home and sleep in *our* bed, my pet. But I can hardly lie down on my good bed now, and think that you may be lying on the bare ground. . . .

Tuesday Morning, Aug. 25th, My Best Love, it is quite cold this morning. We had a pretty severe frost last night. More than half of our cucumber vines are killed. I haven't been out to look at anything else. I expect the corn is injured a good deal. . . .

We have just heard that Luther Roland is dead. He died at Mound City. . . . I should like to know how many of your company have died, and how many you now have doing duty. Father has just brought in some good watermelon and we have eaten all we could. . . . Father says the vines are nearly all killed by the frost. I am afraid they will all be gone before you come home, darling. I don't think I ever saw as cold weather in August before. . . .
Dollie

Tuesday Night, Aug. 25th, 1863
My Own Dear Love,

. . . The latest dispatches say General Davidson was near Little Rock and in sight of Price's pickets. But I don't know whether you are with Gen. Davidson or not. I think not from what you said in one of your letters. I don't know who commands the expedition nor how many troops are gone. Brown said Col. Drake thought there would be about 12,000. . . . It is thought Fort Sumter could not hold out much longer. Wagner and Gregg were silenced and the Charleston people were talking about defending the city street by street from the expected Yankee invasion. I do hope we shall hear before the end of the week that this Southern Gibraltar has fallen. They say Lee's army is demoralized and his men are deserting by hundreds every day. Bragg's army is still worse than his. . . . The draft is being made in New York and was passing off very quietly. No more danger from a Copperhead mob there. And after the draft is enforced in New York City, it can be anywhere. Small mobs in Indiana and Illinois will understand they had as well submit gracefully. Even Gov. Seymour seems to have had quite enough of riots.

I have heard no more about the draft in this state. . . . They are organizing a negro regiment at Keokuk and it is getting well underway. I don't know where the negroes come from.[24] Recruiting officers are named for all the southeastern counties. Nobody objects to it now. . . .

Wednesday Morning, Aug. 26th, My Dearest, Mr. Teater has just been here. John[25] and his wife are staying at Woodside. John says a good many of your men would have been dead before now if it had not been for you. He speaks very highly of you dear one, as everyone else does. Dollie is glad. John says he was pretty badly scared when the battle commenced at Helena, but after he had fired a few rounds he wasn't afraid. He says you are easily excited, but you were as cool as a man could be that day. Darling, it made me shudder yet to think of your danger there. And you may be in worse peril this moment. . . . Teater says he heard in Centerville that your expedition was going to Texas. I am afraid it will love, but they don't know anything about it in Centerville. Teater was there Saturday at the Union county convention. He says he never saw as strong Union feelings, and as much enthusiasm manifested in his life. Provost Marshall Shannon made a speech in which he got after Judge Harris[26] and literally flayed him alive. Harris made a feeble attempt to deny the charges Shannon brought against him, but it only made the matter worse and he gave it up. I have heard several people speaking of the affair as very rich. Teater says badly as he hated Harris he couldn't help feeling really sorry for him. The convention nominated Dr. Udell for the Senate and Capt. Walden[27] I believe for Representative. Anyhow he is a Capt. and a Democrat. . . . The Copperheads are almost in despair. . . . Since I ever knew anything about politics or parties I never saw near as much a predicament. No wonder their visages are long and doleful. . . . Our soldiers *will* whip their dear friends of the South

in nearly every engagement, the Government *will* enforce the draft in New York and wherever else it has a mind to; Jeff Davis *doesn't* take Washington nor Baltimore nor Philadelphia; he doesn't recruit his armies in Ohio and Pennsylvania; France and England don't interfere to save them; our soldiers don't talk of turning traitors and voting the Copperhead ticket, still they will vote! In view of all these things, is it any wonder that they are not joyful but sad? "What a man sows, that shall he also reap."
Dollie

Duvals Bluff, Ark., Aug. 26, 1863[28]
My Darling,
 . . . The railroad running from Memphis to Little Rock crosses [the] White River here. It is not finished from here to Memphis but it is to Little Rock. Probably Gen. Steele intends taking possession of it from here to Little Rock or as much of it as he can. General Davidson is out West some 20 or 30 miles with his forces. . . . The Surgeons are putting up extensive Hospitals here to accommodate the sick. The military says that this place is going to be permanently occupied. . . . We are soldiering now my Darling, no mistake. . . .
 I was weighed this afternoon. My weight is 153 pounds, a little too heavy yet. I ought not to weigh more than 145.[29] Will is well. Lieut. May is well again. . . .
W. F. Vermilion

Thursday Morning, Aug. 27th, 1863
My Dearest Love,
 . . . Old Mr. Black is up from Missouri.[30] He . . . said he wouldn't come back here to live at all. Martha McKinley is married again. Tell Will that I got a letter yesterday from Emily Cox.[31] There is not much news in it, only a few days before she wrote some troops came down from Indianapolis to Mt. Meridian and marched off a number of the leading Copperheads. . . . They are to be tried at Indianapolis for destroying the enrolling books. . . . The rest of the traitors there are all pretty badly scared. She didn't say a word about our folks there. Mary Allen was sick.[32]

I have just read Gen. Grant's report of the Vicksburg campaign. . . . The reading of this report has largely increased my faith in Grant. What wonderful energy he must have! Only to think love that last winter and spring when he was sending out expeditions and digging canals, and the army was mystified and the papers complained that "Grant kept his own counsel," and nobody knew what he meant, he knew no more how he was going to take Vicksburg than you or I? The work was before him and he intended to accomplish it, but *how* was a question that no doubt troubled him far more than it did the busy correspondents who volunteered their advice and criticisms. But through it all I think his courage never gave way. When one plan failed he coolly adopted another — but you must read the report. . . . He can not only *make* history, but he can write it as well. I am afraid you can't get any papers where you are darling, and I am going to send you some more. If you have any they are not Iowa papers and you will like one from home. . . .

Last night was the coldest "spell" we have had yet. . . . I slept under two comforts!
Dollie

Duvals Bluff, Ark., Aug. 28, 1863
My Darling,

. . . We are camped in an old field and it has been just about as dusty as you ever saw till this morning just before day there came a good heavy rain. It commenced about 3 o'clock and rained on till long after daylight. The boys and nearly all the line officers got quite wet though I don't know if we are any the worse off this afternoon for it. . . . We have nothing but a fly which we put up to keep the sun off of us, and a little of the rain. The field officers have good wall tents and everything else that is comfortable. Don't you see it is something to be a field officer? We are now what old soldiers call soldiering. If it is not I don't want an introduction. . . . Will is doing better than he has ever done since we first came into the Service. Davenport is in Keokuk in the Hospital. Hancock is not very well and is not capable of doing the business. He is a good clever old fellow, perfectly willing to do all he can. But Will has all the business — the orderly's business — to do and he pitches in pretty well. If he doesn't watch it we will make something of him yet. He is a good noble fellow. Always kind and always willing. Lieut. Wright is not very well liked but he is a good duty Lieut. The reason the boys don't like him is *he makes them mind* especially when he gets out of humor. He is harder on the boys [than] Lieut. May. He seldom tries to shift the responsibility on me, which is not the case with all Lieuts. and sergeants. . . .

. . . I have nothing more to say about our business. You know more about it than I do. I am not going to get to come home soon enough to attend to it myself. So go ahead love and attend to it yourself. You will make a good businessman yet, won't you? You can I know if you will try. . . .

Tell Mullinix we are soldiering now just as he and I have often talked of. Tell him it is harder work than plowing yet I am able to do my part. There is not a line officer in the regiment but has lost more time from sickness than I have. 29 out of 30 have failed more than I have. Tell him he had better stay at home. The war will soon be over. He will not be likely to be drafted. Out of so many he will not be likely to be the lucky one in the Lottery. There is no man I would rather have in my Company than him, yet I feel that he is needed at home. Many good men are needed there even more than are now there. His volunteering may save some Copperhead from coming. . . .

W. F. Vermillion [*sic*]

Sunday Evening, Aug. 30th, 1863
My Own Darling,

. . . I have not heard a word from you since you left Helena, almost 3 weeks! I know my darling, I grieve too much about you. I ought to be braver for your dear sake if nothing else—but I am not brave my pet. I resolve every day that I will do better and be more courageous, but I fail all the time and I can't help it. If you could have come home a little while I could do better I think. But I know it was not your fault my love. I know I ought not to murmur that you are sent out into more active service, and I don't sweet love. . . . But I love you so much and I am afraid some harm will come to you. . . . I have been writing to Matt today. . . . I got a long and good letter from him. . . . He thinks the war will soon be ended unless the rebels get some foreign aid. He says he wouldn't be surprised to find ourselves involved in a war with England. . . . Most of the boys say they are willing to soldier it 2 or 3 years longer for the sake of a chance to give John Bull a lesson that he will remember. He doesn't think they can "set the Confeds up to housekeeping."

Fort Sumter was about to surrender on the 23rd, the date of the last dispatches. Gen. Gilmore had commenced throwing shells into the city from his batteries *five miles* distant. This had brought forth a bitter remonstrance from Beauregard,[33] and Gen. Gilmore then gave him 24 hours to remove the women and children. This looks like going to in earnest. . . .

Monday Afternoon, Aug 31st, My Dear One, This is the last day of summer. I am glad of it. It has been such a long summer to me. And then every day that passes brings the hour of your return that much nigher. . . . The weather is as beautiful as it can be. The nights are cold but the days clear and calm and bright. They are just such days as you always loved. I never admired autumn weather you know. It is always the saddest season of all the year to me. But if the autumn brings you with it this time I think I shall always love it in future.

I was going to Woodside tomorrow but now Wrights are coming. . . . Father talks of going over to look at our cattle there. He offered me $90 for the 7 that are left over there. I asked him $100. He said he must see them before he gave that. Since then I saw Mullinnix and he says they are not worth that much. There are 2 fine heifers and fine steers — one a yearling. The 2 Zintz steers are not worth much I'm afraid. But I don't want to take less than $100 for them. . . .

Later, It is nearly 10 o'clock my darling, but I want to talk a little to my "Peaches" before I go to bed. The rest are all gone to bed. But I don't want to sleep. Mr. Wright and his wife are here. We have had a long talk, mostly about the war. The old man is as earnestly loyal as anyone you ever saw. And the old lady is now, though I heard last winter that she was not right. It might not have been true. They have told me a good deal of news but nothing very in-

teresting. Affairs there are getting desperate, or rather more desperate. They say John was in the mob that destroyed the enrolling books. He doesn't deny it. They say that father is bitterer than ever; that he said he didn't want to hear a letter from a loyal man read in his house. . . . Henry is all right still. They say he is just as firm in his loyalty as ever a boy was: I knew they could turn him when they could the course of the Mississippi, and not before. . . .
Dollie

Duvals Bluff, Ark., Aug. 30, 1863
My Darling,
. . . Just as I expected the Army of the Potomac is lying idle. . . . It is not the practice of that army to move rapidly or do anything when not compelled to. It seems as though Lee can checkmate any Commander in that Country. When will the condition of things change?

Yesterday I got two letters from you. . . . $225 is a very good price for the 8 head. . . . Let Mr. Hancock have Evans'[34] note if he will take it, no odds how long he wants to pay it in. His note is good. Evans is not. In all probability Evans himself will never pay it. . . .

. . . Neither Thom, John or father has ever written me a line since I came into the Service. They don't want to correspond with an Abolitionist I suppose. All right. If they don't want to have anything to do with that sort of people they had better not write me sure enough. . . .
W. F. Vermilion

Tuesday Afternoon, Sep. 1st, 1863
My Dearest Love,
. . . Old Mr. Wright and his wife were here and we sat up late talking, then I wrote to you awhile after the rest went to bed. . . . I didn't get to talk with them a great deal. I may see them again before they go back. I sent Jane a nice book — one of mine. . . . I am glad I am not there now my darling. There is almost open war in many places in that state. Matters are worse than ever. . . .

Wednesday Morning, Sep. 2nd, Oh darling, what do you think? Jimmy's come! Just as I was writing that last sentence someone said "Good morning" and I looked up and there stood Jimmy! I was glad to see the boy. He came from Lagrange this morning. His eyes are pretty bad, not painful but weak. Hawk Kendall[35] came with him. He looks considerably like a soldier. Almost the first questions he asked were about you and Will. My pet, I can't write now. . . .

Dollie

Thursday Afternoon, Sep. 3rd, 1863

My Own Darling,

. . . Jimmy came yesterday just when we were least expecting him. . . . He is all right except his eyes, and I hope they will get better before he goes back. He has gone over to Mr. Jenison's[36] this afternoon. When Will was here he didn't want to go anywhere hardly; it isn't so with Jim. He is going to see everybody he says, that's what he came for. He is in the best of spirits, likes a soldier's life above all others. Says when the war is over he is going to "settle" in Springfield. He is never coming home to live and work on the farm. . . . He is in earnest about joining the regular service. He has seen some hard service but he won't tell anything about it, only as we ask him something and make him tell. . . . Father got a letter from Mr. Steele today and he says your money is there safe. . . . I was getting a little uneasy about it, it had been a long time coming, but it is all right I guess. Mr. Maiken came up here yesterday to pay me for our cattle. He paid me $225.75. He says he barely saved himself by taking them to Chicago. If he had been a few days later he would have lost considerable. . . . I have put the money away for you sweet love, and I will keep it for you till you come. Don't you remember how saving we used to be of a few dollars my pet, and how little money we had sometimes, and how much you hated to be poor? I think of it dear one and I save the money for you as carefully as I can. My darling shall have plenty of money when he comes home. I have $1250.00 *put away for you love*, and I have some besides. . . . I want you to tell me love what to do with the corn. It is going to be a good price before next year if we can get it taken care of. Some think it will be worth a dollar a bushel before spring but I hardly think that. My only fear is that if *Teater gathers it honestly* it will be stolen from the pen. . . .

Mr. Maiken . . . wanted me to go to Centerville to a great Union meeting next Monday. Senator Harlan[37] speaks. He wants everybody to go from this neighborhood. He says they are actually going to try hard to carry Appanoose County against the Copperheads this fall. He thinks the prospects pretty good if everybody who loves our cause will only *try*. . . .

I have been sewing. . . . I sent by father and bought me a new dress — yellow — the other day, and I am making it up. It is pretty I think. I want some nice dresses to wear when you come sweet pet. They won't do me any good till then. A year ago yesterday we broke up and moved from Woodside. It has been such a long year. I hope the next year will be a happier one for us my pet.

Friday Morning, Sep. 4th, My Love, All this week we have had company and bustle till this morning. Now there is no one here but mother and me. . . . Mother has been very uneasy about you and Will. . . . She says she *feels* like something has happened to you. I never tell her that I am troubled. Yesterday all day she would speak of you every few minutes and say she never wanted to hear from you as badly in her life. She is very childish. I don't know what made her get to thinking so much about you now. If she is anxious about you dear one, how do you think your Dollie gets on? But we won't talk about that love, for your Dollie doesn't do as well as she ought, with such a brave noble husband to encourage her *and love her*. You must not scold me till you come home . . . then you may scold just as long as you please — till I kiss you and make you hush. . . .

Friday Night, Sep. 4th, My Own Love, There is one dispatch that says Steele's Expedition is on White River 45 miles from Little Rock and that the enemy was in front in large force. The pickets were skirmishing every day and a hard battle was expected. . . . There is a rumor that Gen. Blunt has fought a battle . . . and been badly beaten. I hope it is not so, and I think not. Blunt is not the man to be defeated. . . . The news from Charleston is not so encouraging. The "Gibraltar" is not taken yet. I begin seriously to fear that there is something wrong in the management of our forces there. There are complaints that the navy has not done its share of the work. We shall soon know, for whatever is done I remember Vicksburg and try to possess my soul in patience. . . .

Jim is out somewhere tonight. . . . It is too quiet here for him when we have no company. . . . I don't enjoy his visit home like I did Will's. But I ought hardly to say this, ought I love. He is very bitter against Copperheads and traitors. He says some of the best men in his company talk of voting for Tuttle, thinking him all right. I trust they will get enlightened before the election. . . . Dollie

Saturday Evening, Sep. 5th, 1863
My Own Dear Love,

. . . I am dull today darling. I got up before 3 o'clock this morning. Father started just at daylight. You know I never liked to get up early, don't you?

You can't guess sweet pet what I have been doing today! I have been *shooting*. Don't you laugh. Jim has a revolver and he has been learning me to use it. . . . I *can* shoot love. Out target was a little scrap of white paper tacked to the gate post. Jim made the best shot and I the 2 next best. I planted one ball about 2 inches from the center and I think that was pretty well for the first day, don't you? I shall try it again one of these days. How will you like it if I beat you when you come home? Wouldn't I laugh at you more than ever?

Sunday Morning, Sep. 6th, My Love, Father brought me two letters from you. . . . I am so sorry that so many of the men are sick. . . . Don't get sick love. . . . What would we do if you should be sick away out there? Ever since you started from Helena my greatest fear has been that you would be killed or wounded. . . . This is a beautiful September day, calm and warm and hazy. The leaves are beginning to fall, "brown and red." Everything looks so calm and peaceful that I sit here and wonder that there can be war and carnage and suffering in the world. Alas darling, I have only to look at the vacant chair beside me and your letters lying on my table to realize all too painfully the dreadful fact. . . . When I think only of ourselves — of your hardships and dangers, of the dread uncertainty of the future, I am almost wild. . . . But when I remember the peril of our country and the noble cause you are defending, and the thousands of patriots who have sanctified it with their blood I feel ashamed of my weakness, and proud that I am a soldier's wife; and that in giving you to the war I have given a priceless offering to our country.

Evening, Father and mother . . . stopped a few minutes to see Hawk Kendall. He and his wife were coming down to Thompsons' but there were 20 people there and they wouldn't get off, so Miranda cannily sent her little children — one a baby — down here with mother, and then she would have to come.[38] She didn't get along for 2 or 3 hours but the baby was played off on the crowd. It is too bad the way people impose on nearly every soldier that comes home. I know they do it out of proud admiration of the soldier, but they ought to remember that they come home to see their families. Father got your money yesterday. I have put it away for you my darling. We will send Mrs. Hancock's to her and leave the other at Mr. Phillips'. Father says he will see Mr. Dooley. . . .

Don't be uneasy about me, love. I don't work too much. I could have a girl but we don't need one. When I thought you were coming home soon I engaged Lizzy Hickcox to come and work while you stayed, and I will get her whenever you come. Then I can stay with you every minute I can. You tell me to sell our stock. . . . So much corn has been ruined by the frost that people are almost giving away their stock. I guess I shall let father have ours. It is the best I can do. He can buy for less than he has offered me. . . .
Dollie

In camp near Brownsville, Ark., Sept. 5, 1863
My Own Dollie,

On the last day of Aug. we left Duvalls Bluff and on the first day of this month arrived at this place. The last day we marched a distance of 23 or 24 miles. . . . I walked all the way but was tireder than you ever saw me. . . . Then we were ordered out to Bayou Mateo . . . where it was supposed Price and his command were. But when we got there we found no enemy. The advance guard of Cavalry reported having seen a few rebel pickets. . . . We . . . marched back last night — that is got here last night at dark all tired again. Today we are lying idle and rested tolerably well. . . .

I know you work too hard, my Darling. I am not complaining because you are working at your father's for you are living there. But you have money. Hire your hard work done. . . . I don't want you to work yourself to death while I am in the Army. Lieut. Wright has just stopped David Barnhart and John Clark [39] from fighting. I am glad he had it to do, and he doesn't mind it. . . .
W. F. Vermilion

Tuesday Morning, Sep. 8th, 1863
My Own Dear Love,
. . . I went to the Union meeting sure enough. I had the headache in the morning and tried to beg off, but father and Jim wouldn't let me and I'm glad now that I went for it was the grandest day Appanoose County ever saw. Hickcox's and Jenison's girls [40] went with us in the wagon. We started over early and got to Mr. Maiken's just as they were starting with a four-horse team and the buggy. Mrs. Maiken came out and insisted on my going in the buggy with her folks, and as it was easier I willingly agreed to it. We got to Centerville soon after 10 o' clock. The wagons had been pouring in at every crossroad and by the time we got there our procession was nearly a mile long. We paraded around the public square awhile, where there were already crowds of wagons and horses and people, and the men shouted themselves hoarse, and the clouds of dust almost blinded me. Mr. Maiken was just driving out of the line at last to go out of the dust when some man dashed up and told him to hold on, there were *400* wagons just coming in from the South. We got back in line and pretty soon they came pouring in — flags and music and banners; wagons and flags and music and banners in what seemed an almost endless stream. I never saw the like scarcely. Then they formed a procession of wagons *5 deep* and paraded awhile and dust was so thick we could hardly see our nearest neighbor, but people didn't mind that. They were there to celebrate the Union. The meeting started with the singing of "Rally round the flag boys," and they did with a shout that was almost

deafening. Mr. Maiken said we were nothing but black abolitionists anyhow, and whether we were a few shades lighter or darker was of no consequence. Then we went out to the grove and ate our dinner and then was the speaking. Mr. Harlan was not there. They said he spoke 3 hours Saturday at Bloomfield and broke down completely, so that he was not able to come. Dr. Udell made a short and very patriotic speech. . . . Then Mr. Nourse of Des Moines made *the* speech of the day. I wish you could have heard him darling. I wished all day that you could be there. He is almost as fine a speaker as Grimes,[41] and resembles him very much. But he couldn't be heard [by] over half that vast audience so they divided the crowd and half of them went over to another hillside and listened to a judge somebody from Bloomfield. There were still more people than could hear Nourse. I can't tell you much about the speech my love; it was so good that any attempt to describe would not [do] it justice. I *wish* you could have been there, sweet pet. You would have felt that love for the Union was not dead in Appanoose County. It was a *political* meeting too. I often heard the remarks "We're *Stoning* Tuttle today," "We'll Stone Tuttle to death between now and the election," "His *stars* can't save him." I wouldn't have believed it possible to have such a meeting in Appanoose and I begin to think the election is almost safe. I thought . . . how it would cheer your heart on your long, toilsome marches to know how the soldiers were remembered at home. . . .

Later, There was a man here yesterday while I was gone to rent Woodside. He is from Lee County and his name is James A. Gustin.[42] He had been to see the place. . . . He is a sound Union man. . . . He came to the state a few years ago and bought a large farm where he still lives, but times set in hard and he couldn't pay for it and has to give it up next spring. He says he wants to come up here on account of the range for his stock. His only objection to Woodside is that there is no school near. . . . Father is quite taken with him and thinks I had better let him have the place. He had a choice of two farms in Davis County but he didn't like them so well as Woodside. The United Brethren [43] hold their conference this week between here and Moravia, and he told father he could learn all about him by inquiring of the presiding elder of this district. . . . Dollie

Tuesday Night, Sep. 8th, 1863

My Dearest Love,

. . . I have been reading your letter again darling. . . . And you tell me sometimes to burn your letters. Why pet, you don't know how your Dollie loves your letters. . . . When you come home to stay love, you shall have the letters — maybe — if you want them, but till you come I wouldn't burn one of them pet for 10 times their weight in gold. I couldn't my darling, and you won't blame me will you? The dispatches say Rosecrans and Burnside are moving, but where or for what immediate purpose I can't learn. . . . Dr. Udell said Monday in his speech that the war must be ended and the country saved in the next 2 years *or it never could be*. He felt as sure of that as that the sun would rise again. Mr. McClaran and Goldsberry[44] enlisted Monday in the 8th Cavalry. . . . It was said Goldsberry belonged to the K. G. C. I suppose he found that he had fallen into bad company. The Centerville Company in that regiment is not quite full yet. They say Clagget has started his Constitution again.[45] The first numbers are very mild. I think he will likely have a very wholesome regard for the feelings of sick and wounded soldiers. . . . The political campaign in Iowa is getting exciting. The Union men are putting forth all their strength. Grimes and Kirkwood and Harlan and Nourse and Wilson[46] and Bussey . . . and scores of other able speakers are going to every county in the state. There was hardly as much interest manifested before the Presidential election. And that was of hardly more importance to Iowa than this. The results of this election will tell our soldiers whether they are to be sustained and encouraged and protected or not. I don't fear the result in this state. . . . I only wish you were here my darling to help in the good work. Did you hear what General Grant said of Logan?[47] You know he was making telling speeches in Ill. When his furlough was up Grant gave him a further leave of absence, remarking that "While Logan was fighting Copperheads in Illinois he was still doing service in the field."

I am afraid you are not well love. You would weigh more than you do if you were stout I am sure. Oh my pet, don't get sick. John Teater says you were not very well when he left you. . . .

Dollie

Thursday Night, Sep. 10th, 1863
My Dearest Love,

. . . Jim is gone to a "singing" that was got up for him by some of the young folks. . . . There is to be a grand Union rally at Chariton next Wednesday. They are going to try to outdo everything of the sort that has been done. They will have many retired and furloughed soldiers. It will be a nice thing. Baldwin[48] is one of the managers and he was here today to get me to ride in the cavalcade. I told him I wouldn't go myself, but he should have my saddle and any service I could render the girls. . . . I didn't sleep much last night and my eyes are heavy tonight love. . . . If you were here I should not want to sleep a minute tonight. I would want to talk to you and hear you talk all night, and all day too. But you are not here my precious darling. If I sit up here hour after hour I must sit alone to my solitary bed, and meet with my love only in my dreams. Sancho Panza said "Blessed be the man who invented sleep."[49] I say Blessed be the man who invented dreams. . . .

Friday Evening, Sep. 11th, . . . You don't know how it hurts my feelings my precious love to think of your lying out in the rain without anything to shelter you. . . . I hope it doesn't hurt you darling any worse than it does me. When you come home dear one, Dollie will remember all these hardships and danger, and she will pay you then in kindness and love and petting for all of them, if she can. My captain won't be above being petted and spoiled a little, will he. If he is I shall just adopt a plan of "discipline" that is not known in the "Army Regulations."
Dollie

Camp near Little Rock, Sept. 12, 1863
My Own Dollie,

Here we are Dollie in full possession of the Capital of this state. We got here on the 11th inst. The infantry was not engaged.

The rebels were running when we got here. . . . The reports from the front are gloriously good. Our loss is estimated at 60. Indications go to show that we will remain here. . . . In fact if reports

be true we have no enemy to pursue for Price's army has gone up. I await now anxiously for the news from Charleston and Chattanooga.[50] If those 2 places have fallen we are all right. . . .
Will

Sunday Morning, Sep. 13th, 1863
My Own Darling,

. . . I did a large ironing and then we killed a big, fat "porker" and I had that to attend to. I work here, and attend to everything just as if it was all my own. Mother does a good deal but she has almost lost her mind and she is not capable of taking charge of anything hardly. . . . I don't think she can ever keep house by herself again. She used to be a good cook but now she can hardly get a meal that will do at all. She has failed sadly in the last year, and her deafness is much worse. . . . Father is good to me as he can be — a great deal better than he ever was when this was my home. He will do anything in the world for me. I believe he thinks he can't do without me. . . . He asks my advice about his work and all his plans, just as though I knew about such things. Whatever I think best he generally does. This didn't used to be his way. You know when you went away I thought I never would come back here and live. . . . But I get on a great deal better than I expected. It is not like *our home* my darling, but then I know no place can be like home without *you*.

People are excited about the election. . . . LeGrand Byington would like to be elected to the U.S. Senate and the fools he works with at home would like to help elect him. He knows and they know that if they fail in this contest they are all politically buried "more than 40 fathoms deep." It is "now or never" with them. . . . I have faith in a just cause and in Iowa "abolitionists" and I believe it will be all right when the votes are counted. I think every soldier's wife ought to be allowed to vote. . . . I must go and get some dinner cooking. If you could only be here, there would be more than 150 pounds of you dear one. You must weigh 30 pounds more than that. . . .

Sunday Night, Father saw a man from Albia today and he said they had news in yesterday's Hawk-Eye that Little Rock is captured without any hard battle. . . . It is said *all* of Morris Island is now in General Gillmore's possession. Fort Sumter is demolished and Wagner and Gregg captured[51]. . . . What do you think my pet of Jeff Davis calling for negro soldiers, and promising them *freedom* and 50 acres of land each? I thought the "chivalry" hated "small farmers." Won't they soon have "mudsills" among them at this rate? But darling, will the negroes bite at this tempting bait? Will they fight for their oppressors on any terms now? If they will I fear the war is not ended yet. But I hope Jeff is several months too late to accomplish much.

Monday Evening, Sep. 14th, My Dearest Love, One year ago today you started with your company from Iconium. . . . I have a bad headache today. I was very well this morning and was making a bed in the yard to plant my tulips, when the bees grew cross and one stung me on the forehead. I didn't know they could hurt so bad. It has made my head ache all day. They drove me from my work, just like rebel sharpshooters sometimes do our poor soldiers. . . . I saw Will McCully last night. He says Will is having the ague but is getting on finely in this respect, and so is Jake Grimes. Will says you are the *best man in the world.* "He just knows there isn't your equal anywhere." He would have been dead long ago he thinks if it had not been for you. The tears almost came in Will's eyes when he talked about it. . . . Does it not encourage you pet to know that you are *appreciated* among your men? I know you do all you can for them. *I know how good you are* better than poor Will McCully, but does it not make your duties lighter to hear how they talk about you when they come home? I think it does my precious one. Jimmy listened awhile and at last said "I do wish we had a good captain." He doesn't like any of his company officers much, but his captain is the worst. He thought everything of Blue while he lived. . . .
Dollie

In Camp near Little Rock, Ark., Sept. 13, 1863
My Darling,
    . . . On the 10th our troops began to move out of camp 10 miles below here at 3 o'clock A.M. and by 9 all were on the march that were intended to be put in the engagement. On the night of the

9th Gen. Steele had put a pontoon across the river about halfway between ou[r] camp and this place. We had not moved out more than a mile before we heard the report of artillery which we afterward learned was the report of the firing . . . in the contest over the bridge. Gen. Davidson was crossing his Cavalry Division and the rebels were trying to prevent, but he crossed and the rebels gave back. The firing continued occasionally until we got to near the bridge. Gen. Davidson had all of his command, which was about 6,000, on the south side of the river. We marched steadily up the river until we came to the rebel fortifications which we found deserted. They were all over the river and the sharp engagement which Davidson had but an hour before was with the rear guard. . . . The fighting was quite sharp for awhile, but the rebels soon gave way and Davidson marched in to the City and hoisted the *Stars and Stripes*. . . . Steele must have out generaled Price. At least all the prisoners and deserters agree in stating that they intended fighting us until we effected a crossing from below. As soon as the bridge was observed Thursday morning and they ascertained they could not drive Davidson from it they crossed on their pontoons . . . and skedaddled. . . . Brigadier General Kimball — the same who was wounded at Fredericksburg last winter and has since been operating around Vicksburg — has come up with us and is going to take command of one Division of the Army, probably the 2nd. Ours is the 3rd. He is a physician and lived in Martinsville Ills. during the last year I was there. I was quite well acquainted with him. He was an elector for Scott in 1852.[52] He was not much while he was in Ills. But a clever fellow and rather high minded. He was in the Mexican War with Col. Bowles but did not run with him. He took his company into another Regiment and fought until the end of the battle.[53] . . . I am going to call and see him, provided I don't learn that he is too aristocratic. If he is as he used to be he is not. They tell me he is quite a disciplinarian, almost too terrifying. . . .

W. F. Vermilion

In Camp near Little Rock, Ark., Sept. 14, 1863

My Own Darling,

. . . The pursuit of Price I fear will not amount to much. . . . He always gets out of the way, and reports always say "his army is badly demoralized," but he has always managed to get another army together again. . . . It will not be 3 weeks until Price will have another formidable army ready to contest our progress — until we get to him — then he will run and his army will be greatly demoralized. . . . Price never has done any good fighting, never done anything except at Lexington[54]. . . . From present indications the Railroad from here to Duvalls Bluff will be put in running operation just as soon as possible. . . . When the cars get to running we will get mail more regularly. . . . Don't be scared love because Captain Webb[55] died. . . . He had the ague before we got to Clarendon. He continued on duty too long and did not take medicine soon enough. Poor fellow, he left 4 orphan children but plenty to keep them. . . . As to our business Dollie you must do with that as best you can. . . . But money is plenty now and it must be a good time to collect debts. . . .

W. F. Vermilion

Tuesday Night, Sep. 15th, 1863

My Own Darling,

. . . I went to the post office this afternoon but I didn't get any letter, my darling. . . . It was a sore disappointment. But . . . I know it is not your fault, sweet love. . . . What a blessed thing it is my pet that we have *faith* in each other! When I don't get any letters for a long time, like it has been now, it troubles me nearly to death, but I don't doubt you my own love, not for one instant. . . . I have heard of some women who would not write to their husbands in the army, only just as often as they get letters from them. I don't *love* my "Peaches" that way, do I darling? Long suffering East Tennessee is liberated at last.[56] Thank God for that! She is freed from her tormentors, I trust, forever. Our victory is nonetheless important because it was bloodless. Gov. Andy Johnson has come out strongly in favor of immediate emancipation. . . . Everyone here is preparing to go to Chariton tomorrow to the great Union meeting. . . . Jim is going up in the cavalcade. They all went as far as Lagrange this evening. The ladies are to wear white riding dresses, blue scarfs, and red caps. The soldiers their uniforms. They will make quite an imposing appearance I think. . . .

Dollie

Thursday Evening, Sep. 17th, 1863

My Own Darling,

. . . I got a letter from Will today but it is an old one written the 22nd ult. It gives more particulars for your hard march from Helena. . . . Will doesn't grumble but makes very light of marching through the rain and lying on the bare, wet ground all night, with nothing for supper but a bit of meat and crackers. It seemed very hard to me darling, but Jim thinks it was a mere nothing. He says they ought to have been thankful that they had *meat* and crackers and the privilege of eating at all. He has seen the time when he would have given a "greenback" for one cracker, or all he had in the world for as many as he could eat. . . . He says he has been nearly starved and nearly frozen and marched without sleep till he could not stand up any longer, and he got fat on such treatment and isn't a whit the worse for it now. . . .

Friday Evening, Sep. 18th, My Dear Love, I went up to Mr. Sheeks this morning hoping there was a letter there for me, but I was disappointed again. . . . But I saw Isaac Sheeks. . . . He says Capt. Varner and Webb are both dead. Capt. Webb died soon after they started home — or back to Helena, and Capt. Varner just before they reached Keokuk. . . . Sheeks says of the 10 captains who went out a year ago only you and Joy are left. Is it any wonder my love that I am uneasy and troubled? He says you are very cheerful and not a bit homesick. . . . He tells the same story about your being so good to the men darling; about how they all like you. The old lady told me this. She said Isaac thought there was hardly another such man in the world and that he would have died but for your care. This is what they all say my precious darling. I can't tell you half they do say in your praise. If you were here my pet or I knew you were safe, how happy it would make me to hear everybody praise you. But I can hardly bear it now. *I* know how truly noble and good you are, I know it better than they do my husband, and it is because you are so good that I can't live without you. If you never come home to your Dollie her heart will break. . . .

Saturday Evening, Sep. 19th, My Darling, The weather is quite cold. Last night there was very severe frost, and even ice. . . . Cucumbers, pumpkins, squashes and the like are killed. It is going to be a hard winter I fear on many people, almost as bad as the winter 5 years ago. . . .

You ask if I ever hear from father. No love, nothing but what I have told you. Not one of them has ever written me a word or sent me a word by way of message since I left there but Jane. . . . I am sure they have nothing against us but that we love our country and hate treason, and if they throw us away for this we don't want to help it. . . .

Later, I wish I could tell you some good war news but there is no news anymore hardly. . . . I told you there was no news, but have you heard the good election news from Vermont, Maine, and *California?* It is very good love, good enough. California has given about a 20,000 Union majority! Mahoney says he doesn't understand it at all. . . .

Dollie

Little Rock, Ark., Sept. 18, 1863

My Darling,

. . . We send our teams foraging every day. Yesterday the detail brought in quite a lot of sweet potatoes, and the boys of my Company managed to get outside of the pickets some way and get plenty of beef & pork and I believe some chickens. . . . The Quartermaster has been issuing only half rations. . . . The rest the boys have to forage. All I require of them is that they don't get into trouble themselves & get me into it. When orders come around against foraging I inform them of it and tell them what the punishment will be *if they are caught at it.* They understand it, for they told me they got meat of a first rate butcher yesterday. The rebels are having this army to support, all but bread, sugar, coffee and salt. The forage is all taken from the country, and it amounts to considerable, for there are some 10 or 12,000 horses and mules in the expedition. . . .

W. F. Vermilion

Sunday Morning, Sep. 20th, 1863
My Dearest Love,

Jimmy is gone. . . . It is very still and lonesome here now. He is a noisy fellow and kept everything "boiling" as he said while he stayed. He went off in good spirits, though I think he dreaded the parting. He knows something of the chances of war and felt that he might never see home again. I shall miss him for a time sadly, with his careless, noisy racket. But 11 months ago this day I kissed my husband and gave him to his country — and mine — since then no parting can hurt me greatly. . . .

Monday Night, Sep. 21st, My Darling, I have been all over the woods today. I went grape gathering with Martha Hickcox and Lizzie. . . . We went down to Wilson's grove along the path that you and I followed once a long time ago — long before we were married. Do you remember pet going to Denny's one afternoon when you came out here to Iowa the first time? Well, I went along the same little path today. I thought of that walk of ours, sweet love and I could hardly keep from crying. How well I remember how you looked and talked! I loved you then darling. I *thought* I loved you with all my heart, but it was not as I love you now my pet. I didn't know then the brave, noble heart that was offered me. I didn't know how good you were. And because I did not know, I was almost afraid to trust you. *Am I afraid now, my husband?* Darling, God has given me a love worth all the world besides; surely he will not snatch it from me just as I have learned to appreciate the precious gift. Oh, surely he will not bereave me of all, and leave me utterly desolate. . . . I have been reading Mr. Sumner's [57] great speech on the subject of foreign intervention. . . . Mr. Sumner, you know darling, is chairman of the committee on Foreign Affairs, and such a speech from him at this juncture is I think of the utmost significance and his opinion entitled to unusual weight. I have not got all the specifics yet, but he evidently thinks the danger of a war with England or France or both is imminent. I believe he thinks war almost inevitable. . . .

Dollie

"I Listen Every Hour to Hear of a Decisive Battle"

The capture of Little Rock in the summer of 1863 had benefited the Union cause in a number of ways. First, it was the third Confederate state capital seized during the Civil War, giving tangible evidence of the progress of Union arms. Second, possession of Little Rock meant that the Union controlled a significant part of the populated area of the state of Arkansas. The prospect of such control, along with the liberation of much of Tennessee and Louisiana, allowed Abraham Lincoln to announce in the fall of 1863 a plan for reconstructing the nation. Finally, Little Rock's occupation gave the Union a southern base from which to penetrate even further into the Confederacy. Considering the small price in casualties paid by Steele, it was a remarkably economical accomplishment.

Initially, the 36th Iowa shared in the national euphoria over the capture of Little Rock. The occupation of the capital of Arkansas allowed the men to explore a city with a number of points of interest within its boundaries. The newness wore off quickly, however, and the regiment soon settled into a familiar routine of drill and parade. As fall turned to winter, William received the best news possible: he would get to go home to recruit new volunteers.

As previously noted, the 36th Iowa had suffered grievously from disease since its muster into federal service. To make good its losses, the adjutant general of Iowa authorized a detachment of individuals from the 36th Iowa to return home to solicit enlistments. The detail would include Privates Daniel Bashore, Claudius Miller, and George Frush, Corporal Henry Maiken, Sergeant George Hickenlooper, and William Vermilion. William would open a recruiting office in Centerville, and that would allow him to live at home with Mary. In fact, he would see a great deal of Mary, because he hired her to clerk for him while he carried out his duties.

The letters in this chapter cover perhaps the best and worst moments in their correspondence. They both are troubled about the setback dealt the Union cause at the Battle of Chickamauga, and speculate about the effect that it will have on the fall elections in Iowa. But the chapter ends with William giving Mary the best news that he possibly could.

Little Rock, Arkansas, Sep. 21, 1863
My Darling,

. . . I have heard nothing for several days, only the people are coming in quite rapidly to take the oath. In many instances I think only to save their property. I got the papers you sent me and the Dictionary. Thank you for them. I will keep the book. I was so glad to get it.
W. F. Vermilion

Tuesday Night, Sep. 22nd, 1863
My Own Dear Love,

. . . Little Rock is taken, and perhaps you are there now. We have Gen. Steele's official dispatch now, which merely says that his forces occupied Little Rock on the 10th inst. And that the rebels were retreating South, and Gen. Davidson was in pursuit. . . . The latest dispatch says Rosecrans was fighting a terrible battle in Georgia.[1] The rebels fought bravely and the contest was not decided. I have no fear for the result. Rosecrans is never defeated. He doesn't begin to fight *his best* till any other general would be beaten. And the battle is in *Georgia* love. Isn't that a cheering sign? Last year Kentucky and Tennessee furnished the battlefields. The war is going bravely on. . . .

Wednesday Night, Sep. 23rd, My Darling, I am poisoned. . . . We all got among some poisoned vines the other day when we were gathering grapes but I didn't think about its hurting me. I have often been among them and was never poisoned before. It is hurting my eyes the worst. They are swollen and somewhat painful. I was right sick during the night last night. I haven't done anything for it yet. I don't know what to do; and I guess it will get well itself pretty soon. . . .

The stock is all disposed of. We have nothing left now but Rocker and Cassie and Beppo! You must tell me sweet love whether you are satisfied with all I have done. Tell me all you think about it, won't you? I have done the best I could my love. If you had been here you could have done better I have no doubt. All the cattle . . . just come to $336.75. . . .

Dollie

Friday Evening, Sep. 25th, 1863

My Own Dear Love,

. . . The news of Rosecran's defeat has almost been more than I could bear. . . . The old story — 1,200 killed and 7,000 wounded and our army falling back to Chattanooga. The old story of all the rebel armies being unexpectedly hurled upon one of ours and crushing it. Oh, where was Burnside to allow such a misfortune to befall us? I see that Gen. Sherman with his corps has been sent to reinforce Rosecrans. He has 11 Iowa regiments with him. The 6th is one of them. They are probably at Chattanooga by this time, as I suppose they can go all the way by railroad. If those 11 regiments had been there last Sunday we should never have heard the news we have. . . .

Saturday Morning, Sep. 26th, It is said Meade was moving upon Gordonville and a battle was expected this week. . . . I am glad it is, for it is only after a fierce storm of battles that we can hope for the calm of peace. The news from Charleston is meager and not very good. I fear there is little prospect that the "Gibraltar" will fall into our hands soon. But it must after awhile. I wish DuPont [2] was in command of the fleet again. But the best news of all . . . is the announcement in the London Times that the new rebel ironclads will not be allowed to leave the Mersey.[3] The British Government has got awake to the matter at last, and says positively that the new rams shall not get out to sea. I can't tell you darling how glad I am of this for I thought all the time that if they did get out a war with England was inevitable. If they are detained it will be the first sign of a disposition to deal fairly by us that England has shown since the war began. . . .

Dollie

Monday Evening, Sep. 28th, 1863
My Dearest Love,

They have come my darling, 2 good precious letters from you. Oh my husband, you surely never wrote 2 other letters that did as much good as these. I say this my pet, not forgetting my anxiety last winter while you were gone down the Pass, or after the battle at Helena. Then I did not have to do without hearing from you *30 days*. You advise me love, about our business. . . . You don't know how much I have wanted your advice and I am glad of it now though it comes too late. But I am glad because I find you wanted me to do just as I have done almost. I think now that you will be satisfied with what I have done. I hope so darling, for I did my best. I have already told you all about it. If you have got all my letters you know everything I could tell you. I did get $79 for Jake and I think I sold the cattle pretty well and got them all off in good season. I gave up buying any oxen. I am so glad now that I did since you advise against it. If you are pleased my sweet love that is all I ask. . . . I see it stated that there is to be no draft in Iowa as she has furnished about 6,000 troops more than her quotas under all the calls. They are raising the 9th cavalry regiment now. It will soon be full and there is already talk of the 10th. Willis Hays has come home. . . . No doubt he brings news from Matt. . . . Dr. Hays is not at home. He started last week to go to Cape Girardeau to see Josephus[4] who is sick and has been for a long time. But they have got a letter from him since his father started, saying he was much better. By going now the old man has missed seeing Willis, clear. It is a pity. . . .

Dollie

Wednesday Evening, Sep. 30th, 1863

My Own Darling,

. . . It seems that the rebels are determined to risk another battle in the hope of retaking Chattanooga and driving our army out of East Tennessee, the possession of which, they acknowledge, is of vital importance to them. . . . Rosecrans must have a very large army by this time. It is said 40,000 reinforcements have been sent to him from Grant's army — all of Sherman's and McPherson's corps. Monday's paper says that troops were also sent from Meade's Army of the Potomac[5]. . . . I got a letter from Mrs. Brown yesterday and she sent me a bundle of papers by the mail carrier. They are the Union Guard published at Bloomfield and edited by Matt Jones.[6] It is a spicy little paper. I am going to send you 1 or 2 just to let you see what your friend Jones is doing. He is in the fight as well as you love, but his field of labor is widely different from yours. He is a "thorn in the side" of Davis County Copperheads. . . .

Later, Father came back but brought no letter from Matt. He saw Willis however, and learned a good deal about him. He had ague awhile but was doing duty again when Hays left. He would have come home if he could have a furlough. They drew lots to see who would come and Matt didn't happen to be the lucky one. Willis says they are in good spirits and have a jolly time of it generally. Every man in the regiment will vote for Stone. And speaking of this, Mrs. Hays was telling father that she has been watching Mullinnix and she believes he is going to vote for Tuttle. She was there the other day and she was not just pleased with everything. She says if he does vote the Copperhead ticket she will never countenance him again. And that would be right darling, but I think she is mistaken. I can't believe it. . . . The last time I was there I remember his saying he would rather anybody should call him a nigger than a Copperhead. And he has subscribed for the *Nashville Union*[7] and thinks it the greatest paper out. He has just got one of Andy Johnson's late speeches with which he was very much pleased. . . .

We got two letters from Matt, both written while he was sick. He speaks about Dr. Lambert being so kind to him, and seems to like him very well. He says he has plenty to read. They take

4 weekly papers in their tent, and have Comstock's Philosophy[8] besides. They are preparing to give a "rousing vote to Stone" at the election and he wants to know what *we* think of Tuttle and his treasonable platform. He seems to be quite well posted in regard to home politics; says the soldiers admire Tuttle as an officer but *hate* him as a politician. . . .

Dollie

Little Rock, Arkansas, Sep. 30, 1863

My Darling,

. . . The Barracks for the boys are nearly done and I am glad to say all the good wall tents occupied by the field and staff are well floored and that they have built a good stable of plank for their horses. . . . I am also glad to tell you Dollie that the line officers who came here are all living although we have no protection but of the tent fly. It is a little larger than [if] new sheets would be sewed together and stretched over a pole. But I can stand it if the rest of the line officers can.

Will

Thursday Night, October 1st, 1863

My Dearest Love,

. . . October is here now. It was October when you left me, pet. It will soon be a year — it seems *10* to me since I saw you. Don't you remember when you left me you said you would come to see me by Christmas? Oh darling, we didn't know much about war then, did we? I am afraid another Christmas will come before you. . . .

The people here have sent off a petition asking to have father appointed postmaster.[9] We think there is no place else for the Osprey office to go. . . . I tried to get him to stop their petition, but I believe he is very willing to take it. If he is, it will do us no good, as the mail will come but once a week. He has no room for it, and it will be a great deal of trouble. What I shall hate is that it will bring so much company and make so much work, but let him do as he pleases about it. . . .

I see in my paper that Robert Standley of Co. F 36th regt. died. . . . I don't think you had any man of that name.[10] Did you

darling? I hope there is some mistake. I hate for so many of your men to die. I know it troubles you, love. I wish you could bring them all home with you. But your men have fared extremely well, compared with some regts. and companies I heard of. . . .
Dollie

Little Rock, Ark., Oct. 3, 1863
My Darling,

. . . Some say Price is at Arkadelphia with what is left of his army. Reports say they are coming in here and taking the *oath*. The number of 200 a day. General Steele is arming all who wish to defend themselves against the guerrillas. . . . The latest news we have here is to the 17th ult. . . . Some say Rosecrans has been whipped and beaten back from Chattanooga. I can't believe it. I don't want to believe it. But if he ever is whipped he will be badly whipped. . . .
W. F. Vermilion

Sunday Night, October 4th, 1863
My Own Dear Love,

It has been a cold, bad day, but I went to Dr. Hays' for all that. . . . We had a very good time. There were over 70 people there. The house could hardly hold them. They had an excellent dinner, everything that was good. They had sent out a general public invitation to all Union people to come. . . . The old lady was flying around and seemed just in her element. The only thing that troubled her was that the old doctor was not there. Willis looks very well, and seems in the best of spirits. I talked with him a few minutes. He speaks very highly of Matt. Says a better person never wore uniform. He brought home a large picture, having 8 figures on one plate — all the members of their mess. The pictures are all good. Matt is sitting down with his spoon in one hand preparing something to eat. One is holding a cup of hot coffee, one smoking, one reading, some standing around. It is very nice. The boys joined in sending it home to their friends, and it belongs alike to all. We are to keep it by turns. Willis says Matt will not come home now till his time is up, unless the war ends before. I didn't know hardly anybody that was there, but a good many knew me. Everybody nearly seemed to know you. A young lady from Albia wanted to look at your likeness in my breast pin, and said she had often heard of Capt. Vermilion. She told me that Capt. Varner's wife[11] knew nothing of his death till they brought his dead body home, and at the moment she was busy writing a letter to him. Wasn't that dreadful, my darling?

There is no news hardly. . . . It is said now that Sherman is not gone to reinforce Rosecrans. I don't know which dispatch is true. I see that the rebels are watching anxiously to see how our elections go. They say if Vallandigham is elected there is a prospect of peace, and their papers are urging their generals to make some vigorous movements in his behalf. If he is defeated, they say the war must last for years yet. At the time you get this letter, darling, we shall know what the people of Ohio say about it. The traitors are going to claim the election *by fraud* if possible.
Dollie

Monday Night, Oct. 5th, I have been busy all day, or I would have finished this letter before night. This morning father was going to the timber with the wagon, and I went with him to gather hickory nuts. I couldn't find any hardly and didn't stay very long. But I was glad I went. The woods are very beautiful now. The trees have folded away their green summer robes, and clad themselves in the gorgeous tints of October. Their rich crimson, and gold, and purple are beautiful, but saddening. I can't love my old friends so well, in such brilliant dresses. Far dearer to me are the warm showers, and bursting buds, and tender springing grass, and pale wild flowers of May. Poets love to sing of the "golden October," but it was always the saddest of all the twelve to me. It is doubly sad to me now, my love, because you left me in October. I never see the yellow leaves go drifting by but I think of that autumn morning. I think of it too much, sweet darling, but we won't talk about it tonight. We won't talk of anything that will give us the "blues," will we, dear one? It has cleared up again, and the weather is fine now. I am truly glad of it. I have been sewing ever since I came home this morning. I don't do much work that requires me to be still. I don't do all I ought to.

Darling, just now Beppo flew out and barked like somebody was coming. I sat still, and didn't look up, but I *thought* maybe it was you coming. My heart almost stopped beating for a few moments. But I guess it was nothing. Beppo is quiet again. But it has made me so nervous, love, that I can hardly write. Don't laugh at your silly Dollie, will you pet? There! He is barking again, but I won't mind him this time. Father and Mr. Wilson are going to start to Eddyville in the morning. Father is going to sell his wool, and buy salt and coffee, and such things as he needs. Mother and I will be pretty anxious while he is gone. I mean to get some one to stay with us of nights. I shall be afraid to stay just with mother. I know I can't suppose anything would go wrong with us at all, but I am timid and cowardly since you went away. I wouldn't stay alone now like I used to of nights, for a great deal. I never thought hard of being afraid then. I will send this letter by father and he will mail it somewhere for me. Fletcher Evans came home today on a furlough, and found not one of his family left here. I feel sorry for the boy. His mother and father have both died since he went away, Jim has enlisted again, and the girls[12] have taken up and moved to Marion County. Fletcher is going to start there in the morning. He has nothing here but the graves of his parents. He could tell us about Jimmy, if we could go to see him, but I guess he got back all right or we should have heard it. I may get a letter from him tomorrow. If I don't hear from *you* then my darling, I don't know what I shall do. It has been a week now since I heard one word. Sometimes I think you are coming home, and that is why I don't get any letters, but I watch and look for you, and you don't come. My own darling doesn't come. It may be that you cannot come at all, but I don't know anything about you now, my pet, and so I will believe that you are coming soon. Let me have this poor comfort, dear one. There is no news to write. Nothing has happened. Nobody is sick or dead or married that I have heard of lately. Everything goes on just as normal. One day is like all the others. The people all talk about the election. There is more interest manifested I believe than was before the presidential election. And it is right that every patriot should be fully awake now. They say there will be 12 or 15 Copperhead votes given in this township. It is late, my pet, and I must quit writing. My eyes ache. . . . I can't write when I am uneasy. Send me a *big, long letter*, dear, and you shall have a better one than this in reply. Take care of yourself, sweet pet. Be of good cheer. Don't be troubled about me any, but send me all the letters you can possibly, and above all, don't forget to love your own Dollie

Little Rock, Ark., Oct. 4, 1863
My Darling,

. . . Today I have been reading *The Story of the Guards* by Jessie Fremont.[13] The Knapsack Edition is a pamphlet of some 250 pages, price 50 cents. I don't think it is a very great effort but I will send it to you if I can buy it. . . . It is more of History than anything else. I learned more of Zagonyi[14] than everything else. Jessie speaks well of all the Guards, every one, and thinks they have been badly used by the Government. . . . Never before in this Country surely have such brave men suffered so much. And surely never before in this Country did such a man as General Fremont suffer so from the Head of the American Army. . . . I can't help thinking him one of the great men of the age. But we can't always get our men in just such places as we want them. When Fremont was removed Uncle Abraham had not concluded to fight this war with abolitionists and Negroes. Wise men — that is some wise men — saw then that the Government would have to adopt the abolition system, but others professed not to see, so things went badly. What an immense amount of blood and treasure would have been saved to this country if all men could have seen as far as John C. Fremont, but alas for the short sightedness, have we not paid for what all seem to concede now. But why sit here talking all the night of the man we both always admired. Let the blunders of this administration go, for in reality they seem to have been few when we consider the magnitude of the work. No man of this age has had half so much entrusted to his care as Abraham has. Of all men he has had to work, and if he comes through without being mortally wounded he will be the great man of the age. . . .
W. F. V.

Tuesday Night, October 6th, 1863

My Own Darling,

. . . We had company nearly all day. Old Mr. Christie and his wife are here tonight staying with us, because I was afraid to stay alone with mother. . . . It has been a bad day and I couldn't go to Iconium, but I went to Mr. Sheeks' late this afternoon to see if they had brought my mail. Isaac had gone to the office, and was not home yet. . . . Isaac is not much better. He is trying to get his furlough renewed. If he doesn't succeed he will start back in a few days. . . .

Dollie

Little Rock, Ark., Oct. 6, 1863

My Own Dollie,

. . . There must be quite an army here to hold all this country until peace is made, and even then it will require something of a force to keep the country all right. But the Negroes ought to do that with the help of the regular army. While I think of it, don't let Jim go into the regular service if you can help it. . . . He is young now and if he gets attached to such a life he will not be likely to do any good at anything else. It is a noble thing for a young man to volunteer to defend his country when it is in peril, but to sacrifice oneself so far as to go into the regular service is too much [like] a fair young lady going into a nunnery. Keep him from it if you can, for I will assure you he will not find the regular service like being under old John Edwards[15] at Springfield. . . .

All our clothing and tents have come up. . . . So I hope to be comfortably situated tomorrow evening at this time. If I get a good tent I shall have no more spats with Col. Kittredge about the way we have to live. We will turn all our attention to the men's barracks. Ours is not quite covered yet, and we need chimneys in it, for the weather is getting too cool to do without fire. We had a fine brigade drill this afternoon. Col. McLain[16] of the 43rd Ind. is commanding. He drills tolerably well, besides he is a very fine man. . . . But he will soon be sent back to his regiment for there are brigadiers enough here now to command all the brigades we have. Col. Samuel A. Rice — no, Brig. Gen. Samuel A. Rice of Oskaloosa Iowa will command us. . . . We think him a fine officer. In our brigade we have the 77th Ohio. The regiment the 6th Iowa was with so long. It was reported they ran at the Battle of Shiloh.[17] They appear to be a good regt. now. General Salomon of Wisconsin, a Dutchman and the man who really fought the battle at Helena, has come up and is going to take command of our division. There is but one other brigade in the division. . . . Col. Benton[18] of the 29th Iowa is now commanding it, but will soon be sent to his regiment to give a place for another brigadier who has just come up. . . . Everybody in the army Dollie is working for promotion. And it is seldom given to those who deserve it for meritorious conduct. The shrewd wire-worker always gets placed first. . . . General Steele seems to [be] running the thing here all his own way. . . . General Steele is a very passionate commander. He kicks men around just as he pleases. While we were on our way from Brownsville to Mill Bayou we stopped one day to rest. There were 2 roads . . . at that place some 30 or 40 yards apart. The Cavalry and Artillery were passing us on one of these tracks and we were resting on the other where no horsemen had passed. The boys were all lying down. They — or some of them — were lying with their feet in the wagon track. While we were resting there and some of the boys were asleep the General and staff came along. As he came opposite — or through Co. I of our Regt. (Capt. Gedney's)— his horse scared at one of the boys lying by the side of the road. The General stopped and spoke sharply to the man and asked him if he couldn't get out of the road — or if there was not room for him out of the road. He had on no shoulder straps and the man did not know him, so he told him there was but he need not be in such a fit about it. The man then got up . . . and moved a little way out of the road — and told the General he could move or ride on. In a moment Steele jumped off of his horse and stepped up to the man and asked him if he knew who he was talking to. The man said not and added some-thing somewhat impudent. It excited Steele and he kicked at the man's face with all his might, but he threw his gun up and knocked the kick off and put his finger on the trigger. They then had some words, when the General got on his horse and rode off saying the man had insulted him. A day or two afterwards while we were en-camped at Mill Bayou some men went to an old mill near Steele's headquarters and were taking such lumber as they wanted. Steele saw them and ran out with all his might telling them to stop it. He met a sergeant . . . with a heavy load of planks on his shoulder. Steele hit him on the face. The man was either hurt or thought he had better get away from there as fast as possible, so he pitched the lumber off onto the General's shoulder. . . . Segt. Brashar who saw it couldn't tell whether the man was hurt or whether he was only anxious to get away. If I had seen it I know I should have laughed. For all these peculiarities the General is a good fighter. He has managed the army well and I suppose he never intends to become a candidate for the Presidency. . . .

The election is nearly here, one week from today. The boys are talking considerably about the election. Some are going to vote for Tuttle, but I don't think George Stewart will get a vote in the Company, and not 10 in the Regiment. I shall be glad if no one of my Company votes for him. Nimrod Marchbanks told me this, that he would not vote for him if it were to save his life. If Rod doesn't I don't think anyone else would if they half understood themselves. . . .

Green is getting to be as good a cook as we can expect a negro to be. . . . We only agreed to give him $5 per month but he is worth more than that and I think we must give it to him. His old master has taken his wife and children down — or out — towards Texas. Green wants to go out farther and find her if he can. All or nearly all the negroes who live in this part of the country have been taken away. [Slaveholders] are running away from Old Abe's proclamation. At first they said they were not afraid of it but I notice it makes them skedaddle with their Sambos. Texas is reported already full . . . for many have been taken there from East of the Mississippi. . . .

Here in the army many things pass unobserved by me. For instance at the Battle of Helena because I was tired I waited until the 6th before I went over the battleground on our left where there was such a slaughter among the rebels. . . . Now I wish I had gone earlier as many others did. But then all the marks of the severe cannonading were there on the 6th. The old negro church with 100 or more holes through it where the balls had passed through. The stumps are torn to pieces, the grave stones knocked to atoms, the ground torn up and so on. . . .

At 8 o'clock this P.M. we went out to drill again. The ground we drill on is between two large Hospitals. One is in the rebel Seminary. It was occupied by them before we came to this place. The other is in the U.S. Arsenal building. The seminary is a large enough building, with a nice yard. . . . The Arsenal is a very nice place. The rebels carried all the machinery away with them to Arkadelphia. Our Division has taken the building for a Hospital and it makes a very nice one. But as I was saying . . . there is seldom a day passes but a funeral procession passes by while we are on drill. What a thought to one who is capable of thinking. We are drilling, learning to destroy men, and a few of our comrades passing by with the remains of some poor fellow who has fallen prey to this war. Here we stand all in columns for we can't make the next movement until the procession gets by — and there that procession goes. So slow, the music is so solemn. There 3 or 4 fifers and about that amount of drummers with their drums muffled playing and beating the dead march. Next comes 8 soldiers with their pieces all reversed — he is a private, for the escort is composed of only 8 walking so solemnly. Next the ambulance with the corpse and then there are the mourners behind. Sometimes there are only one or two but this time there are 8 or 10. All stepping to that dead march. Slowly they move. We still wait. How many of all that 1,000 men standing by my side give the doleful sounds of that march a solemn thought. Not many I imagine, for before it was past the Col. showed signs of impatience. Then not one in all that number could give it a farewell look. Many gave it looks but only of curiosity. But the mortal part of that soldier passes on not withstanding and the immortal part looked on without pain. Such my Dollie is the last sight we get of many a poor comrade but such is war. . . .

W. F. V.

Wednesday Morning, October 7th, 1863

Good Morning My Love,

Are you well and safe and comfortable, dear? I hope so. We are well. The "bugaboos" didn't get us last night. Christies are just gone home. They are good, kind people. . . . I was up before day this morning. I haven't got my work done up yet, but Lizzie Hickcox was just here and said she had some letters to mail and wanted Rocker to ride to Iconium. I will let her take him, and I can send you this scrap of a letter. She will bring my mail when she comes back. I hate to wait 3 hours for it, but I might have to go all the way to the office myself. I didn't know I could send out a letter today, or I would have written a long one last night. . . . It is no account, but it will tell you I am well. I hardly slept any again last night. I couldn't sleep for thinking of you, sweet love. I think every night maybe you will come before morning. I looked for you last night. I can't help it, pet. I want you to come so much, that it is hardly out of my mind one moment. . . .

Dollie

Wednesday Evening, October 7th, 1863
My Darling,

. . . [Humphrey] May is a candidate for some county office, I forget what, but if he is elected he will move to Corydon. In that event he will want Hancock [19] to keep his farm. . . . But I don't suppose there is much prospect of his election. I have not heard anything from them lately. I wish they would come and see me, I am so lonesome. I have not heard anything from father's folks. . . . I guess Jane will not write any more. I shall not write to them any more unless they do to me. If they don't want to hear from us, sweet one, I don't want to intrude upon them. I wrote to Jane after the battle at Helena, telling them that you were safe, and they have never answered my letters. But we won't be troubled about it, my darling. We will love each other all the more. . . .

Dollie

Little Rock, Ark., Oct. 8, 1863
My Darling,

. . . The weather is still quite cool but I have more a comfortable place than I have had since we left Helena, and where do you suppose I am? We have a Barracks for the men much like those [that] were at Keokuk. The men's bunks are all below and I have a place floored on the loft — up against one of the gable ends. . . . It is small but quite pleasant and warm. The only trouble is the boys' noise. They say I shant stay here — they will drive m[e] away. I am going to see. . . .

Our regiment has lost 3 line officers. . . . First Cap. Webb of Co. K. He lived at Albia. Then Lieut. Spooner[20] of Co. B. He lived at Centerville. And today we heard of the death of Capt. Varner of Co. A. He lived at Albia. All good men and all were on their way north. . . . The war may yet end with many of us lying here under soil once occupied by rebels, but I hope not.
W. F. V.

Friday Night, October 9th, 1863
My Dear Husband,
. . . Father came home from Eddyville last night. As he came through Albia he sold Will's mare, Nelly, and he went back there today to deliver her up. He got $80.00 for her, tell Will, and she is going off to the war. But then he wanted to go back today any-how. Col. Stone was to speak there, and they were making prepa-rations for a grand time. Father wanted to see the future Governor of Iowa. He has not come home yet. . . . I hope when he comes he will bring some good news. We have heard cannon firing today, and I don't know what it is for unless there is good news. The fir-ing, they say, was at Chariton. But there may have been a Union meeting there. . . .
Dollie

Little Rock, Ark., Oct. 9, 1863
My Darling,
. . . My cold was hurting me very much last night so I didn't write much. I took a big dose of opium and had a good time all night but you know one can't sleep much after taking opium late of an evening. . . . I was through the south part of the city and saw more of it than at any time before. Nothing attracted my attention but the cemetery. It is a nice place situated on high rolling ground. It was once an oak and pine grove but the pines have all been taken out leaving nothing but the oaks, such as we have in our grove only they are nicely cared for. The grounds are well laid off and the graves well cared for so far as monuments, tombstones, fencing

and poling and such. There are some as nice monuments as I ever saw in my life. . . .

I am glad you sold Jake and the cattle. You got as much as I could if I had been there no doubt. You are a good trader. Get Mr. Knapp's[21] team to gather the corn with — that is if he doesn't charge you too much. He is a tremendous man to charge Dollie and it will no doubt suit him very well to make his team pay a part of that $100. . . .

W. F. V.

Saturday Morning, Oct. 10th, 1863
My Darling,

. . . Father says the opinion prevails that the rebels will attack Rosecrans again next Tuesday. They think it is part of the plot, and that Bragg will fight that day in order to prevent the Union soldiers from voting against Vallandigham. That would be a trick worthy of them, and one that would suit the traitors at home, perhaps better than it would their rebel brethren in Georgia. I shall not be surprised if something of the sort is accomplished. The copperheads have staked everything on Vallandigham, and if his election be possible they will accomplish it. His defeat will be utter ruin to them. They . . . are bad and desperate men who will hesitate at no scheme of wickedness that will help them to power. It is said that thousands of butternuts are being run into Ohio from Indiana and Kentucky to vote. . . . Matters are almost as bad there as they used to be in Kansas during the border ruffian reign of terror. If we lose the election it will be a terrible blow to me. . . . I shall not sleep much till I hear that the votes are counted. I am not uneasy about Iowa. Iowa is all the time right. I am proud of Iowa. I never want to live in any other state. . . .

Dollie

Monday Morning, October 12th, 1863
My Dearest Love,

. . . I received a letter from Jane Saturday. There is not much news in it. She has had a "rising" in her hand for a long time, so

she couldn't write. She didn't say a word about any of them but Henry. He had been elected sergeant in the home guards, and was at Greencastle drilling. All the loyal young men in the county belong to the home guards. Henry had been looking for a letter from you. She says she never got but one letter from you, but "that was dearer to her than if she had always been used to such a brother." Amanda has had very poor health all Summer. The doctors say she has consumption. She calls her boy Franklin Banks. Jane says her quarrel with Wilcox was a serious affair, and they are parted forever. He got to believe she was corresponding with some soldier. . . . She says "he was hard to read, and it took a long time but she was bent on finding him out." She thinks he never had the love and confidence that she ought to have had, or he would not have hesitated and waited so long. But it is all over now, and he is not breaking her heart at all. I am glad it is over, my love, for I never thought he was half good enough for her. . . .
Dollie

Little Rock, Ark., Oct. 12, 1863
My Darling,
   . . . Tomorrow is the election. . . . Late this evening I learned John Sheeks was going to vote the Copperhead ticket so I called him into my tent and asked him if he wanted a ticket. He told me he had one and from the way he looked I knew he was going the whole hog. . . . But there is one thing that is pleasing Dollie, G. B. Stewart won't get *a vote in my Company*. Or at any rate such men as Bad Marchbanks and John Wafford say they won't. He will get but few in the regiment. But then he ought not to get any — not one in any regiment. What, a soldier vote for George Stewart to represent him in the legislature. Can it be possible any man is in the army who will do such a thing. But then he is just as good as General Tuttle or any other man who is on their ticket. Wait till I get home and I will study politics and give it to them to their heart's content. It is what I long for and the time will come after awhile.
   There, the town clock has just struck 11. . . . It reminds me so much of old times in Chicago. There I went by the clock on the market house. There 11 was common bedtime. . . .

Oct. 13th, Evening, The election is over and the votes for governor counted. Stone gets in this regiment her 306 and General Tuttle 71. My company gave him some 10 or 12 of them but the county ticket got only about half that number. Stewart got "nary votes" from my Company. . . . After the voting had commenced I found such men as John Wafford, Jack Day . . . had been gulling the boys. So I pitched in, not as I would have before at home but as I thought best. I think I saved Stone several votes. It was a thing I hated very much to do but I thought it best to do it. It will not do for an officer to electioneer with his men much. . . . Nimrod Marchbanks voted for only 3 Democrats, on the State ticket Tuttle and Duncome, on the County ticket Sheriff Banks.[22] That did pretty well for him, a full blooded Copperhead when he came into the service. When we started out my Company was pretty nearly equally divided. Now there [are] 11 or 12 who have voted for Tuttle. Bart Maiken was not going to vote this evening. I called him into my tent and . . . told him how it was. . . . Bart wishes the cause as well as I do but he is a very bashful fellow and all the others had voted and many had tried to get him to vote. He refused because he thought his vote would not elect anyone, and then he hated to go to the polls because I think he was afraid he would have to talk to the Board some. When I told him I would go with him he agreed to go. Bart is a good boy and I think I did right in getting him to vote, for no one else could, not even Henry. I thought of the old man and knew he would want Bart to vote so badly. . . .

How much money have you put away now Dollie? It is foolishness to spend much money here when everything is high. Boots such as I must wear this Winter will cost me about $12. Shirts $10, a pair of nice pants $12 to $15. No one has them but the sutler and he must have a big price. Butter he sells at 60 odd cts. per pound, eggs when he has them for 40 to 50 cts. . . .
W. F. V.

Tuesday Night, Oct. 13th, 1863
My Own Dear Love,
    . . . I got Mr. Knapp's horses to gather the corn, and Teater is to store yours away in the crib that Mullinix built. I have told you all the details darling, very fully. I hope you have got the letters. I will

not sell the corn till you come home, or give orders about it. I think there will only be 300 bushels. I hope a good deal more. Corn is already selling at 50 cents. Counting Mr. Knapp's note as money, I have just $1,700 put away for you, my love. And I will keep it for you till you come home, sweet pet, every dollar of it. As to the notes, I didn't know what was best. We have not tried to collect any, but there has been about $50 paid as I have already told you. I thought I would let them remain on interest, if you were willing, and not try to collect any till you come home, as I have so much money on hand. But it shall be as you say, dear one. . . .
Dollie

In camp at Little Rock, Ark., Oct. 14, 1863
My Darling,

The Capital of Arkansas is not a great city after all. . . . It covers a large amount of ground but it is not compactly built. Keokuk is far ahead of it. There is no such a street as Main Street, in fact there is not a fine street in the whole city. In what we would call the business part there are a few very good buildings, but no nice blocks. In the outskirts of the place there are many fine dwellings evidently belonging to wealthy men, but they are mostly built on the Southern style and mostly of bricks. The business part is not pretty. The rest is. The site had once been covered thickly with an oak grove. The trees still stand around all the fine dwellings. . . . In the City now and then there is a frame house built as we build them North. Poor things, they look as though they were away from home. . . . We saw plenty of citizens but talked to only one. He claimed to be an Englishman and he was exempt, or he would have been in the rebel army long ago. . . . When we came in he left the Southern Confederacy for good. In conversation he asked me what I thought would become of the negroes. I told him they were free in all of Arkansas. He didn't like that, and added white men can't work in this climate. Soldiering is harder than working is it not? Yes says he. Well says I, we soldier quite well down here in the Summer. He then said the country would be ruined for the farms are so large white men never can cultivate them all. We asked him if white men would not do more work than negroes. He thought so but still contended that the farms were too large. We asked him

how large they were. Some — one especially that he knew of — who had a farm of 200 acres, and no northern man could ever farm that. We told him that would be an ordinary farm in some places in the north, that farmers in Illinois and Iowa would not be satisfied with that amount. We told him that the northern people would crowd the South and cultivate every acre of the soil and become rich too. That the Yankees would hire the negroes and keep them on the big farms their masters kept them on and that their money and energies would make the South worth more to itself and to the world than it ever had been worth. . . . Why if I had 10,000 dollars and this war would end I could come into the South and lease land of the Government and in 10 years I could make half a million. But don't be uneasy Dollie, I am not going to come. . . . I love the loyal North too well, I love the institutions of the North too well, to exchange them for this country. In connection with home I know nothing but peace and love. In connection with the South I know nothing but Slavery, envy, war, and blood. . . .
W. F. V.

Thursday Evening, Oct. 15th, 1863
My Own Dear Love,

. . . I have not heard much election news yet. Monroe County is all right — has elected every one of her Union candidates. So has Lucas. They say this township gave 50 majority to Stone. But I hear nothing like this from Appanoose. Tuttle is ahead there. Chariton Township gave him 30 majority, Independence 30, and all the others we have heard from small majorities. I think we shall hear all about it tomorrow. But I never had any hopes of Appanoose. I don't think we will ever live there any more, my love. Do you? There are too many traitors there. . . . I know my gallant soldier will never want to live around them, and I don't blame him. There is considerable excitement to hear the news. Old Mr. Ely was here today and told me that several members of his church had voted for Tuttle, and that he couldn't and wouldn't live in the same church with them. The old man got excited talking about them, and at last, stomping his foot, he exclaimed "Oh, I could kill them, the last one of them. Now I don't know as I ought to *kill* anybody, but

I want to knock 'em *in the head.*" A great many people manifest just such a spirit as this. . . .
Dollie

Little Rock, Ark., Oct. 15, 1863
My Darling,

The 36th has made a gallant charge today. This afternoon we charged Battery Greenbacks. . . . Each private got his regular 26, and I got my 255. . . . Lieut. Wright is quite poorly with ague and diarrhea. . . . He had that disease while in the Army of the Potomac.[23] He had some cough when we made our company and he has never got well and in all probability never will as long as he stays in the service. . . . I wish he would get well. . . . He wants to so badly. And then he is making a very good Lieut., full as well as could be expected. He is by far the best Wright I ever saw. . . .

Evening, When we came to look around and think what we would need to put up our furnaces and chimneys we found we have no trowel. So Capt. Fee and I concluded we would go to the City and buy one. . . . So off we went and inquired in every Hardware Store we could find in the City but there were none to be had. . . . At last we espied an old dilapidated brick building that was being repaired. The workman had gone to his dinner and left his tools just as he had last used them. We walked all around the building and Capt. Fee went up on the scaffold but could not see any trowel. We gave it up in despair and went on to look elsewhere. After looking some time in vain we happened to pass the same building again and saw the trowel lying on the wall in one corner. I observed that there was the trowel. Capt. Fee looked up and saw it and observed "I must have that." So up the ladder he went and got it, right in the center of Little Rock in broad daylight. We walked off together, he with the trowel in his hand and I laughing at him. . . .

Night, Several of us have been over to Col. Drake's tent playing Muggins.[24] Capt. Fee was there, and don't you think he had the impudence this afternoon — he was passing the house where we got the trowel and while the fellow was still hunting for it — to stop and ask the fellow to loan him his trowel. . . . Now the stealing of the trowel in the first place didn't amount to much but to get back while the man was working hunting for it was a little too bad. He should be punished. . . .

W. F. V.

Saturday Night, Oct. 17th, 1863

My Dearest Love,

This has been a very disagreeable day. The wind has blown so hard we could scarcely step outdoors without being almost whirled away. It is still blowing and is very cloudy and murky. I am quite well. George Hickcox has just been in, and brought me some good news. Nathan Gilbert[25] is at home, and his mother made a soldier's dinner for him today. George was there, and I charged him this morning to ask Gilbert 100 questions about you. I had an invitation to the dinner, but I couldn't go. He told George that he saw you and Will often, that you were well, and so fat that I wouldn't know you, and that you were the best looking soldier he ever saw in the service. . . . He speaks in the highest terms of you. . . .

Dollie

Tuesday, October 20th, 1863

My Darling,

. . . It is one year today since you left me, my darling. Have you been thinking about it? Are you sad, dearest? For weeks I have dreaded this day. . . . But I have done better than I expected. I have kept busily at work, and tried not to think about it too much. . . .

Father saw Taylor Hancock today, and talked with him about Woodside. If Humphrey is elected collector — I believe that is it — he will stay where he is next year; if not, he wants to rent a farm, and says he will go and look at Woodside. Humphrey is only 47 votes behind at home, and he thinks the soldiers' votes will elect him. In that case he will move to Corydon. . . .

I wish I knew whether you are satisfied with all that I have done. It seemed to be the best I could do. If you can't come home this Fall you must tell me what to do with our corn. Whether I shall sell it this winter, or keep it till Spring. Teater expects to move in February and it might be stolen if left after that. But you tell me,

love. I lost $100.00 by selling our old corn last Spring. But I could-
n't see any farther ahead.
Dollie

Little Rock, Ark., Oct. 20, 1863
Dollie,

. . . The news came into camp yesterday evening that Iowa had
given Maj. Stone on the home vote from 15,000 to 20,000 over
Gen. Tuttle and that [John] Brough had beaten Vallandigham
from 75,000 to 100,000 on the home vote in Ohio. . . .

I heard a sermon preached this afternoon not by our chaplain
nor by any other chaplain but by a negro, and it was preached
to our regiment too. The man was about as large and almost as
white as Mack Eliott of Hoosier,[26] but used better language and
was undoubtedly a more intelligent man and a better preacher. He
looked to be nearly 50 years of age, could read although he had —
I think — always been a slave. His manner of speaking was quite
good — mild and not very loud. He prayed fervently for the President of the U.S., for the Cabinet and for the Congress, and for all
the rulers both military and civil, and finally for the *private sol-
diery*. He touched very lightly and very appropriately on the condition of his own race. Today was the first time he ever spoke to a
congregation of white people and the first time he had ever spoken
in the open air. There were several negroes with him. I suppose
members of his own class and I noticed the most of them would
read the hymns and sing quite well. I wish I could get to tell some
of our one horse rebel preachers in Iowa that there is a slave or a
man here in Little Rock who has always *been a slave* who is now a
better preacher and a smarter man than they are. *Poor insignificant whelps that they are.* How I do love to hate them. . . . Haters of
liberty, teachers of treason, and yet pretending to be guides for the
people. Of all men I think I hate them the worst. . . .

I was down to the Arsenal this evening — not for the first time
but I never paid too much attention to it before. It is a nice place,
much the nicest Public Property in the City. There's some 12 or
15 acres inside the fence, which I suppose contains all the ground
belonging to it. The ground lies very nice, high and slightly rolling.

It is quite sandy with no grass scarcely growing on it. There are plenty of the same nice oak trees that grow all over the city to give plenty of shade. There is a large garden fenced off to itself. I was not in it so I don't know what it contains. In all I suppose there are some 10 or 12 buildings. . . . The large ones appear to be the main machine shops — or were, we are using them now for a Hospital for our Division. . . . The buildings aside from the two large ones have been for Warehouses, Paint Shops, Dwellings, Stables etc. Gen. Rice is occupying the old *United States Headquarters*, a very nice little building. His Headquarters guards occupy the old guard house. Off to the west from the main building along by the side of a large brick building used for a stable, which is painted yellow — and everything in the yard is yellow — stands all in good trim a Battery of 6 or 8 Parrott guns,[27] but this way — dismounted and lying on the ground — is one of the largest bored guns I have ever been close to. It is 10 or 12 inches. . . . I went down there to see one of my boys who is very sick. His name is Prather.[28] He has chronic diarrhea and I am afraid will never get well. . . .
W. F. V.

Thursday Night, October 22nd, 1863
My Dearest Love,

I have not written any to you since yesterday morning. It seems a long time. I have been washing today, and I put off writing till night. . . . I have been troubled all day. Rocker has been quite sick, and I was so afraid he would die. But he seems very much better tonight. Father says he will be all right by morning. I don't know what has ailed him. I think now he was not well yesterday. He wouldn't drink any water, but he ate his corn readily, and I let Martha Hickcox ride him to the post office. This morning he couldn't eat or drink and seemed to be suffering. . . . I shall go down to the barn and see how he looks before I go to bed. I want him to get well so much. Two or three of the neighbors have called in to see how he was. Rocker is a favorite. . . .

I have heard no news since my letter yesterday. . . . I hardly ever hear anything from Iconium. I have not been there — that is, to stop or get off my horse — since Will was home. I never go when

I can help it. I expect you hear more news from there than I do, love. We got a letter from Matt last night. He was at Memphis when he wrote, and he was well. The boat they came up on came very near being burned, but they happened to discover the danger in time. . . .

Dollie

Little Rock, Ark., Oct. 23, 1863

My Darling,

. . . About Mullinix. I will bet you a fine dress that he voted for Tuttle. He could not help it very well. He has not got the firmness Dollie and then Tuttle being a *soldier* will make him all right. But don't get mad at him until you get everything out of his hands. He owes me a good deal you know and you know his disposition. . . .

W. F. Vermilion

Sunday Evening, Oct. 25th, 1863

My Own Darling,

. . . I got a letter from Jimmy this morning. They were expecting an attack from [Confederate Colonel John T.] Coffee and his horde of raiders, every day, and there were no troops at Springfield except 2 companies of the 18th, and a few militia. The citizens were scared almost to death, he said, and were pouring into town with such old arms as they could gather. His eyes were no better, and he thought he would have to quit going on duty. I am afraid the boy will lose his eyes yet. He is so careless of them too. He doesn't try to take care of them, I am afraid. . . . I have yesterday's paper. . . . Rosecrans is removed. I am sorry, though I hope it is all right. . . .

Dollie

Monday Evening, Oct. 26th, 1863

My Love,

My cold is not much better. . . . I don't cough so much as I did yesterday, but it hurts me more. My throat and chest were so sore last night I took some opium, and drank a cup full of syrup made of ginger tea and honey, and went to bed early. I thought I should be well by this morning, but I coughed all night. I couldn't sleep much. I dreamed that you had come home, but only stayed a few minutes. I thought you were in your shirtsleeves, and were so fat you could hardly walk. That was a mean dream, wasn't it pet? You shall stay longer when you come again. . . .

Dollie

~~~~~~

Tuesday Night, Oct. 27th, 1863

My Dearest Love,

. . . Well darling, another man wants Woodside. Whom do you think it is? Jake Fees! Old man Fees talked to father about it. . . . He said Jake was coming to see Woodside and asked if it would be worthwhile. Father told him he guessed not. He believed I would not rent it till I heard something more from you about it. Poor simple Jake. What could he do with his idle, worthless wife, and nothing else? I don't expect he is worth as much now as he was the day he married. I have heard he was doing no good at all. He had better have taken our advice. Mullinnix says Dr. Hays got home with Josephus. . . . The poor fellow is bad sick. They think he will not live. . . .

I have been reading the Tribune a little. Greeley has a good article on elections. He says "*of course* Iowa is all right" and that is every word he has to say about *our* election. I should like to have him rapped over the knuckles for passing over our great victory, of which we are all so proud, and which we deem so important, with a simple "of course." But he is in ecstasies over Ohio. He knew the soldiers' votes would defeat the traitor who "waited and watched over the border," but he never dreamed that a candidate so imposingly presented was actually *not running at all*. He never expected to hear that the home vote gave a 60,000 majority against him. It is something to rejoice over and thank God for. . . . A more terrible calamity could scarcely befall our country than Vallandigham's election. . . . We can already see the fruits of the victory. Gov. Seymour has issued a proclamation at once stating that the President had called for 300,000 volunteers and that *he must have them*, and

New York must not be behind in her duty. We would not have seen such a document as that from Seymour if Vallandigham had been elected. . . .

Dollie

Little Rock, Ark., Oct. 28, 1863

My Darling,

. . . As usual at this time of night the boys are singing their old mournful hymns. They make right good music or at any rate it sounds so to me. It may be simply because it reminds me of so many years ago when I used to go to Church, and when I first learned to know Dollie when I saw her. And then they always make me stop and think and I always think of Dollie. I love to hear them. I love to think of Dollie but why do they sing such songs so much if they don't love to think of home and those they love. And my Dollie the boys here are not forgetting their friends. They think of their wives — those who have them — as much as their wives think of them. They get the blues when they don't get any letters. When they get letters and good news they are cheerful and do their duty without grumbling. Their friends at home ought to write and write often. . . .

There was a fight the other day down at Pine Bluffs. It is about 40 miles below here. . . . Col. Clayton[29] of the 5th Kansas was in command. . . . Col. Clayton whipped them without a doubt. . . .

W. F. V.

Friday Morning, Oct. 30th, 1863

My Dearest Love,

. . . I stopped awhile at Mr. Maiken's. . . . They had heard down there that Trim and Simmons (your men) were both dead.[30] I hope it is not true. It scares me for so many of your men to die, my sweet love. . . . There is very little news in our papers. Now that Rosecrans is removed everybody seems turning against him, and making all manner of charges against him. . . . One is that he has used opium lately to such an extent that his mind is greatly injured.

I am going to send you this week's Hawk-Eye. It is a very good number. I see that the 36th gave only 71 votes for Tuttle.[31] That is pretty well. The 40th gave a *majority* for Tuttle. I am sorry for that and hope still that there is a mistake in the figures. The Gate says the 36th cast just 400 votes in all. I suppose that doesn't include the sick men who were scattered through the hospitals.[32] I hear that Jimmy has left Springfield for *Little Rock*. If this is true you will soon see him. The report is that the 18th will winter in Little Rock.

Dollie

Little Rock, Ark., Oct. 30, 1863
My Darling,

Billy Smith is *dead*. . . . Consciousness never returned from the time he was first taken. . . . He lay all the time with his eyes partly closed. He couldn't open them. Now they are completely closed — to open no more in this world of blood and strife. His race is run, his soldiering here is over, and how I wish we could bury him where the sweet rose could grow over his grave in loyal Iowa. But we can't. Tomorrow we must take him out here on the hill and lay him under the sod where already there are many Union boys sleeping there. He will rest as quietly as they for he was as good a soldier as came to Little Rock. Always ready and willing to do his duty. . . . A. B. Prather died this morning and was buried this afternoon. We have but one other man sick here and he is in the Company and able to be about. His name is Luzader. He lives up by Cozad.[33]

I am glad you got a letter from Jane, though I had begun to fear she would never intend [to] write to us. Write to her and tell her we will keep her as long as she will live with us and do just as good a part by her as I can. Write to her immediately and tell her to tell father's folks what she intends to do. Probably they will object but she is *of age*. . . .

This has been muster day again and quite a day it has been too. The Col. got just *drunk* enough to pitch into the boys. He scolded more than I ever knew on any day before. . . .

W. F. V.

Tuesday Night, Nov. 3rd, 1863

My Own Darling,

... The war news ... seems very good. Hooker has got possession of Lookout Mountain, a very important victory I think for us.[34] Everything is important to us now that tends to the safety and success of the army at Chattanooga. If the rebels could dislodge and scatter that army, no matter at what cost, they would do it. Their not doing it proves their weakness and inability. Some of their own papers say they *must* retake East Tennessee, or their cause is hopeless, that if they are not a "long ways from the borders of Georgia next spring, they will be upon the verge of distraction." I trust Bragg will be a long ways *South* of his present locality next spring! We have news from Charleston up to the 27 ult. Gillmore had commenced shelling the city, and the Monitors were all ready for work. I hope we shall hear good news from there very soon now. If we could only know that the vilest of all traitorous cities was captured, or burned up, I should think we had occasion for devout thankfulness. If it *can* be taken, I think it will be now very soon. But you hear the news, love, almost as soon as I do, so I need not be telling you. ...

Have you ever heard that Iowa's quota under the late call for volunteers is about 9,000? Do you think they can be raised? I believe they will. They will give $302 bounty to new recruits, and $402 to soldiers who have served 9 months and over. This seems hardly fair. ... I think the old soldiers who have done the work should have at least as much as men who turn out now at the 11th hour. ... My sheet is nearly full, and it is quite late. I must make my stew and go to bed. I am so lonely without you, sweet love. I wish you were here. Take good care of yourself. ... Don't get sick. Write to me as often as you can. Don't forget your home, my precious one, nor your own

Dollie

Thursday Night, Nov. 5th, 1863

My Dearest Love,

. . . I spent $2 today, and what do you think I bought? Can you guess? A new bridle! I was just obliged to do this, or not ride any more. I had mended the old one as long as I could. Twice I had to dismount and tie it up lately. Rocker got out of patience with it. Father went to Iconium today, and I sent by him for it.

I don't know whether I can get anything on your debts or not this Fall. Father has so much to do, he can't go out and see many of them. I will get him to dun all he sees. The greater part of them I fear are pretty hard ones. But if he could spare the time a good deal might be collected. He would do it if he could. . . .

Dollie

Little Rock, Ark., Nov. 6, 1863

My Darling,

. . . Just as I predicted about Mullinix. I thought in all probability that he would not vote the Copperhead ticket, but I knew he would go for Tuttle. It has not surprised me one bit and as it didn't affect the result any *I don't care a farthing.* . . . Don't get him mad Dollie or he will charge us for everything he has ever done in his life. . . .

Could I get out of the Service with my present good health, my reputation would be gone. The people at home would despise me and my boys here would never forgive me. . . . It is impossible . . . as much as I love you for me to desert my post and come home . . . with such men as Davenport and Dr. Phillips. . . . I know [it] is a long, very long time to be parted from you. In ordinary time I could not endure it. But we are making History faster than all the writers can tell it. . . .

W. F. V.

Nov. 7th, 1863

My Own Love,

. . . I have just been reading Henry Ward Beecher's Manchester speech. It is good and to the point, but it is not nearly so fine as a literary effort as many of his Plymouth sermons.[35] He is in earnest though, and his speeches have created the greatest excitement and enthusiasm throughout England. No man can plead our cause with the English people better than he. He has made some very happy "hits," for instance. It was told to his prejudice there, that, before leaving this country, he had used threatening language towards the British government. That speaking of intervention he had said: "just let England wait till we have put down this rebellion, and *then*" the report stopped there, but when it was thrown in his teeth, in that very England, he curtly finished the sentence. "And there we will show England how we can forgive an injury and *heap coals of fire upon the heads of those who have sounded us.*" He is doing good service, and I wish him a "God speed" in his work. I read somewhere the other day that there are six of the Beecher family in the service. One is Capt. of a negro Regt. And that brave young Col. [Robert Gould] Shaw who fell in the charge on Wagner and was buried with the negros in one common grave was a member of the Plymouth congregation[36]. . . .

Dollie

Little Rock, Ark., Nov. 8, 1863

My Darling,

. . . Will and some of the boys were down to the City yesterday evening to the Union meeting. Rodgers,[37] Gantt, and others spoke. There was a large audience there, principally soldiers. That doesn't tell much for the citizens. Gantt was elected to the Federal Congress in 1860. Afterwards he turned rebel. But he has been whipped and is loyal now[38]. . . .

W. F. Vermilion

Tuesday Night, Nov. 10th, 1863

My Good Darling,

... Mr. Christie went yesterday to see Josephus Hays. He brings a sad account of him. He thinks he may have 2 or 3 weeks, but more probably not that many days. He has chronic diarrhea. I feel so sorry for him, pet, and for his family. ... Jennings' death was a hard blow for them. His mother told me that the manner of his death hurt her worse than his death itself. Perhaps she only thought that. If they had got Josephus home sooner he might have got well. The poor fellow lay in the hospital several months. He never told them in his letters that he was much sick and they would never have known it — in time to see him — had not his sister in Ills. learned the truth, by some means, and wrote to her father to go to him. He started at once, and a few days after they got a letter from Josephus . . . saying he was all right, and able for his ration. I have no doubt but many a poor soldier dies concealing the truth just this way for fear of causing uneasiness to their friends at home. My darling, if you love you[r] Dollie never deceive her in this way. If you get sick tell me or have somebody tell me. . . . Won't you, my own love? I hope you will not get sick, but I am all the time uneasy about it. I can't help it, dear one. I shall be uneasy till I can clasp my arms around you and know that I have you restored to me safe and well. . . .

Dollie

Monday Night, Nov. 16th, 1863

My Own Darling,

... I have had the blues a very little all day. I have felt so lonesome. This afternoon I laid down my sewing and went to my trunk — *your* trunk, love — and read your latest letters over again. I always do this when I am lonesome. They comfort me, sweet love. I have been grieving because you can't come home, but I won't any more dear, if I can help it. It is wrong, I know, and I want to do only right. If you *could* come it should do me more good than anything else in the world — except having you *come for good.*

You don't know how I long to see you, to hear you, to kiss you, to have my darling here to comfort and dine with and advise me — oh, for a thousand reasons I want you, but I must try to forget self, and think of *duty*. If you cannot come I will not distress you by talking any more about it. I will *love you*, and do the best I can and hope for the "better day" that is surely coming. . . .

Dollie

Tuesday Afternoon, Nov. 17th, 1863

My Dearest,

I wrote a letter to Jane this morning — not a very long one, not a very good one. I didn't feel like writing much. I didn't say a word about the war or politics. I thought it would be better not. I told her what I could about you, and a little about myself. I sent my love, and a few kind words to mother, thanking her for her kindness to me while I stayed there. I did not say a word to any of the rest — except dear little Etty. I promised her ever so many nice little books if she would come to see her "aunt Mary." I bought her a new book last spring, and Jane says she thinks so much of it. Jane will be glad to get my letter. I don't know whether any of the rest will care about hearing from me. . . . But we have plenty of *friends*, and *we love each other*! If they won't love us because we love our country, pet, we can't help it, can we? I am sorry, more sorry than you think, dear, but I can't waver in my duty to you and our cause. I would give almost anything in the world if they were all true friends to us, and could understand us, and believe as we do, and sympathize with us. But they never will, sweet love. Let us not be troubled about it. You shall never want for a *friend* to sympathize with you, and comfort you while your Dollie lives. She loves you more than they ever did, my darling. And she knows you better, and appreciates you better than they ever could. We are enigmas to them; we are not to each other. We are more like each other than we are like them. I am not speaking of Jenny. She is good and true. . . .

There is little news in my papers. There are vague hints and promises that Meade will accomplish great results before his campaign is ended. I hope so, but I can't feel very sanguine. Burnside is superceded by Gen. Foster. The notorious Henderson is elected to the U.S. Senate, for the long term, from Missouri (that is good rhetoric isn't it, my pet?). That is bad . . . but I expected nothing better. B. Gratz Brown[39] is sent for the short term. That is *good*, so far as it goes. I heard that the 18th regiment is at Fayetteville Ark. Mr. Gilbert got a letter from his son[40] this morning. They marched all the way from Springfield. Amasa said their shoes were gone up.

Dollie

Little Rock, Ark., Nov. 21, 1863
My Darling,

. . . The Colonel has made application to send a recruiting party home to recruit for our regiment and has asked that I be allowed to command it. . . . If they come around all right I will take the boat from Duvalls Bluff next Wednesday or Thursday[41]. . . .

W. F. Vermilion

Sunday Night, Nov. 22nd, 1863
My Darling,

. . . Humphrey and Julia and the children and Mrs. Gibbons were here today. We had a very good time. Oh, how I wished you were here! I missed you so much! Julia looks better than I ever saw her. She stayed in the kitchen and helped me to get dinner. We talked more than we cooked, I think, but we had a very good dinner, for all that. I wish you could have had part of it. Humphrey is looking as well as you ever saw him, but I don't know whether he is stout yet. They are going to move to Corydon before Christmas. He says his office is worth about $750.00 a year. I am afraid they will not make the ends meet on that sum, but I think they believe it is ample. They haven't counted all the expenses yet. They want to buy a house, and Julia wants a good one, with several rooms. . . . You will be glad to hear that little Billy May is fat as he can be again. He says he would like to see his "Uncle Doctor," but he would rather have Beppo. . . .

Dollie

Friday Night, November 27th, 1863

My Dearest Love,

. . . It seems scarcely possible, my pet, that all our soldiers can ever return. We have been so wonderfully spared so far, that it scares me to think of what may be in store for Hickcox's, Evans', Smiths, both the Gilberts and both the Mays, while we alone are spared talk about these things tonight, my beloved. I thank God every day I live for His mercy to me. While you are living and well, sweet pet, I feel that I have more cause for thankfulness than any one else can have. It is getting so cold that I must quit writing and go to bed. I will talk to you tomorrow, dear. . . . For tonight, my good love, I must say Goodbye. I will dream of you.

Sunday Night, Nov. 29th, We have plenty of war news now. Another terrible three days battle has been fought at Chattanooga — or near there. Grant has won a great victory and the rebels are routed.[42] This is what my papers say. I hope it is all true. You can tell, my darling, how fervently I hope so. But it may have cost us dearly. The 6th Iowa was in the thickest of the fight, charging [with] killed and wounded. There is no list of the casualties yet. We are uneasy about Matt. I am afraid he is killed, my love. Are not you, too dearest? Father and mother are both very anxious. I got a letter from him to day written on the 16th. They had just been ordered to the front. He was very unwell, had one of his severe colds, and I think he had the blues. He said he had lots to tell me but he had no time then. It might be that that was the last letter he would ever write, but we must hope for the best. . . . If he lived through the coming battle he would send me a better letter. This was the way he wrote, and it made me sad to read it now, while we are ignorant of his fate. He said he had not slept in a tent but once or twice since the last of Sept., and often they had no blankets. It was sleeping in the mountains without a blanket that made him sick. Poor fellow! I can hardly bear to think about it, darling. Hickcox got a letter from Ed. He said Jimmy's eyes were still bad. They had plenty of greenbacks and "*greybacks*," especially the "greybacks." They had had no change of clothing for 28 days, and

didn't know when their knapsacks would come. But they were in fine spirits, and ready for anything. They are a jolly set of "sogers" [soldiers]. . . .
Dollie

Monday Morning, Nov. 30th, 1863
Darling,

. . . I don't mean to be taxed in this county if I can help it. And it will be bad if I can't outwit Bill Evans, their copperhead assessor. I have Rocker and Cassie here, and I ought to pay for them, so I told father to put them in with his stock, as he does for the boys. If the assessor comes to see me then I shall tell him I don't live in this county, and that we are taxed at home. This will satisfy Evans I think, without a doubt. But if it should not, if he makes me give in money and notes I will take their notes for all we are worth, and give in nothing but notes! This will not be wrong, will it, my love? I don't think it will. If the Chariton Township assessor comes to see me, I will give on all the property we have in his county. . . .
Dollie

Tuesday Afternoon, Dec. 1st, 1863
My Own Dearest,

We have more news from the battle at Chattanooga, all good news, too, glorious news; but we learn nothing about Matt. I can only hope that he is safe, but I fear for him, love. I have Saturday's paper but there is no list yet of the lost. General Corse was severely wounded,[43] and Major Innes of the 6th killed.[44] This is all we know yet, only that the Reg't was in several desperate charges, and lost heavily. We may hear in a few days. The mail comes in to night, and father says he is going to the office in the morning before day. He thinks he may learn something of him there. But it is a complete victory, my darling, thank God for that! Our latest dispatches say our forces were ten miles beyond Chickamauga driving the rebels before them. Sixty pieces of artillery and 7,000 prisoners are some of the visible fruits of the victory. Meade too is moving. I listen every hour to hear of a decisive battle in Virginia. It may have been fought already. If Meade is successful, and I believe he will be, don't you think, love, that the rebels will *have* to give up the contest? Don't you think we shall soon have peace? It seems so to me, pet. . . .

You have spoken once or twice about orderly Davenport voting. Mrs. Maiken says he didn't vote. . . . He wrote to his father the *democrats* were not allowed to vote! That the polls were guarded to prevent their voting! She says he didn't vote because he was afraid it would injure his prospects in the company, but he couldn't help showing the venom of the serpent. . . .

I am tired tonight. I made sausage today. They killed a fat porker yesterday, and I grounded it up this morning. I wish you had some. I know you would like it. Mrs. Paschal was here to day. She is making a club for Peterson's Magazine,[45] and she came to get me to subscribe. I didn't do it. I told her I didn't care much for ladies magazines while the war lasts, and then there are others that I would much rather have than Peterson's. I hope she will get her club though, for she is a very good, amiable woman. Everyone who gets a club for a good magazine or newspaper is a good public benefactor so far. I have no news to write, my love. Shall I tell you how our new Senate and Legislature look in figures? Like this: Senate, Union 42, Cop.[46] 4. Legislature, Union 87, Cop. 5. How does it please you, dear? Dubuque, Lee, and Alamakee counties have the honor of sending all the copperheads! George Stewart is kindly allowed to remain at home with his "sickly wife and 5 small children." I hope he feels duly grateful to the soldiers for the favor. . . .
Dollie

8

"Our War Can't Last
Much Longer As It Is
Now Carried On"

When Ulysses S. Grant received the rank of General in Chief of the Armies of the United States on March 12, 1864, he hoped to initiate a campaign to capture Mobile, Alabama. Grant put a high priority on this course of action because he knew that the Confederates could ill afford to lose their last major port on the Gulf Coast. But the War Department informed the nation's only lieutenant general (a rank Grant had held since March 9, 1864) that many of the soldiers Grant intended to use against Mobile were already slated for an operation west of the Mississippi River. These troops, Grant learned, had orders to participate in a military excursion that would soon depart for Texas.

A curious mixture of forces motivated the Union high command in this matter, going all the way back to 1862. First, President Lincoln hoped to influence the behavior of France by placing Union troops in Texas. In 1862 Emperor Napoleon III, ostensibly to collect debts owed to French creditors, dispatched soldiers to Mexico as part of a multinational punitive expedition. While the soldiers of the two other countries soon left, the French contingent remained; it quickly became apparent that Napoleon would use them to support a puppet regime that he planned to create in Mexico. Regarding this as a violation of the Monroe Doctrine, Lincoln had the State Department lodge complaints with France, which Napoleon ignored. Left with no peaceful alternatives, Lincoln decided that the arrival of a contingent of Union soldiers on the border of Mexico might persuade Napoleon to forego his dream of an American empire.

Second, Lincoln also looked favorably on such a campaign because of economic considerations. The Union naval blockade of the Confederacy, coupled with a widespread decision by Southerners not to sell their cotton on the international market, had reduced the flow of that commodity to textile mills the world over. As a consequence, Northern mill owners sought a secure source of the raw material, and saw the control of a rich cotton-producing area as the answer. Lincoln could scarcely disregard the opinion of these powerful individuals who, by and large, were members of his political party. Indeed, in October 1862 Lincoln chose Nathaniel Banks, a political general from the textile state of Massachusetts, to lead an expedition to Texas.

Third, the idea of a campaign up the Red River had become nothing short of an obsession for Major General Henry Halleck, the general in chief of the Union army prior to Grant's promotion. When Lincoln made it clear in 1862 that he wanted a Union military presence in Texas, Halleck decided that only an advance into that state by way of the Red River would suffice. Without ever directly ordering him to pursue that course of action, Halleck cajoled Banks for months about conducting such an operation. Various factors, including the siege of Port Hudson, delayed his response, but in early 1864 Banks finally acquiesced.

No doubt pleased, Halleck began to aid Banks in planning this venture. Suspicious about the military abilities of the former Speaker of the House of Representatives, Halleck sought out help from a general of proven ability: Frederick Steele. Halleck actually contacted the general after Steele's occupation of Little Rock, soliciting his opinion on the best method for placing Union troops in Texas. Steele seconded Halleck's strategy to move into Texas via the Red River by offering him troop support. Accordingly, in the spring of 1864 Banks initiated a two-pronged offensive, based on the assumption that Steele's troops would link up with his main forces at Shreveport, Louisiana.

Steele's portion of the campaign initially succeeded. As he moved southward from Little Rock, forces under his command brushed aside Confederate resistance at Elkins' Ferry on the Little Missouri River on April 3, then dislodged the enemy from a strong position at Prairie D'Ane. By April 15 Steele occupied the southern Arkansas town of Camden, and seemed poised to rendezvous with Banks.

It soon became apparent, however, that Steele had to surmount a huge obstacle before even attempting to move southward. Confederate forces had virtually stripped bare the countryside of southern Arkansas. Steele knew that he needed to secure provisions for both his men and his animals before he could proceed. Therefore, Steele began to send out foraging parties to gather the necessary supplies. One such detachment left Camden on April 23, bound for a Union supply depot at Pine Bluff.

This foraging party included an artillery unit, parts of two cavalry regiments, and three full infantry regiments, including the 36th Iowa. Steele would have given command of the expedition to Colonel Kittredge of that regiment, but illness prevented him from taking the field. Lieutenant Colonel Drake subsequently inherited its command.

Drake seemed an excellent choice for the mission. He had proven his valor on numerous occasions. At the age of 18, while leading a wagon train to California, a group of over 300 Pawnee warriors attacked his party. Undaunted, Drake killed the Pawnee chief with a well-placed shot, causing the Indians to flee. On another occasion, Drake found himself shipwrecked off the coast of California. Coolly keeping his head, Drake managed to find a dinghy, and used the small craft to save a number of fellow passengers. His actions during the war had done nothing to diminish his reputation for courage.

Drake made good progress until Confederate forces under the command of Brigadier General James Fagan intercepted Drake's regiment. Wet conditions in an area known as Moro Bottom had slowed down Drake, which gave the Confederates the opportunity to strike such a blow. As a result, nearly 3,000 troops under Fagan's command attacked Drake's 1,800 on April 25, 1864, near a small cluster of buildings known as Marks' Mills. The battle raged back and forth, as Confederate and Union units were fed piecemeal into the melee as they arrived on the field. The postengagement reports credited the 36th Iowa with fighting bravely, especially Captains Porter, Fee, and Hale, and Lieutenant Charles Birnbaum. But Fagan prevailed. Utilizing his superior numbers, Fagan routed the Union detachment by the end of the day, killing, wounding, or cap-

Charles Birnbaum after his promotion to captain,
ca. 1865. Photograph courtesy of Mark Warren.

turing almost 1,200 Federals — including virtually all of the members of the 36th Iowa on the expedition.

William Vermilion missed this engagement. In fact, he had not participated in the campaign at all. He instead departed for Iowa in December 1863, where he spent the next five months in Davenport recruiting new soldiers. After enlisting 118 volunteers, William left Iowa to rejoin his regiment. Ironically, he departed for Arkansas on the very day that his compatriots met Fagan's troops at Marks' Mills.

Once Vermilion arrived in Arkansas, he took command of what was left of his company. He found 25 men on the roster, but only 13 fit for duty. The other companies in the 36th Iowa had suffered losses similar to those of Company F during the campaign. Because of the depletion of the regiment's officer corps, William led the regiment for almost six months after General Steele seconded Colonel Kittredge for other duty. The losses incurred at Marks' Mills, along with those that occurred as Steele retreated to Little Rock, relegated the regiment to garrison duty for the rest of the war.

The letters in this chapter deal with this woeful period in the history of the regiment. It turned out to be doubly tragic for William and Mary: they also learned of the death of Mary's oldest brother, Matt. Moreover, William feared that the malady which had claimed Matt's life might also strike down Mary. The letters also cover the time when the Union war effort sunk to its nadir. But the period also saw the dramatic successes that saved the Union cause, triumphs that led to Lincoln's reelection. The two were also heartened by the arrival in Iowa of William's favorite sister. The correspondence demonstrates Mary's ability to adapt to the changed circumstances brought on by the war — she continued to take care of their business concerns and work as a clerk. Finally, the letters show a growing realization on their part that they will soon be together forever.

Davenport, Iowa, April 23, 1864
My Darling,
   ... So far we have had a very pleasant time, considering that we have just left our dearest friends behind. At Albia I found our recruits all ready. . . . Hickenlooper[1] had 5 recruits whom he had never reported. . . .
Will

Steamer *Savannah*, Mississippi R., April 27, 1864.
My Darling,

. . . We passed Burlington a little before noon. I saw the state prison at Ft. Madison, and got a good view of the river portion of that City. . . . Late this evening we came on to the Rapids. The boatmen tell me they extend about 18 miles. . . . We are lying tonight at Montrose. On the Illinois side is Navou². . . . The town is situated on a beautifully situated piece of ground (That is bully English). There appears to be but one corner of the old Temple standing. It was built of stone. . . .

W. F. Vermilion

Thursday Evening, May 5th, 1864.
My Dearest Love,

We are just done planting corn "to our house." We had a piece about as large as the garden and we planted it for roasting ears. I "dropped," and father covered it with his plow. We have everything planted now. I am glad of it, for the work seemed pretty hard for me. I am lazy. . . .

I am as uneasy as I can be about you, sweet love. I am afraid you are sick, and I am afraid of the guerrillas along the river. I am afraid you want to go to Little Rock, and will be captured while trying to get to the regiment. I shall not be content one moment till I hear [from] you. . . .

You didn't tell me whether you were taking down any recruits, or how many were on your boat. I should like to know. I wish I knew whether you are going to Little Rock. I don't think you can get to the regiment now. If there was any line open we could hear from them. I often think of Mrs. Drake, how uneasy she must be. I should like to see her. . . .

. . . The volunteers leave in a week, I believe. I suppose Mericle will get a commission. I fear he doesn't deserve it. . . .

Dollie

Memphis, Tenn., May 5, 1864.
Dollie,

We have just seen Capt. Haden — Gen. Steele's Chief of Artillery[3] — and he says Col. Drake was killed at Saline River Arkansas on the 25th ult. He was commanding the train that was captured. . . . I hope it was but a detachment of the regiment that was captured. . . .

W. F. Vermilion

Friday Afternoon, May 6th, 1864.
My Own Darling,

. . . Father went to Iconium last evening. He saw 11 volunteers for 100 days, sworn in.[4] Mr. Stewart was one, and Eads and Mullinnix and John Dykes, and Davy Maiken. I believe these are all I know. Milo Phillips is going; and Steve Benthusen and Frank Gilbert[5] are raising a squad. Mullinnix sent word to me to come and see him before he starts. He said he couldn't come here, as he was going to plant his corn before he goes. I will go I think, for he may want to make some arrangements about his note. I would like if he could. Wouldn't you?. . .

Did I tell you about the nice album Matt sent me? I . . . was greatly pleased with it. It will hold 24 pictures. Poor old fellow! I am afraid *he* will never see it again. Somehow, darling, I *don't feel* like he will ever come back any more. But he may. God only knows. He told us a dreadful secret, love, about poor Jim Hickcox. It shocked me, and I didn't get over it for days. I will tell you but you must never tell *anybody*. It is the "dead secret" of Co. E! Jim was not killed by the enemy, but by *one of his own mess*! Young Cyrus Blue[6] of Lagrange did it. It was an "accident" of course, but *how* it could happen none of them could understand. Matt and Jim were very near each other, and some paces in front of all the others. They had just reached a safe cover — a tree, and log — when they heard the report, and saw the flash of the Blue's gun, and Jim was shot in the back! The poor fellow never knew whence the shot came. Blue took it terribly to heart, at first, and for his sake, and for the sake of Jim's friends, they vowed among themselves to keep it always a secret. It has been better kept than most secrets of that nature could be. I believe Mrs. Hickcox would be crazed if she knew it. I hope she never will. They fought over the dead body two days, and both his legs, and both his arms were shot off, and his head almost. This is part of the "secret," that they never tell. How Blue could come home, and mingle with Jim's friends as he did, and get married, and seem to enjoy himself quite as well as any of them, is the mystery to me. There cannot be much *sensitiveness* about him. You won't speak of it to anyone? You know I can't, pet darling, keep a secret from *you*, but *we* can keep one.

I wrote to Jane yesterday, and last night I got a letter from her. I have good news from her, and *astonishing* news too, my love. She is in Greencastle going to the seminary! What do you think? She went with one of George Hurst's girls — Melissa,[7] and is rooming at Mrs. Hibbs's, and Tom and Isaiah are *paying expenses!* She said she knew I would think it very strange, and she thought it very strange herself. But they wanted to send her, and she wanted to go, and there she is. She seems delighted with everything. . . . She learns rapidly. Is going another term. Are you not glad for *our Jenny*, my love? I am. I think I know just how it came about. Your writing to Jane last winter and offering her a home, and protection, and all the money she wanted has made Tom and Isaiah *ashamed of themselves.* I hope, too, it opened their eyes so they could see themselves as we saw them. They know Jane has slaved and worked for them for years — ever since she was born almost — while she did nothing for you, and none of them did anything for you. And then for you to make such an offer was enough to arouse their pride if nothing else. . . .

May 7th, 1864, My Own Darling, . . . You ask what I think of the Lincoln-Blair arrangement. I think just as you do, love. It is one of the President's most egregious blunders. Not two men have done more to injure our cause than the two Blairs. I have no respect for either. I wonder how long we must suffer for their sins? I am glad to see that the Senate Committee will not sanction the President's course. They have decided that Blair is not in the Service at all, because he held his commission in violation of law. We shall see how

it will end.[8] If the Blairs should go over bodily to the Confederacy we should be about as well off as we are. . . .
Dollie

Wednesday Morning, May 11th, 1864.
My Dearest Love,

I didn't write again last evening, as I said I would, for there was someone here all the time till dark, and then our mail came, and I was so excited over the news that I couldn't write. I sat up reading and thinking nearly all night. I felt like I couldn't go to bed or sleep. . . . We hear that Grant has been fighting 3 days, and the result is hardly yet known. The last dispatch says Lee was falling back and had left 13,000 dead and wounded rebels in our hands. . . . And then there is other news more interesting to me than even this. Some dispatches say that Steele's army has fallen back to Little Rock, followed and harassed by Price, and that he and Marmaduke will join and attack the Rock. Other dispatches say Steele had quite outgeneraled the rebels, had captured Camden, after considerable fighting, and was preparing to move on Shreveport. But I rather think the 36th will come back to Little Rock. I do want to hear so badly, love. . . . One special dispatch from Cairo says: "Col. Drake of the 36th Iowa has reached Little Rock. His wound is doing well, and he will start home in a few days." This is all, dear, but what can it mean, if they have not been in battle, and Col. Drake [has] been wounded? We have rumors in plenty, but we have not heard one word directly from the boys since they started on the expedition. We hear frightful reports constantly. The last one is that Lieut. Wright is killed, and his brother Sam severely wounded. Mother is [convinced] that the whole regiment were killed and taken prisoner. It won't do to begin to believe anything we hear of this sort, but you know love, we are very anxious about them. . . . Col. Drake can give an account of it, if no other way. Perhaps you will meet him, and I hope, for his poor wife's sake, that he isn't badly wounded. She said she always felt that he would be wounded. That was strange, wasn't it, darling?
Dollie

In Camp at Little Rock, Ark., May 11, 1864
My Dollie,

I am in camp again all right, but it is a blue place. There are but 21 of my company here and 4 up the river I believe. The rest are all taken prisoner, that is what are not killed. We know Lieut. May is dead. He was wounded in the leg and died in 3 days. Lieut. Pearson of Centerville saw him die and helped bury him. James H. Ryckman is dead. . . . There are 15 who are *reported* wounded, others may have been killed on the field. . . . Col. Drake was not killed. . . . He was wounded, paroled, and started home yesterday morning. . . . Sergt. Brashar was wounded at Saline River, and Corpl. Duckworth at the Little Missouri. . . . James Kemper is here, and tolerably well. . . .

Vermilion

Little Rock, Ark., May 12, 1864
My Dollie,

. . . Our regiment left their camps here on the 23rd day of March, and it is claimed by our men and conceded by all who I have heard speak of it to have been the best regiment that left here on that expedition. . . . The first fight they were in was at the Little Missouri on the 4th day of April.[9] The regiment had 17 wounded. . . . On the 23rd or 24th Col. Drake was put in command of our Brigade which was composed of the 43rd Ind., 77th Ohio, and our regiment, with a train of between 200 and 300 wagons, and ordered to Pine Bluff for supplies. On the 25th he was attacked by some 5 Brigades of Price's Army. Before our forces had time to do much the rebels moved up and made the attack on the front right and left. But 2 regiments were up at the time — the 36th and the 43rd Ind. The 77th Ohio was in the rear some 4 miles. The 2 regiments fought the whole rebel force until the 77th came up. . . . Colonel Drake was wounded early in the engagement and after he fell there was not much commanding done. Maj. Hamilton did all he could, but the boys fought principally on their own hook until they were forced by superior numbers to surrender by detail. The rebels couldn't get them to surrender by regiment or company. They were forced to hunt them down by ones, twos, and threes and so on, until they finally got nearly all the boys. Lt. May was wounded in the leg — below the knee — early in the engagement. After the battle he was picked up and cared for until he died, which was on the 28th. . . . The boys who escaped think Will Kemper went through all right but made a prisoner. . . . Nimrod Marchbanks was in the fight at Marks Mills, when the trains were captured. After the fight was about over he made his escape and went into Pine Bluff. . . . Will Grissom was taken prisoner by 2 or 3 officers. One of the 1st Iowa Cavalry was taken prisoner at the same time. Will asked the rebel officers if he might ride behind the cavalryman. The rebels said yes so he got up. They had not gone far before they came to a fork in the road. As the rebs turned one way the cavalryman turned the other, and put his spurs to his horse. The rebs drew their revolvers and ordered him to halt but there was no stop to him. They . . . traveled all night and got to Pine Bluff the next day. Luther Landes [10] made his escape too by riding the adjutant's horse out. . . .

Will

Little Rock, Ark., May 15, 1864
My Darling,
   . . . On Friday Night Colonel Kittredge was detached and put on a General Court Martial for the trial of Colonel somebody, "and such other cases as might be brought before the Court." That left me in command of the regiment, or what is left of it. . . .
W. F. Vermilion

Little Rock, Ark., May 20, 1864
My Darling,
   . . . Poor James Hickcox. . . . He was a good soldier and had always done his duty, and what a horrible thing it is. . . . Is Matt sure he is right in thinking he was not killed by the enemy. It is the strangest thing in the world to me how a good, well-drilled soldier could make such a blunder. . . .

   I am truly glad that Jane has met with one streak of good luck. . . .

Two terms are not enough for her though, Dollie. She ought to go for at least a year. By that time she could teach for her living. If she doesn't get to go long enough to get sufficiently advanced to enable her to teach she will have to go back to fathers and work for the rest of them just as she has been doing for the last 10 years — that is if she doesn't go to Iowa and live with us. . . .

Will Vermilion

Little Rock, Ark., May 21, 1864.
My Darling,

. . . If you will look in the Missouri Democrat of last week you will see what the boys say is a good description of the fight at Marks Mills. The boys say Col. Drake was brave but that he deposed and handled his troops badly. . . .

Vermilion

Monday Night, May 23rd, 1864.
My Dearest Love,

I sent you a long letter this evening. I can't write much to night. Mrs. Stewart and Mr. Stewart have been here all day. They came early, and stayed till after supper. They are pretty good spirits, except about John Davis, and they still think he may be safe.[11] They are very anxious to have some account of there from you. They hear so much, and so many contradictions, that they don't know what to believe, but if they could hear from you they would know the truth. They had no news, only at one of their town meetings the other night they tried to get volunteers. There were several young men present, but they wouldn't go. At last 9 girls went up in a body, and offered themselves. Mericle said he didn't know what to do, he didn't like to take them. The girls insisted on going in, but finally said if 4 or 5 young men *of whose names they had a list*, would go in their places, *they would stay at home and plow*! They handed in the list and Mullinnix called off the names. Jake McInich and young Frankhouser[12] were 2 of them, I don't know the other. The *young men* got indignant very! and Frankhouser has since written a scandalous, anonymous letter about the girls. It is thought he did it, at least. Mrs. Stewart says if the girls ever get him in their power it won't take them a minute to hang him. I don't know who all the girls were. Jane Sheeks and the Roy girls, and Delay's[13] are all I know. Mr. Stewart says your life was *seriously threatened*, darling, after that oyster supper. *They were afraid*, and that alone saved you. Dunover was the most open of your enemies. Stewart *heard* him threaten your life. He is gone to Idaho, to get out of reach of the draft. I am afraid Mr. Stewart will never get back, my love. He looks very thin and weakly. He says he is useless here, and if he can go and fight in the place of some strong, brave soldier . . . it will be a service worth risking his life to accomplish. He doesn't see how any man, with a heart in him, can stay at home now. . . . He has a notion that you will be promoted now to a command in some of these new Reg'ts. . . .

Tuesday Evening, There is a new trouble among the people up here. I will tell you because your care for your Dollie last winter may have saved her life. A great many are so alarmed that they may greatly exaggerate the danger. I don't know how that is. You remember when you kept me from being *vaxinated* last winter? And how sore the girls' arms were? Well, everybody nearly was vaxinated with the same kind of virus, their arms never got well, but all the time worse; till, since the very warm weather, a good many are down sick. Their throats particularly are affected. And the people about here say that the doctors say it is *syphilis*— isn't that the name of a terrible disease, my darling?[14] That is . . . what the people here say, pet; you know I don't know anything about it myself. Old Mrs. McCully[15] and her girls are bad. They have consulted Gibbons. All the Pepperses have it. Mr. Bill Peppers[16] went to Centerville a day or two ago to get advice. He says several persons over there have died of it, and one girl has had her arm taken off. I hardly think this can be true. He is almost scared to death. They are trying to burn out the sores now with caustic. Two of Hickcox's little girls have it and their mother is greatly distressed. What do you think about it, dear one? Can it be what they think it is? Can it be *cured*, if it is? . . .
Dollie

Little Rock, Ark., May 26, 1864.
My Darling,

... The boys tell some queer tales of our wounded while they were in the hands of the rebels. ... The rebel wounded complained very much, and as the rebel surgeon said of wounds that were comparatively slight, while our men were cheery and were mirthful who were apparently badly wounded. Some of our boys would sing their camp songs and at the same time pour cold water on their own shattered limbs. Another great peculiarity in our men: each one thought he was going to get well. The rebel wounded generally thought they would die. The boys say they were treated very well, after they were taken to the Hospital. The rebel Hospital nurses attended the men indiscriminantly, paying no attention to who they were. A great many women went to see them. Some were very kind, others asked "What are you-uns all down here fighting we-uns all for," "When you get well you will go home and let we-uns alone, won't you?" There has never been any fighting in that part of the country before, and many of the poor devils thought the whole United States was whipped. ...

The report is ... that General Rice is dead. He was wounded ... in the ankle. From some cause his leg was not amputated. Some few days after I got here he started for his home in Oskaloosa Iowa, and reports say [he] died on the way between Memphis and Cairo. I hope it is not true [17]. ...
W. F. V.

Little Rock, Ark., May 30, 1864.
My Dollie,

... I want to send Lt. Wright a letter. It will be impossible to get one to Will. He is gone south — somewhere into Texas, and we have not been informed to what point. ... Poor fellow, he will have the blues badly, and there is no telling how long he and the other boys who are with him will have to stay. The Government is not exchanging any at this time [18]. ...
Vermilion

Little Rock, Ark., June 1, 1864

My Darling,

. . . This morning directly after breakfast I received an order from General Steele's Head Qrs. detailing me to sit on a "board of officers" to determine the amount of rent the Government should pay an old Gentleman for a building the Q.M. was using which belonged to him. . . . He appeared to be very communicative and went on to tell us all the damage the Government had done him since the Army came here. . . . Among other things they — the military — had torn down a certain plank building and had used it for various purposes — he was particular to enumerate everything. Some he said had been used to construct the Gallow on which the Spy was hung.[19] I simply remarked that that much of it was put to good purpose. The old chap had no more to say. . . .

W. F. Vermilion

Sunday, June 5th, 1864

My Dearest Love,

. . . I have eaten my dinner, and now I will tell you what I did yesterday, love. I am afraid you will hardly be pleased, but if it is wrong you must not scold *much*, sweet pet, for I did what I thought was right. Old Mr. Messenger came here to see me about the mortgage he had on Shepherd's land, and I bought it, dear. His claim, principal and interest, was $164.00. I paid him that, and took the note, and mortgage. I didn't know what to do about it. He was obliged to have money, and couldn't wait for me to write to you, and get an answer. Dr. Shafer[20] wanted it if this is the mortgage you told me Shafer had last winter — and sent word to Messenger last Saturday that his money was ready. . . . He was going there to let Shafer have it if I hadn't bought it. He says that I could attend to it as well as you. Shafer said he didn't want it then, but he sold some land lately, and now wanted it. Messenger came here first, because he is an ultra Union man, with 4 sons in the service, and he said Shafer shouldn't have it, if he wanted it, because he is a cop-

perhead. And he thought, too, that he only wanted it to sell to you and make something. . . .
Dollie

Little Rock, Ark., June 6, 1864
My Darling,
   . . . Gen. Sickles of New York came in last evening and of course there had to be a general review of all the troops at this place to-day. . . . General Sickles was out on horseback. He rode quite well although his right leg is off just above the knee and he uses no artificial leg[21]. . . . His general appearance is sloven, but his countenance shows the man. . . .
William

Little Rock, Ark., June 8, 1864
Dear Dollie,
   . . . A Lieut. belonging to the 77th Ohio came in yesterday. He made his escape 20 miles beyond Shreveport by jumping a fence and running for his life. . . . He brings the news that the boys are generally well. The treatment was hard and the boys were suffering considerably; still, but few were sick and all seemed to be quite cheerful. . . . Their destination was supposed to be somewhere in Eastern Texas. I was unable to hear anything in particular about Will. . . .
Will Vermilion

Little Rock, Ark., June 10, 1864
My Darling,
   . . . The disease you speak about as having followed vaccination must be of a Sufolytic [syphilitic] Nature. I don't know what else it can be and if it should prove to be that there is no telling to what extent it may be spread. The people should be careful, and above all things should not suffer anyone else to be vaccinated. *Be sure and don't have it put in your arm Dollie.* How glad I am we have missed it. . . .
Will Vermilion

Headquarters, 36th Iowa Infantry, Little Rock, Ark., June 15, 1864.
My Darling,

. . . Three rousing cheers for Abe Lincoln for the next Presidency. I have just read the proceedings of the convention. . . . Someone told me this afternoon that Fremont had expected the nomination of the Cleveland Convention.[22] I am sorry if he has. I had hoped he would not. . . .
W. F. Vermilion

Headquarters, 36th Iowa Infantry, Little Rock, Ark., June 22, 1864.
My Darling,

. . . Directly after dinner I played a game [of] marbles. The boys beat me for the first time for several days. Orderly Haver[23] and Corpl. Walker played against me and another man who can't play very well. So we got beaten. . . .
Will

Wednesday Evening, July 6th, 1864.
My Own Dear Love,

I haven't written a word for two days because I was sick, and because I could not write till father came from Centerville and I learned something about that mortgage. I have been so troubled about it, sweet pet. I had made up my mind that it was worthless, and our money was gone sure. I knew I couldn't make anything out of Messenger. But father has come home. Judge Tannehill[24] says the mortgage is perfectly good, and he will get you a deed next term of court. There is no difficulty about it. Darling, I felt 10 years younger when I heard that! It will cost more than I thought — perhaps as much as $25.00 Tannehill says. His fee is $15.00. He said he had to pay two prices for everything he lived on and he would charge anybody else $25.00, but for *you*, because you were in the army, he would do it for the fee he always charged. . . . I have no more care about it till the deed is ready. Besides this there is the advertising, and clerk's fee. Father paid him $15.00 and he sent me

Major General John C. Frémont, ca. 1862. From
Camp-Fire Chats of the Civil War, *by Washington Davis.*

his receipt. He is to pay all expenses, and the rest to go on his fee. I am going to pay this, love, out of the money for those *furs* I don't want now! I will save it all this year, my good pet. Now, that you know the mortgage is good are you very sorry I bought it, darling? Don't you think the land is worth more money? I did wrong to buy it, and it is a lesson that will last me all my life. I have been punished for it, but that did make it right in me. *Can you forgive me for it now, my own love?* I am sorry as I can be, but I *can't* undo it now. I will *never* do so again. I wouldn't suffer what I have for the last 4 days, dear, for anything, but I had done wrong and deserved to suffer. Only say you will forgive me and love me as of old. . . .

I got one [letter] from Matt. He was safe on the 27 ult. His letter hurt my feelings. He says he thinks he has the best sister ever any soldier had, and he thinks more of her than anybody else in the world, and a great deal more. Poor fellow. I wish I was half as good as he thinks I am. He says he doesn't mind the bloody work he has to do, when he reads my letters. I ought to write to him oftener I know. He may have fallen in the repulse two days after this letter was written. . . . Father heard at town that Sherman has at last got the rebels out of the mountains. This is glorious news if it is true. Matt said his Capt. was in the hospital, sick with a *sore arm!* They had some smallpox in the Reg't last spring and nearly all the boys got vaxinated, and some of them would lose their arms. He didn't get it in his arm because he had been exposed before he knew it. . . .
Dollie

Headquarters, 36th Iowa Infty, Little Rock, Ark., July 8, 1864
Dollie,
. . . I thought gold would get up to 100% but it has gone to 250%. . . . There will be a continual fluctuation no doubt until Secretary Chase's successor gets established[25]. . . . Some people grumble about high taxes but I wish Congress would levy a sufficient tax to keep the currency up to par. . . .
Will

Tuesday Evening, July 12th, 1864.

My Good Love,

. . . Father went to see Will Collett this morning. He says Matt was wounded, through his thigh, on the 27th of June.[26] It is only a flesh wound, but severe. He was brought into the hospital three days after just as Collett was starting home. He seemed in fine spirits, and the first thing he said when he saw Collett was: "Well, Bill the same cuss who shot you has shot me now. Just another such a job." He was in good health, and well cared for, and Collett thinks he will do well. He will get to come home as soon as he is able. They furlough all the wounded, who can travel, at the hospital. It was 20 miles from the field where Matt was wounded. We shall look for him home in a week or two more. Collett's wound is precisely similar, and the surgeons told him he wouldn't be able for duty again before cold weather. . . .

You see I have been talking as you say "about nothing." Don't you think I have a happy faculty of amplifying on that subject? If I didn't have, I don't know what you would do for letters, dearest. Do you? I haven't so much as the excitement of a game of marbles to stir my beloved. And then nothing happens up here. It isn't so with you. I am sorry your muster rolls are so much trouble. I wish I were there to clerk for you till you get them all made. Sgt. Brashar said you would have them to make for the whole Reg't as there was no person who could do it but you. That will be too bad for you, won't it?

Evening, I have just written to Jane, and enclosed her $20 more. I thought I would be sure and send enough. I hope she will get it all. I have given her such plain directions that I don't think she can have any trouble if she comes alone. I advised her to come by St. Louis, unless she could get a through ticket at Greencastle to come direct from Springfield to Keokuk. There is a road open but they didn't know it at Greencastle when I was there. I had rather she would come, darling, than to stay and go to school. I think we could all get on together till you come home. I do hope you will come this fall, and I still think you will, my pet. Our war can't last much longer as it is now carried on. Do you think it can, dear? It is not like it was when we stood guard on the rebels' property, and caught their negros for them, and fed their women and children. I believe it will end this year, love. Then when you come Jane will already be here without any trouble to you about it. I didn't say anything about her going to school in this letter. I told her to come to Moravia, and I would meet her or send for her if she would write in time before she started. . . .

Dollie

Little Rock, Ark., July 15, 1864.
My Darling,

. . . There was a meeting of Iowa officers this afternoon at Gen. Bussey's Head Qrs. in regard to the death of General Rice. . . . Just before the meeting adjourned Gen. Bussey brought the subject of the Iowa Orphan Asylum[27] up and stated that the enterprise ought to be brought properly before each regiment at this place. . . . There are but a few of us you know but the boys feel disposed to throw in their mite. There are about 200 of us on duty in this regiment and the boys say we can raise $1,000. If we do anything I will give $25. That is a lifetime share. . . .

William

Headquarters, 36th Iowa Infty, Little Rock, Ark., July 20, 1864.
My Darling,

. . . You have read a great deal about the Southern refugees, and no doubt you think you understand their condition, but let me tell you Dollie you know nothing about it. . . . They are occupying huts that were built and occupied by the soldiers last winter. Some of them are quite comfortable quarters while others are merely shanties with no chinking, and sometimes but little roofing. None of them have any floors, and the occupants have their all as a general thing lying around on the ground. . . . In some instances I saw where the whites and blacks were occupying adjoining huts, and I must say in every instance the latter made much the best appearance. They talk more intelligibly, were the healthiest and cleanest and appeared to have a dozen times more energy. In a few instances I talked — or tried to talk — to the white refugees, but it was very hard to get them to enter into a conversation. They seemed to know nothing to communicate. In other instances I spoke to the negroes of their condition, and in every instance they replied promptly and gave a satisfactory acct. of themselves. They all had employment. At Helena the negroes suffered severely, but here it seems is entirely different. . . .

W. F. V.

Hd. Qrs. 36th Iowa Infty., Little Rock, July 22, 1864.

My Darling,

. . . How I would like to be at home this Summer and next Fall. I would like to talk to the people of Appanoose County especially. I want them to know just what the soldiers think of the men who tried to hold the lever on us last Fall. . . . It is impossible for us to forget the effort they made to disenfranchise the soldiers of that county.[28] Look at the facts Dollie and see if you can blame me for screaming just a little. . . .

Will

Wednesday Morning, July 27th, 1864.

My Darling,

. . . I got a letter from Matt yesterday written the 14 inst. He was doing well. His furlough had been sent off and it would take it 6 or 8 days to get around. He thought he would get started home by the 20th of the month. Their first Lieut was not a veteran and had been mustered out, but he was going to wait a week for Matt so he could help him along. He must be nearly helpless from the way he writes. I shall look for him every day now. . . . Father started to Eddyville this morning and thinks he will meet him. Matt say Co. "E" is almost "played out." There are 7 non-commissioned officers and 5 privates left. Of his mess that numbered 22 at first there is 1 solitary man left. His name is Watson.[29] They had 13 men in the fight at Kenesaw Mountain and 5 of them were wounded. This is a sad history, isn't it, love? What do you suppose they will do with the handful of boys left? Did you ever know a company more nearly annihilated, never to have a man taken prisoner? Willis Hays has got home, but I have no idea he will stay. . . .

... The dispatches say Sherman has taken Atlanta, but I am almost afraid to believe it yet. Anyway, have we not paid dearly for our victory? Gen. McPherson was killed near the city.[30] This is a heavy loss.... We could not well spare such a leader at this time — or at any time. I wish he could have lived to finish his work. But it is right as it is, or God would not have taken him....
Dollie

Camp 36th Iowa Infty., Little Rock, July 31, 1864.
Dear Dollie,
... The latest papers report Sherman in Atlanta.... The same papers say the rebels are getting out of Maryland as rapidly as they went in but that they are taking with them a large amount of property.[31] That doesn't bother me however. If the citizens of that part of the country haven't got courage enough to assist in defending themselves and property, I say they should go by the board.... I am sorry to hear of Matt being wounded, although he will not be apt to suffer as much as he would had he remained at the front and continued fighting as he had been....
William Vermilion

Camp 36th Iowa Infty., Little Rock, Aug. 2, 1864.
My Darling,
... I think a large portion of Mr. Price's Army is north of us probably on their way to Missouri.[32] The rebels are stronger in central and northern Missouri than they have been for 2 years. They are trying to drive us back — or pull us back rather — to that country....
W. F. Vermilion

Head Quarters 36th Iowa Infty., Little Rock, Aug. 15, 1864.
My Darling,
... Capt. Harvey of the 6th Kansas is here on his way home. He has served his 3 years as Capt. and is now going out.... Some 15 days ago he had the bad luck to have nearly all his Company captured.[33] They were on outpost duty at Ft. Smith and were at-

tacked by a Brigade under the rebel Gen. Cooper.[34] The men were nearly all either killed or captured. John Hinton's boy, Isaiah Roy, Cyrus Teater and several others are prisoners. One of the Zintz's and old man McCauley's boy were killed on the field. Noah Scott[35] is a prisoner. Have you ever thought how many Appanoose County men are being *captured* this season. 4 companies of our regiment, one of the 3rd Cavalry and Capt. Harvey's, and then the Company of the 6th Iowa are nearly all gone. . . .
Vermilion

Headquarters, 36th Iowa Infty., Little Rock, Aug. 18, 1864.
My Darling,
. . . I was in the street with Capt. Harvey and we accidentally met Col. Kittredge. Of course I gave him an introduction to the Capt. The Colonel asked how they were getting along. Capt. Harvey replied that he had just lost quite a number of his men. Col. Kittredge told that Kansas men never did anything to cause them to lose men. That they wouldn't fight, and a great deal more such talk. *Capt. Harvey took it in a minute* and retorted by telling the Col. that Kansas had as brave troops as any state and if he didn't think so he had better try it. . . . I ought to have asked Harvey's pardon for introducing him to a man of such low breeding but I didn't.
Vermilion

Camp 36th Iowa Infty., Little Rock, Aug. 23, 1864.
My Own Darling,
. . . We have just learned . . . from Pine Bluff that Major Hamilton and 2 captains of our regiment have just got into that post having made their escape from Tyler.[36] They will be up the first opportunity. . . .

Let us talk about Uncle Abe's affairs. . . . He has been President now for nearly 4 years and he has no more ardent supporter than myself. I have believed and still believe he has the good of our country at heart, since his election as well as before. . . . But my Dollie, if the country were not in the condition it is in, *I should want to vote for someone else.* . . . Other men might have made

errors full as bad as Lincoln's, but I think some men would have shunned the ones he has committed, and even that thought makes one think "Perhaps we had better try some other man." His treatment of the Radicals in Missouri has been a sting to me. . . . Our friends there — the friends of our Government there — are Radicals. . . . Then why, oh why, has he treated them as he does!
Vermilion

Camp 36th Iowa Infty., Little Rock, Sept. 1, 1864.
My Darling,

Capt. Lambert, Capt. Miller[37] and Maj. Hamilton have just come up from Pine Bluff. They were 34 days on the road from Tyler to that place. Company F were all well and none of the boys had died. . . . I go to the City to examine rebel deserters. . . .
Vermilion

Camp 36th Iowa Infty., Little Rock, Sept. 15, 1864.
Dollie,

At last the fall of Atlanta is confirmed, and how glad we are. Sherman is the General of the season. Hardee — the author of the Infantry Tactics [book] we have been using in our army for so long — is dead. . . . The old raider John Morgan has gone up at last[38]. . . . The sky seems to brighten, but there is a great deal to do yet. . . .
Vermilion

Camp 36th Iowa Infty., Little Rock, Sept. 20, 1864.
My Darling,

. . . Lt. Vermilya[39] — of Unionville, Appa. Co. — came in from Tyler yesterday evening. He made his escape on the 17th of Aug., and went to Natchez, and then came up the Mississippi and White River. . . . Some other boys who came a few days ago left the stockade after he did, and consequently bring later news. . . . Peppers was still living though very low.[40] 5 of Co. F had made their escape. The boys didn't recollect their names. . . .
Vermilion

Lieutenant William Vermilya, ca. 1864. Photograph courtesy of Mark Warren.

Camp 36th Iowa Infty., Little Rock, Ark., Oct. 1, 1864.
My Darling,

. . . Col. Drake has returned, looking as finely as I ever saw him, though he is unable to walk without his crutch. . . . He will not be able to take command of the regiment. . . . With 3 field officers belonging to the regiment I think at least one should be here to command. I have been commanding the regiment and 3 companies since the 3rd of June. . . .

Oct. 2, The news from Sheridan is still good.[41] Early must get out of the valley or his army will be ruined. In fact Col. Drake brings the rumor that Sheridan has captured 15,000 of his forces. . . . Vermilion

Tuesday Afternoon, Oct. 4th, 1864
My Dearest Love,

 . . . You were not in very good spirits about the war when you wrote, darling. I can tell that you had not yet thrown off the gloom and doubts that expressed all Unionists for months after the Baltimore convention. Those were dark days, my love. But thank God the clouds are breaking. I trust we shall never see such days again. You are not alone in your views about Lincoln's nomination, pet. I have heard the same things said often. John Hays said the other evening that he would do all he possibly could for Lincoln as he believed every man who loved his country would, but he would have been very thankful for the privilege of voting for someone else. I hear the same thing often. I think it is all for the best as it is, my darling. Lincoln has blundered terribly sometimes I know, but I know he is honest and means well, and could we afford a change now? There is not a man living who could have been in the President's place and committed no errors. He is obstinate *in the right*, sometime, you know. Don't you remember how persistently he adhered to Grant when nearby there in the loyal press deprecated his appointment to command an important Department. Nobody is sorry that he clung to Grant now. His Missouri policy was past finding out, but he *wouldn't* throw Schofield aside. Well, nobody complains of Schofield now. Let us forgive him the wrong — and there is a good deal to forgive, I know — and trust him to finish the bloody work he had to do. No man on earth ought to envy him his place. . . .

I have a bit of home news to tell you that is right good. There were 22 men drafted in Chariton township last week.[42] The draft went off at Grinnell, for our Congressional district. Their quota is 11, but they drafted twice the number. I don't know who are "elected" yet. They expected their "list" last night, but they didn't come. Matt said there wasn't a copperhead to be see at Iconium yesterday. They were afraid to be out doors, I suppose. They were sorely troubled about the men they lost to Johns township last winter. *Some copperheads proposed to get them back by paying them $50 bounty yet!* Mericle went to Centerville yesterday to see if this could be done, Matt thinks. He told a number of them when he came back, that he couldn't do anything. It was too late! Poor Cops! And nobody is sorry for them. I am not much interested but I should like to hear some are drafted. I hope there is not a Union man among them. How they will all "suffer in the flesh" till they know who is doomed. I will tell you as soon as I learn their names. I am glad that some more poor fellows have escaped from Tyler. I wonder if Will were not one of the 5 of Co. "F" who got out. . . . But I fear more of them will die on the way and never be heard of even if the rebels don't recapture them. You never tell me whether the boys say the prisoners are suffering greatly in the stockade or not. I should like to know what they say, dear one. I fear there is no hope of an exchange after all. I do wish they could all get away now while the rebel troops are busy in Missouri. Graham says that Capt. Miller told him in Keokuk that many of their guards were good Union men — better Union men than some of the prisoners. . . .

Dollie

Camp 36th Iowa Infty., Little Rock, Oct. 15, 1864
My Darling,

The time is 9 o'clock at night, and the most of this inactive VII Army Corps is asleep or on duty, and I might add engaged in their nightly revels. This is the hour the dissipated generally select to indulge their ill natures, and could one look into the saloons and houses of ill fame in the City just now I imagine the sights would not be very encouraging to the moral. . . .

Albert Gillman[43] — a recruit that came to my company from Milledgeville — is dead. He was wounded at Marks Mills and has been in the hospital ever since. His wound was getting better but he had diarrhea for a long time. It was that I think that killed him. . . .

We have no news of Col. Kittredge of late. . . . Col. Drake told me yesterday that Kittredge could never command again — that he intended to tell him that he never would acknowledge him as his commanding officer. The most of the officers in the regiment have about come to the conclusion to be abused by him no longer, and if Col. Drake stands up to what he says, something will be done that will rid us of the greatest weight and drawback we have ever had. . . .

Vermilion

Camp 36th Iowa Infty., Little Rock, Ark., Nov. 1, 1864
My Darling,

. . . Do you think it best for Jane to travel around with the youngsters so much Dollie? What girls is she associating with? Be sure and have her keep clear of Nicholson's girls[44]. . . . I want to get her into better society just as soon as we can. . . .

We are looking for Col. Kittredge every day, and when he comes we are going to have an exciting time I think. Col. Drake is getting up charges and specifications against him. . . . In my opinion Col. Kittredge will have to resign or he will be dismissed [from] the service. One of the charges will be drunkenness, one that if proven will dismiss him. I can furnish notes — taken during the Summer — sufficient to do the work. . . . Other officers are beginning to realize what I told them two years ago. . . . It can't make Col. Kittredge any more bitter against me. If it does let him pitch in, for Col. Drake is my friend, and I will assist him all I can. . . .

Nov. 3, There is a rumor in town that Pleasanton has captured Marmaduke and 10,000 men[45]. . . . Price surely can't get out of Missouri and Kansas with his whole army. We have forces enough in that country to either capture or disperse his whole force if they push their advantage as Sheridan does in the Shenandoah Valley. . . .

Vermilion

Camp 36th Iowa Infty., Little Rock, Nov. 8, 1864
My Darling,

We have had an election, and what do you suppose the result is? The regiment has polled 237 votes, and all of them are for McClellan *but 233*.[46] What would Greely think of that do you suppose. He thought the eastern soldiers would cast 4 or 5 for Lincoln to 1 for McClellan. . . . We have given 58 and a fraction for our country to 1 against it. Bully for the 36th Iowa. Yet I am not satisfied. I didn't want any man who has been with this regiment for 2 years to cast a vote on the side of our enemies. But there are 4. I hope they did it through ignorance. There surely can't be a man in our regiment who voted the Copperhead ticket understandingly. There was not a vote cast by a member of my company against our country. . . .

Later. Appanoose Co. extends 69 votes for the Union and 3 for the Copperheads. So we only get a majority of 66. That will help our loyal friends considerably[47]. . . .
W. F. Vermilion

Camp 36th Iowa Infty., Little Rock, Nov. 9, 1864
My Darling,

. . . The war seems to be shaping badly in Sherman's Department. I don't like the idea of Hood getting so far in the rear . . . without having to fight for it.[48] Sherman is after him I know. . . .

Nov. 11, The 29th Iowa has not done as well as was first reported. They gave McClellan 51 votes, and Lincoln 550. . . . Copperheads have no share in this regiment. All of us who have been at home know them too well. Corpl. Walker says they are the meanest set of men he ever knew in his life. The boys who have been at home this summer say I never told them just how bad the Copperheads were in . . . Iconium. Their going home has done the most considerable good. Noah Graham can say the hardest things of them of any man I nearly ever saw. Orderly Davenport can't near sit and listen as the boys read his letter. He goes for Lincoln with all his might. . . .

Major General George B. McClellan, ca. 1862. From
Camp-Fire Chats of the Civil War, *by Washington Davis.*

I am not learned, I am not great, and of course can never know and say great and wise things, as great and wise things have been said in the days of yore. But there is one thing I can say, and say it truthfully as anyone who has ever lived and been blessed with the power to write or speak, and that is I love my Dollie with all my heart. A little longer must we suffer . . . and then I hope the war will be no more, and that freedom will reign throughout the land. . . .

Nov. 12, I have been reading an English story. . . . A young doctor married a young girl of 16. He was a good, everyday fellow. She was romantic, knowing . . . but little of the realities of life. . . . He read his medical books and counted his dollars and wanted his wife to put her time in working with the needle. In one week after they were married they found out that they didn't like to talk to each other. Suppose that had been our condition my darling, what would have become of us in the future? They didn't quarrel, but they did the next worst thing; they didn't talk to each other.
W. F. Vermilion

Camp 36th Iowa Infty., Little Rock, Nov. 19, 1864.
My Dear Dollie,
This morning's mail brought me a letter from Sergeant Grimes. He wrote that Matthew had died at the pest house the night before of Small Pox.[49] What a sad thing my darling, that he should die of that disease and under those circumstances in the fourth year of his soldier life. He was the first of our number to enter the service of our Country, the first wounded on the battlefield, and the first to yield his life in the sacred cause for which we are all contending. It is hard to think of his death as it occurred. All brave soldiers like him who have to die want to die on the battlefield with the Star[s] and Stripes floating proudly over them. . . . But we must submit to the laws of Him who rules in the Hospital as well as on the battlefield. It makes me sad to talk about his fate my darling. I am sorry, truly sorry for you and for your aged mother and father. . . .

Col. Kittredge is here. . . . The charges and specifications against Col. Kittredge have been handed to Gen. Salomon, our division commander. . . . He requested the General to let him withdraw them but he refused and no doubt is not stopping until the case is tried by Court Martial, and then unless the Col. is acquitted the case will have to go to the President of the United States. The case is such that he must be either acquitted or dismissed [from] the service. . . .

W. F. Vermilion

Camp 36th Iowa Infty., Little Rock, Ark., Nov. 28, 1864.
My Darling,

. . . Appanoose County is all right. They have beaten us but 35 on the home vote. We did enough right here in the regiment to overcome that — and considerably over. Their balls and whisky in the cellar last winter didn't do them any good. They are gone up in Appanoose County henceforth and forever more. . . .

The 33rd Iowa is just now the talk of the whole VII Army Corps. They returned from a trip to Ft. Smith on the night before last, and went into their old quarters. Just after night the Division Band, a band of dutchmen brought here from Wisconsin by the dutch Gen. Salomon for the especial benefit of the various dutch organizations of this army, and especially of the 1st Division, went into their camp to give them a serenade. They stopped before Col. McKee's[50] tent and commenced playing. . . . The enlisted men fell upon the musicians and beat them with stones till their flesh was very sore. The Lt. Col., the Major, and the line officers went out and told them that they were sinning against the dutch, the army regulations, and the privileges of bands in general, but they heeded them not, but caused the stones to fly so thickly that the safety of the officers required that they return to the place from whence they came. So the Wisconsin dutchmen, who it seemeth are here without proper authority from the War Department, were left to the mercy of the infuriated 33rd Iowa Infty and their flying stones, and it seemeth that the 33rd Iowa Infty and the stones prevailed, and that the dutchmen composing the band had to go away with their flesh all bruised, and their heads more sore than when they came. Since then it has come to pass that when one soldier meets another soldier in the road or on the streets of the City or in his quarters, they say one to another "the 33rd Iowa hath stoned the dutch blind because the dutch that rodeth in this Department doeth unto the dutch soldier better things than they doeth unto the white soldier. Some who serveth their Country well sayeth one to another: Sing ye to the Lord, for He hath trumped gloriously; the dutchmen of the land hath He caused to be stoned." The 29th Iowa had had some trouble with Gen. Salomon about the same band. Some say the Gen. is not allowed to muster the band and that he tried to collect a tax from the various regiments to pay them, and that the 29th being the first called upon refused to pay. Since then the 29th Iowa has been transferred to another Division. . . . Vermilion

Camp 36th Iowa Infty., near Little Rock, Dec. 9, 1864
My Darling,

. . . Do you remember the morning one year ago my pet? Yesterday evening one year ago I left Eddyville. . . . It seemed we never would get to Albia, and we were longer if possible getting to Moravia. When we got there we thought we were nearly home, and that we would get horses and ride out in a very short time, but there was no one there who thought enough of a soldier to hire him a horse to ride even that far, so we had to foot it as far as Mr. Cuppy's.[51] They had souls in there. They all got up and then the old gentleman went to the prairie and got us horses to ride. We soon rode up to Mr. Maiken's. They had just got up and didn't know me until they saw Henry. . . . I was glad to see them but there was someone else I wanted to see a good deal worse; so I didn't stay long but got a fresh horse, and a very foolish one too, and went ahead. . . . A little further on I got lost, my horse was so mean. I must have gone north of Mr. Sheeks' field. It seemed I was lost a long time but it couldn't have been an hour. At last I got straight, and to Dollie's house. Your father had just got up and started a fire. I went in, and like Mr. Maiken he didn't know me. In a few minutes he recognized me. I asked him where Dollie was. He said she was in bed. He asked me if he should wake her up. I told him he might or I would do it myself. He took the candle and started, but it seemed to me it would be too long for me to wait, so I followed and got the first kiss I had had for nearly 14 months. I will remember that meeting a long time my pet. I thought of it first thing this morning and I have been thinking of it all day. . . .

Maj. General Steele is relieved at last and I am heartily glad. Gen. Reynolds[52] takes his place. . . .

Vermilion

Camp 36th Iowa Infty., Near Little Rock, Ark., Dec. 9, 1864.

Dollie,

. . . Col. Drake has withdrawn his charges and specifications against Col. K. He claims that . . . the prosecuting of the Col. might injure his prospect at Washington. Col. Drake wants to be a Brigadier. Col. K is out here with some 200 men and a junior Col. to him in the City of Little Rock in command of our Brigade. . . . This is owing not to any peculiar prejudice of the commanding General but to the general worthlessness of Col. Kittredge. . . .

Vermilion

Camp 36th Iowa Infty., near Little Rock, Dec. 17, 1864.

My Darling,

. . . The rain is just beginning to fall. . . . It makes me think of 25 years ago when I was a little fellow and wrapped up cozily in the Trundle Bed in pa's old cabin. It was long long ago, and many and crooked are the steps I have been taking since then. . . . If some kind hand had only pointed out to my young feet the proper path, and some wise and good man had taught me how to think and what to think, what a different man I might have been. But 34 years of my life are gone and I find it very hard to change my mode of thinking. . . . But the change *must* be made. More must be done than has been done. Some men may think all men have [had] their growth at the age of 34, but it surely can't be so with me. I must do something yet. . . .

Vermilion

Head Quarters 36th Iowa Infty., Camp near Little Rock, Jan. 4, 1865

My Darling,

. . . Col. Kittredge's trial commences tomorrow. . . . Some 6 or 8 days ago I drew up a request to Col. Drake asking him to use his influence with Gen. Salomon to have the Col. brought before a general Court Martial and tried for drunkenness and general neglect of duty. I obtained the signature of 9 or 10 of the line officers to it, and Col. Drake took it to Gen. Salomon, and he is *putting it through*. . . . The charges are serious and must dismiss him from service if proven, and I think there will be no question as to the proof. The Judge Advocate sent out and required me to serve the notice on the Col. late this evening. I never saw him look worse than he did when I handed him the notice. I couldn't help feeling sorry for him. Still I remember all — everything that I have had to suffer at his hands. Gen. Salomon sent a staff officer out Sunday morning and had him arrested, and turned command over to me. Col. Drake is not able to be here and do the work that is required, and Maj. Hamilton swears by the *Eternal* that he will not command and let Col. Drake remain in the City. I am a Capt. and they can impose upon me and I can't help myself. . . .

Vermilion

Head Quarters 36th Iowa Infty., Camp near Little Rock, Jan. 7, 1865

My Darling,

. . . Gen. Reynolds has issued an order requiring the noncommissioned officers to be reduced to certain proportions in minimum companies. I had to reduce one of my Sergeants who has received his promotion since the organization of the Company. It had to be Orderly Davenport or Sergeant Maiken. *I reduced Davenport* and I am preparing myself to receive all their *curses*. . . .

W. F. Vermilion

Camp 36th Iowa Infty., Little Rock, Jan. 9, 1865
My Darling,

... I suppose Richards will pay his note. Mericle wrote to me a few days ago asking me to give him more time, but I have not answered his letter. I don't think I shall. ... It is nothing to me if the Doctor leaves Iconium. I have no interest whatever in the place or the people. If there was an individual there in whom I felt any interest I should want him to move to another point. ...

Col. Kittredge's trial has been going on today again. ... He is charged with being drunk 6 different times, and then with being drunk "sundry and divers" times. ... The strongest evidence would have been given in proving the last charges, but the court has ruled that these charges are too general, and that the Col. cannot be tried on them. ... But for all that there is going to be some very strong evidence against him. As the case stands now I will not be used to prove but one specification and I understand that Col. [William B.] Mason of the 77th Ohio has testified that the Col. was not drunk on that occasion. I can't see it. I have seen him drunk often. ...
W. F. Vermilion

Camp 36th Iowa Infty., Near Little Rock, Ark. Jan. 20, 1865
My Darling,

... What does Mr. Christie pay you for clerking for him? You should charge him as much as you did me, if not more. ...

Capt. Lambert's wife[53] came to the Bluff yesterday evening and telegraphed him to meet her at the Depot today when her train arrived. She had not heard of the Captain's death. When she arrived at the Depot she saw one of our regiment and asked him about her husband. The soldier told her that he was dead. ... I have not learned what she intends to do. ...
Vermilion

Camp 36th Iowa Infty., Near Little Rock, Jan. 21, 1865
My Darling,

. . . Just after noon yesterday I had laid down to take my accustomed nap. I had hardly got to sleep when the Sergt. Major poked his head in at the door and hollered "Have all your men ready to fall in at a minute's notice. The rebels have captured half of the Cavalry Pickets." At first I thought it was "a sell," but after getting up and making a few inquiries for myself, I ascertained the report to be true. In a very few minutes I received orders to take my Company to the front and occupy the breastworks. It was just beginning to snow quite lively, and I thought it a hard job, but I went out and staid until sundown or later, when I came in and remained until 4 o'clock this morning, and then remained until 7 o'clock. The excitement was occasioned by 30 or 40 guerrillas ambuscading a scout of 16 of the 3rd U.S. Regulars who were returning to their picket post, from a short scout. They made a complete surprise of it, killing, scattering, and wounding the Regulars generally. They all got in towards night however but 4. Several were wounded pretty badly. A party of 40 of the 3rd Wisconsin Cavalry went out some 15 miles towards Benton this morning but saw nothing of the rebels. It is about 3 or 4 miles out where the skirmish occurred. . . .

We have just heard of the capture of Wilmington, or Ft. Fisher rather.[54] Bully for that.
Vermilion

Camp 36th Iowa Infty., near Little Rock, Jan. 25, 1865
My Darling,

. . . The court has found — after mature deliberation — that Col. Kittredge has never been drunk, although 10 or 12 line officers and a score of enlisted men testified to the contrary. . . . Lt. Vermilya saw Col. Drake yesterday and he learned from him that the evidence and the proceedings of the court were being reviewed with the view of having the case remanded for a new trial. If it is done the case will be tried on charges more general. . . .
W. F. Vermilion

Camp 36th Iowa Infty., Little Rock, Ark., Feb. 8, 1865
My Darling,

... Col. Kittredge's case still hangs on. ... Lt. Vermilya made quite a significant remark this evening while at the supper table. Someone brought the Col's case up and the Lt. remarked that he wished to God that the President would make a Brigadier of him, so as to take him away. ... He hates him with all the venom there is in his little nature. He is a good officer, and I like him. ...

We are trying to do something for the Iowa Orphan Asylum. I don't know how much we can raise yet. I am taking a life membership. It is $25. ...

W. F. Vermilion

Camp 36th Iowa Infty., Little Rock, Ark., Feb. 21, 1865
My Darling,

... We received papers up to the 16th inst. They stated that Sherman's Army had captured Branchville and that one column was moving on Augusta and another on Charleston with a fine prospect that the latter city would fall very soon. What a satisfaction it would be to hear of the fall of that cursed place. ... Sherman can and will take it; he can — and I believe will — take every thing in South Carolina. There is no country ... in the world I would rather see devastated by the Army than that state, and I imagine it will require more vigilance on the part of the commanding officers to keep the boys from destroying property than they are in the habit of exercising. ...

W. F. Vermilion

Feb. 24, 1865
Dollie,

... Last evening [the orderly] and I went to the Theatre to see Miss Alice Kingsbury play "Fanchon, the Cricket." She has been here for several weeks and has made quite a sensation. It was a nice play and I felt better after going. "The Child of the Savannah" is to be played in a few nights. . . . Miss Kingsbury is the principal actress in that also. . . .

Vermilion

Camp 36th Iowa Infty., Little Rock, Ark. March 1, 1865

My Pet,

. . . Gen. Soloman is going to put us in the field immediately. He doesn't believe in having us lying around all Summer doing nothing so he has issued an order requiring the Brigade to make 40 acres of garden. The boys are about to mutiny — they say they will dig up the vegetables in place of the weeds if they are compelled to work, but I guess they won't. . . .

Peaches

March 3, 1865

My Dollie,

. . . I received orders at dark from Gen. Reynolds to move the regiment to St. Charles on White River and report to the commander of the Post for garrison duty. . . .

Will

St. Charles, March 9, 1865

My Darling,

. . . We have good news at last my pet, from our prisoners. They are exchanged and were at New Orleans on the 27th ult. . . . Since then Col. Kittredge has received a letter from Adjutant Mahon. . . . He was then on his way home. The other officers were at New Orleans but had drawn 4 months' pay and had a leave of absence of 30 days. They had made an effort to get the men furloughed, but had failed. . . . We are expecting them on the first boat, then I think we must all have a jubilee. I don't know pet, but I will get "inebriated." Will you care?

W. F. Vermilion

Camp 36th Iowa Infty, St. Charles, Ark., March 11, 1865
My Darling,

. . . I saw a letter the other day from Senator Harlan to Col. Drake in which he said the Secretary of War had promised him that day that he would send Drake a *Brevet Brigadier Commission.* . . . So you see the Col's self conceit and perseverance are getting him promoted. It will hurt Col. Kittredge and Major Hamilton badly but I am glad of it. . . . They have always acted as though there were no men in this regiment that didn't live in Ottumwa. . . .
W. F. Vermilion

Camp 36th Iowa Infty., St. Charles, March 13, 1865
My Dollie,

. . . Adjutant Mahon — Col. Kittredge's brother in law — has returned from the prison, and from what the boys say is in very bad repute with the officers and with the men. Lieut. Swiggett of Company "B" gave him a very good whipping before they left the stockade. . . . When they arrived at New Orleans he didn't put up at the same place, and he managed to get off up the river by himself. It is the general wish of the regiment that he will remain at home. I have never had any trouble with him, but he is very unpleasant. . . .

I have been reading some of your letters again today and I believe I found one item on which you wanted information. . . . It is in reference to the risk you run in handling those clothes of Matt's. You ran a great risk my pet but the danger is over now. . . . Smallpox is often communicated in that way. . . .
Peaches

St. Charles, March 15, 1865
My Darling,

. . . I beat Maj. Hamilton. . . . He received his order this morning appointing him A[cting] A[djutant] I[nspector] G[eneral] for the Post of St. Charles. The same order relieved me. Col. Drake and

Major Stephen K. Mahon, ca. 1864. Photograph courtesy of Mark Warren.

I were over at Head Quarters early this morning and the General gave the Col. the order, and requested him to hand it to the Major. . . . A short time afterwards I took all the papers and instructions pertaining to the office over to the Major, but he didn't thank me any; he only swore at me, which I could very well afford to take, as I had won the game. The mere idea of beating him does me more good I believe, than the getting shed of the appointment does. . . .

Some of the officers were down at the landing, and I understand they saw a paper of the 12th and that it quotes gold at $1.70. If that is the case, it is a good indication it is good war news. Those fellows in N.Y. are not letting it come down for nothing. They understand the movements as well as anyone outside the War Department, and they are smart enough to act accordingly. . . .

Peaches

Wednesday Night, March 15th, 1865
My Dearest Love,
. . . Oh, I want to see you so badly, mine love, that I can't put the time off nearly 7 months yet. I feel like you must come before October. Let us hope that you all will get home before then. . . . I rejoice in Gen. Soloman's order "putting you in the field." I like that sort of campaigning for you dear. "Forty acres of garden," sounds like having something to eat. The work won't hurt you, pet (privately I don't believe you'll do much of it, sweet love, you are spoiled a wee bit, I remember — And you shall be worse spoiled when you come home again, for Dollie will be better to you than she ever was, dear one) and the exercise will be fine, and then just think of the onions and cabbages and potatos and early peas, to say nothing of the cucumbers and roasting ears, you will have. Truly, I would like to board with you, pet — but I'd rather board with you here in Iowa. . . .

I think now I did not half appreciate my blessing when you were home with us. I loved you then with all my heart, but it seems to me now I was utterly blind. I think I see more clearly now. Oh, I hope it is not too late. I want to live, sweet love, to do you good, to be of some use to you, and to the world. . . . I think I have spent my life, so far, to as little purpose as any one ever did almost. And how rich have been my blessings! How kind heaven has been to me, my darling!

Dollie

Friday Afternoon, March 17th, 1865
Sweet Love,

. . . I am quite well this morning, only my wound broke out last night and is running. It is sore, and hurts me some. It had seemed well for some time. I think my cold settled in it, or else my sewing for a few days has hurt it. I am used to it, pet, and don't mind it much. My left shoulder has been lame for a long time. I think I strained it while the other one was bad. It is the worst off now. You will think that I am not so very well after all though, if I tell you of my severe ailments, sweet darling. But I am well. My lame shoulder doesn't make me the least sick. I can't go to see Dr. Richards to day, dear. It is so windy and muddy, and I am just going to wear my flannel to Mrs. Maiken's. I will go, pet, just as soon as the weather gets settled so I can get out. Our mail hasn't come yet. Perhaps I shall find it on my way somewhere. . . .
Dollie

St. Charles, Arkansas, March 18, 1865
My Darling,

. . . I saw a *St. Louis Democrat* today of the 14th. . . . There is a confirmation of Sheridan's success. He reports himself near Lynchburg. Also that he has succeeded in destroying the James River Canal.[55] I hope he will soon be able to cut the Lynchburg Rail Road. When that is done what will the poor devils in Richmond do for something to eat, and what do you suppose they do now for something to wear? They have exhibited a great degree of endurance — much more than our army has. Our men have worked, marched, and fought very hard, but they have always had something to eat and wear, and *all* they needed of both as a general thing. And our soldiers receive their pay semi-occasionally, but the rebels never think of such a thing. . . .

St. Charles, Ark., March 21, 1865

My Darling,

... We have drawn new flags, and have just sent them to Memphis to have them inscribed. I don't know just how many battles they will show for us, but I do know — judging by the way Col. Drake called on me awhile ago for money — that it is going to cost something to have it done. We are sending $75.00, which Mr. Wolfe[56]—who has been over there—thinks will about pay it. . . .

Peaches

Friday Night, March 24th, 1865

Mine Own Love,

I wrote you a long letter this morning and took it down to be mailed this afternoon, and now I am going to write again. . . . I can't do anything better than write to my "Peaches." I love to write to him. I have been to Mrs. Maiken's since dinner today. They are all well. Mary said the old lady is in trouble about Henry. He wrote that Walker was promoted to Sergeant, and she thinks Henry has done something wrong and been reduced and Walker put in his place. Mary says she believes in Henry, and she's sure he hasn't done anything. I told her you never mentioned the subject, and I guessed the boys were all right. Are they not, pet? . . .

Sunday Evening, March 26th, I heard that H. H. Swift is dead — died in prison.[57] I am sorry. My wound is still bad. You must not be uneasy about it, my darling, it will get better I wish I knew how to cure it up, but I don't. Its being on the joint I think makes it get sore. Tell me what to do for it, sweet pet, won't you? I know if you had been here it would have got well long ago.

Monday Evening, March 27, Mother seems to be better since Will came home. I think she may get well now he is safe once more. He still looks badly. He has a "bad cough" and diarrhea. The medicine he took seemed to help him though, and I think he will get all right. The doctor said he must not eat buttermilk, and Will thinks that very hard. He will have a little. His appetite is very good, but

not ravenous. People come to see him everyday almost and keep him talking about it all the time. They all want to hear the same story of course, and he is willing to tell it. Bad as their lot was, it was not all together dreary. They had a good deal of fun — which they paid for sometimes. He says they were all dreadfully crass, and would quarrel and fight about almost nothing. Neel [58] whipped Frankhouser one day just because he said that he knew they were going to Camden when they started from the Rock. "He knew entirely too much," Neel said, "and he'd clean him out." There were many funny things that happened. Will doesn't much grudge the experience now it is all over. He says they had nothing to do, but find each other out.
Dollie

St. Charles, Arkansas, March 28, 1865
My Pet,
   . . . Col. Drake and I had a very pleasant time yesterday evening. We talked of home, of the Country, of the war, and then of Col. K and his trial, and we had some good hearty laughs over it, which we can very well afford now that the trial has gone all right. We still receive news from Washington — almost every mail — that he is cashiered. . . . He still lies around camp and looks as though every friend he has in the world was dead. . . .
   Col. Drake's name has been published in the papers as having been confirmed by the Senate as Brevet Brigadier but he has not received the official notice yet. It will have to come through Gen. Canby's [59] Head Quarters, which will take it a good while. . . .
Peaches

Thursday Morning, March 30th, 1865
My Darling,
   . . . Jenny and Will are beautifying themselves. . . . It won't take me long to dress, for the only eyes I care to dress for are not here to see me. *I wish they were.* I used to be wrong about my dress, dear. I thought I must be economical because we were poor, and I wore shabby clothes when you didn't want me to. I am sorry for it now, sweet love. Now we have money enough, but we can't spend it to-

gether, and if I got nice clothes you would not see them, darling. I hope for the good time coming though. Don't you, my pet?....

Dollie

St. Charles, Arkansas, March 30, 1865

Dear Dollie,

. . . St. Charles is situated (or was before it was destroyed by the Army) on the right bank of the White River at about equal distances from Devalls Bluff and the mouth of the river. The rebels sunk a gunboat[60] at this point sometime during the Spring of 1862. . . .

The long looked for papers have come at last and Col. Kittredge has gone home. The order came in yesterday morning and he left in the evening, just after dark, without bidding half a dozen men in the Regiment goodby. He was what we call drunk all day yesterday. He gets his pay up to yesterday, the day he received the order, but his military honors are all gone. He simply ceases to be an officer in the United States Army, by order of the President. . . . I hardly think the Adjutant can remain in the Regiment and do duty, the feeling is so strong against him. He has no friends scarcely left, especially among the prisoners. . . .

Peaches

9

"The Days Are Long and Dreary till You Come Home"

A Confederate officer, recognizing how close his army was to total collapse on the second day of the Battle of Shiloh, compared its condition to a sugar cube saturated with water. Although both looked solid, the slightest push could cause either to crumble. By April 1, 1865, the analogy could also have been applied to the Confederacy itself. One nudge would cause its collapse.

The push came on that very day at Five Forks, a strategic point south of Petersburg, Virginia. A determined attack by a portion of the Army of the Potomac secured that vital position, inflicting losses on Lee's army that the Confederates could ill afford. Grant took advantage of this the next morning, assaulting Petersburg itself. The gains achieved by the attacking Federals forced Lee to evacuate Petersburg. Lee's retreat made it impossible for the Confederates to hold Richmond; it fell on April 3. Six days later, Lee surrendered his army at Appomattox Court House. Other Confederate armies still in the field soon followed suit. By June 1, 1865, all fighting had ceased, ending the Civil War.

If Union troops expected an immediate end to their days in the military, however, most were mistaken. While the War Department mustered some regiments out quite rapidly, others remained in federal service for almost a year until Congress reorganized the U.S. Army.

The 36th Iowa fell in between these two extremes. It continued its stay in Arkansas long after the guns had fallen silent, but was mustered out before serving its entire three-year term of enlistment. William had much to do during those months — due to the court-martial of Colonel Kittredge, he had to serve as the acting commander of the regiment for much of this transitional period. Finally, on August 18, 1865, he learned that he and his fellow Iowans could prepare to return to the Hawkeye State.

The letters of this chapter cover this happiest of all periods for the Vermilions. Only a few of Mary's letters from this period survive, so the focus is almost exclusively on William's reaction to the end of the war. His joy regarding the Union victory contrasts sharply with his sadness over the death of Lincoln. In addition, William describes the awkward situation involving the cashiering of his nemesis, Colonel Kittredge. He also relates a story of a tragic fight that occurred between his regiment and some demobilized Union soldiers. Particularly interesting is the sense William has that reconstruction will not be a seamless process, based on an incident which his unit investigates. As he had done throughout the war, William counsels Mary about medicinal matters — in this case, a painful wound on her shoulder that refuses to heal up properly. But obviously, William devotes the lion's share of his letters to his realization that he will soon be back with his beloved Mary.

St. Charles, Arkansas, April 2, 1865
Mine Pet,
    . . . I forget whether I wrote to you about the death of Morehouse or not. . . . Nowel's son[1] was very bad when we heard from him last. . . . The people had no business to send such boys to me. I wrote to Mericle to not send me any recruits, but it didn't do any good. If those who are so anxious to get such boys into the Service would come themselves, or use their influence to get older men to come, they would be doing the Government nearer justice. . . . The truth is no man has any business in the Army who has not had the measles. That disease ruins more than half of the men who have it in the Army. There are but few men who ever get sufficiently over it to do the duties of a soldier without running great risk of taking disease. . . .
Peaches

St. Charles, Arkansas, April 8, 1865
My Dollie,

. . . I have not said much about the fall of Richmond because you know more about it than I do. But I rejoice as much as you or anyone else can. It is a death blow to the Rebellion, yet the war is not won, and will not be for some time, unless Grant succeeds in capturing a large portion of Lee's Army. . . . But suppose they do go to Danville or into the country west of that point, or even into eastern Tennessee, what can they do? The civil government is gone, their resources are destroyed, and they have not got sufficient power to reestablish the former or to furnish the latter. . . .

April 10, Sweet Dollie, We had a report a day or two ago that Sheridan had captured Gen. Robert Lee, but as I fully expected, that turns out to be a mistake; but Fitzhugh Lee[2] and Custis Lee and 3 or 4 other Maj. and Brig. Generals have been captured[3]. . . .
Peaches

St. Charles, Arkansas, April 11, 1865
Mine Pet,

. . . The news came up this evening that Lee had surrendered himself and [his] army to Grant on terms proposed by Grant. *That ends the war.* Sherman will press Johns[t]on back right into Grant's or Sheridan's clutches. That is if he doesn't surrender before they have time to do it. I look for a general capitulation of all the rebel forces in a very short time, but a large army will have to be held until the States are properly back into the Union. It will take some time to accomplish that. Each State will have to set up and establish a civil government for themselves, and then if they need any assistance the government will have to furnish it, which will keep a large army in the field for a long time. . . .
Peaches

St. Charles, Arkansas, April 16, 1865
My Darling,

   . . . If you love me you must take care of yourself, and when the wound gets healed up you must consider it only half cured, for just as sure as you go to use it, it will break and run. . . .

April 17, My Pet, We have all got the blues today. We got the news yesterday of the Assassination of Lincoln and Seward.[4] We can't help having the blues my pet. I am afraid of Johnson. Still I hope he is all right. . . .
Peaches

St. Charles, Arkansas, April 21, 1865
Mine Pet,

   . . . The present you sent me came in all right — even the cigars. Thank you, Dollie. Not many women would have sent their "Peaches" so fine a present as those cigars are. But I have had so many friends today they are nearly all gone. One was an old acquaintance belonging to the 126th Ills. Infty. His name is Bridges,[5] and he is Surgeon of the Regiment. He read medicine in Marshall at the same time I was reading in Martinsville. I had a good time talking with him. . . .

   We are going to be paid this morning. This forenoon all the troops at this Post are to be formed and marched in procession, with reversed arms and muffled drums, in honor of the late President Lincoln. . . . Our regiment marches in front. . . .
Peaches

St. Charles, Arkansas, April 28, 1865
My Darling,

   . . . Sherman's star has taken a tumble at last and what a pity.[6] I am sorry, but it will not injure him as a fighter. His military fame is too well established. But it only proves the more that a man is not necessarily a Statesman because he is a fighter. . . .
Peaches

St. Charles, Arkansas, May 1, 1865
My Darling,

. . . I would like to talk to you about the sad end of our beloved President. . . . But you must not get discouraged. . . . The war will go on as though we had lost no great man, only I think it will cause many more rebel necks to pull hemp than would have done it had Lincoln lived. . . .

Peaches

St. Charles, Arkansas, May 13, 1865
My Darling,

. . . Gen. Reynolds is busy at the Rock fitting up an expedition to go into Texas, provided the rebels in that part of the Country don't surrender. . . . I have not been able to learn much about the strength of the command that is to go. Some of our officers think we will be sure to go. . . .

Peaches

St. Charles, Arkansas, May 15, 1865
My Darling,

. . . Gen. Thayer[7] received a letter yesterday evening from St. Louis by the way of the Rock and Ft. Smith, said to be signed by Secretary Stanton, that Jeff Davis has been captured, and that he is now in the hands of some of our commanding officers in Georgia.[8] That news made everybody in the camp feel good beyond all conception. Johnson will hang him I hope. He has enough of the "Andrew Jackson" firmness about him to do it I think, but if he has not, publick opinion is sufficiently strong to nerve him up to the proper point. . . .

Peaches

St. Charles, Arkansas, May 20, 1865

Mine Pet,

. . . Gen. Thayer has been ordered to Helena, and Col. Drake has taken command of the Post. Maj. Hamilton is still Inspector General of the Post, and of course can't exercise any command. So you see I am likely to have to command the 36th until the expiration of our term of service. I am still going to retain command of the Company. . . .

Will is getting along first rate. He is actually one of the best fellows in the world. He does nothing wrong except to assist Orderly Brashar in abusing me by making everyone believe that I am one of the laziest fellows in this Command. He must quit that. So must Brashar, otherwise there will be a couple of fellows about their size one of these days soldiering for $16 a month [9]. . . .

Peaches

Head Quarters 36th Iowa Infty., St. Charles, Arkansas, May 25, 1865

Mine Pet,

. . . Some of the 1st Indiana Cavalry have just brought in the guerrilla that shot Gen. Canby last summer here on White River as he was on his way to the Rock.[10] Col. Drake has him in irons and under strong guard. They say he is a very bad looking man. . . .

If you see stated in the papers that your Peaches is promoted, you must not think he is going to be at home soon, for he isn't. I have a Major's commission but I can't be mustered.[11] There are not men enough in the regiment. I didn't want Col. Drake to send for the commission, but he would do it. He thought something might turn up. So I could be mustered, but I have no idea of such a thing. . . . Maj. Hamilton is not going to leave the Service as long as he can get along without doing any hard work, and still draw his pay. The Col. thought when he sent for the commission that he (the Major) would resign in order to accept a clerkship in the Senate, but he is not going to do it. . . .

Peaches

· Tuesday Afternoon, May 30th, 1865
My Dearest Love,

. . . We are all well, but mother. She is much the same. She has
taken a fancy now that if she can live till you come home you can
do something for her. She has more faith in you than in any one
else. She says this is her last hope, now. I don't believe she will ever
get well, my darling. Dr. Gibbons has quit treating her. He said he
could do nothing more. I don't know what can ail her. She almost
lost the use of one arm entirely. I suppose it is some liver disease. . . .

Wednesday Evening, May 31, I was glad to hear that you were . . .
to remain where you are till the "mustering out" comes. I was so
scared over the idea of your going to Texas. I thought I never could
stand it at all if you started there. But you will not have to go, my
pet, or stay at St. Charles either very long. Kirby Smith has surrendered before now.[12] This is the latest news from Texas, that
Smith was negotiating for a surrender. I thought he would have to
do it soon. Sheridan will have 60,000 cavalry in his Department. . . .
I hope the "order" will come to you very soon, dear. I do hope so
for I want to see you so much. The days are long and dreary till you
come, sweet darling. . . .
Dollie

St. Charles, Arkansas, June 4, 1865
Mine Pet,

. . . You must not be too sanguine of our early return. . . . But
it is settled that we will not have to go to Texas. Kirby Smith has
caved, and the war is over. The Government will have to try a few
hundred rebels — and I hope hang that number — and the great
war of the 19th century is at an end. . . .
Peaches

DeValls Bluff, Arkansas, June 13, 1865
Mine Pet,

... Mrs. Drake, Mrs. Fee, and Mrs. Gedney [13] are making their arrangements to meet their "Peaches" somewhere on the road as they go home, and Capt. Fee tells me they are going to try to have you go with them. I suppose they think "Youens" must be good friends because "weens" are, and I don't know my sweet pet but you should be. Their husbands are good friends of mine, and they will all be glad to have you come along. . . . I think we will be mustered out either here or at the Rock, and then sent to Davenport to receive our pay and turn over our property. . . .
Peaches

DeValls Bluff, Ark., June 16, 1865
Mine Pet,

We have had a little excitement in camp since yesterday morning in consequence of the return of Col. C. W. Kittredge with orders from the War Department that he supposed restored him to his former rank and command in the United States Army. He arrived in camp about 10 o'clock A.M. Quite a number of his friends greeted him very cordially. He told them he expected to take command of the Regiment and to have them out of the Service in about 60 days. This morning the adjutant sent for me and informed me that the Col. had assumed command. I reported the matter to Gen. Drake immediately. In an hour or two Col. K sent up his morning report but Gen. Drake returned it at the same time notifying Kittredge that he was not apprised of his being in the United States Service, and he (Drake) could not recognize him as an officer. Kittredge then forwarded his order from the War Department. Drake then referred the matter to Division Head Quarters. Gen. Shaler [14] was absent but his Adjutant General referred the case by telegram to Maj. Gen. Reynolds, and got his decision that the vacancy was filled by the Governor of Iowa commissioning Drake as Col. So I had to take command again and Col. K starts homewards. It has been rather amusing, especially among disinterested persons. . . .
W. F. Vermilion

Friday Evening, June 23rd, 1865
My Dearest Love,

. . . You will come to Davenport I think, pet, without doubt. I want to go there to meet you. I don't know what makes Mrs. Drake and Mrs. Fee talk about my going in company. I haven't seen or heard a word from them since we left Centerville. I should like to go with them though, especially Mrs. Drake, and if we all go we will be able to meet at Eddyville anyhow. I don't think I need write to them about it. I don't mean to "stage" it out if I can help it. Mary Maiken I think will go and I shall go with her to Eddyville. Henry writes to her to come with me, and for his sake and for the old people's I must join company with her you know, that far. I should like there to meet the other party. But this is enough on that subject, isn't it sweet love?. . .

June 25th, 1865, I look for Jimmy the last of this week. I hope he will get here soon. They have given up the projected celebration of the 4th, I believe. They have concluded to wait till you all get home and then have a public dinner. That suits me precisely. They are going to have a barbecue at Lagrange on the 4th. This has been a very long day, sweet love. . . .

Monday Evening, June 26th, Father started to see Lieut. Wright this morning. . . . Mr. Evans was here awhile ago, and he saw John yesterday. He says he isn't mustered out yet, and will not be until you are mustered as Major. He is to be Captain. I don't understand how it can be unless Major Hamilton is also promoted. I suppose he will be however. . . .
Dollie

DeValls Bluff, Ark., June 23, 1865
Mine Pet,

. . . Maj. Hamilton has been returned to the regiment for duty and has relieved me. . . . Col. K I learn has gone North to prosecute his claim still farther. I am not informed as to where he has gone, whether to Washington or to the state of Iowa to see Governor Stone. . . .

3 months will soon pass and ever then will I have time enough to look around and "fix up against winter." I want to go home though my darling, as badly as you want me to; but I will have to await orders. It won't do for me to resign and leave my men just at this time when they need my services worse than they ever have. No other man knows as much about the books and papers as I do. Even if Lt. Wright were to come back it wouldn't do for me to leave, for he wouldn't know much more than anyone who had never seen the Company. . . .

Each evening . . . Capts. Fee, Gedney, and myself take a stroll through town. We always stop at a saloon and get a good cigar apiece, and you had better believe we enjoy a good smoke. They like it about as well as I do, and they like an evening stroll. . . . They are clever fellows and can run a joke as closely as anyone; but for all that I manage to hold my own with them very well. We have made an agreement to take all kinds of abuse from each other but hard licks. . . .

Peaches

June 30, 1865
Mine Pet,

. . . I have just commenced reading "Dugannes Prison Life." [15] I think I shall like it very well, but the Marks Mills soldiers say [he] has not given a true version of that fight. He obtained his information from the Ohio Officers. . . .

Peaches

DeValls Bluff, Ark., July 4, 1865
My Darling,

. . . The 2nd Division of the XV Army Corps arrived here yesterday morning under the command of General Oliver.[16] They are all veterans and recruits, and are the worst demoralized and dissatisfied soldiers I have ever seen. As soon as they landed yesterday morning both men and officers went in for a dr[i]nk. About

9 o'clock A.M. they began to break into groceries and saloons and help themselves, and such another muss as they kicked up I never saw. I noticed one fellow with a keg of liquor on his shoulder making for a hiding place on the double quick.

Gen. Drake says he thought they would kill the Provost Marshal at one time in the morning, but the leader couldn't get enough of his brother "bummers" to assist him. Both officers and men call themselves "Sherman's Bummers" and they made bold to say they were going to clear the town out, that they were not going to be arrested or guarded by the "home guards" as they called the 36th. There were about 70 of our men on guard in town at the time; not enough to keep things quiet. So they made another detail on us for an officer and 35 men. Lt. Smith[17] of "E" Company went down with the detail. I was in the court room when he reported with his men at head quarters, and when I looked along the line I knew the "Bummers" would have a rough time if they didn't become quiet. So they did have a rough time, for in the afternoon two drunken officers were wounded while resisting the guards, and it is reported this morning that one of them, a lieutenant of the 10th Iowa Infty, died yesterday from the effects of a bayonet thrust. I hope he is not dead, yet there were 2 or 3 dozen officers in that division, ranking from Majors down, who ought to be sent home in disgrace. Lt. Smith got into a fight with 2 or 3 of them at once, and came very near getting run through with a sword. But the guards were near at hand, and by their assistance he succeeded in sending 2 of them to jail and mortally wounding the other, which I think is the Iowa lieutenant referred to above. . . .
Peaches

DeValls Bluff, Ark., July 21, 1865
Mine Sweet Pet,

. . . We will move to Centerville just as soon as I get home, provided I can rent or purchase a house that will suit us. I would rather rent for the time being, because when I buy I want to get property that will do us for some time. . . .
Peaches

DeValls Bluff, Ark., Aug. 6, 1865

Mine Pet,

. . . Dr. Udell came over here from the Rock on the day before yesterday evening. He is a Sanitary agent[18]. . . . He brought no special news from Centerville except that the prospect of a Union victory in that Country is not very good. In fact he fears there are movements on foot in the State that may possibly carry the State against us. I expressed myself as having no fears of that, but for all his reasoning seemed very good. In Lee County he tells me, there is a call made by some returned soldiers for another convention. It is signed by between 150 and 200; and they declare they will not support the ticket that is now in the field, simply because they — the candidates — are in favor of striking out the word "White" from the Constitution. He says such men as Judge Trimble[19] are exerting themselves day and night to bring about such a combination of forces as will break the force of the Union Party. They expect to endorse President Johnson's administration, and to differ from the Union Party on nothing but extending the right of Suffrage to the negro, and to nominate men for office who have always been war men, and who have done good service in the field. In Appanoose County he says the Union Party is going to condemn the course the State Convention has taken in the matter. . . . He says the loyal Democrats are not caring so much as the returned soldiers, and some of the old Republicans. If this Regiment were to vote tomorrow, they would go almost to a man against the measure.

As for myself I acknowledge the correctness of the principles but I think it inexpedient at this time. It is not always best to attempt to accomplish all that is right and just at once. The negro can better afford to remain in his present political status for a few years than the loyal people can afford to lose control of the state of Iowa, and perhaps that of the general Government. These are uncertain times, and I think it best for us to travel slowly and be sure we are secure from all danger. We can't tell yet what President Johnson will do. We do know this, however, that he has been over-conservative and that he is creating and establishing an influence in all Rebel states that will be bitterly opposed to the party that placed him in power, and I fear sometimes that he is trying to reestablish his old party, or a new one on anti-negro principles, in order to be the next President-elect. . . . He expects I fear to take a part of the Republican Party and attach it to his Southern organization, and then get the Northern Democratic Party to endorse him[20]. . . .

Peaches

DeValls Bluff, Arkansas, Aug. 10, 1865
Mine Pet,
   . . . The Judge Advocate told me this morning that the General has some citizens now in confinement whom he intends we shall try as soon as the charges can be made out against them. They are accused of abusing some negroes and perhaps of murdering some of them. Some 3 or 4 weeks ago, 2 or 3 negroes came in and complained to the Provost Marshal that after having made a specific contract with their old master to work the old homestead by the halves, and that after they had labored hard and got the crop nearly completed, the old man's son returned from the rebel army and notified them that they should not have any part of the crop, and that they should leave the place immediately, and in order to enforce their order they ejected the negroes from the premises in a very rough manner, and told them — I believe — that if they returned they would kill them. The Provost Marshal sent a party of men out and arrested the guilty persons and had them brought in and confined in the military prison at this place. In a few days afterwards the negroes were brought in to testify against the accused persons at the preliminary trial before the Provost Marshal. Several white citizens came in from the same neighborhood and . . . were very observant of the proceedings and of what the negroes testified to; and in the evening late, I remember myself seeing 2 young men of the party considerably under the influence of liquor. The negroes were restored to their rights on the farm, and the next night . . . some persons visited the farm where the negroes were sleeping quietly in their quarters, and as they thought, secure from all danger, and drove them all, young and old, from their houses, and shot down all who did not succeed in hiding themselves in the

weeds and bushes, so they couldn't be found. The next morning early one . . . succeeded in reaching the Post, and made complaint to the Provost Marshal who sent out a lieutenant and 8 or 10 men as soon as it could be done to inquire into the matter, and arrest the guilty persons if they could be found. The party returned the next day and reported that they found and buried one negro man, and that they saw where another had lain in the grass and bled profusely, but they were unable to obtain any clue to the perpetrators of the crime. The next morning one of the negroes came in wounded in the leg and reported that he was the one who had laid in the grass where the blood was found. The next day . . . another lieutenant and 6 or 8 men were sent out late in the evening with orders to remain overnight and to arrest certain persons if they could be found. The next day the party returned with several persons, some of them women, but I have not learned what evidence the Provost Marshal has of their guilt[21]. . . .

Peaches

Friday Evening, August 11th, 1865

My Dearest Love,

After Maples left the stock got in very badly and Knapp said he hauled out the middle fence — or part of it. They got in a habit of going into the field last year, and that makes the stock worse. But I will see if I can do anything right away, pet. I will go over tomorrow if it doesn't rain. I dread the ride in this hot weather, dear. It will be pretty hard but I think I can stand it. John says he'll go with me. I will tell you everything when I get back. Collins[22] understands perfectly that he was to risk the place just as it was when he took it. I don't think he looks to you for repairs, but I don't want any of the crop destroyed. I will do the best I can, dear. . . .

Jimmy and I had a nice ride today, only it was warm before we got home. We went by Mullinix's but only called at the gate a minute. Allie is well. We stopped at Maiken's too, and found them all right. Mary had just had her fortune told, and it was a very good one so she's in fine spirits. I got two good letters then, and bought muslin to make you two new shirts. I have plenty of time to make them now, and I will not have time to sew after you come you know. . . .

Saturday Evening, August 12, 1865, I am all alone, my pet, and I am glad of it for I want to talk to you, my own sweet darling. Father is mowing and mother has gone out to look at him work. Jenny and Jim have gone, with Ed and Lizzie and Martha down the creek plumming. The plums are getting ripe now. *They* are to have all the *fun* and Jim to have the *plums*. I don't look for more than a bushel. I didn't get to Woodside to day, dear, because Jim couldn't get a horse till after dinner and then it was so hot. I dared not start. We are going Monday. Besides I feared we shouldn't find Collins at home. . . . I was suffering some from my ride yesterday, but I would have risked it if we could have got off early. I have never told you, my pet, how riding affects me in hot weather, because I hated to write about it, and I was hardly sure I knew what the trouble was. I didn't know how to tell you. But last month there was an article in our magazine written by the great Dr. Jackson [23] on Sidesaddles and Horseback Riding for Women which described my case precisely. He says such cases are very common, and the suffering is caused by the strained and unnatural position of the body in the saddle which induces temporary inflammation of the *kidney and bladder*. I knew that was the ailment, pet, but I couldn't imagine what caused it. I was afraid it was a disease that might grow worse and serious. I was relieved of this fear by the article. You can understand it now can't you, my love? I remember suffering in this way once or twice while we lived in Mt. Meridian, but I had almost forgotten it till since you went away. I had one "spell" of it the first summer you were out, and several last summer and this. I never had it bad after riding no farther than Iconium but once. I had washed very hard in the forenoon, and then foolishly ran a little race with Matt after we started. It came on me directly though I only went as far as Mullinix's, and I suffered intolerably for 6 or 8 hours. When Jenny and I rode to Woodside last spring I thought I should almost die. The acute suffering only lasted one night, but I didn't get over it for several days. I have rode no farther than the post office since, and not often there. I never have it only when I ride on horseback in the hot weather. I know no remedy but perfect rest, and cold water. I tried opium, my sovereign remedy in all other ailments, but it only aggravated this. Now you know, sweet darling, why I have not looked after Woodside better, and why I don't visit some of our friends. I went to Julia's, but I'm afraid to stay. I never was very fond of horseback riding, and I mean to quit it entirely when we get moved. Here I have to go sometimes. If I had rode two miles farther yesterday I should have been very sick I think. I don't want you to be one bit uneasy about me, love, for I have told you all now. I wanted to tell you before but hated to do so. I wouldn't tell you now only I'm afraid you think me unpardonably careless about seeing Woodside. It has not been carelessness, my good darling. I would like for you to tell me what you think of what I have told you, dear — but I can wait till you come home if you don't want to write it. Only be sure and don't let it cause you any uneasiness. I am not uneasy about it now, when I am well of it, and don't want to go somewhere. I would try to get father to go to Woodside now, but he is crowded with his haying. So is Mullinix with his oats harvest. And I want to see for myself, dear. It may not hurt me at all. I don't always get sick when I ride. It may be that my general health has something to do with it. I have not been as strong, since you were home, as I used to be. You know what long rides we used to take, pet. I only got tired then. Don't you remember how I used to abuse the saddle and tell you I wanted one "made to order." I don't want any more.

I do think . . . I must save some room for tomorrow and to tell you how many plums I get. Jim is a good fellow, but he's lazy.
Dollie

DeValls Bluff, Ark., Aug. 14, 1865
Mine Pet,
 . . . The order has just reached the regiment restoring Colonel Kittredge and ordering him to take command immediately; and what is the worst of all, it has been done through the influence of Governor Stone. It has pleased His Honor to thrust back upon the regiment a drunken Colonel that his predecessor forced upon us in the first place. . . . I consider it an outrage never to be forgotten that any demogogue who happens to be occupying a high place at home should thrust him back upon us. I can't see what we have ever done that makes us so deserving of punishment. The Governor didn't intend we should know anything about it, but we have it in black and white from the War Department. . . .
Peaches

Thursday Night, Aug. 17th, 1865
Mine Own Love,

I am tired and feel like going to bed, but I should not sleep if I did, without saying a word to my "Peaches." We have had company all day past. The neighbor women, first one, then another. Allie Mullinix came over this morning and b[r]ought home my new carpet. It is nicer than I expected; quite good enough for a bedroom or sitting room. . . . Allie was in fine spirits, only a little spunky at John because he wouldn't let her stay all day. He was working in his field and said she must come home to get dinner! I believe he can hardly bear for her to be gone half a day at a time. It's too mean of him, isn't it. I'd teach him a lesson if I were Allie. As I am Dollie though, and not Allie, if my "Peaches" were selfish in that way I expect I should humor him and spoil him just as she does that ugly John. Women like to think they are appreciated, so if a man wants any amount of self-sacrifice he has to flatter us a little, and behold we are martyrs. . . .

August 18th, 1865, I will try to not have the blues any. But there was no word about an early muster out. I look for a new order that will apply to your case, but it doesn't come pet. I don't think your application to the War Department will do us any good, dear. At least I'm afraid not. They will be able to leave the matter with Gen. Reynolds I should think. They — the boys — are writing home that it is all Gen. Drake's fault that you are held so long. They think he wants to stay, and that he made a false report to Gen. Reynolds, which induced him to retain the regiment. I don't suppose it is true at all. I should think by now Drake would want to come home as badly as anybody. But I guess the boys must talk about something. If you can only keep well, my love, the 4th of October will come. Don't be sad, pet, or despondent, will you?
Dollie

DeValls Bluff, Ark., Aug. 18, 1865
My Dearest Pet,

The good news has come at last. . . . The order came late in the evening on day before yesterday and what a time we had over it. Everybody hollered and threw their hats and chairs and everything else. Captains Gedney and Fee came near tearing my house down. They did break out all the windows. . . .

I will write you on every mail day between this and the time we start, but you had better get ready to *march* immediately. . . . You will have to stop at a first class hotel my pet, and take a room to yourself, so I will have someplace to stop when I get there. . . . The Burtis House . . . is the best place.[24] Stop there, unless I instruct you differently. I am almost sure we will go to Davenport.

Col. Kittredge is not here yet. . . . Some one reported here yesterday that the last boat left him in Memphis drunk. Very likely the report is correct. . . .

Peaches

DeValls Bluff, Ark., Aug. 20, 1865
Mine Pet,

I don't care anything about the affairs in this Department anymore. All I care for is to get out from here. Several other regiments are being mustered out. They are mainly veteran organizations. Ours I believe is the only '62 Regiment in the Department. . . . Oh, how I do wish I were at home, my darling. The time does seem so long but it will come. Goodby, Dollie.

Peaches

Epilogue

Orders finally came for the 36th Iowa to return to the Hawkeye State, and on September 2, 1865, the regiment was mustered out in Davenport. Vermilion still had service to do, however. Apparently Colonel Kittredge had at last caught up with his regiment and regained command, because on September 4 he ordered Vermilion to turn over his company's "stores and equipage." Vermilion accounted for all of his company's gear except for one gun sling, and was duly charged 25 cents for the item. He paid the quarter, and on September 6 received a document releasing him from federal service.

At that moment William Vermilion began the transition from soldier to civilian. While many fellow veterans chose to return to their prewar occupations after the conflict, he did not. Although his letters do not specify the exact reason why he eschewed his medical career, they do give evidence that William had become increasingly frustrated with the inability of physicians during the war to secure even a minimum level of good health for their soldiers. At any rate, Vermilion determined to chart a completely different course of action in the postwar years.

Demonstrating the fluid nature of nineteenth-century America, especially in a frontier state, William became a lawyer. He studied law with his former comrade Thomas Fee, took the bar exam in 1868, and became a licensed attorney. Recognizing the limited potential for a lawyer in Iconium, William decided to relocate to Centerville, thus fulfilling a promise he made to Mary during the war. He became a partner of Judge Harvey Tannehill, and their firm became known as Tannehill & Vermilion. Eugene C. Haynes,

The Vermilion "Dream House," ca. 1890.
Photograph courtesy of C. W. "Bill" Simmons.

who had been a lieutenant in the 6th Iowa, joined the partnership in 1872. The firm thrived, and Vermilion soon became one of the most respected attorneys in south-central Iowa. Edward Stiles, the reporter of the Iowa State Supreme Court from 1867 to 1875, commented that Vermilion's "easy manners and good fellowship" helped him to build a large clientele. Indeed, Vermilion did so well that he and Mary were able to construct a "dream house" on the outskirts of Centerville in 1870. The house still stands, and today is a registered historic landmark.

As his professional life blossomed, so did his personal life. On November 6, 1866, Mary delivered their only child. They named the child Charles William Vermilion, but he would be best known by the nickname "Willie." Willie would emulate his father in two respects: he would attend his father's alma mater, by that time known as DePauw University, and he would become an attorney. Indeed, he would later practice law with his father.

The birth of their son was not the only change that would take place for the Vermilions. Jane Vermilion, William's favorite sister, had decided to remain in the Hawkeye State after the war. When Will Kemper returned to Iowa after his release from Camp Ford in 1865, he was reintroduced to Jane, a young lady whom he remembered only as a small child from his days back in Putnam County. He obviously liked who she had become, because they married in 1867.

One other member of the Vermilion family reentered the scene as well. Like his older brother, Reason Vermilion (now known as Reese) decided to become a lawyer. He moved to Centerville, and became a partner in William's firm. He would practice law in Centerville for a number of years before eventually moving to Wichita, Kansas.

Mary also had a family member move to the area. Her half-brother Tom had recovered from his bout during the war with typhoid fever, and had decided to move his family nearer to his relatives. Consequently, he purchased land in Independence Township in Appanoose County, and relocated there soon after the Civil War.

Adding to the familial bliss was a political triumph enjoyed by William in 1869. The seat representing Appanoose County in the Iowa Senate became vacant, and the local Republican Party asked Vermilion to run for the seat against John Pierson. In a close election, Vermilion defeated his opponent by a margin of 242 votes. Vermilion would serve out his term, but declined to seek reelection in 1873. He did receive a significant honor from his adopted community, however. Because of his military and political service, the Appanoose County supervisors changed the name of the township encompassing Centerville to Vermilion Township — the name it still bears today.

One of Vermilion's best friends from his days with the 36th Iowa also received postwar recognition. Francis M. Drake had returned to Iowa after the war, and had decided to become a lawyer. After passing the bar examination, he became a highly successful attorney in Centerville. He argued many cases before the Iowa Supreme Court, which required him to be absent from his home for long stretches of time. Needing someone to look after his affairs, Drake wrote to William Vermilion for help. Demonstrating how military experience can bond people together, the individual who had once hated Drake promised his friend his "complete cooperation." Drake eventually entered the political arena, running successfully for governor in 1895. During his lifetime he also donated a great deal of money to deserving causes, especially to Oskaloosa College, which hoped to relocate in Des Moines. Largely through his generosity, the college accomplished its goal. In return, the trustees renamed the institution Drake University. Drake also helped fund the public library in Centerville, a facility which today also bears his name.

When his political career ended, William found a new outlet for his energy. Proud of his military service, William became a member of the Grand Army of the Republic (GAR), the postwar Union veterans' group. Historian Stuart McConnell has done a masterful job of analyzing the rise of this organization. He argues that Union veterans formed the group to influence future generations' perceptions of their efforts. Vermilion seems to have joined the GAR in large part for this reason. Indeed, in conjunction with a celebration sponsored by his GAR post, Vermilion delivered a memorable speech in 1882. Unsurprisingly, his presentation was entitled "The Ladies — The Soldiers' Best Friends."

Vermilion also began to dabble in financial matters. Continuing a practice that Mary indulged during the war, Vermilion invested in real estate, both in Iowa and elsewhere. He became the vice president of the Albia National Bank, and served as director of the Chicago and South Western Railroad Company from 1869 to 1876. In addition, he became a partner in an investing firm known as D. G. Campbell. These activities allowed him to amass a fortune of $14,690, according to the 1870 federal census. Much of this wealth came from his real estate holdings, suggesting that Mary had made some wise investments during the closing stages of the Civil War.

As William and Mary's personal lives began to flourish, however, their parents' health was deteriorating. Joel Vermilion died on December 10, 1871, and his wife followed him six months later. Mary had lost her mother nearly three years prior, on July 2, 1868. The loss left her father alone on the family farm, because by that time both of his surviving sons had moved away — Will to Bedford, Iowa, and Jimmy to Fairmont, Nebraska. Heartbroken and lonely, Valentine decided to sell his land and move in with Jimmy. He would live for another decade, finally passing away at the age of 84 on October 14, 1878.

Sadly, another death loomed on the horizon. Mary became ill in the early 1880s, and her condition grew steadily worse. She finally

William F. Vermilion, ca. 1880. Photograph courtesy of Eloise Duff.

passed away on January 3, 1883. William buried her in the Oakland Cemetery in Centerville.

Although he had obviously loved his wife deeply, William soon found a new romantic interest. Kate Day had moved to Centerville after the war with her husband, a Union veteran from Pennsylvania. Her husband had passed away in 1875. The two bereaved individuals found comfort in each other's company. William proposed to her, and they were married on December 10, 1884. In that quaint custom of the Victorian era, she would always address her new husband in their correspondence as "Mr. Vermilion."

By all accounts, William's second marriage was a happy one, but it would not last nearly as long as had his first. Mary had often talked during the war to her husband about William's health, and despite his repeated assurances he had obviously suffered from various maladies as a result of his military service. Throughout the 1880s, his condition gradually deteriorated. It finally declined enough that he applied for a government invalid pension on October 27, 1890. His physician diagnosed a wide variety of ailments, including chronic bronchitis and rheumatism. The combination of infirmities caused his health to collapse eventually. Returning in December 1894 from Des Moines, where he had been pleading a case before the state supreme court, he complained of chest pains. Dr. Sawyer, his old comrade from the 36th Iowa, attended him, and felt that Vermilion would soon recover from his illness. But two days before Christmas in 1894, William passed away while resting in bed.

Vermilion's death saddened the community. All of the county newspapers printed tributes, and the Bar Association suspended regular court session in his honor. Francis Drake returned from Des Moines to pay his respects to the family. Finally, after a funeral presided over by Reverend G. H. Putnam, his son and his second wife laid him to rest in the Oakland Cemetery, beside Mary. Thus the two individuals who had conversed so eloquently about reuniting the nation were reunited in death in the soil of Iowa, their adopted homeland.

Notes

1. During the first months of the Civil War, Iowa Governor Samuel J. Kirkwood and his adjutant general, Nathaniel B. Baker, had overseen the creation of a training camp in Keokuk to prepare the first volunteer regiment from the state for military service. Soon, the rush of Iowans to enlist in new regiments forced Kirkwood and Baker to open other facilities to supplement the original location, known as Camp Elsworth. However, President Lincoln's call for additional volunteers in the summer of 1862 had forced Kirkwood and Baker to recognize the need for even more camps. To that end, Baker ordered the construction of a second facility in Keokuk. Officially opened on August 11, 1862, the camp bore the name of the president.

2. John Wesley May, age twenty-six, of Confidence.

3. William R. Kemper, age twenty-two, of Jackson Township in Monroe County. He was a younger brother of Mary.

4. William H. Dunlap, age twenty-seven, of Eddyville. He was the wealthiest merchant in the community.

5. Built in 1850, the *Die Vernon* was a 255-foot-long steamboat owned by the Keokuk Packet Line. In *Steamboating on the Upper Mississippi*, William J. Peterson asserts that the vessel was "perhaps the fastest craft on western waters."

6. Age thirty-two, of Iconium.

7. Jacob Rowe, age fifty-six, was a plasterer in Keokuk. His wife Olive, age forty-five, had made their large residence at the corner of 6th and Morgan Streets into a boarding house.

8. Prior to the Civil War, local militia units had often chosen nicknames for their outfits. Companies raised during the Civil War, both North and South, continued this tradition. Because the majority of the men in Company F had resided in Chariton Township in Appanoose County, they had decided to call themselves the "Chariton Rangers."

9. The instant. During the Civil War, letter writers often used this term to indicate that an event described took place during the month in which the correspondence had been written. If an event had occurred the month before, they would use the term ultimo, often shortened to ult.

10. McCullough, age eighteen, and Bartlett, age thirty-eight, both of Iconium; Duckworth, age twenty-five, Evans, age thirty-eight, and Luther Roland,

age twenty-one, all from Lucas County; Columbus Jenkins, age twenty-five, of Confidence.

11. During the Civil War, the U.S. Army purchased over 800,000 .577-caliber rifled muskets that had been manufactured at the Royal Small-Arms Factory at Enfield, England.

12. James M. Kemper, age eighteen, of Jackson Township in Monroe County. Mary's youngest brother, he was a member of the 18th Iowa. In October 1862 the 18th Iowa was camped at Wilson's Creek, Missouri, where Union and Confederate forces had fought on August 10, 1861.

13. Woodford and Henry Vermilion, ages forty-two and thirty-four, respectively, were cousins of William. Both lived in Vigo County, Indiana.

14. Kemper and Grimes were both sergeants, which made them non-commissioned officers.

15. The Lorenz Model 1854 was a rifled musket imported from Austria by the U.S. War Department during the Civil War. Because the lockplate, barrel, and fittings of the weapon were treated with a blue-black finish, it resembled the British-made Enfield. Therefore, it was often called the "Austrian Enfield" by Union soldiers.

16. Thomas C. Woodward, age thirty, of Ottumwa; Charles Woodman Kittredge, age thirty-six, of Ottumwa. Kittredge had served as a captain in the 7th Iowa earlier in the war, receiving a medical discharge due to a leg wound that he had suffered at the Battle of Belmont.

17. During the Civil War, the inspector general of the U.S. Army gave a license to civilians to accompany federal forces and sell them goods. Each regiment was entitled to one such individual, known as a sutler.

18. John Sevy, age thirty-three, of Chariton Township in Appanoose County.

19. Henry Vermilion, age nineteen, of Jefferson Township in Putnam County. Henry was a younger brother of William.

20. Horatio Seymour, who had just been elected governor of New York. Seymour was an outspoken critic of the Union cause, especially regarding Lincoln's Emancipation Proclamation. He would later receive a significant amount of the blame for the 1863 New York Draft Riot.

21. Disappointed with the response to the call on July 2, 1862, for volunteers, on August 4 Secretary of War Edwin Stanton announced that the loyal states would have to provide the government with 300,000 militia men, who would serve for nine months. Stanton warned states that a draft would be imposed if states failed to meet their quotas. But Stanton's plan also established a trade-off: one three-year enlistee would equal four men enrolling for nine-month terms. In 1862, Iowa recruited enough three-year volunteers to avoid conscription. In addition, by the time Vermilion enlisted, Iowa's only three-month regiment, the 1st Iowa, had disbanded.

22. Horace Greeley, the founder and editor of the *New York Tribune*.

23. Sarah Jane Vermilion, age seventeen, of Jefferson Township in Putnam County. Jane, often referred to as Jenny in later letters, was a younger sister of William.

24. Prior to the Civil War, a number of prominent Americans had favored relocating freed slaves to Africa, believing that this would make slaveholders more amenable to emancipation. At the time Mary wrote this, Abraham Lincoln still felt that this plan, called colonization, offered the best hope for a peaceful acceptance of his Emancipation Proclamation.

25. On July 11, 1862, President Lincoln had appointed Major General Henry Wager Halleck general-in-chief of the Union armies.

26. Major General Ambrose E. Burnside, commander of the Army of the Potomac; Major General George B. McClellan, former commander of the Army of the Potomac; Major General William S. Rosecrans, commander of the Army of the Cumberland; Major General Don Carlos Buell, former commander of the troops that became the Army of the Cumberland; Major General Ulysses Simpson Grant, commander of the Army of the Tennessee.

27. In May 1861, Brigadier General Benjamin Franklin Butler, the commander of Fortress Monroe in Virginia, had decided against returning slaves who had sought sanctuary inside Union lines to their masters. Butler, a prewar lawyer, justified his decision by asserting that slaves used by the Confederacy were "contraband of war," and thus subject to confiscation. Many Union commanders soon ceased to make an attempt to determine whether runaway slaves had actually done work for the enemy or not, preferring instead to simply protect them all. For this reason, the term "contraband" soon came to apply to any runaway slave.

28. Joshua and Susana Christie, both age sixty-four, of Jackson Township in Monroe County.

29. Major General Samuel Ryan Curtis. The forty-five-year-old Curtis had been a congressman from Iowa at the start of the Civil War, but the West Point graduate resigned from the House of Representatives and reentered the army.

30. On November 15, 1862, a fire started on Main Street in Keokuk in a building owned by a barber by the name of George Cabus. The fire threatened the nearby Billings House Hotel, but local firemen and Union soldiers managed to save that building. Unfortunately, after containing the blaze the firemen attacked a member of the 36th Iowa doing police [Provo Guard] duty on Johnson Street. This set off a riot that was not quelled until later that evening. The Keokuk *Daily Gate City* of November 17, 1862, essentially corroborates William's version of the affair.

31. Joseph B. Gedney, age thirty-six, of Centerville. Gedney commanded Company I in the 36th Iowa.

32. The Estes House Hotel, constructed in 1857, had been appropriated by the military for use as a hospital. It became the center of a cluster of buildings that would eventually be known as the Keokuk U.S. Army Hospital.

33. Charles J. Ball, a lieutenant in the 13th Regiment of the regular U.S. Army. Ball had officially mustered the 36th Iowa into military service.

34. An adjutant is a staff officer who helps the commanding officer with ad-

ministrative duties; line officers are second lieutenants, first lieutenants, and captains.

35. Anna McCarty, age sixty-five, of Warren Township in Putnam County. Mary was her niece.

36. Emily A. McCarty, age thirty. Emily was Julia May's sister.

37. The *Fred Lorenze* was one of the two boats that transported the 36th Iowa to St. Louis.

38. At the start of the Civil War, it became obvious that St. Louis would become a major staging area for Union troops operating west of the Mississippi River. Because of this, in August 1861 Major General John C. Frémont had ordered the construction of a training facility on the western end of land occupied by the St. Louis fairgrounds in 1861. Named for the general's late father-in-law, the installation consisted of spacious buildings 740 feet long and 40 feet wide.

39. James Van Benthusen, age thirty, of Greenville.

40. Officers holding the rank of major, lieutenant colonel, or colonel.

41. Lieutenant Colonel Francis Marion Drake, age thirty-one, of Unionville.

42. Albert A. Hancock, age forty-three, of Confidence.

43. Judge John S. Townsend, age forty, of Albia. He presided over Iowa's Second Judicial District.

44. John Baden Marchbanks, age thirty-two, of Iconium.

45. A Baptist meeting house located in Jefferson Township in Putnam County.

46. Thomas Vermilion, age thirty-five, was William's eldest brother. He operated a store in Mt. Meridian; Reason Rhynerson Vermilion, age twelve, of Jefferson Township in Putnam County, was the youngest of William's brothers.

47. Dr. Washington Brinton, age thirty-nine, of Jefferson Township in Putnam County.

48. John Vermilion, age twenty-five. A younger brother of William, he still lived on his parents' farm.

49. John F. Brothers, age twenty-six, of Franklin Township in Putnam County. Technically, he was not a cousin; his sister Rebecca had married William's uncle, Mason Vermilion.

50. On February 25, 1862, Congress passed the Legal Tender Act, which authorized printing $150 million worth of treasury notes. Because of their color, these notes were called "greenbacks."

51. The *Daily Gate City* was a newspaper published in Keokuk; William Burns, age thirty-one, of Iconium died on November 26, 1862.

52. James F. McCammack, age twenty-three, of Jefferson Township in Putnam County.

53. Age twenty-two, of Jefferson Township in Putnam County. He had married William's sister Martha on October 30, 1861.

54. On December 13, 1862, General Burnside had ordered the Army of the Potomac to attack the entrenched Confederate forces occupying the heights south and east of Fredericksburg, Virginia. The Confederates repulsed re-

peated Union assaults, inflicting 12,600 casualties by the end of the day. On the night of December 15, Burnside admitted defeat and led the remnants of his army back across the Rappahannock River.

55. On December 11, 1862, the U.S. House of Representatives had considered a motion to condemn the process of emancipation as unconstitutional. Although the motion did not pass, a number of observers believed that Lincoln would modify his proclamation to preempt further attacks on his initiative.

CHAPTER 2. *"You Are in Danger Now, Every Day, I Know"*

1. The *Jeanie Deans* was a Mississippi River steamboat during the period of the Civil War.

2. James G. Phillips, age thirty-six, of Moravia. Phillips, like Vermilion, was a prewar physician who chose to raise a company of soldiers rather than enlist as a doctor. Phillips commanded Company C in the 36th Iowa.

3. Julia May's son John William May, age four; Ellindas McCarty, age twenty-three, a younger daughter of Anna McCarty.

4. Sally McGaughey, age seventy-two, of Greencastle Township in Putnam County.

5. Age sixty, of Greencastle Township in Putnam County.

6. After the Union successes on the Mississippi River in 1862, Confederate control of the waterway had been reduced to a section from Vicksburg, Mississippi, to Port Hudson, Louisiana.

7. Matthew W. Kemper, age twenty-six, of Jefferson Township in Monroe County. The oldest brother of Mary, he had enlisted in the 6th Iowa during the summer of 1861.

8. Henry M. Pentecost, age fifty-eight, of Jefferson Township in Putnam County.

9. In 1862, James Robert Gilmore wrote *Among the Pines or, the South in Secession Time*. This book painted a very harsh picture of the slave culture of the South.

10. John Hays, age fifty-four, of Jackson Township in Monroe County; James M. Hays, age twenty-seven, of Lagrange. James Hays was discharged from the army three days later due to medical disability.

11. Matthias S. Reed, age twenty-three, of Centerville. Reed was a member of Company D of the 6th Iowa.

12. Fort Pickering.

13. Brigadier General Alexander Sandor Asboth; Major General Stephen A. Hurlbut; Asboth was actually Hungarian.

14. Greenbury Owen, age twenty-six, and Clowser, age twenty-one, both of Lucas County. Apparently, Owens and Clowser did turn out all right. They served with the regiment through all of its campaigns until they were both captured at the Battle of Marks' Mills in April 1864.

15. Major General Ulysses S. Grant.

16. John Mullinnix, age thirty-four, of Franklin Township in Monroe County. He had lived in Putnam County, Indiana, before moving to Iowa.

17. Captain Thomas B. Hale, age twenty-six.

18. Brigadier General Willis Arnold Gorman, the commander of the District of Eastern Arkansas.

19. At this stage of the Civil War, the two sides had worked out a system for returning prisoners of war that involved the trade of equivalent numbers of captives.

20. Major General William Tecumseh Sherman.

21. William is referring to John B. Wyman. Wyman had been stationed at Helena prior to leading troops into battle at Chickasaw Bluffs, a fight in which he lost his life. Wyman was not a general; he was instead the colonel of the 13th Illinois.

22. Steven W. Merrell, age forty, of Wapello County. During the Civil War the quartermaster provided quarters, transportation, and supplies for his unit.

23. William Lane, age thirty-eight. He was a blacksmith in Greencastle prior to the war.

24. Fees, age twenty, Scott, age forty-five, and Mary Scott, age twenty-two, all of Chariton Township in Appanoose County.

25. Thomas Dykes, age twenty-six, of Chariton Township in Appanoose County; Joseph Bartlett, age thirty-eight, and Mary Bartlett, age eighteen, both of Independence Township in Appanoose County.

26. James M. Blue, age forty-three, of Monroe County.

27. Mary is referring to the Battle of Stone's River, which the Army of the Cumberland under Rosecrans fought on December 31, 1862, and January 2, 1863. Rosecrans suffered 13,000 casualties, but heavy Confederate losses led to their abandoning the field of battle.

28. Hulled wheat boiled in milk and flavored with sugar and spices.

29. McCarty, age forty, of Warren Township in Putnam County; Mary is referring to John L. Cooper, age twenty-three, who had served in the 14th Indiana. He would indeed later enlist in the 2nd U.S. Cavalry.

30. Major General John A. McClernand had taken his XIII Corps and Sherman's XV Corps to attack Ft. Hindman at Arkansas Post, Arkansas.

31. Oliver P. Morton.

32. James F. Robinson, who had been appointed governor in 1862 to replace Beriah Magoffin.

33. Abel McCarty, age thirty-two, of Warren Township in Putnam County. Abe was Anna McCarty's only son; Bridges, age thirty-five, of Marion Township in Putnam County.

34. Isaiah Vermilion, age twenty-four, of Jefferson Township in Putnam County. Isaiah was a younger brother of William.

35. William and Harriet Bourne, ages forty-five and forty-one, respectively. Valentine Kemper had sold them his property in Jefferson Township in Putnam County when he moved to Iowa; thus Mary is referring in this letter to her old house.

36. On New Year's Day, 1863, a Confederate force surprised a detachment of the 28th Iowa just outside Helena and captured twenty-seven members of that regiment.

37. During the Civil War a number of firms manufactured body armor designed to protect the torso of a soldier. Despite Vermilion's assurances, the devices were uniformly ineffective in stopping enemy bullets.

38. Delano R. Eckels, a fifty-seven-year-old lawyer from Greencastle.

39. Age thirty, of Iconium.

40. On January 8, 1863, Confederate forces attacked the federal supply depot at Springfield, Missouri. The 18th Iowa, along with Missouri militia units, successfully defended the installation.

41. Sarah Blue, age twenty-three, of Monroe County.

42. Bill Allee, age thirty-nine, of Floyd Township in Putnam County; Amanda Vermilion, age twenty, of Vigo County. A cousin of William's, she would marry Bill Allee on February 22, 1863.

43. McHenry Wilcox, age twenty-six, of Marion Township in Putnam County.

44. Moses Cousins, age thirty-five, of Albia. Cousins was the surgeon of the 36th Iowa.

45. In 1862 Union Brigadier General Thomas Williams had reasoned that the pronounced loop made by the Mississippi River as it ran past Vicksburg offered an opportunity to divert the course of the river away from the city by digging a canal. He had his troops initiate an effort to accomplish that goal, but soon abandoned it. General Grant, after moving his base of command to the area, had resumed work on the canal.

46. Major General Nathaniel Prentiss Banks, the commander of Union forces in New Orleans.

47. Major General Joseph Hooker, who had assumed command of the Army of the Potomac on January 26, 1863.

48. Brigadier General Clinton Bowen Fisk. After the war, he would found a university for blacks that today bears his name.

49. On January 16, 1863, 1st Lieutenant Humphrey May had submitted his resignation on account of disability. His younger brother, Wesley, received promotion to that rank the following day. Swallow, age twenty-one, of Centerville, had previously held the rank of 1st corporal.

50. A hard, saltless, flour biscuit issued to soldiers during the Civil War. These biscuits were commonly called "hard tack."

51. Colonel Samuel Allen Rice, age thirty-five, of Oskaloosa.

52. Born in Kentucky, Gorman had moved to Indiana at the age of nineteen. After serving in the U.S. House of Representatives, Gorman had been appointed governor of the Minnesota Territory in 1853, and still resided there at the start of the war. Gorman was indeed a Democrat; he was one of that party's candidates for presidential elector in 1860.

53. Esther A. Vermilion, age six, of Jefferson Township in Putnam County. Esther was a niece of William and Mary.

54. John C. Breckinridge, vice president under Buchanan and the candidate of

the southern wing of the Democratic Party for president in 1860; George Sherrill, age fifty-four, of Jefferson Township in Putnam County. He would soon be elected sheriff of Putnam County.

55. Martinsville is a community in Morgan County, perhaps best known today as the home town of legendary UCLA basketball coach John Wooden.

56. Captain John Wright, age thirty-six, and his wife Rebecca, age thirty-three, both of Dahlonega.

57. Brigadier General Benjamin Mayberry Prentiss, who had just been placed in command of the District of Eastern Arkansas.

58. Benjamin Franklin Pearson, age forty-eight, of Centerville. He was the 2nd Lieutenant of Company G.

59. Richard Yates, governor of Illinois; Joseph Holt, who had served as secretary of war during the final months of the Buchanan administration. After Lincoln's inauguration, Holt became the nation's judge advocate general. The U.S. minister to Prussia at the start of the Civil War, Joseph Albert Wright had been appointed by the Indiana state legislature in 1862 to fill out a term in the U.S. Senate.

60. Age sixty-six, of Jefferson Township in Putnam County.

61. In the first successful action of the Crimean War in 1854, Vice Admiral Sir Charles Napier of the British navy had captured Bomarsund, a Russian fortress.

CHAPTER 3. *"I Want to Know Whether Our Government Is Really Worth Dying For"*

1. Andrew Johnson, whom Lincoln had appointed governor of Tennessee in 1862.

2. The Knights of the Golden Circle. This organization was founded in 1854 by George W. L. Bickley in Cincinnati to promote the idea of seizing and colonizing the northern parts of Mexico. During the Civil War, many Unionists suspected the K. G. C. of undermining, directly and indirectly, the efforts of the Lincoln administration to subdue the Confederacy.

3. Bowen, age forty-seven, and Hurst, age twenty-eight, both of Jefferson Township in Putnam County.

4. On February 14, 1863, Colonel Charles Rivers Ellet, commander of the *U.S.S. Queen of the West*, had run aground on the Black River in Arkansas. Bombarded by enemy artillery fire, the crew had abandoned ship. The Confederates soon took possession of the vessel.

5. Charles Ellet, Jr., a civil engineer, had suggested to the War Department that a vessel designed to ram enemy ships could be highly effective on the rivers of the American interior. Given permission by the government, Ellet constructed a fleet of rams, including the *Queen of the West*. His idea bore fruit in June 1862 when his squadron demolished a Confederate fleet at Memphis. Unfortunately, Ellet was wounded in that battle, and later

died of complications. His son, Colonel Charles Rivers Ellet, then took command of his father's ship.

6. Due to a precipitous decline in enlistments, on March 3, 1863, Congress passed the Enrolment [*sic*] Act. This gave the president the power to call for troops if he felt the military situation required it. The law established a system for assigning quotas for each congressional district. If the district failed to meet the requirement, a draft would then take place. But Section 13 of the law allowed an individual to pay a $300 commutation fee, which would exempt that person from the draft on that particular occasion, but not in future calls.

7. John W. S. Bland, age nineteen, of Ottumwa.

8. James Owens, age thirty-three, of Jefferson Township in Putnam County.

9. The fortification called Ft. Pemberton by the Federals (often referred to as Ft. Greenwood by the Confederates) was actually located on the Tallahatchie River.

10. Major General William Wing Loring had indeed lost an arm in the Mexican War, but he was a North Carolinian by birth. Brigadier General Leonard Fulton Ross, of Fulton County, Illinois, commanded the 13th Division of the XIII Corps.

11. Michael H. Hare, age forty-five, of Albia.

12. Thomas Kemper was a son of Valentine Kemper's by a previous marriage. The thirty-seven-year-old lived in Putnam County with his forty-year-old wife Emily and their five children: William, Nancy, Rufus, Henry, and Amy. William was the child who passed away in March 1863.

13. "Seeing the Elephant" was a common Civil War phrase, meaning to see combat for the first time.

14. Brigadier General Lorenzo Thomas.

15. A type of Union warship, made of iron and patterned after the famous *U.S.S. Monitor*.

16. The letter Vermilion is referring to was dated March 23, 1863, and was purportedly written by members of the 29th, 33rd, and 36th Iowa regiments. The text can be found in *Iowa Valor*, by Steve Meyer.

17. James Green Vermilion, born in 1828, and Joel Davis Vermilion, born in 1833, were brothers of William. Both had died shortly before the Civil War: James in 1858 and Joel in 1859.

18. A missionary Baptist church located in Jefferson Township in Putnam County.

19. Martin J. Varner, age thirty-six, of Albia; Edmund L. Joy, age twenty-seven, of Ottumwa. Hale is identified in n.17, p. 342.

20. Isaac A. Rhynerson, age forty-five, of Jefferson Township in Putnam County. A physician, he had served as a Republican representative in the Indiana state legislature before the war. In all probability Rhynerson was well acquainted with the Vermilions, as Reason Vermilion's middle name was Rhynerson.

21. Alzira Mullinnix, age thirty-four. She was the wife of John Mullinnix.

22. Parkhurst, age forty-five, of Centerville; Zintz, age twenty, of Bethlehem; Day, age twenty-six, of Iconium.

23. Thomas Grissom, age forty-eight, of Jackson Township in Monroe County.

24. William Eads, age thirty-seven, of Franklin Township in Monroe County.

25. James Marchbanks, age twelve, of Appanoose County.

26. William N. Teater, age twenty-nine. Formerly of Center Township in Appanoose County, he was living at Woodside while raising a crop for the Vermilions.

27. Age thirty, of Monroe County.

28. On March 25, 1863, Secretary of War Edwin M. Stanton ordered Brigadier General Lorenzo Thomas to begin the process of organizing regiments of African Americans for service in the Union army. As part of his efforts, on April 8 Thomas delivered a speech to white Union soldiers at Lake Providence, Louisiana, explaining the new governmental policy to them.

29. Captain Robert M. Wilson, age forty-seven, of the 22nd Iowa. A resident of Lagrange, he had resigned his commission on April 13. He had lived in Putnam County prior to moving to Iowa; Rachel Wilson, age thirty-four, of Lagrange.

30. John Sheeks, age twenty-five, of Iconium; Harriet Sheeks, age twenty-one, of Iconium.

31. Samuel Sheeks, age forty-nine, and his wife Elizabeth, age forty-six, both of Iconium.

32. Rachel Teater, age twenty-three, of Independence Township in Appanoose County.

33. Nathan Bartlett, age sixty-two, of Appanoose County; Thomas Dooley, age sixty-six, of Iconium.

CHAPTER 4. *"Since I Came Home I Am* Entirely *Satisfied with Iowa"*

1. On May 1, 1863, 160 men of the 3rd Iowa Cavalry left Helena on a scouting mission down the La Grange Road. After driving a small force of Confederates from their front, the Iowans found themselves under attack by a much larger enemy detachment. The Federals suffered losses of three dead, eight wounded, and thirty missing.

2. Breeze, age thirty-three, of Iconium; William Delay, age twenty-nine, of Centerville; 2nd Lieutenant Cornelius A. Stanton, age twenty-one, of Appanoose County.

3. Vermilion is discussing three separate operations in this paragraph. First, on April 30, 1863, General Grant used transports, which had run past the batteries at Vicksburg, to ferry 24,000 of his soldiers to Bruinsburg, Mississippi, south of the Confederate fortress. The Union force had then defeated a Confederate force at Port Gibson on May 1, and on May 2 the federal troops marched towards the Confederate batteries located along the

Mississippi River at Grand Gulf. These fortifications would fall to Grant's men on May 3.

At the same time that Grant was reaching the Mississippi shore, General Sherman was leading a force up the Yazoo River to feint an attack against the Confederate positions at Haynes' Bluff. After making this demonstration, Sherman then moved his force down the Louisiana side of the river and crossed over below Vicksburg to join Grant's force.

Finally, on April 17, 1863, Colonel Benjamin Grierson had started from La Grange, Tennessee, on a sixteen-day cavalry raid through the heart of Mississippi. Grierson's men destroyed fifty miles of railroad track on their journey. Totally confusing the Confederates, Grierson did not return to La Grange, choosing instead to ride all the way to Union-held Baton Rouge. He reached this destination on May 2.

4. Levi Brashar, age twenty-two, of Moravia. Brashar was the 5th sergeant of the company.

5. Orr Kelly, in his book *Dream's End*, provides strong circumstantial evidence that Kittredge's predilection to alcohol was known to Governor Kirkwood at the time that he gave the officer command of the 36th Iowa. Indeed, it seems that Kirkwood almost immediately had second thoughts about his action, but had decided against rescinding his order.

6. Age forty-four, of Iconium.

7. Age twenty-two, of Georgetown.

8. Thomas William Worthington, age thirty-eight, of Moravia.

9. John Phillips, age thirty-seven, of Albia. Phillips had been the postmaster in Albia from 1851 to 1861, and continued to help deliver the mail even after he had been officially replaced.

10. Age thirty-five, of Iconium.

11. Mary Maiken, age nineteen, of Iconium.

12. Vermilion is referring to the *Missouri Democrat*, a popular Civil War-era daily newspaper published in St. Louis. In the last week of April 1863, Major General Joseph Hooker had initiated an ambitious operation in northern Virginia. Leaving 40,000 men at Fredericksburg, he had moved the rest of the Army of the Potomac across the Rappahannock River a few miles upstream into an area known as the Wilderness. He hoped to crush Lee between his two forces, but Hooker let his opponent seize the initiative. Lee conducted a holding action at Fredericksburg, then committed the majority of his soldiers into battle against Hooker near the hamlet of Chancellorsville. The struggle, known as the Battle of Chancellorsville, took place on May 1-3, and resulted in a Confederate victory.

13. In August 1862 Confederate forces under Major General John C. Breckinridge had constructed a formidable set of fortifications at this site on the Mississippi River. At the time that Vermilion was writing, the Union had no troops in the vicinity of Port Hudson.

14. Daniel Wolsey Vorhees represented Indiana's 7th Congressional District,

which included Putnam County, in the U.S. House of Representatives. A Democrat, Vorhees opposed the Lincoln administration's prosecution of the Civil War.

15. Ohioan Clement Laird Vallandigham had served in the U.S. House of Representatives until defeated in 1862. He then became the Democratic gubernatorial candidate in his home state in 1863. A bitter opponent of the Union war effort, Vallandigham toured Ohio in the spring of 1863, delivering scathing speeches aimed at the Lincoln administration. General Burnside, by now the commander of the military district encompassing Ohio, had him arrested on May 5.

16. Age thirty-three, of Centerville.

17. A community in northern Appanoose County.

18. Thomas M. Fee, age twenty-four, of Centerville. Fee commanded Company G.

19. Located on the north bank of the Rappahannock River across from Fredericksburg, Falmouth was the site of the camp where Hooker began his Chancellorsville campaign. In conjunction with Hooker's move against Lee, Major General George Stoneman led a cavalry raid with Richmond as its goal. His campaign, which lasted from April 29 to May 8, was a failure; he achieved none of his tactical goals, and wore out 7,000 horses in the process.

20. On May 11, 1863, Grant was still twenty miles west of Jackson, but moving in that direction.

21. Gray dye became increasingly rare in the southern states as the war progressed. Consequently, Confederate soldiers began to use a combination of natural ingredients to color their clothing. The hue produced was called "butternut." Roundabouts were short, close-fitting jackets.

22. A term used interchangeably during the Civil War with "Union."

23. On May 11, 1863, a Union cavalry detachment from Helena, comprised of the 5th Kansas and the 5th Illinois, ran into a Confederate force while returning to camp. In the ensuing engagement, known as the Battle of Mount Vernon, the Federals suffered losses of one killed and fourteen wounded.

24. This is a reference drawn from *Don Quixote*, by Miguel de Cervantes. In it, good days are marked with white stones, while bad days are indicated by black ones.

25. Wells Gibbons, age forty-six, of Monroe County.

26. Age twenty-three, of Iconium. He was a private in the 36th Iowa.

27. Elizabeth Evans, age twenty-one, of Monroe County; Hancock, age thirty-three, of Monroe County; Davis, age forty, of Jackson Township in Monroe County.

28. At the Battle of Chancellorsville, Confederate Lieutenant General Thomas J. "Stonewall" Jackson had suffered a wound at the hands of his own men. After the amputation of his arm, pneumonia set in. Subsequently, Jackson died on May 10, 1863. On May 7, Dr. George R. Peters shot and fatally

wounded Confederate Major General Earl Van Dorn. Peters had become enraged over the attention that Van Dorn had paid to his wife.

29. One of Iowa's most intriguing Civil War-era residents, Henry Clay Dean had been a Methodist minister early in his life, serving as the chaplain of the U.S. Senate during the sessions of the 34th Congress. He moved to Iowa during the 1850s, where he became a lawyer. An outspoken critic of the war, he campaigned tirelessly for Democratic candidates opposed to the Lincoln administration. On May 15, 1863, a group of convalescent soldiers from the military hospital in Keokuk had arrested the forty-one-year-old for his disloyal speeches.

30. Secretary of the Treasury Salmon P. Chase.

31. Major General John McAllister Schofield. Schofield had indeed superceded Curtis as commander of the Department of the Missouri.

32. William Childs, age thirty-eight, and his wife Phoebe, age thirty-two, both of Independence Township in Appanoose County.

33. Joseph Marchbanks, age thirty-four, and Frances Marchbanks, age twenty-eight, both of Independence Township in Appanoose County; Jane Myers, age thirty. She lived next to the Marchbanks.

34. Sam Davenport, age twenty-two, and Jonathan Davenport, age fifty-two, of both of Chariton Township in Appanoose County.

35. James Harvey Ryckman, age twenty-three, of Centerville.

36. Lieutenant Colonel William F. Wood was appointed colonel of the 1st Arkansas Infantry (African Descent), but he came from the 1st Indiana Cavalry rather than the 46th Indiana.

37. William A. Pile, colonel of the 33rd Missouri, would indeed receive promotion to brigadier general, but not until December 26, 1863.

38. William H. Clifton, age thirty-nine, of Ottumwa.

39. Major General Alexander McDowell McCook, commander of the XX Corps.

40. John May, age sixty-three, of Wright Township in Wayne County.

41. John P. Evans, age sixty-two, of Jackson Township in Monroe County.

42. Andrew M. Roy, age forty-nine, of Benton Township in Lucas County.

43. Alonzo W. Sharp, age forty, of Jackson Township in Wayne County. Sharp, who represented Wayne County in the Iowa legislature, was a Democrat. He supported the war effort, however, and served on a committee to provide relief for the families of soldiers from Wayne County. E. T. Estep, age thirty-three, represented the district that included Wayne and Decatur Counties in the Iowa senate; Dennis Mahony was editor of the *Dubuque Herald* and a leader of the Democratic Party in Iowa.

44. Martingales are the straps on a horse's harness that connect the nose band to the girth.

45. Confederate Major General Sterling "Pap" Price.

46. Charlotte Kittredge, age thirty-one, of Ottumwa.

47. The Third Battery, Iowa Light Artillery, which was recruited primarily in the Dubuque area.

48. The 1st Regiment Arkansas Infantry (African Descent). Organized offi-

cially on May 1, 1863, the unit would later be designated the 46th U.S. Colored Troops.

49. Mary is quoting Isaiah 50:4–9 in the Bible.

50. Brigadier General William Sooy Smith. Smith commanded the 1st Division, XVI Corps, which included Matt Kemper's regiment. Brigadier General James William Denver commanded the 1st Division, XVI Corps, until his resignation on March 22, 1863. Denver, Colorado, was named after him.

51. One of the most prominent abolitionists of the antebellum period.

52. This is a quote from Cervantes' *Don Quixote.*

53. Henry Vermilion had enlisted in the 55th Indiana Regiment of Infantry in June 1862. His regiment, which had volunteered for three months' service, was captured almost to a man at the Battle of Richmond, Kentucky, on August 30, 1862. Paroled by the Confederates, the members of the regiment went to Indianapolis, where they were mustered out of the service. In spite of his ill health, Henry would indeed volunteer again, enlisting in the 133rd Indiana Infantry.

54. On May 25, 1863, elements of the 5th Kansas and 3rd Iowa Cavalries left Helena on a scouting mission to LaGrange, Arkansas. They met determined Confederate opposition at Polk's Plantation four miles outside of Helena and were forced to retreat.

55. The report of the commander of the 3rd Iowa gave his losses as five wounded and two missing.

56. On May 23, 1863, a force composed of the 2nd Regiment Arkansas Infantry (African Descent) and detachments from the 1st Indiana Cavalry and 36th Iowa sailed down the Mississippi River to Napoleon, Arkansas, on a raid. On May 25 the force came under fire from Confederates near Island 65. The Union troops landed and dispersed the Confederates.

57. On October 3, 1862, Confederate forces under Generals Van Dorn and Price had attacked Union troops defending Corinth, Mississippi. After some success the first day, the Confederates attacked again on October 4, but determined resistance under General Rosecrans allowed the Federals to maintain their hold on the city. The Confederates, having suffered 4,800 casualties to 2,350 for the Union, then retreated.

58. Louisa Jane Pennebaker, age thirty, and William G. Pennebaker, age twenty-eight, both of Wright Township in Wayne County. Pennebaker, who lived in Indiana prior to moving to Iowa, had enlisted in the 4th Iowa Infantry in August 1862.

59. Major General Frederick Steele, commander of the 1st Division, XV Corps.

60. Age forty-six, of Independence Township in Appanoose County.

61. Samuel Ely, age forty-four, of Independence Township in Appanoose County.

62. During the summer of 1863, in what is known as the Tullahoma Campaign, Rosecrans did indeed keep Bragg so busy that the Confederate com-

mander could not spare any troops from his Army of Tennessee to relieve the siege of Vicksburg.

63. Manoah Graham, age twenty-eight, of Iconium. Manoah was a member of William's company.

64. George F. Stewart, age forty-five, of Iconium; G. W. Richards, age thirty-two, who had recently moved to the area from Fayette County, Iowa.

65. Lovey Jolly, age twenty-nine, a schoolteacher in Bethlehem in Wayne County.

66. A church located in Confidence.

67. Argo, age thirty-six, and Sam Redenbaugh, age forty-six, of Chariton Township in Appanoose County.

68. John, age forty-four, and Elizabeth, forty, of Jackson Township in Monroe County.

69. Jennings Hays, age eighteen, of Jackson Township in Monroe County. Hays, a member of the 18th Iowa, had died in May 1863.

70. J. C. Fenton, age twenty-seven, of Centerville; Wafford, age twenty-nine, of Independence Township in Appanoose County.

71. Augustus Hamilton, age thirty-six, of Ottumwa.

72. Stephen K. Mahon, age twenty-four, of Ottumwa.

73. Age forty-four, of Wright Township in Wayne County.

74. Age twenty-three, of Osprey. He served in Company E of the 6th Iowa with Matt Kemper.

75. Gastric distress, usually related to a gall bladder or liver disorder.

76. Major General J. E. B. Stuart, a Confederate cavalry commander who had led a force completely around the Union army during McClellan's Peninsular Campaign in 1862.

77. Silas M. Sammons, age thirty-one, and Joseph Y. Funkhouser, age twenty-five, both of Iconium.

78. Major General John Alexander McClernand, commander of the XIII Corps.

CHAPTER 5. *"I Knew Somebody Had Lost Friends, and I Feared It Was I"*

1. Mark Maiken, age eighteen, and John Maiken, age fifteen, both of Iconium.

2. Catherine Ely, age fifty-seven, of Independence Township in Appanoose County.

3. Age twenty-two, of Iconium.

4. Trim, age forty-three, of Iconium; Jason Stock, age thirty-nine, of Jackson Township in Monroe County.

5. Age thirty-six, of Iconium.

6. John Collett, age nineteen, and William Collett, age twenty-three, both of Lagrange.

7. During the Battle of Second Bull Run in August 1862, Major General Fitz John Porter commanded a corps in the Army of Virginia. Ordered by Major General John Pope, the army's commander, to launch an assault against

a Confederate position, Porter decided that the actual conditions on the battlefield would make such an attack suicidal. Porter, no great admirer of Pope as a leader to begin with, therefore refused to obey. When Pope learned of this after he had lost the battle, he had Porter court-martialed for "disloyalty, disobedience, and misconduct."

8. Johnson Branden, age forty-eight, of Chariton Township in Appanoose County.

9. Age twenty-five, of Jackson Township in Monroe County. He was a member of the 18th Iowa.

10. Cyrus Teater, age fifty-nine, of Iconium.

11. William Dooley, of Iconium, gave his age as eighteen when he enlisted in 1862. However, the 1860 census, which was recorded in November of that year, listed his age as fourteen. It can therefore be surmised that William lied about his age to enlist. Lending credence to this theory is the fact that Jacob Dooley, his father, was only thirty-three in 1860, and his mother Margaret was thirty.

12. The *Republican Banner* was a daily newspaper published in Greencastle, Indiana. As previously noted, the Enrollment Act created a mechanism to force states to resort to a draft if they could not meet quotas set forth by the War Department for enlistments by voluntary means. Each congressional district was divided into subdistricts, and an enrollment commissioner was selected in each to record the names of those residents eligible for military service. This proved highly unpopular in many parts of Indiana, and resulted in the incidents Vermilion describes.

13. Age twenty-nine, of Jefferson Township in Putnam County.

14. James Sills, age fifty-four, the enrolling commissioner for Marion Township in Putnam County.

15. Actually, the article Vermilion is citing states that "Lawson Fry, while leaving the house, was fired at by one of the party and seriously wounded, disabling him for life."

16. A high ridge, northeast of Vicksburg, which overlooks the Yazoo River.

17. William Cassaday, age forty-seven, of Wright Township in Wayne County.

18. William Sigler Duckworth, age thirty-four, of Marion Township in Putnam County.

19. On October 8, 1862, a Union army commanded by General Buell fought a Confederate force led by Lieutenant General Braxton Bragg to a standstill near Perryville, Kentucky. The Confederates retreated the next day, allowing Buell to claim a victory.

20. After his success at Chancellorsville, Robert E. Lee received permission to take his army onto northern soil. By the time that Mary was writing, Lee's army had reached southeastern Pennsylvania. The Army of the Potomac followed warily, but Hooker no longer commanded it, for on June 28 Lincoln had replaced him with Major General George G. Meade, a Pennsylvanian.

21. John Taylor Lucas, who served in Company A of the 36th Iowa.

22. Sarah Lucas, age twenty-one, of Wright Township in Wayne County.

23. On June 14, 1863, General Banks ordered a frontal assault on the Confederate fortifications at Port Hudson. The Confederates repulsed the attack, inflicting 1,805 casualties.

24. Daniel Ivens, age forty-five, of Albia. He served as the hospital steward for the 36th Iowa.

25. Age fifty-five, of Jackson Township in Monroe County.

26. Hoping to forestall Union advances in Tennessee, Confederate Brigadier General John Hunt Morgan had organized a raid into Indiana and Tennessee in July 1863. His force crossed the Ohio River on July 8.

27. Joseph Dunover, age twenty-nine, of Iconium. He owned a mill in that community.

28. Lieutenant General Ambrose Powell Hill, who commanded a corps in the Army of Northern Virginia; Lieutenant General James Longstreet, who also commanded a corps in that army.

29. On June 25, 1863, the Union forces besieging Vicksburg detonated two mines under Confederate positions defending the city. Troops commanded by Major General John Alexander Logan then advanced and occupied the crater created by the larger of the two explosions, but retreated a day later. Logan would win the Medal of Honor for his actions during the attack.

30. William Lind, age forty-six, a physician in Wayne Township in Monroe County; Edward Mericle, age thirty-six, a blacksmith in Iconium.

31. William C. Evans, age forty, of Appanoose County.

32. Colonel William Milo Stone, age thirty-five, of Knoxville. He commanded the 22nd Iowa.

33. On July 4, 1863, General Pemberton surrendered Vicksburg and its 31,000 defenders to General Grant. Vast quantities of military stores also fell into Union hands.

34. 5th Corporal James Matthew Walker, age twenty-four, of Centerville.

35. Major General Alfred Pleasonton, commander of the Cavalry Corps attached to the Army of the Potomac.

36. After Grant had moved his forces across the Mississippi River on April 30, 1863, the Confederate secretary of war had ordered Lieutenant General Joseph E. Johnston to proceed to Mississippi to counter the federal offensive.

37. Age thirty, of Corydon.

38. Brigadier General Mosby M. Parsons, a Confederate brigade commander.

39. Catharine Wafford, age thirty-four, of Iconium.

40. Ginny Finton, age sixty-one, of Independence Township in Appanoose County.

41. Major General John Adams Dix, the commander of Fortress Monroe in Virginia.

42. Brigadier General Frederick Salomon.

43. Following his defeat at Gettysburg, General Lee initiated a withdrawal from Pennsylvania on the night of July 4. On the night of July 13, his army began crossing the Potomac back into Virginia. After naval efforts to subdue Charleston had failed, the War Department decided to commit army forces to that campaign. On July 10 troops landed on Morris Island to begin preparations for an assault on Battery Wagner.

44. Maturin L. Fisher, the Democratic nominee for lieutenant governor of Iowa in 1861.

45. According to the 1856 Iowa census, Thomas Osborn had owned a house in Iconium.

46. Isaac Chapman, age forty-two, of Wright Township in Wayne County.

47. The *South-Tier Democrat* was a Corydon newspaper founded in 1858. By 1863, A. O. Binckley and W. P. Morrett jointly published the paper. Morrett was the individual who aroused the ire of the Missouri Unionists, and James Carter was the sheriff who evoked similar displeasure. After the incident Binckley attempted to prevent Morrett from publishing anything about the incident, going so far as to take parts of the printing press and hide them. Morrett managed to produce at least a few more issues of the *South-Tier Democrat*, but the paper folded in September 1863. The *Corydon Monitor*, the first Republican newspaper in Wayne County, took its place one month later.

48. Age sixty-five, of Jefferson Township in Putnam County.

49. The federal assault on Morris Island, begun on July 10, had by July 17 given the Union control of 75 percent of the island.

50. On July 13, 1863, a crowd had stormed the draft office in New York City to stop the process of conscription. Soon the participants began to loot businesses, and then turned their anger towards blacks living in the city. Only the arrival of troops from the Army of the Potomac finally ended the disturbance after three days.

51. J. F. Stewart, age forty-five, Rebecca Stewart, age thirty-six, and Louisa Stewart, age twenty, all of Iconium.

52. Joseph O. Shannon, age thirty-three, of Burlington. A native of Kentucky, Shannon had enlisted in the 1st Iowa at the start of the Civil War. After the expiration of his term of enlistment, he had received a commission as a lieutenant in the 14th Iowa. He was taken prisoner at the Battle of Shiloh and held in various Confederate prison camps for months thereafter. He was finally exchanged and mustered out of the service on November 24, 1862.

53. Nancy Anna May, age seven, of Wright Township in Wayne County.

54. Bellair was an Appanoose County community nine miles southwest of Centerville. In 1871 the Rock Island Railroad laid track one-half mile south of Bellair, and established a station which it named Numa. A community soon grew up around this station, adopting its name. Within a few years, Numa absorbed Bellair.

55. The *Charleston Mercury*, an influential Southern newspaper.

56. Age twenty-three, of Osprey. A member of Matt's company in the 6th Iowa, he was killed on July 11, 1863.

57. Lieutenant Colonel Henry Clay Caldwell, of Keosauqua; Colonel Cyrus Bussey, of Bloomfield. Bussey would later become governor of Iowa.

58. Age nineteen, of Iconium.

59. Abraham Isley and Ezra A. Couchman were both James Kemper's age, and came from the same township.

60. Age twenty-two, of Lagrange. He was a member of Company E in the 6th Iowa.

61. Wells Hickcox, age fifty-five, and his son George, age sixteen, both of Jackson Township in Monroe County.

62. William Gilbert, age fifty, of Jackson Township in Monroe County.

63. Major General Quincy Adams Gillmore, commander of the Department of the South.

64. Mary Hickcox, age fifty.

65. On July 26, 1863, Union forces finally captured General Morgan and 364 of his men near Salineville, Ohio.

66. Age twenty-nine, of Jackson Township in Monroe County.

67. Age eighteen, of Fairfield.

68. As there is no record of a John Sullivan belonging to the 8th Iowa Cavalry, it appears that John Sullivan, Sr., age forty-nine, of Jackson Township in Monroe County, succeeded in his mission to keep his namesake out of the service.

69. William S. Delay, age twenty-eight, of Iconium, and Peter Talkington, age thirty-six, of Appanoose County, did enlist in the 8th Iowa Cavalry. Ben Head and Jake McInich, residents of Appanoose County, were never mustered into federal service.

70. William S. Lambert, age twenty-nine, of Bloomfield.

CHAPTER 6. *"I Will Never Forget All the Bitter Experiences of the Last Year"*

1. 3rd Corporal William H. Shutterly, age thirty, of Moravia.

2. Brigadier General John Wynn Davidson.

3. Alpheus R. Barnes, age twenty-five, a merchant in Albia; Bryant, age fifty, of Centerville.

4. Mary Rhynerson, age thirty-nine, of Putnam County.

5. After the Lincoln administration had begun to accept African American regiments into federal service, Jefferson Davis retaliated by threatening to execute any captured white officers who led these units. In addition, Davis stated that captured black soldiers would be enslaved. Lincoln countered with an executive order on July 30 announcing that he would execute one Confederate prisoner for every Union captive killed illegally, and he would

force Confederate prisoners to do hard labor in equal numbers to black captives put into servitude.

6. On June 7, 1863, a Confederate force attacked a mixed detachment of white and black Union troops at Milliken's Bend, Louisiana. Observers from both sides credited the black soldiers with fighting tenaciously. On May 27, 1863, Union forces, including two African American regiments, had assaulted the Confederate works at Port Hudson. Although the attack failed, black soldiers again won praise for their gallantry.

7. James P. Evans served in the 6th Iowa until being discharged for disability on September 18, 1862. The twenty-five-year-old resident of Osprey soon recovered, and became a member of Company F in the 8th Iowa Cavalry; Isley, age eighteen, of Monroe County; Hall, age twenty, of Moravia.

8. Brigadier General James Madison Tuttle, age thirty-nine, of Van Buren County.

9. Myran Swift, age fifty, of Franklin Township in Monroe County; George Swift, age eighteen, of Lucas County.

10. The first major federally financed road, the National Road ran from Cumberland, Maryland, to Vandalia, Illinois, along the route that U.S. Highway 40 takes today. The road went through Mt. Meridian and Putnamville in Putnam County.

11. LeGrand Byington, a Democratic Party leader from Iowa City.

12. Henry K. Steele, who ran a dry goods store in Albia.

13. Nancy Carpenter, age thirty-one, of Chariton Township in Appanoose County.

14. Hannah Tucker, age thirty, of Chariton Township in Appanoose County.

15. Vermilion's taxes in 1863 came to $3.48.

16. On August 1, 1863, George Cyphert Tally, a young Baptist minister, led a group of people opposed to the war to South English, where the Keokuk County Republicans were holding their convention. Shots were exchanged by the two sides, killing Tally and wounding others. Upon learning of the incident, Governor Kirkwood dispatched troops to the community and traveled to the county seat of Sigourney to deliver a stern warning to anyone advocating disloyalty.

17. Chester C. Cole, who had run for Congress against Samuel Curtis in the Vermilions' district in 1860.

18. Joseph A. Hinton, age fifty-six. He ran a carpentry business in Lovilia.

19. James Matthew Hays, age twenty-eight, of Lagrange, had served in Company E of the 6th Iowa until his discharge in December 1862. His younger brother, Noah, was recruited for the 8th Cavalry, but was rejected by a physician when the regiment was mustered into service.

20. Sylvester H. Sawyer, age thirty-one, of Unionville.

21. Major General James Gillpatrick Blunt, after defeating a Confederate force at Honey Springs in the Indian Territory on July 17, 1863, pursued the retreating foe to the Arkansas River. While at that location in August,

he learned that the Confederates were attempting to gather a large body of troops to oppose him. But Mary's faith in Blunt was well-founded — rather than retreat, Blunt chose to go forward, and eventually advanced his army to Ft. Smith, Arkansas.

22. Samuel and Jane Wright, ages sixty-seven and sixty-five, respectively, of Warren Township in Putnam County.

23. Age twenty-one, of Moravia.

24. On July 27, 1863, the War Department had authorized the recruitment of an African American infantry regiment in Iowa. Originally designated the 1st Iowa Infantry (African Descent), it became the 60th Infantry Regiment, United States Colored Troops, on March 11, 1864. Many of the volunteers came from Iowa, and the rest were recruited from other northern states.

25. John Teater, age twenty-six, of Centerville.

26. Amos Harris, age thirty-eight, of Centerville.

27. Nathan Udell, age forty-six, a physician from Centerville; Madison M. Walden, age twenty-six, of Centerville. Walden had been the captain of Company D in the 6th Iowa until he resigned in December 1862. He then became the captain of Company H in the 8th Iowa Cavalry.

28. De Valls Bluff, Arkansas. The Union army would make this location a major supply base.

29. When William was mustered on October 4, 1862, he stood five foot ten inches and weighed one hundred forty-five pounds.

30. Alexander Black. The fifty-four-year-old Black had owned a farm next to Valentine Kemper's in Monroe County before moving to Missouri in 1861.

31. McKinley, age twenty-three, of Union Township in Wayne County; Cox, age twenty-six, of Marion Township in Putnam County.

32. Age fifteen, of Marion Township in Putnam County.

33. General Pierre Gustave Toutant Beauregard, the commander of the Confederate forces defending Charleston.

34. John C. Evans, age sixty, of Jackson Township in Monroe County.

35. Elijah L. Kendall, age thirty-seven, of Washington Township in Lucas County.

36. Rufus Jenison, age fifty-eight, of Jackson Township in Monroe County.

37. James Harlan, age forty-three, of Mt. Pleasant. Harlan, first elected to the U.S. Senate from Iowa in 1854, had, like William, attended Indiana Asbury University.

38. The wife of E. L. Kendall was actually named Lucinda instead of Miranda. She and her husband had five children under the age of twelve.

39. Barnhart, age twenty, of Iconium; Clark, age twenty, of Iconium.

40. Nora and Nancy, ages twenty-three and seventeen, respectively, daughters of Rufus Jenison.

41. Charles B. Nourse, who represented Polk County in the Iowa legislature;

James Wilson Grimes, of Burlington. Elected governor of Iowa in 1854, Grimes had been selected by the state legislature for a seat in the U.S. Senate in 1858.

42. Age thirty-eight, of Keokuk.

43. A religious denomination with a German pietistic background.

44. Robert McClaren, age thirty-two, of Moravia; Robert Goldsberry, age thirty-nine, of Iconium.

45. Thomas Clagget edited the Keokuk *Constitution*. Apparently the soldiers in the army hospital in Keokuk did not enjoy his views on the war, for on February 19, 1863, they had destroyed his press by throwing it into the Mississippi River.

46. James F. Wilson, of Fairfield. At the start of the Civil War, Samuel Curtis resigned his seat in the U.S. House of Representatives to accept a commission in the army; in the special election to replace Curtis, Wilson ran against J. E. Neal. Wilson won, carrying Monroe County in the process, but lost Appanoose County by 300 votes.

47. Major General John Logan, one of the few successful politician-generals of the Civil War.

48. Benjamin Baldwin, age twenty-three, of Jackson Township in Monroe County.

49. This is another reference drawn from *Don Quixote*.

50. In late June 1863 General Rosecrans had initiated a campaign against the Army of Tennessee, under the command of General Bragg. Without fighting a major battle, Rosecrans forced Bragg to evacuate Chattanooga on September 9 and retreat into Georgia.

51. The Confederates had abandoned Forts Wagner and Gregg on the night of September 6. The next day Union Admiral John A. Dahlgren, commander of the federal fleet at Charleston, had called for the surrender of the badly damaged Ft. Sumter.

52. Brigadier General Nathan Kimball. The forty-year-old Kimball, like William, had attended Indiana Asbury University. In 1852, Winfield Scott was the Whig candidate for president.

53. During the Mexican War, Colonel William A. Bowles commanded the 2nd Indiana Infantry at the Battle of Buena Vista. During the fight Bowles ordered his men to retreat, a move which left the entire American army in jeopardy. William is correct that Kimball rallied his company of the 2nd Indiana and continued to do battle.

54. On September 19, 1861, General Price had used the highly unorthodox, but extremely effective, technique of having his men advance behind cotton bales soaked in water toward the federal positions defending Lexington, Missouri. When his troops came within 100 yards of the Union lines, the commander of the Lexington garrison surrendered the town.

55. John Webb, Jr., age thirty-six, of Albia.

56. As Rosecrans moved his force in an attempt to capture Chattanooga in the

summer of 1863, General Burnside directed a simultaneous campaign to take Knoxville. Burnside succeeded in his effort on September 2.

57. Senator Charles Sumner of Massachusetts.

CHAPTER 7. *"I Listen Every Hour to Hear of a Decisive Battle"*

1. Mary is referring to the Battle of Chickamauga, fought September 19–20, 1863.

2. Rear Admiral Samuel F. Du Pont, who had commanded the South Atlantic Blockading Squadron until relieved in July 1863 by Rear Admiral John A. Dahlgren.

3. In 1863 the Confederate government had contracted to have two steam-driven ironclad rams constructed at the Laird facility in Liverpool, England. James D. Bulloch, the Confederate agent in England, cleverly disguised the transaction to make it appear that the Pasha of Egypt was purchasing the ships. Charles Francis Adams, the American minister to England, saw through the ruse and demanded that the British government confiscate the vessels in accordance with international law. The British refused his request until news of the string of Union victories in the summer of 1863 reached England; consequently, on September 3, 1863, British authorities seized the unfinished rams, ending the diplomatic crisis.

4. Willis Hays, age twenty-three, of Lagrange; Josephus Hays, age twenty-one, of Lagrange. Josephus was a member of the 1st Iowa Cavalry.

5. Major General James Birdseye McPherson, commander of the XVII Corps. After Rosecrans retreated to Chattanooga following the Battle of Chickamauga, the War Department transferred the XI and XII Corps from the Army of the Potomac to him to help rectify the situation.

6. Maston H. Jones, age thirty-five, of Bloomfield.

7. The *Nashville Union and American* was a daily newspaper published from 1853 to 1866.

8. In 1846 John Lee Comstock had written *A Manual of Natural Philosophy: With Recapitulatory Questions on Each Chapter: and a Dictionary of Philosophical Terms.*

9. From June 30, 1851, to April 9, 1855, Valentine Kemper had served as the postmaster of Mt. Meridian in Putnam County.

10. Vermilion's company included a soldier named John Standley, who was with the regiment as Mary was writing.

11. Matilda Varner, age thirty-eight, of Centerville.

12. John Fletcher Evans, age twenty-three, of Jackson Township in Monroe County. He served in the 18th Iowa with James Kemper; John C. and Mary Evans; James P. Evans; Sarah and Luella Evans, ages twenty-four and sixteen, respectively.

13. Jessie Benton Frémont was the wife of Major General John C. Frémont. In 1863 she wrote *The Story of the Guard: A Chronicle of the War*, a book that

discussed a military unit formed by her husband in 1861 and known as Frémont's Body Guard.

14. Major Charles Zagonyi, the commander of Frémont's Body Guard. Zagonyi was later promoted to colonel, and served as the commander of cavalry under Frémont in Virginia.

15. Colonel John Edwards, age fifty, of Chariton. The Speaker of the House in the Iowa legislature prior to the Civil War, Edwards commanded the 18th Iowa during the conflict.

16. Colonel William E. McLean.

17. Although the evidence is somewhat contradictory, it appears that the 77th Ohio did indeed flee the battlefield at Shiloh in disorder on April 6, 1862.

18. Colonel Thomas Hart Benton, Jr., named for his uncle, the first senator from Missouri.

19. Marion Taylor Hancock, age twenty-one, of Wright Township in Wayne County.

20. Lemuel L. Spooner, age twenty.

21. Jacob Knapp, age thirty-three, of Appanoose County.

22. John Francis Duncombe, age thirty-two, of Ft. Dodge. He was the Democratic candidate for lieutenant governor in 1863; John Banks, age thirty-three, of Centerville.

23. After the firing on Fort Sumter, a number of individuals who had attended Indiana Asbury University formed a militia company and offered their services to the state of Indiana. This unit, known as the Asbury Guards, became a part of the 14th Indiana Infantry. The regiment then joined the Army of the Potomac. John Wright, who had attended Asbury, went back to Indiana and enlisted in the Asbury Guards, but was later discharged for medical reasons.

24. Also known as All Fives, Muggins is a variation of dominoes.

25. Age twenty-four. Gilbert was a member of the 1st Iowa Cavalry.

26. McCamy Elliott, age fifty, of Jefferson Township in Putnam County. Elliott was a Baptist preacher in that county.

27. Robert Parker Parrott, the superintendent of the West Point Iron and Cannon Foundry, had invented a muzzle-loading artillery weapon prior to the Civil War. Such pieces were called Parrotts in his honor.

28. Andrew B. Prather, age twenty-six, of Lucas County.

29. On October 25, 1863, Confederate forces under the command of General Marmaduke attempted to capture the town of Pine Bluff, Arkansas. The Union garrison, consisting of the 5th Kansas Infantry and the 1st Indiana Cavalry, repelled the assault. Colonel Powell Clayton, age thirty, remained in Arkansas after the war. In 1868 he was elected governor, and in 1870 was chosen for the U.S. Senate.

30. Both men were quite ill when Dollie was writing; Trim would die November 4, 1863, and Sammons on January 18, 1864.

31. The official record of Iowa shows that the 36th Iowa cast seventy-three votes for Tuttle.

32. Counting the ballots of all the members of the 36th Iowa who voted, the regiment gave two hundred ninety-nine votes to Stone and seventy-three to Tuttle.

33. Perry G. Luzader, age twenty-seven, and Elijah Cozadd, age thirty-eight, both of Independence Township in Appanoose County.

34. On October 26, 1863, Union forces had commenced a series of operations to establish a secure supply line into Chattanooga. As part of the plan, on October 29 General Hooker's corps (sent west from the Army of the Potomac) attacked and defeated a Confederate force defending Raccoon Mountain, a precipice which dominated the supply route.

35. Beecher, age fifty, was perhaps the most influential American clergyman of the nineteenth century. The pastor of the Congregationalist Plymouth Church in Brooklyn, New York, he had embarked on a lecture tour of England in 1863 to explain the Union cause to that country.

36. Mary is correct on two counts. First, Shaw was thrown into a common grave with the fallen African American members of the 54th Massachusetts at Battery Wagner. And second, at one time prior to the Civil War Shaw's family had lived on Staten Island, and had often attended services at Beecher's church in Brooklyn.

37. Anthony Astley Cooper Rogers. The forty-two-year-old would be elected to the U.S. House of Representatives the following year under the plan of reconstruction implemented by Abraham Lincoln, but the members of Congress denied the Arkansas delegation their seats. Rogers also won election to Congress in 1868, and served one term.

38. E. W. Gantt had won election to the U.S. House of Representatives from Arkansas in 1860. At the start of the Civil War he became a colonel in the Confederate army, but switched his allegiance to the Union in 1863.

39. Major General John Gray Foster, age forty, of New Hampshire. Foster would indeed replace Burnside in command of the Department of the Ohio, but not until December 9, 1863; John Brooks Henderson, age thirty-seven, a Democrat turned Unionist; Benjamin Gratz Brown, age thirty-seven. A prewar Democrat, Brown had raised a Union regiment at the start of the conflict, where he served with distinction. He would be the Democratic candidate for vice president in 1872.

40. Amasa Gilbert, age nineteen, of Lagrange. He was a member of the 18th Iowa.

41. Vermilion was detached from duty on Wednesday, November 25, to take a recruiting party to Iowa to solicit volunteers.

42. Following the capture of Lookout Mountain on November 24, Grant had ordered an assault the following day on the Confederate positions along Missionary Ridge. Avenging their defeat at Chickamauga, members of the Army of the Cumberland stormed up the slopes and captured the enemy works.

43. Brigadier General John Murray Corse, age twenty-eight, of Burlington. The former major of the 6th Iowa, he was severely bruised by a spent bul-

let in the assault on Missionary Ridge. He would recover, and later in the war was the recipient of the famous "Hold the Fort: I am Coming" message from General Sherman.

44. Major Thomas J. Ennis, age twenty-two, of Lyons. Ennis was only wounded in the assault on Missionary Ridge. He would recover, but eight months later would die in the Battle of Atlanta.

45. Harriet Paschal, age twenty-nine, of Jackson Township in Monroe County; a monthly publication that first appeared in print in January 1849.

46. Copperhead was a term used during the Civil War to denote a person opposed to the Union war effort. Since many Copperheads were Democrats, Mary is using the term here to denote the number of Democrats elected to the Iowa house and senate.

CHAPTER 8. *"Our War Can't Last Much Longer As It Is Now Carried On"*

1. George Hickenlooper, age thirty-eight, of Monroe County. The second sergeant of Company K in the 36th Iowa, he had represented his company in the recruiting party commanded by William.

2. Searching for a location where his congregation could find security, Joseph Smith, the founder of the Church of Jesus Christ of Latter-day Saints (LDS), had constructed the town of Nauvoo in 1840 as a haven for his people. Four years later Nauvoo had a population of 15,000, making it the largest town in Illinois. Neighboring Illinoisans not affiliated with the LDS Church resented its power, and a group of them lynched Smith in 1844. The church members (called Mormons by outsiders) decided to abandon Nauvoo, eventually moving to present-day Utah in 1846–47.

3. Captain Mortimer M. Hayden, age forty-four, of Dubuque. The commander of the Dubuque Battery, he had been placed in charge of Union artillery on Steele's abortive expedition.

4. On April 23, 1864, President Lincoln called upon the loyal states to furnish 85,000 volunteers for one hundred days' service. The regiment Mary is referring to would be designated the 46th Iowa.

5. Dykes, age twenty-four, of Independence Township in Appanoose County; Maiken, age forty-eight, of Chariton Township in Appanoose County; Phillips, age twenty-nine, of Independence Township in Appanoose County; Steven E. Van Benthusen, age thirty-six, of Wright Township in Wayne County; Gilbert, age twenty-four, of Jackson Township in Monroe County.

6. Age twenty.

7. Mellissa Hurst, age twenty-four, of Jefferson Township in Putnam County.

8. Congressman Francis Preston Blair, Jr. had helped keep Missouri in the Union in 1861. He had received an appointment as a brigadier general, and had won promotion to major general for meritorious service. Missouri reelected him to Congress, but federal law prevented him from taking his seat because of his military rank. Lincoln allowed the forty-two-year-old Blair to return his commission, hoping that the House of Representatives

would choose Blair as the Speaker. When this did not occur, and after Blair made speeches denouncing Secretary of the Treasury Chase, Lincoln gave Blair his commission back. Questions were raised in the Senate about the propriety of this action, but Blair did resume his position in the Union army. Montgomery Blair was the older brother of Francis Blair, Jr., Lincoln's first postmaster general. Both Blairs struck abolitionists as less than enthusiastic about fighting a war to strike a blow against slavery.

9. The Battle of Elkins' Ferry.

10. Martin Luther Landes, age twenty, of Lucas County.

11. John Davis, age twenty-three, of Iconium. Captured at Marks' Mills, he would survive his incarceration.

12. Jacob McInich, age thirty-five, of Jackson Township in Monroe County; George Frankhouser, age twenty, of Chariton Township in Appanoose County.

13. Delilah Delay, age nineteen, of Chariton Township in Appanoose County.

14. During the Civil War, the smallpox vaccine used to inoculate individuals would occasionally still have the live smallpox virus in it. This would cause the person receiving the vaccine to develop smallpox. In its initial stage, smallpox creates symptoms in a victim similar to those that a person suffering from syphilis will display. For that reason, many doctors of the period assumed that vaccine processed from an individual suffering from both smallpox and syphilis would result in not only inoculation against smallpox, but the transferral of syphilis as well.

15. Elizabeth McCulley, age fifty-six, of Independence Township in Appanoose County.

16. Age thirty, of Independence Township in Appanoose County. He and his wife had four children, ages five through ten.

17. Rice did not die on the journey back to Oskaloosa, as William had heard. Unfortunately, the able and popular general never recovered, and passed away at his home on July 6, 1864.

18. In 1862 Union and Confederate authorities had created a system for exchanging prisoners of war. This agreement worked smoothly until 1863, when the Davis administration announced that it would not treat black Union soldiers, or their white officers, as legitimate prisoners of war. The Lincoln administration countered by ending all prisoner-of-war exchanges.

19. On January 8, 1864, Union authorities in Little Rock had hanged David O. Dodd, a seventeen-year-old Confederate spy.

20. Frederic Messenger, age sixty-four, of New York in Wayne County; David L. Sheppard, age twenty-seven, and David Shaffer, age fifty-five, both of Chariton Township in Appanoose County.

21. Major General Daniel Edgar Sickles had lost his right leg because of a wound he suffered on the second day of battle at Gettysburg.

22. By early 1864 a number of Northerners, including many German Americans, had grown discontented with Lincoln's leadership during the war. As

a consequence, they called for a national convention to convene in Cleveland on May 31 to address that issue. After adopting a thirteen-point platform, the group had nominated Frémont for president on the Radical Democracy ticket. But on June 7, 1864, the Union Party convened its national convention. Comprised of Republicans and prowar Democrats, this group nominated Lincoln for president, and adopted a platform calling for the abolition of slavery.

23. George Haver, age thirty-one, of Appanoose County.

24. Harvey Tannehill, age forty-two, of Centerville. He also served as the recruiting coordinator for Appanoose County.

25. In June 1864 Treasury Secretary Chase offered Lincoln his resignation, as he had done twice before. Much to his surprise, Lincoln accepted. Lincoln then appointed Senator William Pitt Fessenden of Maine as secretary of the treasury. Fessenden held the post until Congress reconvened in December 1864; Lincoln then nominated Hugh McCulloch to fill the position.

26. On June 27, 1864, General Sherman had ordered an assault on the Confederate positions defending the area around Kennesaw Mountain, Georgia. The role of the 6th Iowa was to drive the Confederates from a vantage point known as Pigeon Hill. The attack failed, and Matt Kemper received a wound to his hip.

27. Recognizing that many children would be left orphans by the Civil War, a number of prominent Iowans formed a committee to help establish a facility to take care of the unfortunate youngsters. Through their efforts, a home was opened in Farmington in Van Buren County in July 1864, with a similar dwelling place under construction in Cedar Falls. The group hoped, however, to build a much larger domicile in Davenport, and to that end asked Iowa regiments for contributions. This eventually led to the building of the Annie Wittenmyer Home, on the grounds of Camp Kinsman.

28. In the 1863 Iowa state election 318 Appanoose County soldiers cast ballots in the field, but the Appanoose County Board of Supervisors invalidated them. Proving that the 2000 presidential contest was not the first time that the judicial system affected an election, the Iowa Supreme Court decided against the supervisors, ruling that all votes legally cast should count. Unlike the 2000 election, however, the U.S. Supreme Court did not overturn the state court's 1863 decision.

29. George R. Watson, age twenty-six, of Lagrange.

30. McPherson had been killed on July 22, 1864, during the Battle of Atlanta.

31. On July 5, 1864, Confederate Brigadier General Jubal Early had crossed the Potomac into Maryland with a force of 14,000 men. He reached the outskirts of Washington on July 11. The timely arrival of troops sent by Grant from Petersburg deterred Early from attacking the city, and by July 14 the rebels had fallen back into Virginia.

32. A former governor of Missouri, Sterling Price had never lost sight of his

dream to wrest his state from federal control. With this in mind, in the summer of 1864 he led a mounted force of 12,000 through Arkansas, entering Missouri on September 19.

33. Elijah Elliot Harvey, age thirty-six, of Bellair. During the Civil War a number of states had sought Iowa volunteers for service in their own regiments. Harvey, a veteran of the Mexican War, had recruited individuals from the Appanoose County area to form a company for the 5th Kansas Regiment. In 1862, his company was transferred to the 6th Kansas Cavalry. On July 27, 1864, a Confederate force decimated this regiment at Mazzard (or Massard) Prairie, Arkansas.

34. Brigadier General Douglas H. Cooper, who had been instrumental in recruiting Native Americans for the Confederate cause.

35. Marion Hinton, age twenty-four, of Appanoose County; Roy, age twenty-one, of Benton Township in Lucas County; Teater, age thirty-eight, of Independence Township in Appanoose County; Joshua Zentz (or Zintz), age twenty-five, of Independence Township; Thomas McCauley, age twenty-two, of Independence Township; Scott, age twenty-one, of Walnut Township in Appanoose County.

36. Camp Ford, the largest Confederate prisoner-of-war camp west of the Mississippi, was located near Tyler, Texas. The men of the 36th Iowa captured at Marks' Mills were incarcerated there.

37. John Lambert, age thirty, of Albia. He commanded Company K of the 36th Iowa. Allen W. Miller, age twenty-six, of Unionville. He commanded Company C of the 36th Iowa.

38. William is correct that Lieutenant General William J. Hardee, a Confederate corps commander, had written *Rifle and Light Infantry Tactics* in 1855, but his assertion about the demise of Hardee was premature. Morgan on the other hand, was killed on September 4, 1864, in Greenville, Tennessee.

39. William F. Vermilya, age twenty-seven. Because of the similarity of their names, a few documents pertaining to Vermilya are held by the National Archives in William Vermilion's military file.

40. Daniel Peppers, age twenty-three, of Appanoose County. He had actually died August 29 at Camp Ford.

41. On August 5, 1864, General Grant had placed Major General Phillip Sheridan in command of the Middle Military Division, with orders to raze the Shenandoah Valley. As Sheridan advanced into the fertile region, Jubal Early attempted to thwart the Union campaign. But at Winchester on September 19, and at Fisher's Hill on September 22, Sheridan had soundly defeated the Confederates, forcing Early to retreat further up the valley.

42. On July 18, 1864, President Lincoln had issued a call for 500,000 volunteers. For the first time, Iowa did not meet its quota, and as a consequence had to resort to a draft. Estimates vary, but perhaps 4,000 men, including substitutes, were drafted.

43. Albert Gilman, age nineteen.

44. Martha Nicholson, age twenty-one, Melvina Nicholson, age eighteen, Nancy Nicholson, age sixteen, and Mary Nicholson, age fourteen. They were sisters who lived in Jackson Township of Monroe County.

45. Sterling Price had met with success in his campaign in Missouri, arriving on the outskirts of Kansas City after suffering only one setback. But on October 23, 1864, Union forces under Generals Pleasonton and Curtis defeated him decisively at the Battle of Westport. Price retreated into Kansas, where on October 27 Pleasanton routed him at Mine Creek. James Dunlavy of the 3rd Iowa Cavalry captured General Marmaduke at this battle.

46. The 1860 census results caused Iowa to gain four electoral votes. That meant that every soldier in the 36th Iowa could vote for eight separate electors. Vermilion's tabulation is off in a few instances: in the race between Dan Anderson and Jarius Neal, Anderson received 234 votes, while four were cast for his Democratic counterpart, and in four electoral races, only 235 votes were cast. But Vermilion is correct that no elector pledged to McClellan received more than four votes.

47. In 1864 the civilian voters of Appanoose County went for McClellan by a vote of 920 to 874.

48. After evacuating Atlanta, Confederate Lieutenant General John Bell Hood had moved his troops into Alabama, hoping that Sherman would follow. But Sherman gave up the chase by late October 1864, prompting Hood to take his army into Tennessee.

49. Matt had made a full recovery from his wound, and was on his way to rejoin his regiment when he was struck down with smallpox. He died in the quarantine ward of the military hospital in Keokuk on November 8, 1864, and was buried at Oakland Cemetery in that city.

50. Colonel Cyrus H. Mackey.

51. Thomas Cuppy, age fifty-three, of Moravia.

52. Major General Joseph Jones Reynolds.

53. Jane Lambert, age twenty-nine, of Independence Township in Appanoose County.

54. By 1865 Wilmington, North Carolina, was the last major port east of the Mississippi that Confederate blockade runners could use. On January 15, 1865, elements of the Union army and navy captured Ft. Fisher, which protected the port, thus rendering Wilmington useless to the Confederacy.

55. In February 1865 Grant had ordered Sheridan to destroy the railroads and canals in the vicinity of Lynchburg, Virginia. On March 2 Sheridan's force completely routed the remnants of Early's command at the Battle of Waynesborough, then proceeded to carry out Grant's wishes.

56. Because the 36th Iowa had lost both its national and regimental flags at Marks' Mills, it had to requisition new ones. The regimental flag — dark blue with a red stripe and gold fringe, stars, and lettering — is on display in the rotunda of the Iowa State Capitol Building in Des Moines. J. S. Wolfe, the sutler of the 36th Iowa, arranged for the flag's embroidering.

57. Henry H. Swift, age twenty, of Iconium. Captured at Marks' Mills, he would survive his incarceration.

58. William K. Neel, age thirty-three, of Iconium.

59. Major General Edward Richard Sprigg Canby, commander of the Military Division of West Mississippi.

60. The *C.S.S. Maurepas.*

CHAPTER 9. *"The Days Are Long and Dreary till You Come Home"*

1. Andrew J. Morehouse, age eighteen, of Iconium; Thomas J. Nowles, age eighteen, of Appanoose County, and his father, John, age forty-seven.

2. Major General Fitzhugh Lee, Robert E. Lee's nephew, did not surrender until the formal capitulation of the Army of Northern Virginia at Appomattox Court House on April 12, 1865.

3. On April 7, 1865, Union forces cut off a portion of the retreating Army of Northern Virginia at Saylor's Creek. Among the captured Confederates were Lieutenant General Richard Stoddert Ewell, Major Generals George Washington Custis Lee and Joseph Brevard Kershaw, and Brigadier Generals Dudley McIver DuBose, Seth Maxwell Barton, Montgomery Dent Course, Eppa Hunton, and James Phillip Simms.

4. On the night that John Wilkes Booth assassinated Lincoln, Lewis Paine attempted to do the same to Secretary of State William Seward. Paine wounded his target, but Seward survived.

5. Vernon R. Bridges, of Mattoon, Illinois.

6. On April 18, 1865, Sherman and General Johnston had concluded negotiations for a general treaty of peace between the warring sides. It would have arranged for the surrender of all Confederate armies, and would also have allowed the seceded states to come back into the Union after state officials had merely sworn allegiance to the United States. Secretary of War Stanton found these terms too lenient, and ordered Sherman to simply negotiate the surrender of troops under Johnston's command.

7. Brigadier General John Milton Thayer, commander of the District of the Frontier.

8. Troopers of the 4th Michigan Cavalry had captured Davis on May 10, 1865, near Irwinville, Georgia.

9. By 1865 privates earned sixteen dollars a month. Vermilion is therefore jokingly hinting that he may have to reduce Sergeants Brashar and Kemper to the rank of private for insulting him.

10. While on an inspection tour of Arkansas, on November 6, 1864, General Canby had received a serious wound at the hands of a Confederate sniper. On May 24, 1865, a detachment of soldiers from the 1st Indiana Cavalry captured a Confederate guerrilla by the name of Joseph Morgan near Arkansas Post. Based on the testimony of two witnesses, the Federals believed that Morgan had been the one who shot Canby.

11. Vermilion's official record states that he was promoted to major on May 11, 1865, but never mustered at that rank.

12. On May 26, 1865, General Edmund Kirby Smith had surrendered all forces under his command in the Trans-Mississippi Department.

13. Mary Drake, age twenty-nine, of Unionville; Maria J. Fee, age twenty-seven, of Centerville; Sarah Gedney, age thirty-seven, of Centerville.

14. Brigadier General Alexander Shaler, who commanded a division in the VII Corps.

15. In 1865 A. J. H. Duganne, the colonel of the 176th New York, wrote *Camps and Prisons: Twenty Months in the Department of the Gulf.*

16. Brigadier General John Morrison Oliver.

17. Allen A. Smith, age forty-one, of Wapello County.

18. Early in the war Governor Kirkwood called for a state agency to help provide for the medical needs of the Union army. Accordingly, a group of individuals formed the Iowa Sanitary Commission in October 1861, based on the model of the U.S. Sanitary Commission. In addition to this group, Iowa also had other agencies operating in the state with similar purposes. To rationalize these humanitarian efforts, the various groups met in Des Moines in November 1863 and decided to combine operations under the banner of the Iowa Sanitary Commission. This newly formed group appointed Dr. Udell as one of its three field agents on January 20, 1864.

19. Henry H. Trimble, age thirty-seven, of Bloomfield.

20. William is referring to a resolution adopted by the Iowa Republican Party at its state convention in June 1865. Initially, Resolution Four would have based voting on "loyalty to the Constitution and Union," but an amendment changed the resolution to a call for removing the word "white" from the article in the Iowa state constitution concerning voting. Historian Robert Dykstra has demonstrated conclusively that the idea of extending the vote to black adult males proved unimportant in the state election in Iowa in the fall of 1865, but William was correct in one sense: Appanoose County voted against black suffrage when the issue appeared on the state ballot in 1868.

21. Major General O. O. Howard, the head of the Bureau of Refugees, Freedmen, and Abandoned Lands, received a letter dated August 2, 1865, from his representative in Arkansas reporting this incident. I have been unable to determine the outcome of the legal proceedings.

22. Henry Maples, age forty-nine, of Caldwell Township in Appanoose County; J. W. Collins, age twenty-nine, of Troy Township in Monroe County.

23. James Caleb Jackson. Born in 1811, Jackson wrote on a multitude of health-related subjects and championed the abolitionist cause, but is best known today as the creator of granola.

24. Founded by Dr. J. J. Burtis, the Burtis House was Davenport's largest hotel, containing 150 rooms. It was located at the intersection of 5th and Iowa Streets.

Bibliographical Note

The Civil War remains a subject of great interest to the American public in general, and to academicians in particular. Much has been written about the subject, and much continues to be published. In writing this book, therefore, I was able to consult a wide range of primary and secondary materials.

The 36th Iowa contained a number of individuals who left letters, diaries, or manuscripts, which I put to use. The William F. Vermilion Collection at the Mandeville Special Collections Library, University of California, San Diego, holds a wealth of correspondence written by or to William Vermilion during the Civil War and the postwar period. The collection also contains a diary that Vermilion kept. The letters of Newton Scott, a private in the regiment, can be found on the Internet at ucsc.edu/civil-war-letters/home.html. The letters of Minos Miller, another private in the regiment, were used as the basis for a master's thesis by Larry Philbeck (University of Arkansas, 1990). Benjamin Pearson's diary was published in toto in the *Annals of Iowa*. Samuel Swiggett wrote *The Bright Side of Prison Life* (Baltimore, 1897), which primarily focuses on his experiences at Camp Ford. Among the items in the Vermilion Collection is a diary of an unidentified member of the 36th Iowa. Although I am not absolutely certain, I believe the diary belonged to Sergeant Albert Hancock. The State Historical Society of Iowa Archives contains diaries written by Captain Allen Miller and Private Hiram Pratt, and letters written by Private James Murphy. Finally, Will Kemper, William Vermilion's brother-in-law, wrote a number of letters that are housed at that same facility. In addition, a few of his letters to his sister, Mary, are contained in the Vermilion Collection at UCSD. Will also wrote quite a few other letters which were put up for electronic auction in 1999. Unfortunately, the price of even one of these letters soon escalated beyond the humble means of this New Mexico public employee, thus depriving me of the chance to examine them.

I was also able to utilize other primary sources in preparing my book. The Vermilion Collection contains not only Mary's correspondence to her husband, but also holds letters of hers from both before and after the Civil War. In addition, Mary kept a diary during two trips that she took in her lifetime, both of which Eloise Duff was kind enough to share with me. Mary's account of her first trip to Iowa makes for particularly interesting reading. Matt Kemper, another brother-in-law of William's, wrote several letters that are housed at the State Historical Society of Iowa Archives. Finally, that facility also holds a letter that Mary's father wrote to a son by a previous marriage.

Many authors have written books that pertain to the military experiences of the 36th Iowa. I would highly recommend *Dream's End* by Orr Kelly (New York, 1998). This is a fascinating examination of the experiences of two brothers, one of whom served in the 36th Iowa. Brief but useful accounts of the 36th Iowa can also be found in a number of other books. Lurton D. Ingersoll's *Iowa and the War of the Rebellion: A History of the Troops Furnished by the State of Iowa to the Volunteer Armies of the Union, Which Conquered the Great Southern Rebellion of 1861–1865* (Philadelphia, 1866), gives a summary of the activities of every regiment supplied by Iowa during the war, as does *Roster and Record of Iowa Soldiers in the War of the Rebellion, Together with Historical Sketches of Volunteer Organizations, 1861–1866*, 6 volumes (Des Moines, 1908–1911), prepared by the Iowa Adjutant General's Office. The latter book also allowed me to establish the ages and residences of the members of the 36th Iowa. A similar type of work is Edith Wasson McElroy's *The Undying Procession: Iowa's Civil War Regiments* (Des Moines, 1964), as is Scharlott Goettsch Blevins, *Iowa Volunteer Militia* (Davenport, 1995). Finally, A. A. Stuart's *Iowa Colonels and Regiments: Being a History of Iowa Regiments in the War of the Rebellion and Containing a Description of the Battles in Which They Have Fought* (Des Moines, 1865), while focusing on those individuals from Iowa who attained the rank of colonel, provides a useful account of the activities of the 36th Iowa. It also gives a different perspective on the dismissal of Colonel Kittredge than that found in William's letters.

A number of books based on the letters and diaries of individual soldiers from Iowa provided useful, specific information that aided my understanding of Civil War battles west of the Mississippi River. These include: Barry Popchock, ed., *Soldier Boy: The Civil War Letters of Charles O. Musser, 29th Iowa* (Iowa City, 1995); Mildred Throne, ed., *The Civil War Diary of Cyrus F. Boyd, Fifteenth Iowa Infantry, 1861–1863* (Milwood, N.Y., 1977); Charles Larimer, ed., *Love and Valor: Intimate Civil War Letters Between Captain Jacob and Emeline Ritner* (Western Spring, 2000); Almon Wilson Parmenter, *1864 and 1865 Diaries of Almon Wilson Parmenter: A Union Civil War Soldier Mustered Out Aug. 24, 1865, in Company C, 32nd Iowa Volunteer Infantry, 3rd Division, 16th Army Corps* (San Jose, 1994); Kenneth Lyftogt, ed., *Left For Dixie: the Civil War Diary of John Rath* (Parkersburg, Iowa, 1994); Kathleen Davis, ed., *Such Are the Trials: the Civil War Diaries of Jacob Gantz* (Ames, 1991); Harold D. Brinkman, *Dear Companion: Civil War Letters of Silas I. Shearer* (Ames, 1995); A. F. Sperry, *History of the 33rd Iowa Infantry Volunteer Regiment 1863–6* (edited by Gregory and Cathy Urwin, Fayetteville, 1999); Ted and Hugh Genoways, *A Perfect Picture of Hell: Eyewitness Accounts by Civil War Prisoners From the 12th Iowa* (Iowa City, 2001); and Edwin C. Bearrs, ed., *The Civil War Letters of Major William G. Thompson of the 20th Iowa Infantry Regiment* (Fayetteville, Ark., 1966). Steve Meyer's *Iowa Valor: A Compilation of Civil War Combat Experiences From Soldiers of the State Distinguished as Most Patriotic of the Patriotic* (Garrison, Iowa, 1994) is a comprehensive anthology of accounts left by soldiers from a variety of Iowa regiments. These works all aided immeasurably in my research.

Conducting research about the Civil War in general, I have used a wide range of Civil War histories. Any historian writing about that conflict must start with the 128-volume *War of the Rebellion: A Compilation of the Official Records of the Union and Confederate Armies* (Washington, D.C., 1880–1901), and the 30-volume *Official Records of the Union and Confederate Navies in the War of the Rebellion* (Washington, D.C., 1897–1927). A useful general history of the Civil War is Shelby Foote's trilogy *The Civil War: A Narrative* (New York, 1958–1974). Bruce Catton's 3-volume work, *The Centennial History of the Civil War* (Garden City, 1961–65), also proved helpful. The Confederate side is covered in great depth in Frank Moore, ed., *The Rebellion Record* (New York, 1977). Albert Shannon provided a useful overview of Union recruiting in *The Organization and Administration of the Union Army, 1861–1865* (Cleveland, 1928). Finally, although not as lengthy as the other works I used, James McPherson's *Ordeal by Fire: Volume II, the Civil War* (New York, 1993) did add greatly to my understanding of Civil War matters.

Works which examine specific aspects of the 36th Iowa's services include: Reid Mitchell, *The Vacant Chair: The Northern Soldier Leaves Home* (New York, 1993); Jack D. Coombe, *Thunder Along the Mississippi: The River Battles That Split the Confederacy* (New York, 1996); Steve Cottrell, *War in the Ozarks* (Wilmington, N.C., 1995); Henry Steele Commager, *The Blue and the Grey: The Story of the Civil War as Told by Participants*, 2 volumes (New York, 1950); Robert Shalhope, *Sterling Price: Portrait of a Southerner* (Columbia, 1971); Frederick Phisterer, *The Army in the Civil War, Volume XIII: Statistical Record of the Armies of the United States* (New York, 1885); Eugene C. Murdock, *One Million Men: The Civil War Draft in the North* (Madison, 1971); Hondon B. Hargrove, *Black Union Soldiers in the Civil War* (Jefferson, N.C., 1988); Washington Davis, *Camp-Fire Chats of the Civil War: Being the Incident, Adventure, and Exploit of the Bivouac and Battlefield, as Related by Veteran Soldiers Themselves* (Chicago, 1889); Alonzo Abernethy, ed., *Dedication of Monuments Erected by the State of Iowa* (Des Moines, 1908); Ivan Musicant, *Divided Waters: The Naval History of the Civil War* (New York, 1995); Robert L. Kerby, *Kirby Smith's Confederacy: The Trans-Mississippi South, 1863–1865* (New York, 1972); Elmo Ingenthron, *Borderland Rebellion: A History of the Civil War on the Missouri-Arkansas Border* (Branson, 1980); Jay Monaghan, *Civil War on the Western Border, 1854–1865* (Boston, 1955); William Brooksher, *War Along the Bayous: The 1864 Red River Campaign in Louisiana* (Washington, D.C., 1988); Edwin Bearss, *Steele's Retreat from Camden and the Battle of Jenkins' Ferry* (Little Rock, 1967); Curt Anders, *Disaster in Damp Sand: The Red River Expedition* (Indianapolis, 1997); Ludwell H. Johnson, *Red River Campaign: Politics and Cotton in the Civil War* (Kent, 1958); Kay Sakaris, *Rebel's Hell: Little Rock's Yankee Prison* (Pasadena, Texas, 1993); James Atkinson, *Forty Days of Disaster: The Story of General Frederick Steele's Expedition into Southern Arkansas, March 23 to May 3, 1864* (Little Rock, 1955); Chester Barney, *Recollections of Field Service with the Twentieth Iowa Infantry Volunteers, or, What I Saw in the Army* (Davenport, 1865); Wiley Britton, *The Civil War on the Border 1861–1862* (New York, 1899); Alvin M. Josephy, *War on the Frontier* (Alexandria, Va., 1986); John L. Ferguson, *Arkansas and the Civil War* (Little Rock, 1965); Anne J. Bailey and Daniel E. Sutherland, *Civil War Arkansas: Beyond Battles and Leaders* (Fayetteville, 2000); Leo E. Huff, *Confederate Arkansas: A History of Arkansas in the Civil War* (Fayetteville, 1964); Homer Mead, *The Eighth Iowa Cavalry in the Civil War* (Augusta, Ill., 1925); James A. Fowler, *History of the Thirtieth Iowa Infantry Volunteers: Giving a Complete Record of the Movements of the Regiment From its Organization Until Mustered Out* (Mediapolis, Iowa, 1908); The Iowa Sanitary Commission, *Report of the Iowa Sanitary Commission: From the Organization of the Sanitary Work in Iowa to the Close of its Service at the End of the War* (Dubuque, 1866); Sharon Lee DeWitt Kraynek, ed., *Letters to my Wife: A Civil War Diary From the Western Front* (Apollo, Pa., 1995); *History of the 43rd Indiana Regiment* (Terre Haute, 1903); and Henry H. Wright, *A History of the 6th Iowa Infantry* (Iowa City, 1923).

Information about military affairs in general came from a number of different sources. Bell I. Wiley's *The Life of Billy Yank: The Common Soldier of the Union* (Indianapolis, 1952), although fifty years old, still provides an excellent overview of Union soldiers' military experience. Gregory Coco's *The Civil War Infantryman: In Camp, on the March, and in Battle* (Gettysburg, 1996) is similarly useful. Specific details about the Union military were obtained from Frank R. Freemon, *Gangrene and Glory: Medical Care During the American Civil War* (Champaign, 2001); Stuart McConnell, *Glorious Contentment: the Grand Army of the Republic, 1865–1890* (Chapel Hill, 1992); William B. Edwards, *Civil War Guns: The Complete Story of Federal and Confederate Small Arms: Design, Manufacture, Identification, Procurement, Issue, Employment, Effectiveness, and Postwar Disposal* (Secaucus, N.J., 1982); Henry E. Simmons, *A Concise Encyclopedia of the Civil War* (New York, 1965); Patricia Faust, ed., *Historical Times Illustrated Encyclopedia of the Civil War* (New York, 1986); Chris Bishop and Ian Drury, *1400 Days: The Civil War Day by Day* (New York, 1990); Mark Mayo Boatner III, *The Civil War Dictionary* (New York, 1959); Jon L. Wakelyn, *Biographical Dictionary of the Confederacy* (Westport, Conn., 1977); and J. W. Carnahan, *4000 Civil War Battles* (Fort Davis, Texas, 1971).

Because much of the correspondence between William and Mary pertained to matters outside the military domain, I consulted a wide variety of sources that provided information about other aspects of nineteenth-century America. The Seventh Census of the United States, 1850, the Eighth Census of the United States, 1860, and the Ninth Census of the United States, 1870, allowed me to identify a number of individuals to whom William and Mary refer in their letters. General information on the state of Iowa came from Robert R. Dykstra, *Bright Radical Star: Black Freedom and White Supremacy on the Hawkeye Frontier* (Cambridge, 1993); David L. Lendt, *Demise of the Democracy: The Copperhead Press in Iowa 1856–1870* (Ames, 1973); Edward H. Stiles, *Recollections and Sketches of Notable Lawyers and Public Men of Early Iowa*

(Des Moines, 1916); T. D. Eagal and R. H. Sylvester, *The Iowa State Almanac and Statistical Register for 1860* (Davenport, 1859); Morton M. Rosenberg, *Iowa on the Eve of the Civil War: A Decade of Frontier Politics* (Norman, 1972); James I. Robertson, Jr., *Iowa in the Civil War: A Reference Guide* (Iowa City, 1961); Rick W. Sturdevant, "Girding for War: Conditions Underlying the Response of Iowa Counties to Troop Calls, 1861–1862" (master's thesis, University of Northern Iowa, 1974); Hubert H. Wubben, *Civil War Iowa and the Copperhead Movement* (Ames, 1980); S. W. M. Byers, *Iowa in War Times* (Des Moines, 1888); Leland L. Sage, *A History of Iowa* (Ames, 1974); Robert I. Vexler, *Chronology and Documentary History of the State of Iowa* (Dobbs Ferry, N.Y., 1978); Benjamin F. Gue, *History of Iowa*, 4 volumes (New York, 1903); Robert Cook, *Baptism of Fire: The Republican Party in Iowa 1838–1878* (Ames, 1994); and Henry and Edwin Sabin, *The Making of Iowa* (Chicago, 1916). Resources on Indiana during the Civil War period include: W. H. H. Terrell, *Indiana in the War of Rebellion* (Indianapolis, 1960); Janet B. Hewett, ed., *The Roster of Union Soldiers 1861–1865: Indiana* (Wilmington, 2000); James C. Veatch, *The Soldiers of Indiana in the War for the Union* (Indianapolis, 1869); Frank L. Klements, *The Copperheads in the Middle West* (Chicago, 1960); Giles G. Hoffer, "Disloyalty in Indiana During the Civil War" (master's thesis, University of Mississippi, 1941); and Thomas Earl Rodgers, "Northern Political Ideologies in the Civil War Era: Indiana, 1860–1866" (Ph.D. diss., Indiana University, 1991). I also consulted histories of Iowa and Indiana communities, such as Jesse W. Weik, *Weik's History of Putnam County, Indiana* (Indianapolis, 1910); Carol Zenor, "Putnam County in the Civil War" (master's thesis, DePauw University, 1956); *Biographical and Historical Record of Putnam County, Indiana* (Chicago, 1887); Frank Hickenlooper, *An Illustrated History of Monroe County, Iowa* (Albia, 1896); *The History of Monroe County, Iowa* (Chicago, 1878); Theodore Stuart, *Past and Present of Lucas and Wayne Counties, Iowa* (Chicago, 1913); *Biographical and Historical Record of Wayne and Appanoose Counties, Iowa* (Chicago, 1886); and *The History of Appanoose County, Iowa* (Chicago, 1878).

While the military endeavors of William Vermilion are important, I believe that Mary Vermilion's experiences are equally significant. This led me to look at analyses of the war's impact on women, the family, and the domestic front in general. Consulting a wide range of works on the social history of the nineteenth century, I started with *Frontierswomen: The Iowa Experience* (Ames, 1981), the seminal work by my former advisor, Glenda Riley. I also consulted her *Prairie Voices: Iowa's Pioneering Women* (Ames, 1996). Other works that I used include: Anne C. Rose, *Victorian America and the Civil War* (New York, 1992); Catherine Clinton and Nina Silber, eds., *Divided Houses: Gender and the Civil War* (New York, 1992); J. Matthew Gallman, *The North Fights the Civil War: The Home Front* (Chicago, 1994); Eileen Conklin, *From the Home Front to the Front Lines: Accounts of the Sacrifice, Achievement, and Service of American Women, 1861–1865* (Gettysburg, 2001); Elizabeth Young, *Disarming the Nation: Women's Writing and the American Civil War* (Chicago, 1999);

Ann Douglas, *The Feminization of American Culture* (New York, 1977); Karen Sanchez-Eppler, *Touching Liberty: Abolition, Feminism, and the Politics of the Body* (Berkeley, 1993); Lyde C. Sizer, *The Political Work of Northern Women Writers and the Civil War, 1850–1872* (Chapel Hill, 2000); and Jean Yellin and John Van Horne, *The Abolitionist Sisterhood: Women's Political Culture in Antebellum America* (Ithaca, 1994).

Finally, many Iowa and Indiana daily and weekly newspapers from the era have been preserved on microfilm. The most useful ones for my purposes included the *Keokuk Daily Gate City, Burlington Hawk-Eye, Fairfield Ledger, Iowa City Republican, Iowa State Register,* and *Putnam County Republican Banner.*

Index

Middle Military Division (Union), 365

Military Division of West Mississippi (Union), 366

Miller, Allen W., 290, 293, 365

Miller, Claudius, 229

Minnesota Territory, 343

Mississippi, 62, 127, 139, 168, 197, 347, 353; Bruinsburg, 346; Friar's Point, 114; Grand Gulf, 347; Greenwood, 77; Haynes' Bluff, 347; Jackson, 95, 105, 173–74, 176, 197, 348; Natchez, 290; Oxford, 42; Port Gibson, 346; Senatobia, 111; Snyder's Bluff, 146, 174, 176, 352; Vicksburg, 34, 39–43, 50, 53, 57–58, 62–63, 75, 80, 89–90, 93–94, 96, 99, 103, 108, 114–15, 117–18, 130, 133, 141, 144, 146, 152, 154–56, 158, 163–64, 167–68, 175, 177, 187, 198, 203, 208, 213, 222, 341, 343, 346, 347, 350, 352, 353; Yazoo City, 70, 173

Mississippi River, 19, 31, 33, 52, 62–63, 68, 88, 131, 156, 211, 240, 266, 271, 290, 341, 343, 347, 350, 353, 358, 365, 366

Missouri, 19, 25, 75, 124, 133, 166, 172–73, 197, 207, 262, 288, 290, 292, 293, 294, 354, 357, 360, 362, 364, 365, 366; Cape Girardeau, 231; Kansas City, 366; Rolla, 124; Saint Louis, 8–10, 19, 31, 49, 57, 82, 109, 134, 183, 285, 317, 340, 347; Springfield, 142, 163, 177, 212, 238, 253, 256, 262; Wilson's Creek, 338

Missouri Democrat, 347

Monitor, U.S.S., 345

Moon Lake, 63

Morehouse, Andrew J., 314, 367

Morgan, John Hunt, 165, 171, 176, 188, 290, 353, 355, 365

Morgan, Joseph, 367

Mormons. *See* Church of Jesus Christ of Latter-day Saints

Morrett, W. P., 354

Morton, Oliver P., 54, 59, 72, 165, 342

Mullinnix, Alzira, 82, 111, 128, 326, 329, 346

Mullinnix, John, 39, 42, 66, 84, 91, 111, 117–120, 124, 126–28, 142, 150, 186, 190, 209–10, 232, 246, 253–54, 258, 272, 277, 326, 327, 328, 329, 342

Myers, Jane, 101, 349

Napier, Sir Charles, 60, 344

Napoleon III, 188, 266–67

The Nashville Union and American, 232, 359

National Road, 192, 356

Neal, J. E., 358

Neal, Jarius, 366

Nebraska: Fairmont, 334

Neel, William K., 311, 367

New Hampshire, 361

New York, 14, 167, 171, 175, 198, 206–7, 255, 281, 308, 338, 354; Brooklyn, 361

New York Post, 73

New York Tribune, 73, 85, 254, 338

Nicholson, Martha, 294, 366

Nicholson, Mary, 294, 366

Nicholson, Melvina, 294, 366

North Carolina, 168, 345; Wilmington, 303, 366

Nourse, Charles B., 217–18, 357

Nowles, John, 314, 367

Nowles, Thomas J., 314, 367

Oakland Cemetery, 335, 336, 366

Ohio, 44, 171, 198, 207, 235, 244, 251, 254, 322, 348; Cincinnati, 75, 344; Salineville, 355

Ohio River, 165, 353

Oliver, John Morrison, 322, 368